Miners & Mariners
of the Severn Gorge

Miners & Mariners of the Severn Gorge

Probate Inventories for Benthall, Broseley,
Little Wenlock and Madeley 1660-1764

edited by

Barrie Trinder & Nancy Cox

PHILLIMORE

2000

Published by
PHILLIMORE & CO. LTD.
Shopwyke Manor Barn, Chichester, West Sussex

© Introduction and Listings: Barrie Trinder and Nancy Cox, 2000

ISBN 1 86077 126 2

The publication of this book
has been sponsored by
UNIVERSITY COLLEGE NORTHAMPTON,
UNIVERSITY OF WOLVERHAMPTON.

Assistance from
THE WALKER TRUST,
THE PARISH COUNCIL OF BARROW AND BENTHALL,
FRIENDS OF THE IRONBRIDGE GORGE MUSEUM,
THE KEN AND DORINDA JONES TRUST
is gratefully acknowledged.

Printed and bound in Great Britain by
THE CROMWELL PRESS
Trowbridge, Wiltshire

CONTENTS

List of Illustrations	vi
Preface and Acknowledgements	vii
Subscription List	ix
Introduction	1
The four parishes	2
The inventories	7
Coal getters	17
Coal users	21
The river trade	24
The ancillary trades	33
Social structure and urban growth	36
The practice of agriculture	43
Money and property	53
Housing	54
Material culture	56
Women's work	73
Conclusions	79
A List of people from the parishes of Benthall, Broseley, Little Wenlock and Madeley whose wills or administration bonds are deposited in the archives of the Diocese of Hereford in Hereford Record Office, 1660-1764	87
The Inventories of Benthall	119
The Inventories of Broseley	143
The Inventories of Little Wenlock	239
The Inventories of Madeley	265
Glossary	327
Bibliography	333
Index of subjects and places	339
Index of names of appraisers and others mentioned in Inventories and the Introduction	353

LIST OF ILLUSTRATIONS

(between pages 22/23)

1. The Severn Gorge parishes, 1748
2. The Severn Gorge, c. 1776
3. St Bartholomew, Benthall
4. St Lawrence, Little Wenlock
5. View of the mouth of a coal pit, 1788
6. The Old Furnace, Coalbrookdale, 1758
7. Lead smelter at the Bower Yard, Benthall, 1788
8. An ironfounder, 1837
9. Iron Bridge near Coalbrookdale
10. Bower Yard boatyard, Benthall, in the 1850s.
11. Bow haulers pulling a barge through the Iron Bridge, 1789
12. Cast Iron Bridge over the Severn at Coalbrook Dale, 1782
13. A ropemaker, with his 'engine'
14. A tallow chandler dipping candles

(between pages 54/55)

15. A cabinet maker
16. A cooper
17. Packhorses passing through Coalbrookdale
18. The beehive and sun dial, St Bartholomew, Benthall
19. A sled
20. Benthall Hall
21. Dale End at the foot of Lincoln Hill
22. Stone cottages
23. The cast-iron tomb of the Eustace Beard
24. Fragments of early 18th-century china
25. An early 18th-century chamber pot
26. A woman drawing water from the River Severn

Acknowledgements: Aberdeen Art Gallery, 2; Ironbridge Gorge Museum Trust, 5-17, 19, 21, 24-6.

PREFACE AND ACKNOWLEDGEMENTS

THIS VOLUME results from the work of an adult education class organised by the Shropshire County Council Adult Education Service which met in Telford between 1972 and 1982. It also incorporates research undertaken by parallel classes, some of which continued until 1996, in Bishop's Castle, Bridgnorth, the Clee Hills area, Ludlow, Much Wenlock, Newport, Richard's Castle, Shifnal and Shrewsbury, under the auspices of either the county council or the University of Birmingham School of Continuing Studies. These classes were intellectually stimulating both for tutors and students. In the educational jargon of the late 1990s, this book can be regarded an an 'outcome' of the class.

Much of the book has been ready for printing for more than 15 years and our first acknowledgement must be to the members of the class who patiently transcribed and analysed the inventories, and contributed much from their varied knowledge and experience to the understanding of the documents. We do not have a definitive list of those who attended the class but would like to record the contributions of those who were members over long periods, several of them throughout the 11 years when it met. These include Mrs. J. Bearn, Miss J. Beddow, Mr. J. Bott, Mr. D. Boulton, the Rev. P. Clay, Dr. M. Dawson, Mr. P. Dunn, Mr. J. Fowler, Mr. G. Herbert, Mrs. F. Jacobs, Mr. K.B. Jones, Mrs. M. Kirby, Mr. J. Lenton, Mr. O.G. MacDonald, Mr. V. Needham, Mr. J. Paget, Miss B. Pope, Miss U. Rayska, Miss V. Robinson, Mr. P. Tilley, Mr. T. Wastling and Mr. E.H.J. Wood. We apologise to any class members whose names have been inadvertently omitted. We would like to record our particular gratitude to Dr. J.J. Cox who, in 1973, devised the punched card system used to analyse the inventories. It is also appropriate to thank those who provided accommodation for the class, Mr. J. Kennedy, librarian at Madeley in 1972-73, and subsequently Mr. A. Shapter and Mr. J. Wilson, who were responsible for the adult education programme at the Telford College of Arts and Technology (then the Walker Technical College) in the years when the class met in the college library.

Several organisations and individuals have provided the resources which have enabled the volume to be published. We acknowledge with gratitude the sponsorship of University College Northampton and the University of Wolverhampton, and the enthusiastic support of Professor Peter King and Professor Malcolm Wanklyn. The book has also been generously supported by the Walker Trust, the Friends of the Ironbridge Gorge Museum, the Ken and Dorinda Jones Trust, and the parish council of Barrow and Benthall.

Photocopies of the inventories and related ducuments were made at the Hereford Record Office during the 1970s before the probate records were fully catalogued. We are grateful to the staff of the record office for their patience and co-operation, and to the county archivist for encouraging the project.

Some parts of the book were collated and typed at the Ironbridge Institute during the 1980s, and we acknowledge with pleasure the contributions of Janet Markland and Carol Sampson (now Carol Harris), and also of Dr. David Higgins and other members of the archaeology team that worked from the Institute. Our understanding of the documents was increased by the use made of them by the editorial staff of the *Victoria County History* in Shropshire, by Judith Alfrey and Kate Clark, Nuffield Research Fellows at the Institute in the late 1980s, and by several former Master's degree students at the Institute, in particular by Miriam McDonald and Dr. Peter Wakelin. John Powell, librarian of the Ironbridge Gorge Museum, has strongly supported the project and has provided much assistance with illustrations. The preparation for publication of parts of the text has been aided by the computing skills of the research centre at University College Northampton.

When *Yeomen and Colliers in Telford,* the first volume of the research class's work, was published in 1980, the hope was expressed that the inventories of the Severn Gorge parishes would be published 'in the not-too-distant-future', but financial support was not forthcoming until the late 1990s. We would like to thank Noel Osborne of Phillimore & Co. Ltd. for having faith in the project, and hope that the result will be of interest and value to readers and satisfying to members of the class and sponsors.

BARRIE TRINDER
NANCY COX

October 1999

Note, - References to inventories in the Introduction and Index are indicated by the numbers of the inventories concerned in italics, thus: Richard Benthall *(13).*

SUBSCRIPTION LIST

Dr. Rod Ambler
Dr. Ralph S. Atherton
Pauline Bradburn
Janet E. Bull
Cyril Leonard Burden
John Churm
Neil Clarke
Sue Cleaves
Jim Cooper
Ruth Crofts
Tom Danks
Margaret Davies
Janet Doody
Bill and Heather Duckett
John Easthope
Peter Edwards
Keith Ferrington
J.A. & J.M. Fletcher
Gillian Dangerfield Fox
Ron W. Gibbs
Mrs. Margaret Gillberry
G. & G.E. Groves
Susanne Hemming (née Fletcher)
Dr. David Higgins
C.M. Hobson
Max Hodnett
Mrs. Joyce Hughes
Sheila Jelley
David Johnson
Ken Jones
P.W. King

E. Joyce Latham
J.B. Lawson
Mark Legge
David Lloyd, M.B.E.
Bob Machin
Stuart Massey
Bob Meeson
Mr. & Mrs. N.S. Meeson
Mr. John M. Midgley
Mrs. Madge Moran
Sam Mullins
Maureen Lilian Newport
Sylvia M. Norris
Helen M. Oliver
John L. Parker
Mrs. P.A. Paterson
Mr. A.D. Payne
Stephen Perry
Ian Mark Pritchard
Chris & Mike Rayner
Dr. John Richards
Peter F.C. Roden
Dorothy J. Rolfe
Mrs. J. Royston-Tonks
Dr. M.E. Speight
Angela Sterry
Nigel Talbot
Timothy N. Trown
K.F. Wilde
Dr. M.E. Wilson

INTRODUCTION

'There are great hills all about which I passed over, full of Coale Pitts', wrote Celia Fiennes when she passed through the vicinity of the Severn Gorge in 1698.[1] Even then, more than 80 years before the construction of the Iron Bridge, the district around the Wrekin seemed unusual to an Oxfordshire gentlewoman. The region's celebrity has revived in the past 30 years. People from all over the world visit the parishes in the Severn Gorge in Shropshire to admire the Iron Bridge and the ruins of blast furnaces, to see how porcelain, tiles and clay tobacco pipes were made, and to pose questions about the landscape of industrialisation, an extraordinary blend of nature and art, in the 18th-century sense of that term. It is customary to portray the history of the Severn Gorge as a saga of the heroic achievements of ironmasters and engineers, but their exploits depended on the skills of others, and the objective of this study to examine some aspects of the lives of those others, to examine the developing industrial economy and the changing material culture of the communities of the Severn Gorge in the century after the restoration of Charles II, and to do so by analysing the wills and probate inventories of those who lived and died in Benthall, Broseley, Little Wenlock and Madeley between 1662 and 1764.

Probate inventories provide evidence on a range of historical questions. They throw light on the economic structure of the area, showing the predominance of mining and the river-carrying trade in the Severn Gorge parishes, and the significance of those who used coal, and those who provided the materials used in pits and on barges. They show how the pattern of agriculture was shaped to meet the demands of an industrialising society. From inventories and wills it is also possible to study the family economy, to gauge the extent to which households were self-sufficient, to pose questions about the role of women, and to measure the rate at which people adopted innovations in their homes.

This study is part of a broader strategy developed in the 1970s to make all Shropshire's probate inventories available for study. Many people were involved as members of adult education classes and local historical societies in the transcription of probate records from most towns in the country and many rural areas. A study of inventories from Dawley, Lilleshall, Wellington and Wrockwardine in the northern part of the Coalbrookdale Coalfield was published 20 years ago,[2] and this collection would have appeared much sooner had resources been available for its publication. The material has already been used by Trinder in two preliminary surveys in the 1980s, by Cox in an analysis of retailing patterns, by Wanklyn who discussed the occupational data in 1982, by Alfrey and Clark in an analysis of housing patterns in 1993, by the *Victoria County History* and by Stamper in a survey of Shropshire gardens.[3] Several other avenues of research have been influenced by the study of inventories in Shropshire: the Portbooks Programme, the Dictionary of Traded Commodities, research on the food industry and on retailing, and articles on the nature of inventories and other probate documents.[4] We believe that this material should be available for all kinds of study, for primary school projects, family history investigations, student dissertations in many disciplines and research at the highest levels. We are conscious that this study has been dependent on mid-20th-century technology, the photocopier, the typewriter and the punched card, even though the final preparation of the text has utilised personal computers and scanners. We realise too that probate records are just one source for the history of the industrial communities of the Severn Gorge, and that historians of the 21st century, aided by information technology with capabilities as yet unimagined, may be able to integrate this material with data from registers, company accounts and other sources. We are also aware that only the first fumbling steps have been taken towards the integration of probate records with archaeological sources, to link the words in these documents with real cottages, potsherds, tobacco pipes and iron pots. Nevertheless we regard the publication of this collection as worthwhile. The texts will bring alive to many people the lives of those who lived through the early stages of industrialisation and only the availability of the texts will make it possible to pose questions not imagined by the current editors or by this generation of historians.

The Four Parishes
The four parishes analysed in this study were all rich in minerals which were exploited during the 17th and 18th centuries. All four were part of the Borough of Wenlock, and thus of the Diocese of Hereford, even though Madeley and Little Wenlock are located north of the River Severn, and surrounded by parishes in the Diocese of Lichfield.

TABLE I

The four parishes compared

	Benthall	Broseley	Little Wenlock	Madeley	Total
Acreage	770	2550	1460	2750	7610
Proportion of acreage (%)	11	21	32	36	
Hearths in 1672	90	235	61	174	560
Proportion of hearths (%)	16	42	11	31	
Households 1672	32	94	36	61	223
Proportion of households (%)	14	42	11	31	
Estimated population 1676*	362	1190	261	677	1659
Proportion of population 1676 (%)	15	48	10	27	
Population in 1801	636	4832	980	4758	11206
Proportion of population 1801 (%)	6	43	9	42	
Number of inventories 1662-1764	63	266	49	148	526
Proportion of total (%)	12	51	9	28	

* Calculated from the Compton Census using the standard multiplier of 1:5.

Broseley was the most populous of the four parishes. Wanklyn has noted the extraordinarily rapid growth in the population of the parish in the 17th century and the early 18th century. A count of burials indicated an increase of more than 250 per cent between 1660 and 1760 and, contrary to national trends, there was a decline in the age of marriage between the first three decades and the last three decades of the 17th century.[5] The increase was associated with a rise in the number of strangers and sojourners recorded, particularly between 1690 and 1730. The most eminent was John Thursfield, the potter, who, as a sojourner, married Eleanor Morris of Broseley on 20 April 1729. Thereafter he was accepted as a parishioner, and the baptisms of his eight children are recorded without additional comment. There was a trickle of migrants from the Welsh Borderland, and Francis Mason, buried in 1705, was described as 'a strange poor boy from Diddlebury'. New surnames, hitherto unknown in the parish, appear on almost every page of the register, four in 1701 and two in 1703. Most collier and barge owning families were well established in the parish— 68 per cent of collier surnames and 64 per cent of those of bargemen had appeared before 1650, and 95 per cent of colliers and 90 per cent of bargemen by 1680. Incomers tended to be tradesmen like blacksmiths, weavers and shopkeepers. Only 58 per cent of the surnames of those following such occupations were established before 1650, and only 69 per cent before 1680. As industry developed there was an increasing demand for ancillary services and the outsider could establish himself most easily in occupations where skills or capital were more significant than local knowledge or contacts, but the families engaged in the two key occupations from which this study takes its name were already well-established in 1660.

Broseley was divided among five or six principal landowners, but an appreciable amount of land was held by small freeholders. The Weld family of Willey Hall, and from 1748 their successors the Foresters, held property in the parishes, and increased their holdings through the 18th and 19th centuries, but there were also estates based on Whitehall, a large house near the parish church and on two mansions near the river, the Calcutts and the Tuckies. The latter estate was owned in the period under review by the Langley family, whose members occupied several other large houses including the Wood House *(47)* on the hillside above the Tuckies, and the Amies, reputedly their ancestral home. The tortuous manorial descents of Broseley have been explained with clarity in the *Victoria County History*.[6]

Broseley consisted of three principal settlements. The ancient centre west of the church was developing urban characteristics before 1700, and in 1779 a market hall was erected. To the north west lay Broseley Wood, a settlement where, in the early 17th century, migrant miners built cottages which stimulated the increase in the population of the parish. It was remarked in the early 1680s that 'the ancient commons of Broseley is now in greatest measure built-up and enclosed by poor people and has become a country town'.[7]

INTRODUCTION

The third area of settlement in Broseley, along the banks of the Severn, probably achieved its maximum extent by 1800, and remained much the same when it was recorded on the tithe map and the deposited plan for the Severn Valley Railway, both surveyed in the mid-1840s, and on the censuses of 1841 and 1851. By 1861 many dwellings had been demolished to make way for the railway. In 1851 there were almost 300 houses along the river bank between the stream near the Iron Bridge, which forms the boundary with Benthall, and the Wood Bridge Inn downstream of the road that crosses Coalport Bridge. Within this mass of dwellings, today known loosely as Jackfield, there were recognised sub-settlements, some of which are mentioned in the wills and inventories. According to the 1851 census enumerators there were, moving in a downstream direction from the Iron Bridge, 20 houses in Ladywood, 14 in Upper Passage Ferry (near to the present road bridge), 57 in Coalford (still a current street name), seven in Holly Groves, 34 at Lloyd Head, eight at The Knowle, four at The Rock, eight at Jackfield Rails, one at Calcutts, 38 at Jackfield (near to the present Tile Museum), 48 at Salthouse, 19 at Tuckies, five near the *Duke of Wellington Inn* (by the present Memorial Foot Bridge), 21 at The Werps, eight at the Old Rope Walk, five at Preens Head and two by Coalport Bridge.

Benthall, a parish of only 770 acres, formed a single estate whose owners until 1720 were actively involved in exploiting its minerals. After the death of Richard Benthall *(13)* it passed, after 26 years of litigation, to Ralph Browne of Caughley, who left it to a step-daughter who had married into the Harries family of Cruckton near Shrewsbury. The estate was sold in 1844 to Lord Forester, but Benthall Hall returned to the ownership of a branch of the Benthall family from 1934, and passed to the National Trust in 1958. The ancient settlement was centred on Benthall Hall and on the adjacent parish church, rebuilt in 1667, but during the period covered by these inventories cottages were built by colliers, bargemen and potters in the valley of the brook which divided the parish from Broseley, along what was to become the principal access on the south bank of the Severn to the Iron Bridge.[8]

Between Benthall and Much Wenlock lies the extra-parochial area of Posenhall, some of whose inhabitants—there were only 18 in total in 1811—regarded themselves as parishioners of Benthall. Others are said on their probate documents to be 'of Much Wenlock', and transcriptions of their inventories are deposited in Shropshire Records & Research with those of that town. In 1841 Posenhall comprised a farm, an earthenware pottery and five cottages.[9]

Madeley was the largest of the four parishes but not the most populous until after 1800. The manor was held in the 17th century by the Brooke family; Sir Basil Brooke, pioneer of steelmaking at Coalbrookdale, was a Roman Catholic and a Royalist. He died in 1646 but the family's estates were forfeited in 1652. They were subsequently recovered, but after being held for a long period by two minors, the manor was split in 1727 between the Smitheman and Giffard families. It is evident from many sources that it was easy for incomers to settle in Madeley after 1660.[10]

Madeley consisted of three principal settlements. The topography of the ancient centre along High Street has the characteristics of a medieval new town, but its market had lapsed by 1700, and the inventories do not suggest that there was a significant community of retailers in Madeley before 1764. The most populous part of the parish was Madeley Wood on the slopes leading down to the river, centred in the early 18th century on the green near the *Golden Ball* public house, first licensed in 1728, an area that was substantially altered by the building of the present road up Madeley Bank between 1806 and 1810. There were at least 40 leasehold properties in Madeley Wood in the 1770s. The area retains much archaeological evidence of its squatter origins, but its two substantial early 17th-century mansions, The Lloyds and Bedlam Hall, have long since been demolished.[11]

The other principal area of settlement was Coalbrookdale, an area separated from the manor in the 16th century, comprising the valley of the Calde Brook, used throughout the period under review to power iron-works, some associated settlement along the river bank extending from the present Dale End towards the site of the Iron Bridge, and the farm at Strethill on the boundary between Madeley and Buildwas. Although Sir Basil Brooke had made important developments in metallurgical technology at Coalbrookdale in the 1630s, it remained a small settlement when Abraham Darby I leased property there in the first decade of the 18th century. More houses were built between 1710 and 1750, and the character of the settlement is depicted in engravings published in the 1750s. Much property was held in small parcels, and probate records show that some 18th-century ironworkers occupied their own houses in Coalbrookdale.[12]

Little Wenlock was the only one of the four parishes not bounded by the Severn, but it lies on the coal measures and had links by road, pack-horse track and later by wooden railway to the river, which justifies its inclusion in this study. The manorial estate had been bought by Francis Forester in 1623, and the Foresters steadily acquired more property in the

INTRODUCTION

parish during the period under review and into the 19th century. The Old Hall, the Manor House and the Stone House, all centres of estates within the parish, still stand near the parish church. Two mining hamlets were established by the early 18th century, Huntington to the north east and Coalmoor to the east.[13]

The Inventories

The probate records for the Diocese of Hereford for the period before the Civil War do not survive. This study analyses 526 inventories from the four parishes made between 1660 and 1764. Probate records for the second half of the 18th century have been studied in some detail, and it is clear that the inventory of Jonathan Oakes of Broseley *(114)*, submitted when probate was granted on his will on 26 June 1764, was the last probate inventory made in the four parishes. The selection of 196 inventories published includes all those of outstanding interest and provides a consistent sample of occupations, levels of wealth and places of residence, although some with individual items of note have necessarily been omitted. The analysis in the Introduction is based on all 526 inventories. Wills have also been examined and are summarised where they are of particular interest. The list includes all the individuals for whom there are probate records in Hereford between 1660 and 1764, whether or not inventories survive with other documents. The spread of inventories over time is reasonably consistent. The total for the 1660s is lower than for subsequent decades, doubtless because it took several years for the ecclesiastical courts to resume operation after the Protectorate, and the earliest inventory actually dates from 1663. The low total of 31 for the first decade of the 18th century is the only substantial deviation from the mean of 53 inventories for each of the full decades. Inventories survive for 16 per cent of the adults buried in Broseley in the 1670s, and for 6 per cent of the rather larger number who were interred between 1700 and 1710. It is clear that the practice of making inventories had not diminished in the area in the 1750s, and that its demise in the following decade was relatively sudden.

The collection raises several questions about the ways in which inventories were made and estates administered. It is usually supposed that the wills of people who left property in more than one diocese were proved at the Prerogative Court of Canterbury, but the four parishes under review lay on a diocesan boundary, probably determined in the seventh century, and in at least one instance property is recorded in the Diocese of Lichfield as well as in Hereford. The inventory of Frances Baxter *(115)* widow of a minister of Little Wenlock made in 1663, includes goods at Haughton in the parish of Shifnal in Lichfield diocese, as well as possessions in her home parish. Items regarded by appraisers as fixtures were not normally recorded in inventories, but it seems to have been accepted that it was appropriate to include 'furnaces', large pots set in the walls of brewhouses or kitchens.[14]

Real property is not normally listed on inventories, but leases that were still current could be the subjects of bequests and were included. Leases on lives, which continued while named individuals were still alive, were commonplace in Shropshire, and the inventory of Noel Edwards *(77)* includes the reversion of a lease 'as long as the lives continue'.

Two inventories, unusually, provide evidence of causes of death. Ralph Bradley in 1669 was drowned in the River Severn, while Mary Yates *(175)* in 1687 was murdered, and some of her possessions were in the hands of the Lord of the Manor. Most inventories were made within a few days of the death of the deceased and submitted to the court where probate was sought within a few months. The collections contains a few exceptions: those of Henry Price of Madeley, who died in 1727 but whose inventory was made in 1749, Thomas Preen, who died in 1746 but whose inventory was made 10 years later, and Robert Yeates, whose inventory was made six years after he died in 1677.

Some accounts have survived with other probate documents and provide insights into funeral customs and the care of the sick. A pound had been spent on attending Ann Williams alias Hypkes who died in 1673, 'before her sickness', ten shillings were paid for attendance on her during her illness and £1 4s. 0d. for her funeral. The inventory of William Baugh *(134)* shows that some of his goods had been sold by the parish overseers.

A selection of 265 of the 846 inventories submitted to the local ecclesiastical courts from the parishes of Dawley, Lilleshall, Wellington and Wrockwardine between 1660 and 1750 was published in 1980, and provides many points of comparison with the present study.[15] The development of mining in the parishes to the north was less advanced than in the Severn Gorge parishes, although there was some exploitation of coal around the outcrops at Ketley and on the properties of the Charlton family in the parish of Wombridge, from which no inventories survive.[16] Many inventories have been analysed from other parts of Shropshire which provide further points of comparison.

When this work was carried out the probate records of the Diocese of Hereford had not been calendared, but we are reasonably confident that all

INTRODUCTION

the records for the four parishes have been identified. Records were identified from the index then available, and all bundles from the boxes then numbered 59-206, covering the period from 1662 to 1764, were checked. All the wills relating to the four parishes between 1764 and 1810 were also examined. Bundles labelled 'Wenlock' were checked to see whether they related to Little or Much Wenlock. Inventories for Much Wenlock were transcribed by a class tutored by Sam Mullins in the early 1980s, and transcripts are available in Shropshire Records and Research. The registers sometimes include two entries for the same person, usually for intestates. No attempt has been made to integrate with this collection probate records from the Prerogative Court of Canterbury held in the Public Record Office. Matthews in 1928 listed 28 records for the four parishes in the period 1700-49: three for Benthall, six for Broseley, four for Little Wenlock and 15 for Madeley.[17]

TABLE II

Distribution of Inventories by Parish and Decade

	Benthall	Broseley	Little Wenlock	Madeley	Totals
1660-69	1	12	5	10	28
1670-79	7	35	2	15	59
1680-89	14	27	4	20	65
1690-99	7	22	4	11	44
1700-09	4	14	2	11	31
1710-19	7	21	9	15	52
1720-29	7	37	6	20	70
1730-39	2	29	7	7	46
1740-49	5	32	3	9	49
1750-59	7	29	4	24	65
1760-64	1	8	3	6	18
Totals	63	266	49	148	526
Proportions (%)	12	51	9	28	

TABLE IIIa

Inventories: Analysis of Values (i)

Values	Benthall	Broseley	Little Wenlock	Madeley	Total	Proportion of total (%)
Under £5	8	45	6	29	88	16.73
£5-£9	11	35	-	17	64	11.98
£10-£19	20	95	17	47	179	34.03
£20-£49	12	39	7	19	77	14.64
£50-£99	7	23	12	18	60	11.41
£100-£199	4	16	6	9	35	6.65
Over £200	1	13	1	9	24	4.56
Total	63	266	49	148	526	

TABLE IIIb

Inventories: Analysis of Values (ii)

Values	Benthall	Broseley	Little Wenlock	Madeley	Total	Cumulative (%)
Under £5	12.7	16.92	12.25	19.59	16.73	
£5-£9	17.46	23.16	-	11.49	11.98	2.71
£10-£19	31.74	35.71	34.69	31.76	34.03	62.74
£20-£49	19.05	14.66	24.29	12.84	14.64	77.38
£50-£99	11.11	8.64	24.49	12.16	11.41	88.79
£100-£199	6.35	6.02	12.24	6.08	6.65	95.44
Over £200	1.59	4.89	2.94	6.08	4.56	

All figures are percentages

INTRODUCTION 11

Study of large numbers of inventories has shown that valuations are generally consistent and logical, a conclusion that applies to this collection as much as to any other.[18] There are many indications of informed appraisal. Thomas Boycott, who appraised four yeomen and a yeoman's widow in Little Wenlock between 1713 and 1729, was probably a butcher, like others of that name in Little Wenlock and Wellington. If so he would have known what he was doing when he priced William Wheelwright's *(127)* three cows at £3 apiece in 1714, but the four of another William Wheelwright *(128)* in 1717 at only £2 10s. 0d. each. The name Smitheman is found at the foot of 15 inventories in Little Wenlock and Madeley, mostly of farmers. John Smitheman *(119)*, who died in 1689, was a rich yeoman and doubtless at least some of the appraisers were his descendants. Although the Smithemans' inventories are not always helpfully detailed, they show considerable variation in pricing, there being, for example, no standard value for a cow, and it may be assumed that prices are realistically related to worth. The two mercers' inventories provide no detail of stocks. Thomas Oliver *(51)* is recorded as having 'Clothes stuffs and all other mercery in ye shop' worth £149 1s. 2¼d., and Robert Hill *(39)* had 'Ware and implements' worth £45 14s. 2d., but the odd pence, indeed the odd farthing, confirm that the stock was valued with care. The names of one of the appraisers of each inventory, respectively Christopher Morrall and Edward Simons, do not appear on other inventories in the four parishes, and they were probably mercers with expert knowledge brought in from elsewhere because no local disinterested trader was available with appropriate expertise.

The possessions of waterman were also expertly appraised, although the valuation of vessels may at first sight appear haphazard (see below). Of the 56 people who owned vessels larger than mere boats, all but five were appraised either by a known fellow waterman, or by someone with a name indicating that he belonged to a barge-owning family, a Beard, Benbow, Easthope, Hagar, Pugh or Transome. The vessel on the inventory of William Day *(17)* was 'adjudged by an experienced waterman', and the barge of William Ashwood *(152)* 'by the judgement of a skillful carpenter'. It is impossible not to conclude that such men knew what they were doing, and thus, when George Easthope valued the *vessel* of Richard Brook *(142)* at £40 in 1760 and the two *barges* of Edward Yates at £56 three years later, he was making a distinction that would have been recognised by fellow workers on the Severn.

The names of just over a thousand people appear as appraisers on the 526 inventories. Most are found on just one or two documents, but the name John Hartshorne occurs 63 times, and there are several others which occur more than 12 times. It is usually impossible to determine whether two signatures refer to the same person since names were sometimes signed by other appraisers or written out by clerks making fair copies. There is a further complication in the Severn Gorge—the use of aliases. Broseley parish registers abound with examples. The inventory of Rebecca *Phillips* was taken in 1676, but Rebecca *Reynolds* was buried. Samuel *Cumbersome*, for whom probate was granted in 1749, was called Samuel Hill when his infant son was baptised and buried in 1736, and there are other references over many years which suggest that 'Cumbersome' was a nickname bestowed on members of the Hill family which was sometimes used as a surname. Nevertheless a study of appraisers can reveal much that is significant.[19]

The proportion of appraisers signing by mark varies from parish to parish—17 per cent in Broseley, 10 per cent in Little Wenlock and 8 per cent in Madeley. The last two figures are comparable with those for the parishes to the north—11 per cent in Wellington and Wrockwardine, 9 per cent in Dawley and 7 per cent in Lilleshall. The difference between the two areas widens in the 18th century. Throughout the coalfield the level of illiteracy increased in the 1670s but steadily diminished in the next 50 years, rising again in the 1730s and '40s. The rise is more marked in the Severn Gorge than in the parishes to the north.

Interpreting these figures is difficult, and the reasons for changes may differ from parish to parish. The rise in illiteracy in the 1670s may be explained by a breakdown of education during the Civil Wars, but no research has been undertaken which can confirm this hypothesis. In the northern parishes it was clearly unacceptable by the end of the 17th century fore a well-to-do yeoman to be illiterate, and he either learned to write or concealed his incapacity. In Little Wenlock and Madeley something of the same sort occurred but rather later. It is unsurprising that both Richard Wheelwright in 1684 and George Wheelwright in 1691 signed by mark, but it is remarkable to find a yeoman still doing so 30 years later. Maurice Hayward died as an old man in 1746 when he was living in someone else's house, so there is no way of knowing whether he was a man of substance, although it seems likely. Between 1719 and 1731 he made 10 inventories, mostly of the relatively rich, but he is recorded as making his mark on three of them, although by the 1720s most yeoman's estates were appraised by men who could at least write their own names. This improvement in literacy amongst the farming community was balanced by an increasing proportion amongst the population of colliers and bargemen amongst whom illiteracy may have been less of a stigma.

Study of the appraisers of the inventories of Dawley, Lilleshall, Wellington and Wrockwardine showed that the interactions between them and with other parishes were complex, although the role of Wellington as the market centre was evident.[20] In the Severn Gorge parishes it was assumed that the river might be a unifying factor in the life of the community. With the exception of Little Wenlock, which had links with Wellington, it appeared that the Gorge was a landlocked society, difficult of access by road, whose contacts were with other riverside settlements. A study of the appraisers suggests that for some sections of the community the river was a barrier, and the tensions between those living on either side, and possibly between those living in different parts of Madeley and Broseley, were as strong as those observed by Hudson and King in textile-working parishes in the Pennines.[21] Of some 520 appraisers' names, only 45 (8 per cent) appear on both sides of the river, and the proportion of the 190 names that appear on more than one inventory is only 24 per cent. Of the 45 people who appraised on both banks more than half were involved with trade on the river. Examination of the places mentioned in the Broseley parish registers shows as many references to towns along the river, such as Shrewsbury, Bridgnorth, Bewdley and Tewkesbury as to places on the opposite bank. Broseley had most links with other settlements on the south bank of the Severn, particularly with such parishes as Linley, Barrow, Willey and Much Wenlock.

On the north bank, it is evident that people in Madeley and Little Wenlock had more contacts with Dawley, Wellington and Wrockwardine than with the parishes south of the river. This is at first sight surprising, since people in Madeley, Broseley and Benthall were all concerned with the barge trade, and all four parishes were constituent parts of the Borough of Wenlock. While there was no bridge linking the two banks of the river in the Gorge until 1780, there were numerous ferries and the day-to-day commercial contacts between the communities on the two banks were considerable. Nevertheless, it appears that the relatively sparse retailing facilities within the four parishes were concentrated in the centres of Madeley and more especially Broseley, and that people did not cross the river to find the services of mercers, chandlers, butchers, weavers and tailors.

As in other parishes, people in Benthall, Broseley, Little Wenlock and Madeley described themselves on their wills, and were described by appraisers on their inventories in two ways, by status, indicated by the terms 'esquire', 'gentleman', 'yeoman', 'husbandman' and 'labourer', or by principal occupation, by such words as 'trowman', 'ropemaker' or 'master collier'. The distinction between the two kinds of description is obvious at the upper

TABLE IV

Comparison between appraisers in the four parishes and those in the parishes to the north

	Total	% of names also appearing in Lilleshall	% of names also appearing in Wrockwardine	% of names also appearing in Dawley	% of names also appearing in Wellington
Benthall	84	3.5	3.5	1.0	11.0
Broseley	280	3.0	4.0	2.5	8.0
L. Wenlock	73	3.0	8.0	10.0	25.0
Madeley	174	3.0	7.0	7.0	12.0

end of the social scale. Richard Benthall *(13)* was an esquire, but, as a landowner, unsurprisingly made his living from agriculture, practised on a considerable scale, and from the exploitation of minerals. Benthall's inventory is the only one in the collection relating to an esquire, but there are nine relating to gentlemen, five to members of the Langley family *(22, 47, 53, 55)*, which suggests that the term was used with precision. There are 46 inventories, 10 per cent of those for men relating to yeomen, a lower proportion than the 18 per cent in the parishes to the north. Unsurprisingly the highest proportion of yeomen—45 per cent—is in Little Wenlock, the most agricultural of the four parishes. The inventories of most yeomen in Little Wenlock show that they made their livings by farming. The word 'farmer' does not occur on any probate document in the four parishes during the period under review. The inventories of 16 yeomen were valued at less than £20, showing that the term did not necessarily indicate wealth. Nor was it exclusively linked with farming. Richard Roden *(69)* is described on his will as a yeoman, but made his living by keeping a shop. George Deuksell *(170)* enjoyed the status of a yeoman, but made his living by carpentry. Distinctions at the lower end of the social scale were made only rarely. There are only four inventories for husbandmen and seven for labourers. Francis Rushon *(138)* who died in 1665 was described by his appraisers as a husbandman, but it is evident that he made most of his living as a cooper. Samuel Smith of Benthall who died in 1697 was curiously described on his inventory as shoemaker and bachelor. The occupation of the male head of household was by no means the only source of sustenance for families in this period and, while occupational groups are examined in this study, the main emphasis is on the analysis of activities, of farming rather than of farmers, of pig-keeping, flax-processing and brewing, in such a way that all means of making a living are given due consideration.

Only 64 inventories, just over 12 per cent of the total, list goods owned by women, rather less than the 19 per cent in the parishes to the north. The proportion is consistent in the Severn Gorge parishes, varying by no more than 0.1 per cent in inventories made before and after 1700. The proportion of inventories relating to women in Benthall, Broseley and Madeley varies only between 12.4 and 12.8 per cent, and only in Little Wenlock, where the figure is 8 per cent, does it significantly differ from the mean. It is curious that it is so low in the most agricultural of the four parishes, while in the largely agricultural parish of Lilleshall it is as high as 26 per cent. It is possible that the relatively low proportion of inventories relating to women in the Severn Gorge parishes was the consequence of variations in practice between the courts of the dioceses of Lichfield and Hereford.

Of the 64 women's inventories, 45 related to widows and only five to women clearly identified as spinsters. Most were of low value—13 were totalled at less than £5 and 35 at less than £20. Only three exceeded £100 in value. Most women's inventories seem to have been made because the deceased held assets in money or property. This happened at both ends of the social scale. It applied to all three women with inventories valued at more than £100. Dorothy Starkey in 1668 had moveable possessions worth £357, of which £330 consisted of money owing to her, the remainder of the items comprising a comfortable but unremarkable household. The inventory of Elizabeth Corbett in 1759 totalled £323, most of which was accounted for by chattel leases, money due on mortgages and cash. Mary Ogden *(62)* in 1717 had possessions worth £116, of which £80 was the value of a lease. All three women owned gold or silver. The inventories of poorer women show a similar picture. Margaret Hartshorne in 1753 had just a legacy of £15, while Elizabeth Stanley in 1721 had one of £10. Eleanor Eele in 1701 had only a lease, and a lease accounted for most of the value of the possessions of Joyce Smith in 1749. The principal assets of Ann Hallen in 1756 were arrears of rents, and desperate debts accounted for almost all the value of the inventory of Ann Mullart in 1685. Joyce Edwards in 1765 had a modest share in a colliery enterprise.

Some inventories provide more revealing insights into the place of women in society. The language in that of Catherine Hartshorne *(11)* reveals much about early 18th-century assumptions about the role of servants of the gentry. Two women, Mary Oakes in 1726 and Ann Dawley *(45)*, appear to have been responsible for working barges on the Severn, and the Gloucester Portbooks reveal that several women from the Gorge were involved in the long-distance trade on the river. Several women were engaged in businesses when they died; Hannah Hartshorne *(82)* in weaving, Mary Clemson *(189)* in ropemaking, Margery Swift in 1726 in farming, and Mary Penn *(87)* in running a shop. The example of Margaret Justice of Wellington, who died in 1687 after establishing a mercer's business following the death of her shoemaker husband, shows that it should not be easily assumed that women were simply continuing with enterprises which had been run by their deceased husbands.[22]

The language used in Shropshire inventories has been discussed elsewhere.[23] This collection raises questions about the currency of particular terms. The expression 'tugar ware', which probably refers to baskets (i.e. utensils made by tugging), is used on only four inventories, all from Broseley and three of them *(62, 63)* made within six months by six different appraisers, and the other ten years later. Three of these inventories *(63, 74)* also refer to 'latten ware', probably meaning beaten brass.

One of the most interesting uses of language in the collection is the reference in the inventory of Robert Yates *(154)* to 'money in bancke', written in 1677, some 17 years before the founding of the Bank of England, and many decades before there was a bank, in the sense of an institution taking funds on deposit, in Shropshire. The *Oxford English Dictionary* quotes an instance from 1646 of the word being used figuratively to mean money in store, 'blessings in hand and in bank'. The word was not, therefore, unknown, but it must have been exceedingly uncommon, for this is the only use yet to be noted in any of the many thousands of Shropshire inventories that have been transcribed.

The word 'maid', which in recent times in Shropshire has referred to a clothes horse, is used four times in the collection in a way unknown to the *Oxford English Dictionary*, but with a meaning similar to that which can be deduced from inventories in Shifnal and Bridgnorth. Every reference in this sense is from after 1700. It appears that the word usually meant an iron utensil on which something which might be hot could be placed. Maids in Bridgnorth and Shifnal are associated with pans, dripping pans, toasters and smoothing irons, and there are references to 'a maid to hang a frying pan upon',[24] and to an 'iron maid'. The maids owned by Richard Cox *(179)* and John Goodman *(183)* were both in fireplaces, and follow this pattern, but that of Samuel Burrows *(98)* was in the pantry with dairy equipment, and that of Joseph Whitefoot *(91)* was in what appears to be a lumber room with a spinning wheel and some old books.

Several terms relating to farm animals have to be interpreted in their context, and many have rather different meanings from modern usages. The word 'colt' appears on occasion in all parts of Shropshire to have applied to a young bovine rather than a young equine creature. The best instance in the collection is on the inventory of John Smitheman *(119)* where 'three colts' appear within the hierarchy of a herd of cattle, with colts belonging to mares listed separately. Similarly the word 'bullock' seems often to relate to an ox being trained for draught purposes rather than to a castrated animal being fattened to provide beef.

Another intriguing word is 'cratch' which appears seven times in the collection. The word is most familiar when it means a hurdle, of the kind used for keeping together a flock of sheep, or a wall-mounted manger in a stable. It seems to have been applied to hurdle-like utensils of many kinds in 18th-century Shropshire. Edward Owen *(182)* and William Pearce *(94)* had bacon cratches, which appear to have been the frames suspended from kitchen ceilings to which joints of bacon were tied. Edward Nash *(60)* had a cratch with his coopery ware, which may indicate that it was what is known elsewhere as a cheese cratch, a device used to allow whey to drain away from curds in cheese-making. The cratch in the house with hooks in the inventory of William Maybury *(161)* must have been something different, while the joined cratch owned by John Dawley *(49)* in 1689 could have been a livery cupboard. The word also appears to have been used for a bottle rack, and for a rack which kept together a shoemaker's tools and lasts. The term 'handle cratch' in the inventory of Sampson Buckley *(59)* combines two confusing terms. A handle in this sense was a rod to which teasels were fixed for raising the nap on woollen cloth. It would appear that a handle cratch was a stand on which such rods could be placed, since raising the nap was a wet process.

Coal Getters

Mining was the most economically significant activity in the Severn Gorge between 1660 and 1760. There are inventories for 67 miners, colliers or master colliers, 13 per cent of the total number of inventories for the four parishes. A few were only indirectly involved in mining. Richard Benthall *(13)* the landowner clearly gained much of his income from minerals. Mary Clemson *(189)* the ropemaker had wheels and winches, weighing equipment, four carts and a sled which she would not have needed for making ropes, and was probably involved in mining. William Eardley (or Yardley) *(177)* of Madeley Wood who died in 1729 was described on his inventory as an 'engineer', which probably means, at that date, that he was working the steam engine which pumped water from the mines in the Lloyds.[25] Thirty-four of the 67 miners' inventories were from Broseley, 26 from Madeley, four from Benthall and three from Little Wenlock. There were miners in all four parishes throughout the period covered by the inventories, but the proportion of miners' inventories increased in the 18th century. Before 1700 11 per cent of the inventories related to mining, but there were 46, 14 per cent of the total, between 1700 and 1764. Most miners were poor; the inventories of 32, 48 per cent of the total, were valued at less than £10, and 49, or 73 per cent were valued below £20. Four miners' inventories were valued at more than £200. Thirty-four of those who dug coal were described on their wills or inventories as 'colliers'; seven were called 'ground colliers', distinguishing them from 'wood colliers' or charcoal burners, and nine were simply called 'miners'. Mining was to a large extent an heriditary occupation, and the expression 'born a collier' was used in the area in the 19th century. The miners' inventories include those of four Pearces, four Bodens, four Evanses, three Hollands and three Coxes.

Six of those involved in mining were known as 'master colliers'. With two exceptions, they were not exceptionally wealthy. They appear to have directed the operations of mines leased from landowners. The reference to a lease granting rights of passage for carrying coal to the Severn in the inventory of John Adams *(27)*, exhibited in 1691 some 18 years after his death, shows the importance to coal producers of access to the river. There was a distinct change in the pattern of mine operation in the area in the 1750s, when ironworking companies began to lease rights from landowners, and to operate the pits through sub-contractors called charter masters. The master colliers were in some respects the forerunners of the charter masters of the late 18th and 19th-centuries, but their contracts appear to have been with landowners, not with the operators of blast furnaces. The only inventory for a master collier in the 17th century, that for Thomas Potts taken in 1692, includes no interesting detail, but is significant in that it describes Potts as a yeoman, while in his will he calls himself a master collier. Three master colliers were members of the Pearce family. John Pearce *(58)* in 1709 had goods worth the exceptional sum of £318. His house was small, if comfortably furnished, and much of his wealth was in the form of debts owing to him. Richard Pearce *(79)* in 1732 was even wealthier, with moveable goods worth £483. He was farming on a considerable scale, with six cows, dairy equipment and crops of grain. His inventory includes nothing relating directly to mining, but his will shows that he was a partner in a coalwork with a Mr. Ashwood, a Mr. Pursell and a Mrs.

Crompton, from whom £94 was due, one of several debts which comprised much of his wealth. William Pearce *(94)* in 1742 was owed only £5 and had no mining equipment other than saddlery for pack horses. His will shows that he had shares in coalworks at Gitchfield in Broseley. Samuel Evans *(81)* who died in 1733 was a Quaker, and requested that he should be interred in the Friends' burial ground at Broseley. His inventory suggests that he was involved in brickmaking, and his wealth, like that of fellow master colliers, was largely made up of debts due to him. The inventory of John Palmer *(193)* of Madeley Wood shows a comfortable house but provides no details of his mining activities. His will shows that he lived at Astons Leasow, that his family home at the Lake Head in Madeley Wood had been let to Edward Yates, that he had leased the Tuckies estate in Broseley from John Wase, and that his wife Mary held a life interest in the Old House in Madeley Wood inherited from her father Thomas Danks. The will also shows that Palmer had a brother, Robert, who was probably the Madeley Wood timber merchant who in 1780 built the first bridge at Preen's Eddy, the precursor of the present Coalport Bridge.[26] James Harrison *(36)* who died in 1677 might also be regarded as a master collier. His inventory includes mining equipment worth more than £10, and his will reveals that he was operating a coalwork in partnership with Mercy Bromley and Samuel Langley. Other inventories show that financial interest in coal workings were sometimes of modest scale and spreading widely through the community. Thomas Williams in 1733 had a lease of coals from George Weld worth only £3 5s. 0d., John Beddow in 1736 had a title to a coalwork worth £7, and a Broseley widow, Joyce Edwards, in 1765 had 'A small interest in a Colliery at present worth nothing but may be worth hereafter £20'.

Ten of the published inventories provide evidence about colliery equipment *(5, 13, 25, 29, 36, 58, 81, 92, 132, 158)*, and they do much to illuminate the operation of mines in the Severn Gorge. It is evident that quite poor miners like Edward Jones *(92)* as well as master colliers owned tools and equipment. The most detailed inventory, that of John Pearce *(58)* of Broseley made in 1709, details his possessions at his foot rid (or adit). His equipment less the value of his horses was worth £5 12s. 0d. He had a wind (or windlass), with blocks (bloakes) worth 5s., and a hauling or rope for it worth 14s. A pit rope belonging to James Harrison of Broseley *(36)* in 1677 was valued at £1, and four ropes with three 'tunbarrels' (*turn*barrels or windlasses) on the inventory of Samuel Evans *(81)* of Broseley in 1743 were worth £1 10s. 0d. Hand tools included mandrells *(small picks)*, shovels, spades, wedges, augers, bills, axes and hammers. Coal was usually handled in baskets, seven of which were listed on the inventory of Edward Jones *(92)* and two on that of William Smith *(20)* in 1752. It is evident that, as in the celebrated engraving by Robertson of a Broseley horse gin in 1788, a blacksmith's shop usually formed part of pithead installations. An anvil and other smiths' tools appear on the inventory of James Harrison *(36)* and bellows with a hammer on that of Francis Evans *(132)*. Three inventories mention the primitive railways which were developed in the Severn Gorge from the first years of the 17th century to carry coal from pitheads to the river banks. John Holland's *(158)* colliery equipment in 1690 included rails, while John Pearce *(58)* in 1709 had eight wagons worth 2s. 6d. each, and 150 pairs of wagon wheels worth only 4d. each, together with 50 yards of wooden railway track worth 11s. Pit wagons, probably for use underground, and wagon rails also appear on the inventory of Edward Jones in 1742. Other references to wagons are ambiguous and may apply to road rather than railway vehicles. Horses at coal mines like the mare and colt worth £3 at John Pearce's footrid, or the three horses at James Harrison's mine, could have been used to operate gin mechanisms like those at the mine of William Oakes *(25)*, or for haulage or road or rail wagons. Richard Barker, a Madeley collier whose possessions were appraised in 1731, had a necessary but humbler item of colliery equipment, a pound of candles.

The families of those who mined coal gained their subsistence from many sources other than mining. Ten miners had cows, 16 had pigs, seven made milk or cheese, 37 brewed their own beer, 12 had spinning wheels and seven had yarn in their homes. They were also to the forefront in acquiring luxury goods. Eleven had pottery and nine had looking glasses. Eighteen, 27 per cent of the total, had clocks, whereas only 15 per cent of the inventories as a whole include them. They inventories of Edward Boden *(159)*, John Bayley *(167)*, Edward Thomas *(191)* and William Botteley *(196)* are good examples of self-sufficient miners' households.

Much of the coal mined in the four parishes was conveyed by wooden railways to riverside wharves where it was taken by bargeowners on credit for sale to customers in settlements downstream of the Gorge, the trade often known as the 'Severn Sale'. Some was carried to other customers by packhorse. Edward Cox *(61)* in 1714 had six small horses for carrying coal, worth £3 each, quite a high value for working horses. Some saddlery for pack horses was the only item on the inventory of the master collier William Pearce *(*1742*)* that linked him with mining. The likeliest employment for the five horses and mares owned by the Little Wenlock blacksmith and farmer John Fletcher *(125)* would have been in the carriage of coal.

Coal Users

Iron ore was smelted in blast furnaces in and around the Severn Gorge from the late 16th century. The ironmasters who worked them used ore mined from the carboniferous measures and locally-quarried limestone, but for the most part used charcoal as their fuel. In 1708 Abraham Darby I leased the blast furnace at Coalbrookdale and moved to Shropshire from Bristol, and the following year began to smelt iron using coke produced from coal rather than charcoal,[27] but it was not until the 1750s that the consequences of this innovation stimulated the construction of many more furnaces. In the period covered by the inventories blast furnaces were working at Coalbrookdale, Willey and Leighton. The inventories provide evidence that iron ore was being extracted in Benthall and Broseley. Some of the iron ore for the Coalbrookdale furnaces in the 1720s and '30s was obtained from the south side of the river and ferried across.[28] John Pearce *(58)*, the Broseley master collier, had 'a lading of Ironstone' worth £4 in 1709. The inventory of the landowner Richard Benthall *(13)* in 1720 includes 'ironstone ready got' worth £24 2s. 6d. William Smith *(20)* in 1752 appears to have been extracting iron ore by open cast methods. His inventory describes him as a quarryman, and his 'tools and materials belonging to Iron Stone Works' were worth £5.

The inventories supply only a modest amount of evidence about the relatively small number of people who worked at the ironworks in the Severn Gorge. William Maybury *(161)* who died in 1704 was probably a member of the family who for several generations worked the Upper Forge in Coalbrookdale, and a descendant of the Thomas Maybury, hammerman, whose name was inscribed there in 1669.[29] No inventory survives for Cornelius Hallen who died in 1746, a member of a celebrated ironworking family, specialists in forging frying pans, who operated the Lower Forge in Coalbrookdale. John Jones *(190)*, forgeman of Madeley, probably of Coalbrookdale, died in 1754. His inventory reveals nothing about his work, simply showing that he lived in a well-furnished house, where his chattells were worth £16 12s. 0d. George Thomas *(195)* was the son of the better-known John Thomas, the Quaker potfounder, who followed Abraham Darby I from Bristol to Coalbrookdale in the early 18th century and also died in 1760.[30] George's inventory reveals a modest house with a kitchen and parlour on the ground floor, two bedrooms above, a cellar below, and an adjacent brewhouse. His will shows that this was his own house in Coalbrookdale, which passed to his wife for her own lifetime and then to his son, also George, but his daughter Hannah, author of a well-known memoir of the Darbys, was to receive the brewhouse, together with part of the plot of land on which the house stood, which was to be marked off with quicksets. The will of John Thomas provided for George Thomas's rights of access to his house to be preserved through properties left to his siblings. George Thomas's will shows that Walter Parker, his witness, appraiser of his inventory, and witness to his father's will, was his immediate neighbour. The wills of several Coalbrookdale ironworkers in the second half of the 18th century similarly suggest that those who worked at the furnaces and forges for long periods acquired modest properties and formed a modest 'aristocracy of labour' within the enterprises of the Coalbrookdale Company. Walter Parker made his will in December 1769, and left three freehold tenements in Coalbrookdale, in one of which he lived. Thomas Rose of Coalbrookdale, smith, owned three tenements in Madeley Wood when he made his will in 1767. Michael Parker, ironfounder of Coalbrookdale, apparently not a direct descendent of Walter Parker, held the lease of a small terrace when he made his will in 1799. John Slicer, iron potfounder of Coalbrookdale, held no property, but had deposited a bond of £50 with one Robert Horton for distribution amongst his offspring some ten months before he made his will in 1760.[31]

Roger Downes *(172)*, whose will was proved in 1720, was a brassfounder, who like John Thomas had followed the first Abraham Darby from Brisol to Coalbrookdale, where Darby was working brass as well as iron. Downes's inventory shows that he had tools, including moulds, vices and lathes, a quantity of coal, for use in his workshop, a brass pot, which from its position in the inventory could have been one of his products, and 144 'cocks' (i.e. taps), 'in the rough', apparently cast but not finished. After brass manufacture ceased at Coalbrookdale, Downes and his successors continued to sub-contract for the ironworks, in particular fitting brass taps to the iron pots made in the foundry. Abraham Darby I died in 1717, and when Downes died three years later £10 was due to him from Thomas Bayliss, the notorious administrator of Darby's estate.[32]

Lead as well as iron ore was smelted with coal in the Severn Gorge. A visitor in 1744 found the fumes from the lead works 'vastly poisonous and destructive to everything near'. Four smelters operated in the Gorge during the 18th century, but not all at the same time. The only indication of the industry in the probate records is the rather uninformative will of Christopher Pritchard of Madeley, lead smelter, who died in 1753. Pritchard possibly worked at a smelter near Dale End.[33]

Martin Eele was the late 17th-century pioneer of the destructive distillation of coal in the Severn Gorge. It is unfortunate that no probate documents survive for Eele himself, and that the inventory of his widow,

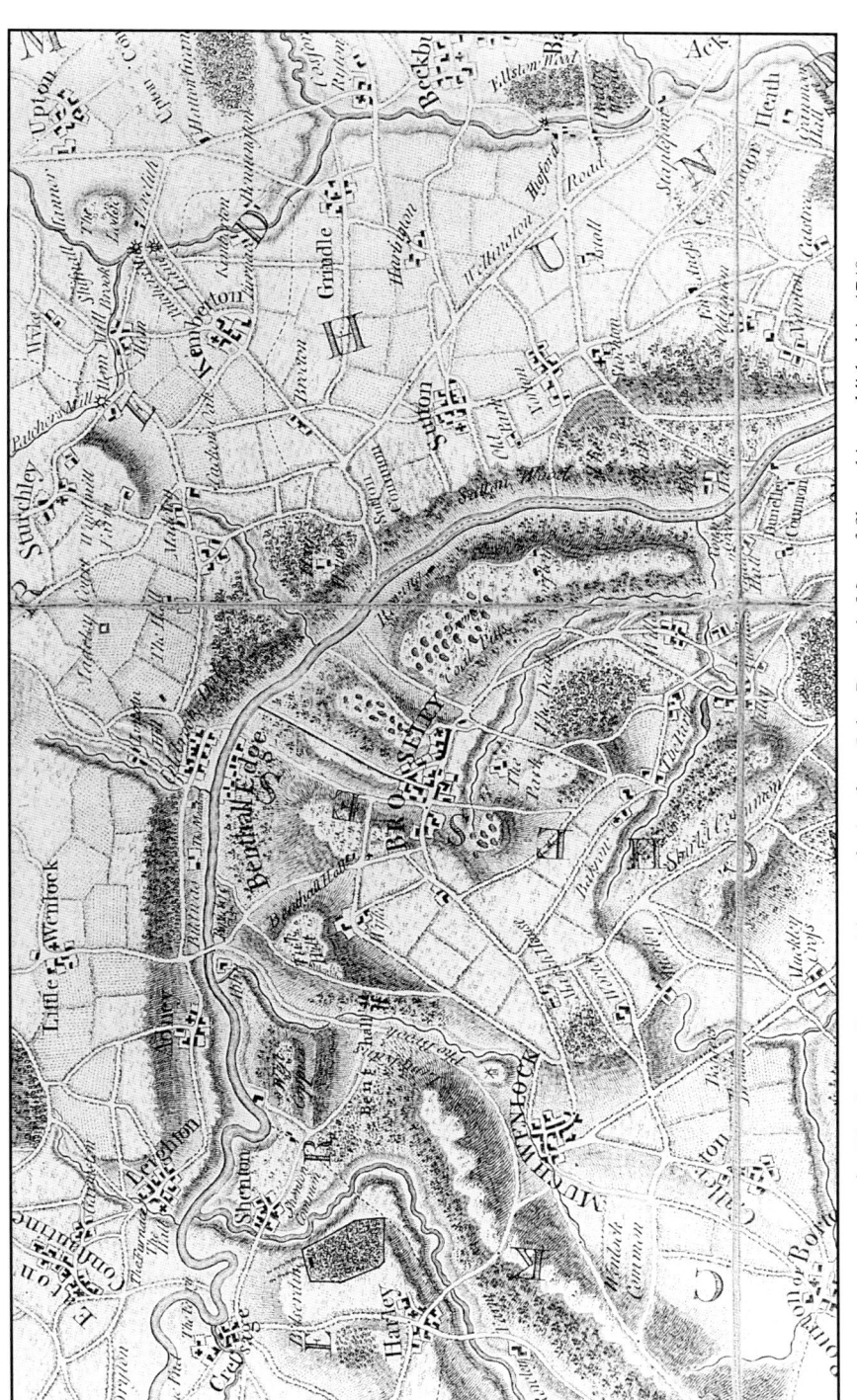

1 The Severn Gorge parishes as depicted on John Rocque's Map of Shropshire published in 1748.

2 The Severn Gorge before the construction of the Iron Bridge. The land in the foreground on the right is in Madeley. Broseley is on the left bank when viewed in this upstream direction, but the smoking chimneys in the distance are those of the lead smelter across the boundary with Benthall. From William Williams, *A View of the Reiver Severn at Madely near Coalbrook Dale*, c. 1776.

3   The parish church of St Bartholomew, Benthall.

4   The parish church of St Lawrence, Little Wenlock.

5   George Robertson, *A view of the mouth of a Coal Pit near Broseley in Shropshire* (1788) showing a horse gin, a wooden railway, a blacksmith's shop and packhorses tended by a woman, all features of collieries included in the inventories.

6   The Old Furnace, Coalbrookdale, as depicted in Francis Vivares and George Perry, *The Upper Works at Coalbrook Dale* (1758).

7 The lead smelter at the Bower Yard, Benthall, as depicted on George Robertson, *The Iron Bridge from Lincoln Hill* (1788).

8 An ironfounder, like John or George Thomas, from *The Book of English Trades* (1837 edition).

9 Samuel Ireland's picture *Iron Bridge near Coalbrookdale*, painted before 1800, shows a barge or trow with a topsail to the left, and a 'boat' on the right bank.

10 Small barges of the kind used in the Upper Severn coal trade moored at the Bower Yard boatyard, Benthall in the 1850s.

11 Bow haulers pulling a barge through the Iron Bridge, from Thomas Burney, *A View of the Iron Bridge, Coalbrookdale* (1789).

12 The windlass in the prow of a barge moored near the Iron Bridge, from F. Edgcombe, *A View of the Cast Iron Bridge over the Severn at Coalbrook Dale* (1782).

13 A ropemaker, with his 'engine', from *The Book of English Trades* (1837 edition).

14 A tallow chandler dipping candles, from *The Book of English Trades* (1837 edition).

Eleanor Eele, who died in 1701, provides no information about the business.[34]

Limestone was worked in the Severn Gorge in the 17th and 18th centuries both for burning with coal in kilns to produce lime for building and agriculture, and for use as a flux in blast furnaces. The only indication in the inventories of its extraction is the 'limestone ready got' which belonged to Richard Benthall *(13)*.

The inventories confirm that many bricks were being made in the Severn Gorge by 1700, a trade which also consumed large quantities of coal. John Lloyd *(146)* in 1675 and John Smitheman *(119)* in 1689 both had considerable numbers of bricks, the former having roofing tiles as well. Richard Benthall *(13)* had a clamp of bricks worth 10 guineas, and the master collier Samuel Evans *(81)* in 1733 had bricks, tiles, crests and gutters.

The existence of potters in the Severn Gorge in the first half of the 18th century, making ware broadly similar to that being produced at that time in North Staffordshire, has been demonstrated from both documentary and archaeological evidence,[35] but no inventories survive for potters from the Gorge as such. Subsequent probate evidence shows that there were numerous potters in Broseley and Benthall, including Aaron Simpson, John Bell, Richard Cotton and John Miles. The only potter's inventory in the collection is that of Thomas Cartledge *(136)* of Little Wenlock which gives the impression of a rather rustic pottery. Cartledge kept a few cattle and a couple of pigs and brewed his own beer. He had two workshops, with a lathe in the new one and a potter's wheel in the old one, and kept finished wares in both. Another Thomas Cartledge was working as a potter at Coalmoor, Little Wenlock in 1767.[36]

Broseley was renowned for its clay tobacco pipes from the 17th century. Wakelin and Higgins have shown from the Gloucester portbooks and from archaeological evidence that pipes made in Broseley tended to be sent to towns which lacked their own pipe manufacturers, and that they were sent to and have been found only rarely in Bristol, where pipemakers abounded. Until the mid-18th century Broseley pipes were made from local white clay, like that listed in the inventory of Richard Benthall *(13)*. Pipes were made in moulds of two halves. The stem was bored out after the bowl had been smoothed and finished. The maker's mark was stamped, usually on the heel (that part of the pipe below the stem), or on the stem itself. Making moulds was a skilled task, but most pipemakers appear to have made only one sort of pipe, and probably bought in their moulds. The 'implements and tools for the art of tobacco pipe making' of Thomas Roden *(71)* were listed in detail, and include six or more types of mould—the differences probably lay in the style of the heel and the length of the stem. Examples remain of just one type of pipe made by this Thomas Roden. They have tailed heels, and were probably made from the 'peak heel' moulds listed on the inventory. Thomas Roden's son Samuel made pipes from clay that had been imported, probably from Dorset or the Isle of Wight. The inventory of Thomas Hartshorne *(19)* of Benthall is one of the most detailed of those for people of modest means, but his tobacco pipe tools were worth only 12s. 6d., and were accompanied in his workshop by equipment for brewing, spinning and gardening. Thomas Hartshorne had a son, John, who was also a pipemaker, and appears to have appraised the goods of at least three other pipemakers. One of them, Thomas Taylor *(84)*, had a shop with screws, moulds, grates and boards, similar to those of Thomas Roden and, like Roden, he had 'slob benches', a term which probably indicated a working surface made of slobs (or slabs, or planks) of timber, characteristically made dirty by the use of liquids. Other inventories are less informative. Thomas Hughes in 1735 had tobacco pipe tools worth 10 shillings, and the tools of William Morris *(106)* were worth a guinea. Samuel Head *(97)* had a slob bench in his workshop, and was probably a pipemaker, although the inventory reveals no details of his trade.[37]

Coal was the basis of the economy of the Severn Gorge parishes in the century before 1750, but relatively small quantities appear to have been consumed locally, a situation which changed with the construction of nine blast furnaces in the area between 1755 and 1758. Local domestic use is considered below (see pp. 56-57). Most of the coal mined before 1750 was distributed along the River Severn, and, after the miners, the most significant occupational group in the Gorge were the agents of distribution who worked on the river.

The River Trade

River traders were more numerous than miners in the Severn Gorge and of similar economic importance. The inventories made in the riverside parishes of Benthall, Broseley and Madeley between 1662 and 1764 include 73 which relate to people who worked on the river, 11 in Benthall, 47 in Broseley and 15 in Madeley, just over 15 per cent of the total. The proportion of bargemen amongst the population appears to have remained constant during the period. Sixty-four inventories list vessels which worked on the river. Barge owning seems to have been a distinct occupation in the 18th century, but before 1700 several people engaged in other occupations owned and operated barges. William Oakes *(25)*, a collier who died in 1669, had a boat itemised with the tools for his coalworks, and the two William

INTRODUCTION

Ashwoods *(152, 160)*, blacksmiths of Madeley Wood, each had a barge recorded on their inventories, most probably the same vessel. The latter William Ashwood was described on his inventory, which listed a smith's shop, as a blacksmith, but as a trowman on his will. In other sources those who worked barges were often distinguished by the prefix 'Owner'. The somewhat inappropriate term 'mariner' was applied to river traders in several probate documents and appears on at least one memorial.

The inventories include references to 91 boats, some of which, like those in the Ashwoods' inventories, may be the same vessels appraised at different times. More or less precise values are given for 66 individual vessels. The inventories throw some light on the distinction between trows and barges on the Severn. If the word trow referred to a distinctive type of vessel, it probably indicated one that could sail safely on the lower river below Gloucester, and thus reach Bristol, Chepstow or Lydney. The Gloucester Portbooks suggest that relatively few vessels from the Severn Gorge worked regularly on the lower river. Owners of vessels are described as *trowmen* throughout the period, but the first reference to a *trow* is on the inventory of Thomas Beard *(7)* in 1706, in which the appraisers, including the trowman Eustace Beard, distinguished a 'middle-sized trow' from a 'small barge'. Trows are mentioned on 20 inventories after 1700. It is evident that some appraisers consciously distinguished trows from barges, and that when the distinction was made a trow was more valuable, and presumably larger than a barge. Only three trows were valued at less than £20, while most of the rest were worth more than £30, a value exceeded by only one barge. The most valuable vessels listed are the trow belonging to Andrew Dodson *(8)*, worth £80, and that of Edward Owen *(182)*, worth £70. Some appraisers, like those of John Poole *(83)* and Benjamin Buckley *(85)*, used 'trow' and 'barge' as synonymous terms. The term 'frigate' is used on two inventories in 1729 and 1734, but it is uncertain just what distinguished a frigate from a barge or a trow. The inventories show that barges with top sails were used by owners from the Gorge. John Rowlands in 1753 had a 'top mast barge' worth £20, and the possessions of Jonathan Oakes *(114)* included a main mast, a top mast, cross trees and a main yard, as well as blocks for raising top sails.

The inventories identify and name the following vessels:

Two vessels, the *Jonathan* worth £40 and the *Thomas* worth £2 10s. 0d. in the inventory of Richard Brook *(142)* in 1669

Two barges, the *Elizabeth* worth £12 and the *Primrose* worth £16 on the inventory of Adam Stokes *(34)* in 1675

Two barges, the *Walton* worth £9 and the *Joyce* worth £2 10s. 0d. in the inventory of Hugh Jones *(48)* in 1689

A barge called the *Joan* which belonged to Richard Eaves in 1692

The trow called the *Eastop* and the barge called the *Nicholls* on the inventory of Edward Lloyd *(164)* in 1709

The will of Edward Owen *(176)* who died in 1728 shows that the barge mentioned in his inventory was called the *Edward*

The trow called the *John* worth £25 which belonged to John Yates *(107)* in 1757

There are 10 references to 'boats' as distinct from barges. The term was used precisely, and was sometimes qualified as in the 'long stock boat' listed amongst the possessions of Edward Owen *(182)* in 1734, or the 'foot boat' which belonged to Oliver Easthope in 1680. All 10 boats were worth less than £3. Such vessels are illustrated in several engravings of the river. They could have been used for moving small consignments of goods between a long-distance barge and other vessels to wharves, for carrying bowhaulers or for passengers.

Some owners evidently allowed their vessels to fall into disrepair in their old age. A barge belonging to Joseph Martin who died in 1726 was 'overworn'. The appraisers of the estate of William Day *(17)* found his trow 'much damaged, decayed and out of repair'. It was worth only £12, but when making his will, only 16 days before he was buried, he expected that it would realise £40 which was to be invested for the benefit of his children. A barge and a boat belonging to Francis (or Stukely) Oakes in 1721 were sold to be cut up, and apparently realised £6 15s. 0d. as scrap. One of four barges belonging to John Poole *(83)* was described as 'worn out', and another had been cut up to realise £2 15s. 0d.

The range of equipment needed to operate a barge on the Severn is defined in the inventory of Thomas Gower *(75)*, which included three vessels, and the ropes, masts, sails, shafts, oars and planks used with them. Thomas Eastope in 1675 had old ropes valued at 3s. 4d., and Timothy Crompton *(29)* old rigging worth five shillings. Ann Dawley *(45)* had pitch, tar and okum, doubtless for caulking her barge. Richard Eaves in 1693 had a mast, a sail and some rigging itemised separately from his barge. John Poole *(83)* had a main mast, a top mast, a tarpaulin and an anchor. William Lewis *(26)* had a barge chest itemised with an unstocked anchor. John Oakes *(96)* also had a barge chest, worth five shillings. Benjamin Buckley

(85) had a windlass barrel and windlass, probably used to raise and lower the mast of a vessel when passing through bridges. The most detailed list of equipment occurs in the inventory of Jonathan Oakes *(114)*, which, ironically, does not include a barge. Oakes had ropes, shrouds, dead-eyes, a cedger (i.e. a small anchor), a hawser (i.e. a tow line), blocks, sails, planks, a windlass and masts. A shroud is part of the rigging of a ship, a set of ropes attached to the head of a mast which relieves the lateral strain on the mast. A dead-eye was a block with three holes drilled in it used for extending a shroud.

Vessels were built in the Severn Gorge throughout the period when the navigation prospered, the last yard closing in the early 1860s.[38] Only one inventory provides any evidence about the trade. George Eastope who died in Madeley in 1682 was a shipwright, but the inventory provides no details of his occupation, save that he had a chest and tools worth 10 shillings.

Three ferries crossed the river between Madeley on the north bank and Benthall and Broseley on the south side. Edward Reynolds *(93)*, whose inventory was compiled in 1743, was described as a dyer, but he obviously operated one of the ferries since his meagre possessions included an old passage boat, valued at only £1 3s. 0d., together with a plank, possible for gaining access to the boat, worth 5s. Reynolds shipped iron ore across the river for the Coalbrookdale partners in 1729-31. In other parts of the country dyers used boats to rinse cloth in rivers, and it is possible that Reynolds had combined the two occupations.

Until the construction of towpaths along the Severn between Shrewsbury and Framilode between 1790 and 1810 vessels were pulled up the river by gangs of bow haulers. The inventories identify two individuals who may have earned their livings this way. Thomas Eastop of Benthall who died in 1673 living in a two-room dwelling with possessions worth only £3 16s. 0d. had ropes worth 3s. 4d. which may have indicated that he worked on the river. John Poole *(70)* died in 1724 and is described as a 'labouring waterman'. His possessions included two lines and a rope, between them worth 19s. 6d., which could have been used for hauling vessels, and two barrows which could have been used for loading cargoes. Bow haulers were usually regarded as poor, an impression borne out by the value of Poole's possessions, only £1 18s. 6d., and by his 'very mean' clothing.

The inventories provide several glimpses of cargoes in transit on the Severn. William Lewis *(26)* in 1670 had 17 tons of alabaster worth £5 19s. 0d., and two tons of coal at 'Brimshill' (i.e. Bristol) worth £1. Alabaster is usually a translucent form of calcium sulphate or gypsum, best known as a material from which funerary monuments were carved. The principal sources in England are at Tutbury, Staffordshire and Chellaston, Derbyshire. It seems likely that the alabaster was en route from the east Midlands to Bristol where there were carving shops which worked it. The inventory of Edward Jefferies, a Bridgnorth waterman who died in 1673, also lists a parcel of alabaster.[39] Coal mines in the Bristol area supplied local domestic needs, but Lewis's inventory confirms the evidence of the Gloucester Portbooks that small consignments of Shropshire coal were taken to the city, doubtless for specific industrial purposes. The inventory of Ann Dawley *(45)* lists coal worth 7s. 6d., while that of Richard Brook *(142)* included limestone worth £4 and timber worth £5. Another aspect of Severn trading is illuminated by the £5 debt owing to John Hagar *(144)* from a merchant in Bewdley.

Bargemen formed an increasingly distinctive occupation group between 1660 and 1760 but throughout the period they augmented their livings by other means. Three 17th-century bargemen, Richard Brook *(142)*, John Hagar *(144)* and William Benbow *(30)*, farmed on a considerable scale. Hagar, at Strethill Farm, cultivated five sorts of grain with a plough team of oxen, had a dairy herd of 12 and a flock of 82 sheep. Nine others kept cows, mostly single animals tended for their milk. Pigs were kept by 29 bargemen, 32 had brewing equipment, 11 had spinning wheels and seven had yarn or unspun hemp in their homes.

Bargemen were pre-eminent amongst those who furnished their homes with luxuries. Thirteen had clocks and Edward Owen *(182)* had a weather glass. Eight had pottery and 11 had looking glasses. As a class those who sailed the Severn were not especially wealthy—48 of the 73 inventories were valued at less than £50, but, rather like the shepherds of Montaillou,[40] they were accustomed to go to distant places, some of them to Bristol, second city in England, and obviously acquired a taste for novelties which they conveyed back to their native places. While most bargemen were poor, there were 12 whose inventories exceeded £100 in value. Most appear to have been amongst those who traded to Bristol, and homes like those of Andrew Dodson *(8)*, George Bradley *(12)*, Edward Owen *(182)*, Benjamin Buckley *(85)* and William Yates *(101)* show that a comfortable living could be obtained from trading on the river.

In a trade that involved extended families, it is hazardous to suppose that a person mentioned in one source is the same as someone named in another. Nevertheless it is significant that at most no more than 20 of the bargemen whose inventories appear in this collection are recorded in the

Gloucester Portbooks, either as merchants or masters. This accords with the view that only a minority of the barge-owners from the Gorge sailed the tidal section of the Severn to reach Bristol, and that most were concerned with the coal trade above Gloucester.[41]

Many of the barge-owning families represented among the inventories had connections with the river over two centuries or more.[42] The inventory of George Armstrong in 1740 included two old vessels on the Severn, worth only £12 between them, suggesting that he was amongst the poorer barge-owners. His will identifies them as *The Adam* and *The Adams*, suggesting a link with another family well-known on the river, and they were left to his widow. There were doubtless links between George Armstrong and other bargemen of the same name. A Benjamin Armstrong was carrying for the Coalbrookdale Company in 1721, and a Henry Armstrong, waterman, was living in Benthall as late as 1861.

The Benbow family was also active in the Severn trade over many generations. William Benbow *(30)* in 1673 had barges worth £8, but gained part of his living from cows, sheep and the spinning of flax. Francis Benbow in 1710 had a small barge and just a few animals. The name is repeated in the records of the river throughout the 18th century. A Francis Benbow was carrying coal from George Weld's wharf in Jackfield in 1748. In 1752 a Francis Benbow, owner, was living at Tarbatch Dingle in Broseley, and had married Joyce Onions, whose family had property there. In 1796 a Francis Benbow of the Rovings, in Barrow parish, boatbuilder, went bankrupt, in consequence of which two large vessels, one uncompleted, were offered for sale.[43] Benbows were also active in the river trade at Bridgnorth.

The Buckley family had a similarly long connection with the river. John Buckley died in 1681-2 leaving a barge worth £15. Benjamin Buckley *(85)* in 1740 and Ambrose Buckley *(109)* in 1758 both left barges amongst their possessions. The will of George Buckley, proved in 1742, is not accompanied by an inventory, but it shows that he owned two vessels, the *Francis & Sarah* and the *Sweepshore*, which were to be sold for the benefit of his wife and sons, and the will of Andrew Buckley, trowman, who died in 1740, shows that the family leased property in Holly Groves in Jackfield. John Buckley, waterman, was living at the Werps, another part of Jackfield, in 1841.

Similarly Silvanus Ball *(95)*, whose inventory in 1743 included two vessels worth £60, was a member of a long-established family of river traders. Another Silvanus Ball was carrying coal from George Weld's wharf in 1748, and a man of the same name died in 1776, leaving three cottages at the Woodlands in Broseley to his sons, another Silvanus, Samuel and Benjamin. The will of a William Ball who had a brother called Silvanus was proved in 1758.

The inventory of Hugh Cullis *(16)* made in 1729 is the only trace in this collection of a prominent river-trading family. Hugh Cullis's inventory includes no barges, but in his will he left his house and vessels to his son Thomas. A John Cullis was carrying for the Coalbrookdale Company in 1719-20. An Edward Cullis was a leading Shrewsbury barge-owner in the 1790s, and four households of that name were living alongside and working on the Severn in Broseley in 1851.

The inventory of Timothy Crompton *(29)* taken in 1672 is the first evidence of the involvement of the family on the river. The Cromptons (or Crumptons) were for long associated with the ferry that until 1909 crossed the Severn at the site of the present road bridge, and an Adam Crumpton in 1654 had built the *Dog and Duck* public house from which the ferry operated.[44] The inventory of John Crompton in 1735 records two old boats together worth only £3, which suggests that he could have been operating the ferry. In the 1720s and 1730s he was carrying iron ore from Broseley and Benthall across the river for the Coalbrookdale Company. In the 1790s Adam Crumpton and his son, also Adam, from the ferry boat, were carrying coal for the Madeley Wood Company, and a William Crumpton was recorded as proprietor of the ferry boat in 1851.

The Oakeses were one of the most active river-trading families. Roger Oakes was described as a trowman when he died in 1669. Francis Oakes, known as Stukely, left an old barge and an old boat in 1721. Francis 'Stukely' Oakes was carrying coal for the Madeley Wood Company in 1794, together with another Francis distinguished by the nickname 'Snig' or 'Snigsy'. A Francis 'Sprink' Oakes had been carrying coal from George Weld's wharf in 1748. Members of the family in the Salthouse area of Jackfield were still engaged in the river trade in the mid-19th century, and others lived at Bridgnorth, where by the 1750s they operated the town's principal boat-building yard. In 1786 a trow belonging to Owner Oakes of Broseley, loaded with iron, sank in the Severn estuary near to the Old Passage.[45]

Perhaps the most prominent of the barge-owners were the father and son, both called Edward Owen *(176, 182)* of Madeley Wood, who died in 1728 and 1732. The senior Owen left two trows and a barge called the *Edward*, with two small boats. He provided in his will for one trow to be sold for the benefit of his widow, and for his son to work the other, together with the barge and the small boats. The junior Owen owned at the time of his death vessels to the value of more than £200, including 'the great trow at Gloucester' worth £70. His inventory shows that he lived in some luxury, with chairs covered with leather and turkey work, maps, pictures, a weather glass and Bristol wares that included a punch bowl. Edward Owen, working a vessel called the *Sarah*, was the principal carrier for Abraham Darby I of the Coalbrookdale ironworks between 1708 and 1713, when Thomas Williams of Broseley took over the work. The Owens resumed carrying occasional loads for the Coalbrookdale Company in the 1720s, and it appears that from 1723 they took over the carriage of castings and pig iron to Bristol, as well as taking goods to Bewdley, Worcester, Tewkesbury and Gloucester, and sometimes to Shrewsbury. The junior Owen's widow, Elizabeth, continued to carry for the Coalbrookdale Company after her husband died. The Owens were related to the Beards and to other barge-owning families and remained active on the river into the second half of the 19th century.[46]

The Beards were the most extensive of the families involved in the Upper Severn trade. Thomas Beard *(7)* in 1706 owned a middle-sized trow and a small barge together worth £60, and is the first of the family who can be positively identified as working on the river, although they were already well-established in the Severn Gorge. Eustroyus (i.e. Eustace, a name much used in the family), son of Thomas and Phelicia Beard, was baptised at Broseley on 4 May 1631, and a Eustace Beard, possibly the same person, married Mary Armishaw in the same parish in 1674. One of Thomas Beard's appraisers was also a Eustace Beard, probably the same man whose inventory was made in 1726. This Eustace Beard *(14)* had no vessels, but possessed ropes, sails and other materials 'for a waterman's use'. He may well have retired and passed his boats to his son, another Eustace born about 1700. The Coalbrookdale Company accounts show that a Eustace Beard was carrying for them from 1724. Subsequently this Eustace Beard became one of the company's most trusted contractors.[47] He regularly took Coalbrookdale goods to Bristol, and from time to time conveyed money for the company. He carried down river much of the pig iron from the first blast furnace at Horsehay when it came into operation in 1755. This Eustace Beard died in 1761 and is commemorated by an iron tomb in Benthall churchyard. In his will made in 1759 he left a house and garden on land purchased from Richard Phillips to his daughter and her husband, James Owen, also a bargeman who carried for the Coalbrookdale Company, who had built a new house on part of the premises. The Owens had a son who bore the family name Eustace. Eustace Beard probably retired from the river about 1756 when he was succeeded by his son Richard. His brother, also Richard, lived in Madeley, was described as a 'mariner' on his will, and left property to his namesake nephew. The Beard family continued on the river till the very end of the navigation. By 1797 James Beard was operating from Pool Quay where he died in 1839. Thomas Beard of Jackfield was the author of a commonplace book which is amongst the most informative sources on the barge-owning community, while Thomas Beard of the Werps, where the family had held land there at least as early as 1797, was owner of the last commercial barge to work on the Upper Severn, which, loaded with bricks, sank after hitting Bridgnorth bridge on 25 January 1895.[48]

Curiously neither the will nor the inventory of Thomas Williams *(76)* reveals that he had been one of the most distinguished bargemen on the Severn. The inventory shows that he had a comfortable if not especially luxurious home, but evidence of his wealth is provided by the properties listed in his will. Williams had carried iron from Coalbrookdale to Bristol between 1716 and 1725 in the *William & Mary*, and his sons, Thomas and Jonathan, also worked on the river.[49]

Most of the other barge-owning families represented in this collection had similarly long connections with the river. The family of Andrew Dodson *(8)* of Benthall, who owned the most valuable single vessel listed in this collection, subsequently settled at Cound Lane End, and one of their barges was the first to be drawn by a horse into Shrewsbury when the towpath was completed in 1810. The inventory of John Oswald, or Oswell, taken in 1728, lists two old vessels on the Severn. Another John Oswell who died in 1786 left two trows,[50] the *Joseph & Mary* and the *Molly of Benthall*, and his will shows that his daughters had married into the Benbow, Beard, Wild and Yates families, all of whom worked on the river. Oswells were still living at the Werps and working on the river in the 1870s. George Phillips who died in 1706 left a vessel valued by his two bargemen appraisers, a Beard and a Benbow, at £13. No inventory remains for Thomas Phillips of Broseley who died in 1743, but a William Phillips was carrying coal for the Madeley Wood Company in the 1790s, and a trow belonging to a Mr. Phillips of Broseley had its rigging blown off when upstream from Gloucester in October 1802, which resulted in the drowning of one of the crew.[51] There were also barge-owners called Phillips in Bridgnorth, and Robert Phillips, a waterman, was living in Frankwell, Shrewsbury, in 1841. The inventory of John Poole of Broseley *(83)* made in 1739 provides some of the most detailed evidence in the collection about the river trade. It was probably this John Poole who between 1736 and 1738 was carrying iron for the Coalbrookdale Company to Bewdley,

Bridgnorth, Shrewsbury and Tern Forge. Members of the family also worked vessels from Madeley, Bridgnorth and Bewdley. John Wilde *(100)* was living in Gloucester when he died in 1747 but had previously been resident in Broseley. Coalbrookdale Company records show that he was carrying iron to Gloucester in 1732 and bringing back deals from Bristol in 1737. Wildes were associated with the river for more than a century after his death, and were still working boats from cottages in the Werps and Holly Groves in the mid-19th century. William Yates *(101)* of the Bowling Green in Broseley who died in 1748 had two trows, named in his will as the *John* and the *Frances*, worth between them more than £100, showing that he was one of the most prosperous bargemen of his time. His son John Yates *(107)* who died in 1757 was less wealthy, and possessed just one vessel, the *John*, then valued at £25. His descendants throughout the next century were amongst the leading barge-owners of the Severn Gorge, their involvement with the trade probably ending in 1869 with the dissolution of the partnership of John and John William Yates of Ironbridge, maltsters, hop merchants, barge-owners and farmers.[52] Similarly long links could be demonstrated for the Dawley, Easthope and Lloyd families.

Fishing was important on the Severn. The construction of fish weirs and by-pass channels to go round them led in the Middle Ages to the formation of islands which can still be identified. The equipment for one such weir is listed in the inventory of Edgar Dyos of Little Shrawardine taken in 1661. Some fishing on the Severn, like that on the Upper Thames for which Fisher Row in Oxford was the base, was done from boats.[53] John Yates *(143)* of Madeley Wood had fishing nets and a fishing boat worth £1, and Edward Jones *(24)* also had a fishing net.

The Ancillary Trades
Mining and the river trade depended on several crafts practised on the surface and on dry land. The presence of so many skills in the Severn Gorge in the century after 1660, allied to the availability of fuel and transport, proved a stimulus to the growth of large-scale ironmaking in the second half of the 18th century.

Ropemaking provided materials for both miners and bargemen, and is illustrated in two inventories. George Fletcher *(131)* of Little Wenlock was a relatively poor man, whose possessions included 'instruments &c. belonging to ropemaking' worth £1 14s. 6d. Mary Clemson *(189)*, the widow of a ropemaker, had more equipment 'belonging to a Ropier's business', including an 'engine', the device used to twist and braid hemp from which the maker drew the rope. She also had a wheel and winches, a sled and four carts 'belonging to the works', suggesting that she was involved in mining.

Tallow chandlers, makers of candles, flourished in the Severn Gorge because candles were the means of lighting mines. Inventories, spread evenly through the period, survive for seven candlemakers from Broseley, four of whom were called Whitmore, and two from Madeley. John Sherratt *(147)* was a wealthy man, able to keep a riding horse, although much of the value of his estate was in debts due to him. He had a workshop, with a furnace worth £2 10s. 0d., with a stock of tallow, wick yarn and completed candles worth £10. Henry Bowdler in 1719 had a chandling shop in Madeley Wood, in which the moveable stock was worth £10, but his appraisers supply no details of it. The moveable estate of Robert Whitmore *(63)* was worth over £1,200, and the goods in his shop, tools and candles for sale, were worth £30. Richard Gears *(66)* had possessions worth nearly £160, of which over £90 consisted of book debts. His stock included half a ton of tallow worth £20, a copper furnace in which to melt it, and wick yarn worth £1 19s. 0d. Nevill Edwards *(105)* had tallow worth a pound, but the presence on his inventory of four lame horses and an old blind mare suggests that he was also following some occupation other than candlemaking. The appraisers of John Whitmore *(38)*, William Whitmore *(74)*, Robert Whitmore and Andrew Pugh refer to their equipment or stock but provide no details. The inventories show that candlemaking, usually an urban trade, was significant in the Severn Gorge, that the chandlers in Broseley and Madeley made tallow candles by dipping, and that some of them achieved significant wealth.

Blacksmiths fulfilled several functions within the four parishes. In the agricultural context of Little Wenlock, John Fletcher *(125)* farmed on a considerable scale, and there is nothing in his inventory, except the description of his occupation, to show that he was a blacksmith. The inventory of James Boarder, the only other Little Wenlock blacksmith, is simply a list of debts. In the Severn Gorge blacksmiths might be closely engaged with mining or the river trade, or they might turn to manufacturing nails or locks. Two William Ashwoods *(152, 160)*, probably father and son, worked as blacksmiths in Madeley Wood, and died respectively in 1681 and 1696. The inventories of both record a barge, probably the same vessel. The shop of the first contained two pairs of bellows, two anvils and a beam and scales for weighing, altogether worth £3 1s. 0d., only tenpence more than the bellows and other tools valued in 1696. Edward Amiss *(52)* of Broseley worked on a larger scale with tools worth £7 13s. 4d. and a stock of iron worth £12. The inventories of the other

INTRODUCTION 35

two Broseley blacksmiths, Charles Davis and John Harriotts, provide no details of their work. The most interesting blacksmith's inventory is that of Thomas Rowley *(192)* of Madeley, which included new bar and rod iron, scrap, some of it old horseshoes, coal for the hearth, hammers, punches, files, a screw plate, a studdy for making nails, a grinding stone, three anvils, one worth £3, a pair of bellows worth two guineas, a vice and a shoeing box. The inventory of Thomas Glasebrook, another Madeley Wood blacksmith, lists tools worth only ten shillings. Edward Hartshorne *(6)* of Benthall combined the trade of blacksmith with keeping an inn. His shop included bellows, an anvil, a vice, some tongs and other tools worth altogether £7 5s. 0d.

Blacksmiths were closely associated with nailing. William Ashwood *(141)*, a Madeley nailer who died in 1667 and was probably a kinsman of the two blacksmiths of the same name *(152, 160)*, had hammers, studdies, bores and other tools worth £1 10s. 0d. Thomas Lee *(54)* of Broseley had nails and tools in his nailer's shop worth £3 15. 0d. Making locks was a similar but more intricate trade. The only indication in the inventory of John Hemlock of Broseley in 1673 that he was a locksmith was the presence of an anvil worth 18s., but the contents of the workshop of Thomas Teece *(73)* included bellows, an anvil, hammers and files. The son of Francis Wilkes, a Broseley collier who died in 1757, had taken up the locksmith's trade, but, significantly, had moved to work at Monmore Green, Wolverhampton. It seems likely that both nailers and locksmiths were operating like similar tradesmen in market towns, supplying local demand, rather than, like those of the Black Country, catering for distant markets.

A more skilled metal-working trade was that of the gunsmith. The inventory of James Smitheman *(165)* includes an anvil and vice, a boring bench with nine bits, and coals, doubtless for use in a hearth. It is often assumed that gunmaking was an essentially urban trade, in which skilled makers of locks, barrels and stocks co-operated, but inventory evidence from several parts of Shropshire shows that individual gunsmiths apparently carried out most of the processes themselves in such remote locations as Farlow and Bromfield. It is likely that Smitheman was supplying local rather than national markets.

A dozen inventories of carpenters or cabinet makers *(1, 35, 98, 99, 111, 163, 170, 178)* survive in Benthall, Broseley and Madeley, all of them valued at less than £50, and six at less than £20. Nine provide values for tools, varying between two shillings and six pounds, with one set kept in a chest. John Doughty *(178)* in 1728 left 'a case of drawers not finished', together with rails and spars, and Samuel Burrows *(98)* in 1745 left 'two chests of drawers not finished, together with fenering (i.e. veneering) stuff', indicating that polite furniture was being made in the district. It appears that the making of furniture could be combined with the execution of woodworking jobs for local mines. Burrows also had a boring rod and its bits worth 10 shillings which seems expensive. It might have been used for boring tree trunks to make drainage pipes for mines of the kind uncovered in several open cast workings in Shropshire. A study of the diaries of John Clifton, carpenter of Oundle in the mid-18th century, shows that he combined heavy building work with cabinet making,[54] and it is likely that this was also so in the Severn Gorge, with demands from mine owners providing a third source of revenue.

Barrels were used in mining and on barges and almost every household in Shropshire had coopery ware (see below) but only one inventory of a cooper survives, that of Francis Rushon *(138)* of Madeley taken in 1665, which records that he had 'timber for cooper's use' worth £13 13s. 4d. William Evans of Posenhall who died in 1724 was a wheelwright but his inventory reveals nothing of his trade except that he had tools worth £1 1s. 6d.

Baskets were the usual containers for minerals *(20, 58, 92)* and were used by butchers *(135)* and for many household purposes. No inventories survive for basket makers, but baskets were certainly made in the Severn Gorge. Charles Gwyn who died in 1798 or 1799 had a basket shop and a little shed by his house in Broseley where he kept tools, his stock of completed wares, twigs, a cistern in which they were soaked, and he also had land on which he cultivated trees to provide twigs.[55] It is likely that craftsmen like Gwyn were also involved in the production of twiggen or seggen chairs (see below).

Social Structure and Urban Growth
The inventories illustrate in some detail the ways in which landowners profited from the exploitation of minerals and how urban communities developed in Madeley and more particularly in Broseley to serve the needs of the mining population.

Richard Benthall *(13)* is the only person in the four parishes with the rank of esquire whose inventory survives. He was the son of Philip Benthall who died in 1713, and grandson of Lawrence Benthall, a prominent Royalist in the Civil War of the 1840s. Richard Benthall was buried in the chancel of the church of St Bartholomew which stands near Benthall Hall.[56] His inventory was not the most highly valued in the collection but it was appraised at over £500, and provides an interesting view of the ways in which a landed gentleman was profiting from industrial development. The house was comfortably and fashionably furnished. The parlour contained a bureau, a clock and 16 cane chairs and its walls were hung with pictures and maps. The hall was occupied by several tables and adorned with obsolete firearms. There was a smoking room with facilities for playing backgammon, and a closet where a few things remained that had apparently belonged to Philip Benthall, who had died seven years previously. Specialist rooms included a dairy, a starching room, a cheese chamber with no cheese, a wet larder, a brewhouse, a room for making pastry, two butteries, an ale cellar and a small beer cellar. There was a copious supply of equipment for working the garden, an extensive agricultural enterprise with stock worth over £100 and growing crops worth more than £50, and the estate also yielded coal, iron ore, limestone, red clay for brickmaking and white clay for tobacco pipes. The inventory of John Smitheman *(119)* which relates to the Manor House in Little Wenlock and those of the Langley family *(47, 53, 55)* provide further evidence of families who owned mineral rights.

The inventories also illustrate the lives of servants to the gentry. Catherine Hartshorne *(11)*, spinster, maidservant to the Benthall family, died in 1712 with possessions worth just over £25, of which three quarters consisted of wages due to her. Her clothes, with other 'necessary linen belonging to a servant maid', were worth £5. Curiously she was the owner of four sheep. Thomas Gears who died in 1715 was a male household servant and more than 80 per cent of the value of his inventory was represented by debts owing to him, probably unpaid wages.

The church is the only profession for which any number of inventories remain. There are inventories for two vicars of Madeley, a rector of Broseley and a rector of Little Wenlock. All were modestly involved in farming, doubtless on glebe land. The least wealthy was Michael Richards, vicar of Madeley, whose inventory made in 1671 was worth only £37 10s. 0d. He lacked a horse but had books worth £15. Benjamin Taylor *(162)* who died in 1704 was rather wealthier and the inventory appears to relate to the Old Vicarage which still stands next to the parish church.[57] His study of books was worth £100, rather more than that of most Shropshire clergy, and other items suggested that he lived comfortably: silver plate, a watch, five guns and a set of Russia chairs (see below). Robert Ogden *(41)* of Broseley, whose inventory was worth nearly £400, was the wealthiest of the clergy. Like Taylor he appears to have been a learned minister, with books worth over £90. His is one of the few inventories to list vestments—gowns, cassocks and other apparel worth £20. The most detailed clergyman's inventory is that of William Whyston, rector of Little Wenlock, who died in 1713. His dwelling included a school house, perhaps indicating that he once supplemented his income by teaching, but by the time of his death it appears to have become an additional brewhouse, and the tutors listed in it were implements for working flax. His library was worth only £2 10s. 0d., but he had two musical instruments, a cittern and a fiddle, and kept a horse of modest value. His household was equipped for making beer, butter and linen, was well supplied with beef and bacon, the presence of 11 yards of black cloth suggests that self-sufficiency extended to the making of cassocks.

The only professional man other than the clergy to be recorded in the probate records of the four parishes was a doctor, Caesar Hawkins, born in 1662 and a descendant of a Caesar Hawkins who commanded a troop of Royalist cavalry in the Civil War. He was resident in Broseley in 1688 when his son, also Caesar, was baptised. He moved from Broseley to Ludlow, probably in 1706, and died in Ludlow the following year. His probate documents refer to him as 'of Broseley', but his inventory appears to relate to his household at 43 Broad Street in Ludlow. It includes a chaise worth £10 which would probably have been of little use in Broseley. It makes no reference to any surgical instruments. His widow, Mary, remained as head of household at 53 Broad Street until 1714, but by 1717 this position was held by her second son, another Caesar Hawkins and also a surgeon. Mary Hawkins died at Ludlow in 1721 and between Easter 1723 and 1724 her son moved to an elegant new house, 8 Mill Street, where he remained until his death in 1750. His son, the fourth Caesar Hawkins, born in 1711, also entered the medical profession, was surgeon at St George's Hospital, London between 1735 and 1774, and later Sergeant Surgeon to the King.[58]

Hawkins's role in Broseley was probably assumed by Isaac Wyke who died in 1755, a surgeon, clearly Jewish, with a large family, and a colossal brass mortar and pestle, each of which was claimed to weigh more than 160lbs. He was succeeded in his practice by his son Jacob Wyke, one of the promoters of the Iron Bridge, who died in 1780.[59]

No lawyers are represented in the collection. The first of any consequence in the region appears to have been Thomas Addenbrooke of Buildwas, who handled the legal matters relating to the construction of the Iron Bridge and died in 1787. The only teacher for whom any probate record survives is Josiah Hatton of Madeley, writing master, but no inventory remains. It is some indication of the urban status of Broseley that Jacob Kitchen, chief officer of Excise, died there in 1780.[60]

INTRODUCTION

Eight inventories survive for general purpose retailers in the Severn Gorge. The growing urban status of Broseley is confirmed by the presence of six retailers in the parish. While none had possessions on the scale of the Wellington mercers,[61] it is evident that retailing was established in Broseley by the second half of the 17th century on a scale unequalled elsewhere in Shropshire outside the ancient market towns. Thomas Crew *(23)* in 1668 had a modest shop for fabrics and haberdashery, with small quantities of woollen, linen and cotton fabrics, ribbons, tapes and thread, two dozen bodices, some gloves and a selection of pins and knives, the value of the whole stock amounting to just over £20. The short inventory of Thomas Jones in 1672 includes 19 yards of coarse blanketing and four and a half yards of woollen cloth which suggests that he was a retailer. Robert Hill *(39)* was identified as a mercer in 1679, and had stock worth £45 14s. 2d., with debts listed in his shop book worth almost as much. Thomas Oliver *(51)* in 1692 was also described on his inventory as a mercer. He had fabrics and haberdashery worth nearly £150, and grocery worth over £25—the highest stock value of the Broseley retailers, although a modest figure by national standards. The other Broseley shops were on a smaller scale. George Bayley *(64)* in 1718 was identified as a shopkeeper on his will, and his inventory listed 'soap and tobacco and small things to sell' worth £1 5s. 5d., as well as scales and weights. Richard Roden *(69)* in 1724 was described on his will as a yeoman, but his inventory makes it clear that he kept a shop in which his stock was valued at £15. Mary Penn *(87)* was a widow who kept a shop with stock and fittings worth £38 3s. 0d.

No inventories survive for shopkeepers in Madeley itself, although the High Street was a medieval urban plantation. The inventory of Richard Pritchard *(194)* shows that there was a modest general store in Coalbrookdale as early as 1759. Pritchard was not a wealthy man—his possessions in total were worth only £15 17s. 0d. His stock included fabrics of modest value, swanskins, linseys, flannels, fustians and checks, cottons, linens, as well as haberdashery, handkerchiefs buttons and thread, socks, knitted caps, children's stays, coffee and tea.

There are five butchers' inventories in the four parishes, all from the 18th century. William Boycott of Little Wenlock who died in 1709 farmed on a modest scale, with a herd of 11 cattle, a flock of nine sheep and two pigs, but his inventory lacks butcher's equipment. The inventory of Richard Taylor taken in 1744 is similar. William Boycott's son, Thomas *(135)* had no animals other than a mare, but his inventory lists a cleaver, a chopper, two knives and a pair of steelyards. It is likely that the Little Wenlock butchers served the market at nearby Wellington, with which road links were better than those with the Severn Gorge. Both the other butchers' inventories date from 1739. That of Richard Stratton of Madeley provides no useful detail, but John Beddow of Broseley had two cleavers and a pair of steelyards in his shop.

Innkeeping appears to have been a by-occupation in the Severn Gorge in the 17th and 18th centuries. Only one inventory survives for anyone described as an innkeeper—that of Richard Mason *(72)*, in which only the presence of a smoking room in the house and three full barrels in the cellar indicates his occupation. Internal evidence on the inventories of several other people suggests that they combined innkeeping with other occupations. Edward Hartshorne *(6)* of Benthall was a blacksmith, but the presence on his inventory of five lodging beds and brewing equipment suggests that he kept an inn. Thomas Lee *(54)* of Broseley, a nailer, had two steel mills for grinding malt and a cellar with beer and ale to the value of £20, well beyond the requirements of the thirstiest of normal households. Andrew Dodson *(8)* was a trowman, but 'drink' to the value of £12 suggests that like his later kinsmen at Cound Lane End he combined innkeeping with river trading. George Bradley *(12)* was also a trowman. His 15 'common chairs belonging to the use of the house' and five lodging beds suggest that he kept an inn, as in all probability did the waterman Francis 'Stukeley' Oakes, who in 1721 had three lodging beds and ten chairs 'broken and whole'. Other likely innkeepers include Edward Lloyd *(164)* a trowman, the Madeley miners John Holland *(158)* and Michael Hotchkiss, who had butter and cheese worth £10 and ample brewing equipment, Robert Benbow *(28)* who had a signpost outside his house, brewing vessels and an overworn malt mill, Richard Gears *(66)* a candle maker, and John Mayor *(65)* who had lodging beds, and apparently combined innkeeping with an occupation in which he employed a working mare.

Only one inventory survives for a miller, that of Mark Henworth *(181)*, which provides no information about his business. There were 16 mill sites in the four parishes on tributary streams of the Severn and, while some had been taken over for ironmaking, several remained in use for corn milling until the 20th century.[62]

Shoemaking was the most common of urban crafts. Inventories survive for six shoemakers, all of them living south of the Severn. Samuel Smith of Benthall who died in 1697 had working tools worth 7s. but none of the inventories of the five shoemakers from Broseley provides significant information about the trade.

Glovers in Shropshire towns often worked as curriers, dressing the skins of sheep, pigs and deer. There are three glovers' inventories in the collection. That of Thomas Wheale of Posenhall taken in 1686 affirms that he was a glover but reveals little about his trade, except that his tools were worth £4. Henry Carrington *(86)* had a workhouse with some undressed skins, leather ready for working, completed gloves worth £5 and tools worth five shillings, as well as some chalk worth two shillings which may have been used to dress leather. The inventory of Joseph Carrington, glover, in 1746 provides no details about gloving, and that of Benjamin Cox of Madeley in 1710 suggests that he worked in leather, but does not reveal how.

There are inventories for seven tailors, the earliest in 1684, the last in 1759. Five were from Broseley, where their presence in the 17th century is further evidence of the parish's urban status. Francis Gears *(50)* had three pairs of shears, three pressing irons and 12 ells of cloth, and appears to have made shirts and cravats. John Evans *(44)* had a smoothing iron, but it was listed with domestic utensils. The remaining tailors' inventories reveal nothing of the trade.

Inventories remain for nine weavers, five in Broseley and four in Madeley. Roger Jones in 1668 and Thomas Cookson in 1725 each had looms worth £2, together with their gears or heddles, the wires through which the warp was passed. Morris Shaw in 1717 had implements of his trade worth £4 but the only indication that he was a weaver comes from his will. Hannah Hartshorne *(82)*, apparently a weaver's widow, had three looms in a new shop in a house which also included an old shop. William Hall *(110)* had three looms in a workshop and two old ones in a work house, valued altogether at £7. Hall also had a long wheel, for spinning wool, a little wheel for spinning linen yarn, and a pair of swifts, lightweight reels, usually of adjustable diameter, upon which skeins of yarn could be placed for winding. John Blest in 1694 had only gears in his workshop to indicate that he was a weaver. John Cowper *(150)* in 1680 had a weaver's shop with two looms, and John Edmunds in 1743 a single loom worth five shillings. The inventory of William Cludd *(174)* shows that he had three looms in his shop, with gears for weaving both linen and woollen fabrics, together with a warping bar, the roller on which the warp would be measured when ready for weaving, a trough for sizing warp, and a quill wheel for winding the weft. Elsewhere in the house was a long spinning wheel worth two shillings. All seven were doubtless *custom* weavers, taking in yarn spun in local homes (see below) and weaving it into fabrics which could be used for clothing and in the kitchen, dairy, brewhouse and bedroom. On a small scale custom weaving survived in Shropshire, although not in the Severn Gorge, for most of the 19th century.[63]

Sampson Buckley *(59)* who died in Broseley in 1711 stands apart from other textile workers in the Severn Gorge for whom inventories remain. He was a clothier, although upon a modest scale. He had 60lbs. of wool, and scribbling horses and cards upon which fleece wool could be disentangled before carding and spinning. He was able to comb long staple wool that could be spun into worsted or jersey yarn. He had just one spinning wheel, but 50lbs. of woollen yarn and 20lbs. of jersey or worsted yarn, suggesting that his spinning was mostly done by outworkers. His snap reel might also have been used for spinning. The wool and yarn had doubtless been weighed on one of his two pairs of scales. Bulkley had only two looms and could well have employed outworkers to do most of his weaving, since his facilities for finishing cloth were on a larger scale. He had four tubs which could have been used for scouring woven cloth. He had a press, three furnaces, one of which, worth £10, must have been of considerable size, and a vat for dyeing. The latter would have been used for woad, producing blue cloth. His bag of fustic would have been old fustic, enabling him to produce yellow cloth with an alum mordant, and his logwood would have enabled him to dye cloth black with copperas as a mordant, or blue with alum. The barrel of 'archill' would have been filled with the lichen better known as orchilla (*rocella tinctoria*), which produces a violet dye as well as the litmus used in chemistry laboratories. The bag of argill was probably argol, crude potassium hydrogen tartrate which was used by dyers as an 'assistant' to accelerate the formation of solutions and make colours fuller. His potash was a crude form of potassium carbonate, a mild alkali obtained from wood ash, used for scouring materials in cleansing, and in adjusting the acidity of dye baths. Potash might have been applied to cloth on the dubbing board. The handle cratch would have been a frame to which some of the six dozen (more probably six dozen dozen or six gross) teasels would have been attached for raising the nap of a piece of cloth, which would have been laid out on the shear board so that the nap could be cut with one of the six pairs of clothier's shears. The clothier's rack was a tenter frame on which the piece of cloth would be stretched. Bulkley was thus able to perform most of the tasks necessary for producing coloured cloth from raw wool, but he was operating on a small scale when compared with the dyers in Wellington or contemporary clothiers like Moses Law and George Bickerton in Bridgnorth.[64] It is possible that Edward Reynolds *(93)* (see above), described on his inventory as a dyer, had at one stage in his life operated a similar business.

Henry James *(148)* was described as a 'bowyer', the only meaning for which given in the *Oxford English Dictionary* is a maker of bows for firing arrows, which seems an unlikely occupation in Madeley in 1676. It is possible that he made drills for the use of woodworkers or miners, or he may have been a bow hauler on the Severn. His inventory is uninformative.

The inventories identify several building workers. George Grice and Francis Woseley of Little Wenlock were described as masons on their inventories, but neither includes masons' tools, and both were farming, the latter on a significant scale. The inventory of another mason, Joseph Whitefoot *(91)* of Broseley, provides a detailed picture of his household, but the only indication of his trade is the presence of tools worth 10 shillings. Unlike the Little Wenlock masons he was not engaged in farming. Thomas Crowther *(89)* in 1741 had a glazier's vice, a board, probably for cutting glass, and some old glass in his shop, but they were worth together only just over £2. Inventories in Shifnal provide a more detailed picture of the glazier's trade.[65]

The Practice of Agriculture
Many of those who lived in and around the Severn Gorge in the 18th and 19th centuries kept animals and cultivated crops, but made parts of their livelihoods by other means. To study agriculture in the region is therefore to examine a range of activities, not to analyse a distinct occupational group. There were several yeomen in the area who might, in the 20th century, be described as 'farmers', although that term was not used in the period, but probate records show that agriculture in the four parishes was shaped to a considerable extent by the demands of the trades related to coal.

Horsekeeping was the activity in which agricultural and industrial concerns overlapped most significantly. Except for the wealthy, keeping horses in Shropshire was most commonly an aspect of farming. In the parishes to the north of the Severn Gorge, which were largely agricultural, horses are recorded on 48 per cent of inventories, and in the farming parishes of Stottesdon and Wheathill the figure is 45 per cent. By contrast only 20 per cent of the inventories for Shrewsbury include horses, and most of those are from farms in the Shrewsbury Liberties, and in Bridgnorth, a town which possessed scarcely any arable land, the figure was 12 per cent. In the four parishes of the Severn Gorge horses appear on 23 per cent of the inventories, a figure which is reasonably constant over time, but differs markedly between the parishes. There were least horses in Broseley where the level of agricultural activity was lowest, and most in

Little Wenlock where it was highest. Horses were used alongside oxen on the large farms in Little Wenlock, but there are some indications that the parish's farms also supplied animals that were employed in working gins and carrying coal.

Table V

Proportions of inventories including horses

	1660-1699	1700-1764	Total	Proportion (%)
Benthall	5	6	11	30.5
Broseley	21	24	45	16.0
Little Wenlock	9	23	32	65.0
Madeley	17	16	33	22.3
Total	52	69	121	23.0

The inventories of the Little Wenlock farmers Francis Parton *(129)* and the two William Wheelwrights *(127, 128)* taken between 1714 and 1728 all include horses alongside oxen, and other references to four, five, six or seven horses with 'gears' similarly indicate animals that were used in the fields. The inventory of John Goodman *(183)* of Madeley appears to distinguish between horses used in cultivation and those used on the road. Goodman has six drawing horses worth just under £4 each, presumably for use in his fields, three wagon horses each valued at £2 presumable for use on the road, and a mare, probably his riding horse. Richard Pearce *(79)* had three wain horses and five old mares worth in total just over £25.

Other horses were clearly used to draw or deliver coal or iron ore. Richard Parton *(118)* and John Fletcher *(125)* both had mares with pack saddles, and Edward Cox *(61)* had six small horses worth £3 each for carrying coal. Pack horses are illustrated on two of George Robertson's engravings of the Severn Gorge published in 1788, and the 19th-century writer John Randall described old people's recollections of packhorses carrying iron ore to the blast furnace at Leighton in the first half of the 18th century.[66] The six 'carring' horses owned by Roger Thresslecock *(133)* might have been used for the carriage of coal. James Harrison *(36)*

INTRODUCTION

and William Oakes *(25)* both had horses for working gins, and it is probably that some of the other 'working horses' listed in inventories, particularly those associated with gears rather than saddles, were used for this purposes.

Some individuals kept horses for their personal use. The tallow chandler John Sherratt *(147)* had a 'riding nag' worth, with her saddle and bridle, £3 6s. 8d., and the Coalbrookdale shopkeeper Richard Pritchard *(194)* had a horse worth £3, also with its saddle. Most mares or nags worth between £3 and £5 appear to have been used for riding. Two inventories refer to horse-drawn passenger vehicles. Caesar Hawkins, the surgeon, had a chaise alongside his five horses, but it was probably kept in Ludlow rather than Bridgnorth (see above). The unwheeled litter suspended between the two mares owned by the Broseley clergyman Robert Ogden *(41)* was doubtless a more practical means of transport in the Severn Gorge.

Thee were no horses of high value in the four parishes, such as sometimes appear on the inventories of gentry. Even at Benthall Hall *(13)* the mean value of the six horses was less than £3. The inventories provide a few details of individual horses. Joseph Reynolds *(10)* had a stallion, and James Colley in 1709 some geldings. Robert Hill *(39)* rode a grey horse and John Burgwyn *(121)* a bay mare. Some horses were in poor condition. Edmund Gray *(130)* had a lame mare and Eliabeth Owsley a lame horse, but Nevill Edwards *(105)* had five old mares, four of them lame and the other blind. The sorriest animal and the least valued appears to have been the 'old mare almost dead of a fistula' worth only five shillings, listed by the appraisers of Mark Henworth *(181)*.

The cattle inventories (see below) in the century after 1660 show that the pasturing of cattle diminished in importance in the Severn Gorge parishes. The proportion of inventories with cattle fell from 57 per cent in the 1660s to 5.5 per cent in the 1760s. The mean for the period 1660-1750 was 28 per cent, which compares with 60 per cent for the parishes of Dawley, Lilleshall, Wellington and Wrockwardine.[67] In Little Wenlock 33 inventories for the whole period (67 per cent) listed cattle, a figure comparable with that for Lilleshall (70 per cent), another parish where coalmining was confined to a limited area. The least cattle were in Broseley where they are listed on only 39 (14.6 per cent) of the inventories.

Most keepers of cattle kept four or fewer beasts, and only in Little Wenlock were there significant numbers of people who could reasonably be described as dairy farmers with herds of more than ten animals. William Green *(116)* had 19 beasts as well as six draught oxen. John Smitheman *(119)* had 17, and George Wheelwright *(128)* more than 21. Some parts of Madeley were relatively unaffected by mining and provided opportunities

TABLE VI
Inventories listing cattle

	Benthall	Broseley	Little Wenlock	Madeley	Total	Proportion (%) with cattle
1660-69	1	3	4	8	16	57.14
1670-79	3	10	2	5	20	33.9
1680-89	4	8	3	7	22	33.85
1690-99	1	2	3	5	11	25.00
1700-09	1	1	2	5	9	29.03
1710-19	2	1	7	7	17	32.69
1720-29	3	5	3	1	12	17.14
1730-39	-	2	4	2	8	17.39
1740-49	1	5	2	2	10	20.41
1750-59	-	2	2	2	6	9.38
1760-64	-	-	1	-	1	5.55
Totals	16	39	33	44	132	
Proportion (%) with cattle in each parish	25.39	14.60	67.35	29.73	25.10	

for keeping sizeable herds. Audley Bowdler *(169)* had 22 dairy cattle as well as a bull stag, his six cows in milk being worth no less than £8 10s. 0d. each, which compares with a mean value of £2 18s. 4d. for dairy cows in the 15 herds listed in the same decade in Dawley, Lilleshall, Wellington and Wrockwardine. Bowdler's farming activities can also be traced through the Madeley parish Easter Books which show that he had 20 cattle, 10 of them cows in milk and the remainder calves in 1683.[68] The number of cows in milk varied between six and ten in the following 31 years, while the size of the herd fluctuated between 10 and 24 beasts, the mean size for the 19 years for which figures are available being 17. Roger Roe *(171)* left a herd of 20 cattle in which the six cows in milk were worth £3 10s. 0d. each. The herd of Richard Benthall *(13)* was valued in 1720 at over £93 which suggests that it numbered more than 30 animals. The median sizes of herds reflect the general level of agricultural activity in the four parishes, 9.5 beasts in Little Wenlock, 7 in Madeley, 4.5 in Benthall and 3 in Broseley. No less than 59 of the cattle keepers (45 per cent) had four beasts or fewer, most of them following occupations other than farming. The inventories provide little information about the kinds of cattle kept. William Evans *(4)* had four 'Welch kine' while Audley Bowdler's *(169)* bull stag was probably an animal castrated when fully grown for fattening. As in other areas it seems that the term 'bullock' sometimes indicated a young gelded beast being trained to work in the fields, as in the 'five oxen and four bullocks' listed in the inventory of Francis Parton *(129)*.

Dairying equipment is listed on 69 inventories, some 13 per cent of the total, a lower proportion than in Dawley, Lilleshall, Wellington and Wrockwardine, where the equivalent figure is 18 per cent. It is evident that many of those engaged in coal mining or similar trades who had enough land to keep a cow made their own butter and cheese. Some of the farms in Little Wenlock were not unlike the dairy farms of Lilleshall or Wrockwardine or those of the north Shropshire plain generally. George Wheelwright *(128)* had mitts (i.e. tubs) and bowls for milk, and cheese vats. William Wheelwright *(127)* had milking pails, cheese tubs and two wooden coolers. Edmund Grey *(130)* had cheese vats and tubs and a cheese press, and the appraisers of Roger Thresslecock *(133)* also distinguished between the cheese tub and the cheese vats in his milk house. The gawns mentioned in several dairies were ladles which originally measured out a gallon of liquid. Some keepers of cows made cheese, but the quantities recorded are small with those of parishes that specialised in dairy farming. A 'parcel of cheese', worth £13 6s. 0d. in the inventory of William Wright of Little Wenlock in 1720, probably weighed about half a ton, and was the largest value recorded. Roger Roe *(171)* the previous year had 57 cheeses worth £3 5s. 0d., a mean value of 1s. 1½d. Other values for individual cheeses ranged between 2s. each for the eight left by Thomas Watkiss in 1684 to 10d. for the 12 on the inventory of a Little Wenlock butcher *(135)* in 1709. Butter is less frequently mentioned, although a Broseley inventory of 1684 *(43)* mentions a 'goanr', perhaps a gallon of it.

Sheep farming was of relatively little importance in the area, only 6.65 per cent of the inventories listing sheep, compared with 25 per cent in the parishes to the north. Many flocks were small but that of Richard Benthall *(13)* was worth £17 5s. 0d. and probably contained more than 200 animals. Otherwise the largest flocks recorded were those of John Hagar *(144)* who had 82 animals worth £12, James Colley in 1709 who had 52 worth £11,

TABLE VII

Inventories listing sheep

	Benthall	Broseley	Little Wenlock	Madeley	Totals	Proportion (%) with sheep
1660-69	-	-	2	-	2	7.14
1670-79	-	1	-	2	3	5.08
1680-89	1	4	1	1	7	10.77
1690-99	1	-	1	-	2	4.55
1700-09	-	-	1	2	3	9.68
1710-19	2	-	4	2	8	15.38
1720-29	2	2	1	-	5	7.14
1730-39	-	-	1	2	3	6.52
1740-49	-	-	-	1	1	2.04
1750-59	-	-	1	-	1	1.56
1760-64	-	-	-	-	0	-
Totals	6	7	12	10	35	
Proportion (%) in each parish with sheep	9.52	2.63	24.49	6.76	6.65	

William Samson in 1688 who had 39 worth £5 and George Wheelwright in 1713-14 who had 38 worth £6 5s. 0d. No other flock exceeded 30, nor do the values of any unnumbered flocks suggest that they contained a larger number. The mean size of the 12 numbered flocks in Little Wenlock was no more than 17. Audley Bowdler *(169)* of Madeley had no sheep when his inventory was taken in 1714, but the parish Easter Books show that he was certainly keeping sheep between 1702 and the time of his death. The Easter Books also show that in the first half of the 18th century William Roe *(168)*, Roger Roe *(171)* and John Goodman *(183)* were amongst the Madeley farmers who provided winter pasture for sheep from parishes

INTRODUCTION

to the east like Worfield and Claverley where 'sheep and corn' farming was practised.[69] The only inventory to provide information about the kind of sheep in the area, that of John Boden *(185)*, lists six small Welsh sheep.

Pigs were commonly kept in the Severn Gorge and are listed on 151 (29 per cent) of the inventories, but pig keeping declined after 1720. Pigs are listed on 40 per cent of the inventories taken between 1660 and 1719, but on only 16 per cent of those taken after 1720. The value of a pig depended on its age and weight, and appraisals vary between five shillings and £1. Of the 151 pig keepers, about a quarter kept only one pig. The nature of domestic pig keeping is captured by the listing of 'a small sow at the Door' on the inventory of James Weaver in 1734. More than half the pig keepers also kept cattle. Only four inventories record herds of pigs worth more than £5. Richard Benthall *(13)* had swine worth over £10, Thomas Lee *(54)* had nine worth £1 each, William Oakes *(25)* had swine to the value of £6, and Edward Edwards *(68)* had five hogs and eight store swine worth £5. Roger Roe *(171)* who was working a substantial farm in Madeley in 1719 had a single fat pig worth £1 15s. 0d., which appears to be the most valuable animal listed. Many appraisers used the word 'pig' to refer to the young offspring of sows, and referred to mature animals as 'swine'. The inventory of Edmund Gray *(130)* lists two swine worth £1 10s. 0d. each, and four pigs worth only 5s each.

The inventories suggest that poultry were not commonly kept in the Severn Gorge. They are mentioned on only 19 inventories, 3.6 per cent of the total, with no significant variation over time. It is likely that, as in the parishes to the north, hens, ducks and geese were often ignored by appraisers.[70] Poultry are commonly included in inventories in Shropshire in the 16th century. The highest value was 12s. 6d. recorded for the assorted flock of the farmer Roger Roe *(171)* in 1719. Geese are mentioned on four inventories *(127, 132, 168, 171)* and were usually valued at slightly less than a shilling each. There are two specific references to cocks and hens. Roger Roe *(171)* had six ducks worth 5d. each, and also kept a stock of feathers, the accumulation of which must have been a significant factor in the economy of poultry keeping. It seems that few people in the Severn Gorge kept bees, which are listed on only three inventories *(40, 170)*.

A variety of crops was cultivated in the Shropshire Coalfield. Acreages are not often quoted in Shropshire inventories generally, and references are very rare in the Severn Gorge. Edward Edwards *(68)* had 10 acres of growing corn worth £1 an acre, and 3½ acres of wheat appear on the inventory of John Rogers in 1754. Gathered crops are as likely to be listed as those still growing. Sometimes crops are located in specific places, like the barley worth £8 10s. 0d. in Cressethays Barn, Little Wenlock that belonged to John Smitheman *(119)*. Francis Parton *(129)* had a mow of hardcorn and one of oats and barley in his corn barn, with fodder for his animals in a hay barn. It is evident from several inventories that some grain crops remained 'in the straw' or unthreshed many months after they had been harvested.[71]

The principal winter crop in the four parishes was corn, listed on 22 or 11 per cent of the inventories. It was intended principally for breadmaking, and was usually a mixture of wheat with rye, which might be called muncorn, maslin, mixed corn, dredge or hard corn. There are only 11 specific references to wheat and only two to rye in all the 526 inventories. It is evident that most appraisers of substantial farms followed a regular hierarchy of crops, listing first the winter corn, then the spring-planted crops, Lent grain *(68)* or Lent tilling *(170)*, which might or might not be listed individually, and then the hay. Thus Joseph Reynolds *(10)* had:

> 23 strikes sowing of Wheat and measeling £14
> 12 strikes sowing of Barley £5 8s. 0d.
> 5 strikes sowing of Pease £1 16s. 0d.
> 18 strikes sowing of Oats £4 10s. 0d.
> 1 strikes sowing of Vetches 5s.
> Hay £7

Richard Benthall's *(13)* growing crops are listed in the order; wheat, muncorn, barley, peas, oats, vetches, almost exactly the same as the inventory of Francis Turner in 1671 which lists muncorn, wheat, barley, peas, oats. The appraisers of William Roe *(168)* regarded growing corn as synonymous with wheat and rye.

The time of year when an inventory was taken will naturally determine how crops are described, but it is clear that the thoughts of most appraisers of the growing of gather crops followed similar patterns. Several inventories provide opportunities to measure winter against spring-sown crops. Roger Roe had 47½ strike of gathered corn and 111 strike of spring crops, but the latter were worth only £10 5s. 0d. compared with £7 17s. 0d. for the smaller quantity of corn. Joseph Reynolds *(10)* had 23 strikes of growing corn worth 12s. 2d. a strike, and 36 strikes of barley, peas, oats and vetches worth only 7s. 6d. a strike. It seems therefore that the areas devoted to spring crops were larger than those used for winter corn, but that the corn crop was considerably more valuable, relative to its size. Nine inventories provide values for gathered corn, eight of them giving values between 2s. 2d. and 3s. 6d. per strike, only one, a small quantity *(122)* being significantly outside that range at 1s. 6d. By contrast the value in July of a strike of corn sown in the winter and ready to be harvested was more than twelve shillings *(10)*. The inventory of Roger Roe *(171)* suggests that a thrave of grain in the Shropshire Coalfield was the equivalent of 1.5 strikes.

The principal spring crop on sizeable farms was barley grown for malting, but perhaps used also for cattle feed. It is specifically mentioned on only 26 (5 per cent) of the inventories, but would have been included in the Lent tilling on others. It is consistently the most valuable of the spring crops relative to the amount sown. Only four inventories give precise values per strike, which range from 1s. 10d. to 2s. 6d., but a strike sown in the spring could be worth 9s. when ready to be harvested in July *(10)*.

Oats are listed on 31 (6 per cent) of the inventories, principally those of substantial farms. Some inventories *(127)* list oats with hay, suggesting that appraisers usually saw them as fodder. Four inventories give values per strike for oats, ranging from 1s 2d. to 2s. A growing crop of oats in March *(80)* was worth 1s. 8d. for every strike sown, but a similar crop in July *(10)* was valued at 5s. per strike.

Peas were also grown as a fodder crop and are listed on 16 inventories throughout the period under review. There are just three values for gathered peas, ranging from 9d. to 2s. 6d. per strike. Field beans appear to have been grown only rarely. There are two references, one in the 1660s and one in 1719. There are five references to vetches between 1690 and 1720, and just one to clover, on the farm of Francis Parton *(129)* of little Wenlock in 1728, a well-organised establishment with 24 head of cattle and seven horses.

Hay was the most widely-used fodder crop, occurring on 70 (13 per cent) of the inventories. There are ten references to ricks of hay which varied in value between 10s. and £2 7s. 6d., two to lads of hay, respectively worth 13s. 4d. *(28)* and £1 *(171)*, and three measure hay by weight, two tons worth £1 10s. 0d. per ton *(187)*, 12 tons worth 15s. 10d. per ton and 12 tons worth a guinea a ton. The largest quantity of hay was held by William Roe *(168)* whose store was valued at £38.

The inventories provide copious evidence that hemp and flax were grown in the four parishes, but for the most part they were cultivated on small patches of land, as they were elsewhere in Shropshire. Roger Thresslecock *(133)* had flax worth £1 that appears to be a growing crop, and Edward Herbage in 1725 had a rick of hemp, but there are few references to unharvested flax and hemp, perhaps because they were harvested by pulling up the plants, that is by breaking the ground, which may have meant that, like root vegetables, they were not normally listed on inventories. A Wrockwardine farmer in 1744 had a growing crop of flax worth £30, but this was exceptional.[72] The growth of hemp and flax and their subsequent processing into fabrics is more logically considered as part of the material culture of the district rather than as an aspect of its agriculture.

Only nine inventories list manure, usually calling it muck or compost. Values per load seem consistent. Luke Twyford *(166)* had 30 loads worth a shilling a ton, and Thomas Beddow *(80)* in 1733 had 20 loads valued at the same rate, while in the previous year the same appraiser had valued about 20 loads belonging to Richard Pearce *(79)* at 1s. 1d. per load. The largest quantity, valued at £2, was owned by Richard Benthall *(13)*.

Inventories of the larger farms provide some details of the commonly listed 'implements of husbandry'. Ploughs and sometimes plough timber *(43)* are listed on 12 inventories, one of which *(168)* refers also to a coplate, suck and coulter. Harrows and sometimes parts of harrows *(183)* are listed on 13 inventories. Thomas Beddow *(80)* and Audley Bowdler *(169)* had rolls, presumably for breaking up clods, amongst their implements. John Goodman *(183)* had a hopper and three inventories list sleds *(116, 118, 171)* while another mentions a wheelbarrow.

Wains are listed on 13 inventories, and wagons which appear to be for use on roads or in the fields rather than on railways on three. Several inventories itemise wains with ploughs and harrows, suggesting that they were considered principally as a means of carriage on a farm. The inventory of John Rutter *(9)* distinguishes between implements of husbandry and those for wagoning, suggesting that the word wagon may sometimes have implied road carriages. The inventories show that wain bodies were detachable from their wheels. Roger Roe *(171)* had a wain body, but no wheels while John Rutter *(9)* had wheels but no body. Rather fewer people, only 14, had carts or tumbrils which might also be separated from their wheels *(116)*. Some appraisers *(171, 183)* seemed to see little difference between a cart and a tumbril, although the latter usually meant a tip cart for manure, like the 'dung cart' itemised elsewhere *(47)*. The inventories of William Roe *(168)* and Roger Roe *(171)* provide some details of harness.

The larger farms in the district employed draught oxen until well into the 18th century. There are five references to oxen before 1700 and nine between 1700 and 1728 when the last was recorded on the inventory of Francis Parton *(129)*. There are two references in Benthall, three in Broseley, eight in Little Wenlock and one in Madeley. John Rutter *(9)* and Richard

Benthall *(13)* each appear to have had two teams of four beasts and six Little Wenlock farmers *(116, 125, 127, 128)* each had six oxen. All the owners of oxen except Francis Adams *(22)* also kept dairy cattle. Oxen were valued between £2 10s. 0d. and £4 5s. 0d., rather less than in parishes which specialised in arable cultivation. The inventories for Little Wenlock farmers in the second decade of the 18th century suggest that both oxen and horses were used for ploughing and hauling, but it seems likely that the use of oxen had ceased by 1750.[73]

People in the Severn Gorge used a variety of hand tools in agriculture and horticulture. Apart from the specialist tools used in mining and in crafts like blacksmithing and carpentry, the inventories record numerous spades and axes, the usual value for the latter being 4d. Tools for cutting wood or scrub included five mattocks *(13, 80, 171, 187)*, two hatchets *(19)*, two broomhooks *(19, 80)*, nine bills *(33, 80, 82, 171, 187)*, one of them a 'forest bill', and a cleaver. For horticultural use there were six rakes *(13, 19, 80, 91, 112)*, two of them specifically 'garden rakes' and two 'dressing rakes', two pairs of garden shears and a hoe. For harvesting there were four scythes *(19, 134, 171)*, a reaping hook *(134)* and five pitch fork or pike evils *(19, 91, 171)*. The inventories also record two hand saws *(132)*, two hammers, a mall and a shovel. The tools used in the garden of Benthall Hall included a watering pan, a garden scythe, a pair of garden shears, a rake, a hoe and a wire riddle. A tool that is curiously missing is the flail, the only means of threshing grain in the period under review. Flails included no metal parts and may have been made up of any pieces of wood that happened to be at hand. There is one reference to a winnowing sheet *(162)*.

There are too few well-balanced farms in this selection of inventories to enable conclusions to be reached on best farming practice. These few, like that of Joseph Reynolds and those of the Wheelwright family of Little Wenlock *(122, 126, 127, 128)*, need to be interpreted in a broader regional context. Within the narrower setting of the coalfield it is evident that much pastoral and arable farming was practised by families who gained parts of their livings by other means, and that the demands of coal miners for haulage and fodder were felt even on the largest farms.

Money and Property
One of the purposes of making an inventory was to provide a basis for the settlement of debts owed by and owing to the deceased, and the only items on some brief inventories are debts due, often for relatively small amounts. Debts are listed on 141 inventories, 27 per cent of the total, although it seems, and this is confirmed by evidence from elsewhere, that less attention

was paid to debts after 1700 than previously. Debts are included on 40 per cent of the inventories taken before 1700, but on only 19 per cent of those made in the 18th century. Most debts are qualified as good or bad, or alternatively as sperate or desperate, which meant the same thing. One inventory *(153)* defines 'desperate' as 'in doubt to be recovered'. Some debts were the result of normal trading, like the book debts owed to the carpenters Samuel Burrows and John Doughty *(98, 178)*, the ropemaker Mary Clemson *(189)*, the locksmith Thomas Teece *(73)* and the mercers Robert Hill and Thomas Oliver *(39, 51)*. More detailed debts are listed in the inventories of the collier Samuel Evans *(46)* and the bargeowner Adam Stokes *(34)*. Unpaid wages comprise the debts in the inventories of the domestic servants Catherine Hartshorne *(11)* and Thomas Gears. Debts of a more formal nature might be described as bonds, to which there are 26 references, or as being 'upon specialty', that is under a special contract or obligation. Such debts were not necessarily secure. Mary Yates *(175)* and George Buttery *(120)* were amongst those who had bonds that were desperate. Some debts, like the £100 credit due to George Wheelwright *(128)*, appear to have been investments, and some, like the money at use listed on the inventory of Noel Edwards *(77)*, certainly were. There are two references to mortgages, and two to rents due. Two inventories refer to annuities, one of them to 40s. per annum settled on an old life, obviously not that of the deceased, and two more to legacies. There are many references to ready money, or money in the purse or pocket, which in the case of Samuel Langley, gentleman, who died in 1698, totalled £100.

Inventories tend not be informative on matters relating to property. It was usual only to list property held on leases which could be bequeathed. The leases listed in this collection nevertheless demonstrate differences between property-holding in the four parishes. Leases appear on 28 inventories from Broseley, but on only four from the remaining three parishes.

Housing
Evidence from the inventories suggests that the size of dwellings in the Severn Gorge was much the same as in the parishes to the north, more than half the houses containing five rooms or less. The main living room of a dwelling was most commonly called the 'house' or 'house place' and contained the cooking facilities. There might be another ground-floor room, quite often called a 'parlour'. The earliest reference to a parlour, on the inventory of Roger Evans *(139)* of Madeley in 1665, is to a sleeping room, but no beds are listed in the earliest parlours of Benthall, Broseley and Little Wenlock *(6, 25, 119)*. The bedrooms on the upper floor were usually

15 A cabinet maker, from *The Book of English Trades* (1837 edition).

16 A cooper, from *The Book of English Trades* (1837 edition).

17 Packhorses passing through Coalbrookdale, from F. Vivares, G. Perry and T. Smith, *A South West Prospect of Coalbrookdale* (1758).

18 The beehive and sun dial in the port of the church of St Bartholomew, Benthall.

19 A sled, from W. Pickett, *Iron works, Coalbrookdale* (1805).

20 Benthall Hall.

21 The untidy pattern of settlement at Dale End at the foot of Lincoln Hill in a photograph of the mid-19th century. Most of the housing visible would have been built before 1764. The long terrace is Nailer's Row, leased by the partners in the Coalbrookdale ironworks in 1733, and the dispersed cottages beyond it are probably older.

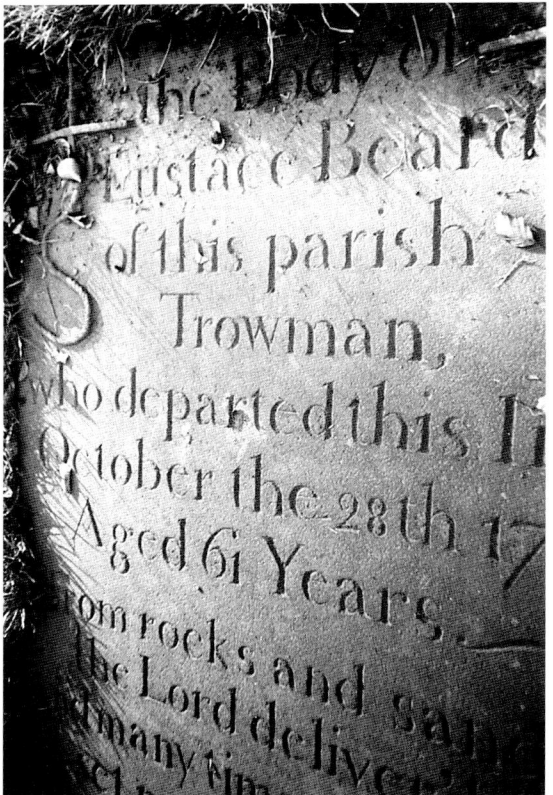

22 A close-up of some of the cottages of stone construction, probably of 17th-century date, visible in plate 21.

23 The cast-iron tomb in Benthall churchyard of the Eustace Beard who died in 1761.

24 Fragments of early 18th-century teapots and a tea cup recovered from excavations of waste tips in Jackfield.

25 An early 18th-century chamber pot re-assembled from sherds excavated from a waste tip at Jackfield.

26 A woman drawing water from the River Severn near the Iron Bridge, from M. A. Rooker, *View of the Cast Iron Bridge near Coalbrook Dale* (1781).

described as chambers. Downstairs most houses had space for activities involving water, which might be called a brewhouse, a wash house or a shire *(155, 157, see below)*. A few houses contained named rooms, a blue room and a red room in the home of the shopkeeper Mary Penn *(87)* and a red chamber in the house of the tallow chandler Richard Gears *(66)*. Some houses had accommodation for servants *(66, 86, 87, 98, 140)*, in one case *(129)* called the 'Fellows' Room'. There were lofts above the chambers in some houses and one inventory *(35)* lists loose boards on the loft.

Table VIII

Numbers of rooms in houses

Number of rooms	Houses where rooms can be counted Total:263	Benthall %	Broseley %	Little Wenlock %	Madeley %	All four parishes %	Dawley* Lilleshall Wellington Wrockwardine
1-3	65	23.33	31.09	7.14	22.09	24.72	23.76
4-5	92	43.33	30.26	46.43	34.88	34.98	34.50
1-5	157	66.66	61.35	53.57	56.97	59.70	58.26
6-10	94	26.67	36.97	42.86	34.89	35.74	35.95
Over 10	2	6.67	1.68	3.57	8.14	4.56	5.79

* From B. Trinder & J. Cox, *Yeomen & Colliers in Telford* (1980), p.15.

The most distinguished of the houses whose contents are listed in this collection is the 16th-century Benthall Hall *(13)*, which is described room by room. The interior was altered in the 19th century, when for a time it contained two dwellings, and it is difficult to match the present-day rooms with those in the inventory.[74] The inventory of John Smitheman *(119)* relates to the Manor House at Little Wenlock.

Wills rather than inventories provide the best evidence for the dwellings of the miners and mariners of the Severn Gorge. It is evident that many families owned or leased cottages which they extended into short, often unevenly-built terraces to accommodate succeeding generations. Edward Boden *(159)* of Madeley Wood in 1691 had a house in the Lloyds in which he lived, another that he had repaired, and a new building that he had added to it. John Bayley *(167)* in 1710 had a cottage which had been purchased from the manorial estate and divided into three dwellings, the chief part in which he lived, the little room and the cock loft over it occupied by his youngest son, and two rooms in the middle with a buttery, which formed the home of his eldest son, and he provided for his daughter to have the brewhouse, the chamber over it and 'the little shop before the door'. William Botteley *(196)* divided his house in Madeley Wood between his son Thomas, who received the kitchen, cellar and parlour, and his son James who had the little room, the room over it and the brewhouse. Like other testators, he was concerned with the division of the garden, where landmarks included a brook, the edge of the waste, the neighbouring dwelling of Amran Styche and a filbert tree. This kind of concern to avoid disputes between offspring is most evident in the will of a Broseley barge-owner, John Dyer, made in 1795,[75] in which he left pigsties to two sons, and added that if he should build another his third son was to have it, 'which will prevent all disputes arising among my sons'. The way in which such cottages were built is illustrated by the will of John Brook made in 1720. He instructed his son John that he was to build for his widow a new house,

> with good and well-burnt brick ... to contain 16 foots in length, 13 foots in breadth within the walls, and 12 foots high in the wall from the ground to the wall-plate with two good and sufficient fireplaces ... and also a shear to go the length of the said building and an oven for the use of the same ... The roof of the said house and all the timber to be therein used to be all good sawd timber and to be covered with good and sufficient tile'.[76]

Material Culture

The inventories can be used to build up a picture of the hearth, the focus of the kitchen. It was predominantly furnished with iron utensils, the 'necessary ironware belonging to the use of the fireplace', as it was defined in the inventory of John Mayor *(65)*. A few fireplaces were more ornate. That of William Whyston *(124)* was ornamented with brass nobs, while William Morris *(106)* in 1753 had steel fire irons. All the homes recorded in this collection were within easy reach of coal supplies. Coal was the universal household fuel, so commonplace that it was scarcely ever listed. Ann Richard *(156)*, significantly a poor widow, had coals in her house worth 3s. and William Whyston *(124)* had a coal box, but otherwise the inventories record little information about the domestic uses of coal. There are several references to other fuels. William Roe *(168)* had a small quantity of charcoal, doubtless for malting. Edward Hollingshead in 1717 had two boxes of firewood, perhaps for kindling, while Edward Herbage in 1724 had faggots, bundles of furze used principally in bread ovens. In other parts of Shropshire like Bishop's Castle, which lay at a distance from collieries, all kinds of fuel—wood, furze or coal—were carefully recorded. The use of coal is indicated by the prevalence of grates in the inventories of the Severn Gorge. A grate was a basket fabricated from wrought-iron bars which was needed when coal was burned in order to ensure adequate supplies of air. Wood was usually burned on the flat bed of a fireplace. Coal was handled with tongs and with fire shovels. There are sufficient cleavers listed with fire irons *(19, 30, 46, 76, 79, 91, 111, 149, 161, 164)* to suggest that some may have been used for breaking coal rather than for chopping meat, and coal hatchets *(164)* were certainly used for that purpose. Combustion could be encouraged by the use of bellows, or, in a well-appointed house like Benthall Hall, with a poker *(13)*, and the bars of the grate might be cleared with fire slices *(6, 29, 36, 37, 42, 44)*, although that term could sometimes mean a simple fire shovel. The area of a fire could be contracted by the use of iron cheeks or wings. An inventory of 1676 listed 'two Iron Cheeks yt keep up the coals'. At the back the fire might be restrained by a cast-iron plate *(18, 19, 116)*, and iron plates might also be found under and in front of the fire *(148, 179)*. The fireplace of Roger Evans *(139)* includes both an iron back and an iron plate. Beneath the grate might be racks or niggards *(126, 130, 174, 179, 180)*, or at the front a purgatory *(85, 99, 101, 103, 197, 182, 189, 190)* from which unconsumed pieces of fuel could be recovered. The inhabitants of some households were protected from the dangers of the fire by fenders which might be of iron *(103, 193)* or brass *(182)*.

The open fireplace was the principal means of cooking.[77] Some inventories include andirons *(103, 139, 163, 166)*, sometimes of brass *(7, 182)*, which were trestles on which revolved spits or broaches, tapering iron pins piercing meat that was to be cooked. Skewers *(94, 137, 182)* had to be used to ensure that the meat did not fall off the spit. William Whyston *(124)* and Silvanus Ball *(95)* had sets of skewers. Small fire-dogs called creepers might be placed between the andirons. An alternative method of operating a spit was to place it on a pair of cob-irons, often called cobberts and sometimes gobbards, which were long bars with hooks, which could be rested against the front of a fireplace at an angle of about 45 degrees. A spit was turned by a jack, which might be operated by the updraught of hot air from the fire, or by a clockwork mechanism, and might be of iron *(9, 59, 91)* or brass *(101, 103)*. Edward Owen *(182)* in 1732 had a dog wheel that probably operated a spit. Such wheels are listed on 15 per cent of the 18th-century inventories in Bridgnorth, but this is the only one mentioned in the Severn Gorge and only one appears in the 846 inventories for the parishes to the north. Meat could be basted while it was cooking with a spoon which might be of iron *(46)* or brass *(85, 100)* or with a ladle *(155)*. A dripping pan was used to catch the fat that dripped from the meat. It was usually of iron or tin plate *(91, 94, 188)* but Luke Twyford *(166)* had a stone one. The *brandards* found in the fireplaces of Richard Benthall *(13)* and Margaret Evans *(149)* were probably *brandreths*, trivets which stood on three legs, which might have triangular or circular tops. The term *brandart* was used in Shrewsbury, and it may refer to the same item as a 'maid' (see above).[78] Above the fireplace there was often a crane, most commonly called a pot gail (or geel), but sometimes a sway or swail *(91, 107, 110)*, from which pots were suspended by links, hooks or hangers *(28, 30)*. Francis Parton *(129)* had chains to hold pots on the fire. Meat boiled in pots could be removed with flesh forks, to which there are five references, all after 1710. Skimmers were used to remove the dross which accumulated on the surface of the stock in which meat was cooked. There were enclosed facilities for heating water in some homes, an 'iron furnace in the wall' *(113)*, an 'iron furnace and iron marmet both in ye wall' *(76)*, and an 'old marment in the wall' *(73)* of a kind that might have been regarded as fixtures by some appraisers.

Food might be prepared with a hacking knife *(36, 125, 149)* or a chopping knife *(91, 100, 112, 133, 183, 184, 188)* and might be cooked over the fire in a variety of utensils. Numerous inventories list iron pots and kettles, for which the foundry in Coalbrookdale became famous after 1709, the latter being open vessels akin to present-day 'kettles' for making jam. Posnets, saucepans with long handles and three legs which usually stood over hot ashes, might be of brass *(120, 161)* or iron *(120)*. Marmites (or marments, or marmits) were pots that might be used for stewing meat and were usually of iron *(34, 76, 80, 103, 130, 174)*. Chafing dishes *(118, 128, 130)* were used to heat small quantities of food, and were placed over chafers, tray-like dishes containing hot ashes or charcoal. Various sieves were used in the kitchen as well as the brewhouse (see below). John Goodman *(183)* had 'a parcell of sieves and riddles', while Richard Cox *(179)* owned a flour search and a cleansing sieve, and William Baugh in 1759 was the owner of a 'soy bowle' (i.e. sie bowl), a form of sieve chiefly used for straining milk.

Mortars and pestles were important in the preparation of food. They are listed on 38 inventories, 7 per cent of the total, spread evenly across the period. Four of the 38 list two mortars and pestles each. It appears that cast-iron mortars, made by the Darbys of Coalbrookdale after 1709, were already known in the area in the 17th century. Of the 11 mortars listed before 1700 whose material is identified, there were three of brass and eight of iron. Of 13 similarly listed in the 18th century only one was of brass, ten of iron and two of wood, at least one of which was used with an iron pestle. Most mortars and pestles were doubtless used in preparing food, but one of the inventories to list two was that of the only doctor in the collection.

Evidence about diet comes from several sources within the inventories. The range of crops grown in the district and the types of animals kept indicate possibilities and constraints. References to foodstuffs are relatively rare since most were perishable. Some deductions can be made from domestic utensils about the kinds of food that could have been prepared.

Dairy products formed an important part of the diet of those who lived in the Severn Gorge. Most of the dairy products listed in the inventories are in the households of farmers who produced them on a commercial scale. Nevertheless it is evident that cheese and butter were made in many homes whose occupants were not primarily concerned with dairying, and in some where no cows were kept.

While no inventories survive for specialist bakers, it is evident that bread was commonly baked in the district, and some bread ovens survive in older houses. Many households had stores of corn. Silvanus Ball *(95)* had a quantity of corn for bread worth £3, while William Green *(116)* had two garners for storing grain, and William Morris *(106)* had a meal tub. Bread was probably made from autumn-sown crops of corn in which wheat and rye were mixed (see above). Two inventories *(36, 171)* mention peels, the shovel-shaped wooden tools used to insert and remove bread into and from an oven. A plate to draw bread *(161)* perhaps served the same function. It is likely that part of people's diet consisted of porridge-like farinaceous gruels, the likeliest materials for which would have been stored in receptacles like the oatmeal box on the inventory of Frances Baxter *(115)*. It is evident that grain was used in other ways, in the form of biscuits or wafers, griddled on wafering irons *(59)*, as cases for pasties or patties baked in pasty or patty pans *(57, 107, 182)*, or as coverings for puddings cooked in pudding pans *(125, 131, 181, 187, 191)* or pudding roasters, or pies baked on pie plates *(124)*.[79]

The inventories for the Severn Gorge, like those from the parishes to the north,[80] show that beef and pig meat were preserved by salting, and that joints were hung, sometimes from cratches *(94, 182)* in kitchens or brewhouses. John Hagar *(144)* had two ready-killed cows in his house. Salt might be stored in salt boxes *(13, 80, 91, 98, 109, 121, 162, 183, 191, 193)* or coffers *(161)* and applied to meat on a salting bench *(106)*. The meat would be kept for a time in a salting tub *(119)* or powdering tub *(13)*. Joints of bacon are listed on 23 inventories. The value of flitchens or little flitches varied between 5s. and 8s. 4d., and that of flitches between 6s. 8d. and £1. Pork as well as bacon was preserved in this way. Samuel Burrows *(98)* had two flitches of pork worth 15s. in his pantry, and two flitches of bacon worth £1 in his kitchen. Joints of salted beef also hung in the kitchens of the Severn Gorge. The inventories include 15 references to preserved beef, all of them before 1740. The collier Edward Cludd *(180)* had a side of pork and a piece of beef, which, with some cheese, were worth only three shillings. Numerous references to mustard pots and pewter salt cellars and two listings of pepper boxes suggest that meat was usually well-seasoned at the table. It is evident that open fires were used for toasting apples and cheese *(107)*.[81]

Beer was the most commonly consumed beverage in the Severn Gorge. It was made and drunk in taverns and in many homes (see below). There are few references to other kinds of alcoholic drink , but John Lloyd *(146)* had cider, which was much traded on the Severn, and some wine, while Edward Owen *(182)* had quart and pint measures for wine. The presence of two stills *(15, 166)* and of gill measures for brandy shows that spirits were made and consumed in the area. The posset cup in the inventory of Mark Henworth *(181)* suggests that some people knew the delights of posset, a highly alcoholic form of egg custard. By the end of the 18th century people in the Severn Gorge were notorious for their excessive consumption of tea, but there are few indications that this was happening before 1764. Tea and coffee were amongst the stock in Richard Pritchard *(194)* little shop in Coalbrookdale in 1759, and in the same year John Yates *(107)* had a coffee pot, but no other inventory lists a tea pot, a tea board, a coffee cup, a canister or any of the other apparatus associated with tea or coffee drinking. It is likely that in the part of England most celebrated for clay pipes much tobacco would have been consumed, but this is not reflected in the inventories. The shopkeeper George Bayley *(64)* was selling tobacco, and Richard Cox *(179)* had four old tin tobacco dishes worth a halfpenny each.

The table, after the fireplace, was the principal object of attention in the living rooms of the Severn Gorge in the early part of the period. There are some references, chiefly in agricultural households, to the 'table boards and frames' *(45, 117)* at which diners sat on forms, commonly found in the parishes to the north,[82] but most of the inventories in this collection simply list table boards or long tables *(9, 13, 14, 58, 122, 129)*. The earliest reference to an oval table is on the inventory of Andrew Langley *(47)* in 1687. They became commonplace during the first half of the 18th century. The first mention of a round table is in 1693 *(6)* but they remained comparatively rare. Mennes Langley in 1699 *(55)* was the first person recorded with square tables which also became quite common. Tables became more sophisticated in the 18th century. The inventories include three dressing tables *(10, 86, 182)*, a folding table *(84)*, oak tables *(91)*, side tables, a slate table *(182)*, a table with a leaf *(188)* and a table with slate in the leaf *(94)*. The 'pairs of tables' listed in four inventories *(13, 47, 51, 156)* were folding boards that could be opened up for such games as backgammon. There are numerous references to table cloths which might be coarse *(107, 174, 183)*, hurden *(94, 149, 180, 182, 187)*, huckaback *(183)*, hempen *(37, 71, 139, 149, 187)*, flaxen *(59, 76, 94)*, diaper *(59, 182)* or damask *(94)*, and tables might also be covered with carpets *(151)*.

Sophisticated table cutlery was not widely used in the Severn Gorge. In the 17th century only ten inventories mention table cutlery, all of them referring to spoons. After 1700 spoons are mentioned more frequently and there are three unambiguous references to table knives and forks: one at Benthall Hall *(13)*, one on the inventory of John Goodman, a modestly wealthy Madeley farmer, and one on that of Edward Holland, a very poor collier.

A desk in this collection most commonly means a portable box which could be locked up, as in the spice desk listed on an inventory in 1699, but the desk in the writing closet of Mary Penn *(87)* in 1740 probably provided a surface for writing as did the 'bewroe' (bureau) in Benthall Hall *(13)* and the desk being made by Samuel Burrows *(98)*. John Palmer *(193)* had a book case alongside his writing desk in his parlour, while Benjamin Buckley *(85)* had a writing table with a stone in the leaf.

Chairs became more commonplace and more elegant in the Severn Gorge between 1660 and 1760, as they did elsewhere in England. In many 17th-century households it was the custom to sit at table on benches or stools, like the buffet stools and the cushion stools owned by Frances Baxter *(115)* in 1663, the three-footed stools which belonged to John Morris in 1680 or the seggen stools in the Benthall home of Maurice Hartshorne in 1682. William Lewis *(26)* in 1670 had two twiggen chairs, and from the 1680s seggen chairs, with seats woven from rushes, became commonplace. Timothy Turner in 1691 had three sedge-bottomed chairs with cushions. Similar chairs were still in use in the 1750s when Mary

Clemson *(189)* had six of them and Edward Sansom had ten. Other, doubtless more comfortable chairs came into use. Robert Hill *(39)* in 1679 had six chairs that were green, which may describe the colour of their upholstery, or may indicate that they were turned from green wood. John Smitheman *(119)* in 1689 had a dozen leathern chairs worth 4s. each, while the Rev. Benjamin Taylor *(162)* had six 'Russia' chairs, which probably had seats of 'Russia', a durable leather impregnated with oil distilled from birch bark, although they might have been of Russia matting made from the inner bark of the linen tree, or the word could even have been a corruption of 'rushen' meaning made from rushes. Four years later Judith Holmes *(57)* had chairs with seats of turkeywork, a form of embroidered fabric. There were increasing numbers of joined chairs, that is chairs made by joiners, and the inventories of those who enjoyed a measure of wealth indicate increasing comfort and an expanding range of choice. Richard Benthall *(13)* in 1720 had an easy chair and 13 cane chairs. Edward Owen *(182)* in 1734 had two leather chairs with cushions, two Turkey chairs, six ash chairs, four black chairs and a child's chair. James Garmson *(99)* in 1745 had a wainscot chair, although it was probably an heirloom rather than an up-to-date luxury. The inventory of Silvanus Ball *(95)* in 1743 is the first to list chairs with braided seats, and several appraisers in the 1740s and 1750s distinguished between such chairs and those with ash, wooden or sedge bottoms. The inventory of John Palmer *(193)* in 1759 is one of the few to group elbow chairs with other dining chairs. He had two, one listed with five and the other with six wood chairs. Two inventories *(15, 169)* record nursing chairs.[83]

Containers of various kinds—chests, coffers, trunks, boxes, cupboards and presses—are listed in most household inventories. They might be used to store linen *(83, 85, 86, 87, 95, 102, 113, 150, 164, 186)*—William Biddle in 1671 had a trunk and linens worth £1, a coffer of linens worth £1 10s. 0d. and a box of linens worth £2—or its raw materials—Andrew Langley *(47)* had a chest with dressed hemp in it while others had chests containing yarn and wool. Robert Whitemore *(63)* in 1718 had linen in chests and yarn in coffers. The word 'press' in this collection almost always means a cupboard, unless it is qualified as in 'cheese press', and the inventory of Thomas Boden *(188)* in 1750 suggests that the two terms were synonymous. John Wilde *(100)* in 1747 had a wainscot press. A hanging press, hanging cupboard *(10, 151, 174)*, standing press *(36, 51)* or standing cupboard *(47)* was a wardrobe. Dorothy Haines in 1738 had a little 'press cupboard' which was a kind of wardrobe with two doors. There are two references in the 1750s to corner cupboards. It is evident from the inventory of Samuel Burrows *(98)* made in 1744 that cabinet makers in the district could make chests of drawers. The earliest items of this kind are the cupboard with drawers and the press with drawers in the inventory of Andrew Langley *(47)*, made in 1687. Edward Owen *(182)* in 1732 had a chest of drawers which appears to have matched a dressing table, and by the 1740s chests of drawers were commonplace.

Thomas Weale in 1686 had a trunk marked 'TW', worth 10 shillings, which appropriately was bequeathed in his will to his neighbour Thomas Wellins. Other containers included leather trunks, a leather portmanteau *(13)*, a little guinea box *(78)*, a wainscot chest *(186)*, a dale (i.e. deal) box, a deal chest *(184)*, a large oak chest *(110)*, a wainscot chest *(186)*, two paper boxes *(191)*, a knife box *(193)*, a straw hamper and some straw hutches *(30)*. There were numerous salt boxes as well as a salt coffer *(161)* and a salt chest, and several candle boxes. There is one reference, in the inventory of Dorothy Starkey in 1668, to a livery cupboard, a small container, often with fronts and sides of turned balusters, designed to contain the food and drink that people took to their sleeping rooms, and one on the inventory of Thomas Jarman in 1689 to a livery table on which such a cupboard was placed.

The dresser, a chest of drawers surmounted by shelves on which household utensils could be displayed, was the dominant feature of most kitchens in the Severn Gorge by the 1750s. One of the most regular appraisers, John Hartshorne of Broseley, most commonly listed first the contents of the kitchen, and almost invariably noted the dresser first. As in the parishes to the north, the word 'dresser' was occasionally used in the 17th century *(5, 41)*, and items of furniture intended for the display of utensils were certainly then in use. A Madeley inventory of 1682 refers to a dresser with shelves, with brass and pewter as the next item, and there are four references between 1682 and 1699 to brass benches. Dressers with drawers, frequently with pewter frames, as the flights of shelves were described, became commonplace after 1730. They occur on 22 per cent of the inventories in the 1730s, 37 per cent of those taken in the 1740s and 46 per cent of those made between 1750 and 1764. They were particularly common in the homes of miners and mariners. One Little Wenlock inventory *(131)* reveals that the dresser it listed had three drawers. The shelves were evidently intended for display, and their presence indicates that some households had more brass and pewter utensils than were required for day-to-day use, and that some capital had been invested in these items. A typical entry on the inventory of William Morris *(106)* in 1756 refers to 'One dresser of drawers, a pewter frame, and the pewter thereon'. There are some references to other displayed items. A Broseley inventory of 1732 *(79)* included not only a pewter frame and a dresser with drawers but also an old glass frame and six earthen plates. An inventory of 1748 *(101)* associated 'a dresser of drawers and pewter frame and pewter thereon' with 'copper furniture upon the chimney piece'. Prized possessions were displayed in other ways. An inventory of 1743 *(94)* listed glass and earthenware on the chimney piece. There are four references *(57, 66, 166)* to glass crates and one *(55)* specifically to a 'case for glasses'. By the 1840s middle-class observers of working-class homes noticed mantelpieces displaying pottery rather than pewter, and the 'shelf with delph upon it' on the inventory of Ambrose Buckley *(109)* in 1758 is perhaps an indication of the beginning of this custom.

Beds in the Severn Gorge were similar to those found in the parishes to the north.[84] A 'bed' in the inventories is usually a fabric container, or 'tick', that was stuffed with feathers, flocks (which usually means rags) or chaff. It was placed on a mat, usually woven from rushes or straw, that was supported by a cord or cords attached to a bedstead or frame. The various parts of a bed, the bed itself filled with feathers, the wooden bedsteads with their cords, and the mat which rested on them, together with the bolster, rug and blanket which lay above, are succinctly itemised in the inventory of John Leadbeater *(103)*. The inventory of Richard Benthall *(13)* illustrated the range of items which might be associated with beds in wealthy households.

Many bedsteads, particularly those referred to as 'joint' or 'joined' beds, were what would now be called 'four-posters', with posts supporting a cover or tester and rods on which curtains were hung. Several inventories provide significant details of beds which illuminated the less detailed entries in others. The modest inventory of John Dawley *(49)* includes three iron curtain rods with two cloth woollen curtains, two bed boards, a seggen mat and twill bed ticks filled with both flock and feathers. William Pearce had yellow curtains on his bed, and Thomas Boden *(188)* had red, while John Leadbeater *(103)* had a bedstead with green hangings and another with blue hangings. John Yates in 1757 had a bedstead with blue hangings and some coarse cloth which was apparently intended for use as hangings. There are several references to beds with canopies rather than full-length covers. Inventories of 1675 and 1708 *(34, 57)* refer to half-headed bedsteads and others to half tester bedsteads *(156)*. It was frequently the custom for beds on castors, truckle or trundle beds to be kept when out of use underneath the full-size 'high' or 'standing' bedsteads, perhaps for the use of children or servants. In an inventory of

1679 *(3)* a standing bed is itemised with a truckle bed, and one of 1692 *(51)* lists a high bed with a truckle bed under it. The best room in the house of Thomas Williams *(76)* in 1729 had a feather bed on a pair of joined bedsteads, and on it a blanket, a coverlet, a bolster and a pillow, with hanging above. Also in the room was a pair of old truckle bedsteads on which lay two flock beds, a blanket, a coverlet and a bolster. The coverings of the bed in the next room included a spotted rug. There were quilts on the beds of William Pearce *(94)* in 1742. One of the crudest sleeping places appears to be the two old flock beds lying upon nailed boards noted in a Broseley inventory of 1679 *(37)*. Only one inventory in the collection gives the weight of a feather bed, the old and much damaged bed in the home of Richard Pearce *(79)* which weighed 60lbs. In other areas beds were commonly weighed, and could contain over 100lbs. of feathers.

On top of the bed lay pillows and bolsters stuffed with the same range of materials as beds, contained in pillow beers or cases *(103)*, together with blankets, coverlets or bed hillings *(6, 22, 51, 57)*, and sometimes rugs or quilts. Sheets were of linen or hempen, and the quality was often made clear by the appraisers as fine *(85, 173, 183)*, flaxen, fine hempen *(84)*, hempen, hurden, coarse hurden *(84)*, overworn hurden *(85, 113)*, twill *(115, 118)*, noggen *(120, 161)* or simply coarse. The will of John Harris *(32)* is one of many which shows the value that was attached to linen sheets, and people's awareness of the distinctions between particular grades. Thomas Williams *(76)* had one pair of flaxen sheets, three of hempen and three of hurden. By contrast William Beddow in 1761 had 'six pair of coarse herden sheets overworn' worth 10s. 6d., and the inventory of John Hartshorne in 1737 listed 'poor ordinary bedding' worth 10s. An inventory of 1741 includes three pairs of hurden sheets valued together at 6s., and one pair of flaxen sheets worth 4s. Dorothy Hartshorne in 1692 had flaxen sheets worth 5s. a pair, hempen worth 4s. a pair and hurden worth 2s. 8d. a pair. Napkins, towels and other linens associated with personal hygiene were made from the same range of fabrics, and linens of all sorts were often known collectively as napery ware.

Since bed linen was highly esteemed, it is not surprising that sheets were listed carefully, and it is possible to deduce from many inventories how many sheets were available for each bed in a house. In the parishes to the north of the Severn Gorge analysis of such figures showed that standards of sleeping comfort improved in the first half of the 18th century as households came to have four sheets per bed rather than the two per bed usual before 1700.[85] In the Severn Gorge parishes it appears that most households already had about four sheets per bed in the 17th century, and there was no significant change after 1700. Of the 557 sheets identified by fabric, 13.6 per cent were flaxen, 27.8 per cent hempen and 58.6 per cent hurden, a proportion which remained constant throughout the period.

TABLE IX

Sheets and beds

	Inventories which detail number of sheets and bed	Number of beds	Number of sheets	Ratio of sheets per bed
1660-69	4	9	53	5.9
1670-79	18	45	194	4.3
1680-89	14	42	226	5.4
1690-99	6	14	51	3.6
1700-09	6	22	116	6.7
1710-19	10	33	126	3.8
1720-29	12	34	142	4.2
1730-39	15	39	172	4.4
1740-49	16	42	194	4.6
1750-59	11	24	91	3.8
1760-64	3	6	26	4.3

Warming pans are listed on 88 inventories, and it is evident that their use became more general after 1700. They are mentioned on 18 17th-century inventories, 6 per cent of the total, but on 75, or 36 per cent, of those made between 1700 and 1764. Seven of those listed were of brass, while 16 were curiously described as 'old'. Randle Holme in 1688 described the function of a warming pan as 'to receive either hot coals or an iron heater in it, which being shut close with a cover for the purpose, the maid warms her master's bed', the implication being that a warming pan was essentially something used by those wealthy enough to employ servants. The inventories from the Severn Gorge suggest that a substantial proportion of the population in the 18th century warmed their beds in this way.[86]

INTRODUCTION

Soft furnishings were to be found in at least some of the houses in the Severn Gorge in the period under review. There are seven references to carpets which were normally coverings for cupboards or chests, one of them to a green example *(22, 29, 41, 146, 151, 159, 164)*. Most curtains were hung on beds, but there is at least one specific reference to window curtains as early as 1679 *(41)*. An inventory in 1676 *(149)* refers to curtains made of Kidderminster stuff, the woollen fabric for which the Worcestershire town was celebrated before it became a centre for carpet manufacture in the mid-18th century. Where floor coverings existed they were generally called rugs, and there are references to red examples in 1688 and 1691 *(121)*, although some rugs were bed coverings.

Houses were lit by candles which were made in the district (see above). Except for the inventories of tallow chandlers, the only inventory to list candles is that of Richard Barker in 1719, who had just a pound of them. There are numerous references to candlesticks, most commonly of brass or pewter, but also of iron *(124, 127, 129)*—probably spirals of wire—in the 18th century. The inventory of Edward Owen *(132)* lists snuffers with his five brass candlesticks. Sampson Bulkley *(59)* also had snuffers, as well as two sconces, bracket candle-holders fitted to the walls of one of his bedrooms, while Roger Evans *(139)* had a hanging candlestick. The inventories include 11 references to candle boxes *(10, 71, 80, 84, 91, 96, 179, 182)*, all from the 18th century and mostly of tin plate. Lanthorns, of which six are mentioned *(91, 109, 124, 171, 182, 183)*, also appear only on inventories made after 1700.

Pewter was omnipresent in the households of the Severn Gorge as it was in every part of England.[87] It is listed in every inventory in which the level of detail is sufficient to reveal its presence. There were pewterers in Shrewsbury, Ludlow and Newport, and pewter was doubtless taken to homes in the Gorge from the 30 or so manufacturers in Bristol. Pewter was used for plates, dishes, cups, tankards, flagons and candlesticks, for pint and quart measures, for mustard pots, salt cellars, salvers, pie plates, porringers, posset cups *(181)*, chamber pots and brandy gills. Two stills are listed, one in the kitchen of Luke Twyford *(166)*, whose house also included a pewter room, and one, with a lead bottom, amongst the possessions of Frances Baxter *(115)*. Appraisers in the Gorge only rarely valued pewter by weight. Richard Pearce's *(79)* pewter in 1732 weighed more than 100lbs. and was valued at 7½d. per lb. Edward Thomas *(191)* in 1755 had 20 lbs of pewter valued at 6d. a pound. The appraisers of Edward Owen *(182)* in 1732 quoted the weight of his 13 dishes, valuing them at just less than 8d. per lb., but not his other pewter. Richard Rutter *(31)* had two *counterfeit* dishes, of pewter wrought with ornamental designs that looked like silver. Two described pewter as 'old' or 'overworn' and probably implied that it was ready for re-cycling.

Brass, like pewter, was present in almost every household in the Severn Gorge. It was used for fire irons, pots, saucepans and kettles, for candlesticks and snuffers, chafing dishes, skellets *(128)*, warming pans, basting spoons, skimmers, mortars and pestles, pepper boxes and drug boxes. Maslin kettles *(14, 180, 187)* were made from a special kind of brass which probably had a higher than normal copper content.

Copper usually appeared in English households as one of the constituents of brass, and lead as a constituent of pewter, but a few items made from the two metals are listed. Humphrey Bowdler *(140)* had 'leaden ware' worth £1. There are three references to copper cans *(59, 178, 182)*, one to a copper pan *(189)* and one to a copper candlestick *(59)*. John Leadbeater *(103)* and Edward Owen *(182)* had copper saucepans, and William Yates *(101)* had copper 'furniture' displayed with brass objects on his chimney piece and elsewhere in his kitchen, and a copper pot, distinct from one made of brass, in his brewhouse. Thomas Beddow *(80)* had a copper furnace which his appraisers described as 'very old', by which they could have meant ready for re-cycling.

Some inventories list silver plate and a few refer to gold plate. There are 11 references which do not specify the nature of the items, and one *(53)* to a large piece of gold. Eleven inventories include silver spoons *(13, 19, 25, 37, 77, 115, 140, 156, 166)*, and there are seven references to silver cups or tankards *(19, 25, 47, 77, 146)*, four to silver bowls *(25, 47, 140)* and one to a silver tobacco box *(47)*.

Ironware, whether wrought iron, the products of the blacksmith, or cast iron from foundries, was used in every household for fire irons, cooking utensils and smoothing irons. Items made of tinplate, thin sheets of wrought iron coated with tin, began to appear in English households during the 17th century and became commonplace after 1700. The inventories from the Severn Gorge confirm that tinplate goods were used on an increasing scale. The appraisers of George Wheelwright *(128)* in 1714 categorised a proportion of his goods as 'tinnen ware'. There are references to tinplate utensils on 12 inventories between 1662 and 1699, 3.6 per cent of the total, but they are mentioned on 67 inventories, 20 per cent of the total between 1700 and 1764, and on 28 per cent of those made between 1740 and 1764. The proportion of inventories listing tinplate goods is rather higher than in the parishes to the north, another instance of the more rapid take-up of innovations in the Severn Gorge. Tinplate utensils included tobacco dishes, candle boxes, pudding pans, pasty pans, dripping pans, plates with covers, broilers, one of which was worth 3s. 6d., dredgers, colanders and tundishes (or funnels).

Earthenware was being made on a considerable scale in the Severn Gorge in the period covered by the inventories. Archaeological evidence, particularly that which came from the examination of spoil tips and limited excavations in the 1980s,[88] confirms that pottery was becoming more attractive during the first half of the 18th century as the quality of delftwares and slipware was enhanced. The household use of pottery increased steadily in the century covered by the inventories. Ten of those taken before 1700 list pottery—only 5 per cent of the total, but after 1700 it is mentioned on 44 inventories—16 per cent of the total. These are higher figures than those for the parishes to the north but less than the 22 per cent recorded in Bridgnorth. There are two references, in 1686 and 1718 *(47, 64)*, to chinaware—this would have been imported Nanking ware since the technology of porcelain manufacture had not been perfected in Britain at this date. The 'whiteware' on the inventory of Robert Ogden *(41)* in 1679 may also have referred to porcelain. There are four references between 1717 and 1750 to Tickney or Ticknall ware *(69, 188)*, a type of earthenware, often black-glazed, which took its name from Ticknall in Derbyshire. Similar black-glazed ware was made in Broseley and Benthall, and the term may refer to the type of ware rather than strictly to its place of origin. The inventories include 12 references to delftware *(95, 96, 97, 102, 103, 104, 109, 129)*, the earliest in 1728. Delftware took its name from the Dutch city, and was distinguished by the use of a glaze made white and opaque with tin oxide, but it was made in England from the 16th century, and the name is currently used for all English ware of this kind. Delftwares were made in Bristol throughout the period covered by the inventories. The Bristol punch bowl owned by Edward Owen *(182)* in 1732 is the best example in the collection of how luxuries reached the Severn Gorge from the second city in the kingdom. The Hall Warren Collection in the Ashmolean Museum includes several Bristol punch bowls which must resemble Owen's. The inventories show the uses to which earthenware was put—there are examples of mugs, cups, basins, dishes, plates and jugs and a solitary mustard pot *(188)*. Pottery was slowly replacing pewter for practical purposes, and it was becoming, like pewter, something to be displayed. William Pearce *(94)* had glass and earthenware on his chimney piece, and Ambrose Buckley *(109)* in 1758 was displaying delftware on a shelf.[89]

The use of glass in the household slowly increased. Bottles are listed on 18 inventories, the proportion scarcely varying over time. Mennes Langley

(55) had 96 worth 1½d. each, and Joseph Whitefoot *(91)* had 72. Drinking glasses, first listed in the second decade of the 18th century, are mentioned on 17 inventories, 6 per cent of the total between 1710 and 1764. The 12 drinking glasses owned by Charles Smith in 1738 were valued at a penny each, and those in the home of Joseph Whitefoot *(91)* were accompanied by a decanter.

Many of the commonplace objects found in the households of the Severn Gorge were made of wood. Appraisers sometimes categorised wooden items as coopery ware, joiner's ware or turned ware *(22)*. Kitchens, dairies, butteries and brewhouses were filled with tubs, half barrels made by coopers, described in one inventory *(73)* as the 'wooden vessels belonging to the buttery'. They were known by various names, some of which were used only in limited areas.[90] In the Severn Gorge they were most likely to be called tubs or mitts, which were used for kneading dough for bread or for handling curds in cheese making, and were, according to one inventory *(58)*, distinct from stunds which were used for similar purposes. The word 'hoop' can also mean a tub, as in the measuring hoop on the inventory of John Goodman *(183)*. The numerous piggins were small half barrels with single extended staves for handles, which could also be used for measuring. People commonly ate from trenchers, wooden plates, probably regarded as turned ware. William Whyston *(124)* and Roger Thresslecock *(133)* each had 36. George Wheelwright *(128)* had 48 worth a penny each, and George Parton *(137)* 11 worth together 1s. 6d. Several inventories *(79, 80, 119, 125, 174)* list wooden bottles. Baskets were made in the Severn Gorge by specialist craftsmen (see above) and were used in many homes. Richard Cox *(179)* had a round-handled basket. William Whyston *(124)* had baskets distinguishable from hand baskets. John Harper *(187)* and Roger Evans *(139)* each had straw whiskets. There are four references to the long shallow baskets called whiches *(47, 115, 162, 171)*, one of which was used to store corn.

Few but the wealthy owned books. They are recorded on 40 inventories, 8 per cent of the total, and the proportion diminishes in the 18th century. Seventeen of the references are on inventories valued above £100. No book titles are listed other than some Bibles. Analysis of inventories elsewhere in Shropshire shows that books were found chiefly in towns. In Bridgnorth, only a short distance from the Gorge, books appear on 22 per cent of the inventories, and they are listed on 12 per cent of those from the parishes to the north. Only two inventories included musical instruments. Mennes Langley *(55)* had a flute and a hunting horn, while William Wyston had a fiddle and a cittern. The proportion of inventories mentioning instruments is usually higher in towns. Nevertheless in 1788 a Madeley Wood collier was in possession of a barrel organ which he suggested his executors should sell to pay off his debts.[91]

People in the Severn Gorge began to adorn their homes with pictures during the first half of the 18th century. Only one inventory before 1700 lists pictures, but there are eight references between 1700 and 1739, and 15 between 1740 and 1764. This is broadly similar to the pattern in the parishes to the north. The inventories provide few details but pictures were clearly cheap. William Yates *(101)* had a variety of prints and pictures, six of the latter being appraised at 2d. each, the same value as that accorded to six pictures, perhaps the same ones, on the inventory of Edward Yates in 1757. Four inventories, all appraised after 1710, include maps *(98, 182)*, apparently displayed like pictures, and there is one reference to a globe *(91)*.

One of the indications of the 'consumer society' that was developing in the first half of the 18th century was the use of looking glasses. They were relatively rare before 1700, but appear on 40 inventories, 16 per cent of the total between 1700 and 1739, and on 18, 22 per cent of the total, between 1740 and 1764, a higher proportion than in the parishes to the north. Looking glasses varied in size and value. Henry Carrington *(86)* had a dressing table glass, and Matthew Gittings in 1759 a large looking glass worth 10s. 6d., while William Whyston *(124)* had two, one worth 5s. the other worth £1. These appear to have been substantial items of furniture, whereas the two small looking glasses worth a shilling owned by Richard Guest in 1737 and that worth 9d. owned by James Weaver in 1735 were doubtless of the kind held in the hand.

The diffusion of the clock and watch during the 18th century brought profound changes to English society.[92] This collection of inventories shows that timepieces were more widely diffused through the population in the industrialising society of the Severn Gorge than in the more agricultural parishes to the north, in the port of Bridgnorth or in the remote market town of Bishop's Castle. Elliott has shown that clockmaking became established as a regular occupation in Shrewsbury and other Shropshire market towns in the decades after 1710[93] and by 1773 there was a clockmaker in Madeley. The evidence furnished by the inventories accords well with this observation. Before 1710 only 16 clocks or watches are listed—only 7 per cent of the total. They are mentioned on 57 inventories, 26 per cent of the total in the next 40 years, and on 23, or 28 per cent of the total, between 1750 and 1764. It is evident that all social classes were coming to pay attention to time. Five clocks are recorded in the inventories of colliers during the 1750s. Most clocks—75 of the 81—are appraised separately from other items, which makes it possible to gain some idea of prices. The mean value of the rather random range of timepieces recorded before 1710 is £1 11s. 7d., but that of clocks appraised in the next forty years is rather higher—£1 14s. 2d. Prices subsequently fell and the mean value of clocks between 1750 and 1764 is £1 8s. 8d. The inventories provide some details about the nature of timepieces. Richard Benthall *(13)*, William Smith *(20)*, Richard Pearce *(79)* and Edward Owen *(182)*, all wealthy men, had silver watches. Benthall also had a repeating clock, while John Ball *(56)* had an old clock with its weights and line, and Richard Pearce *(79)* had a clock case worth 7s. 6d. without its mechanism.

TABLE X

Clocks: percentages of inventories recording clocks in six districts of Shropshire

	1660-1709	1710-1749	1660-1749
North Telford	2.72	20.05	10.3
Severn Gorge	7.04	26.27	15.4
Bridgnorth	6.00	18.02	12.09
Shifnal	6.03	18.05	10.9
Newport	2.79	12.03	6.8
Bishop's Castle	5.55	11.86	8.39

The inventories provide relatively little information on clothing, although references to the deceased's undetailed wearing apparel are commonplace. The only item of interest in relation to women's clothing is the 'wearing apparel with other necessary linens belonging to a servant maid' listed on the inventory of Catherine Hartshorne *(11)*. The inventories of George Buttery *(120)* and John Harper *(187)* both list boots, the latter's worth 4s. Luke Twyford *(166)* had a pair of silver buckles. Eustace Beard *(14)* and George Wheelwright *(128)* both had new cloth ready to be made into suits. Two inventories give some indication of a man's stock of clothing. William Maybury *(161)* had a hat, a wig, two pairs of breeches, two coats, one old and one new, and two shirts, one flaxen and one hempen, worth altogether £2 12s. 0d. Richard Cox *(179)* had a coat, a waistcoat, a pair of breeches, two shirts, shoes and stockings worth 12s. 6d. Some wills provide not only details about garments but indications of how wearers valued them. The amazingly detailed will of John Harris *(32)*, a collier of modest means who died in 1674, carefully divided his most valued clothing amongst his sons-in-law, a 'synamond' (i.e. cinnamon) suit, a grey suit, a green coat and a pair of woollen drawers.

Three men had gold rings when they died. Richard Benthall *(13)* had five, Thomas Haddon in 1682 had two, and Thomas Oliver *(51)* had one with a silver pin. Francis Adams *(22)* had a signet ring and Mennes Langley *(55)* and Robert Ogden *(41)* had rings of unspecified materials. Four women had gold rings. The most valuable was that of Ann Simpson *(102)* worth 17s. 6d., and the least that of Mary Goodman in 1671 valued at 5s.

Few of those who lived in the Severn Gorge between 1660 and 1764 kept weapons. Only 22 inventories, 4.2 per cent of the total, refer to weapons, and of these 10 were specifically guns for birding or fowling, valued between 2s. and 18s. but mostly at the lower end of that range. The Rev. Benjamin Taylor and Richard Benthall were among the five people who had pistols *(13, 91, 98, 119, 162)*. Ann Richards *(156)* in 1689 had an old musket and an old sword, perhaps relics of the Civil War. Mennes Langley *(55)* had two rapiers for fencing valued at 4s. the pair, and a sword with its belt and hanger worth £1, which had perhaps been intended for other purposes. William Maybury *(161)* and Richard Benthall *(13)* also had swords. Francis Adams *(22)* in 1668 had armour and a crossbow as well as guns.

Women's Work

The inventories make it possible to define some of the household tasks that were commonly regarded as the province of women. The domestic processing of hemp or flax was universally regarded as women's work. A Stottesdon inventory of 1667 refers to 'implements of huswifry with flax undressed'.[94] Flax (*linum usitatissimum*) and hemp (*cannabis sativa*), the raw materials from which linen cloth is made, were widely grown in the district, but on odd patches of land rather than as a principal field crop. A map of Little Wenlock in 1727 shows 10 small plots called hemp butts in and around the core of the village.[95] Flax, hemp and yarn were commonly itemised together. Harvested flax is mentioned in 19 inventories, 4 per cent of the total, and hemp on 32, 6 per cent of the total. 110 inventories, 21 per cent of the total, list spinning wheels, hemp, or flax, but in this case the proportion is higher in the 18th than in the 17th century. Before 1700 evidence for domestic production of yarn appears on 15 per cent of the inventories, but on 26 per cent of those between 1700 and 1764, and on 20 per cent of those made in the last 15 years of the period. It is evident that domestic spinning remained commonplace in the second half of the 18th century in the Severn Gorge as it did elsewhere in the Midlands. George Eliot's *Mill on the Floss* is set in north Warwickshire in the second decade of the 19th century, and in it Mrs. Tulliver refers with some exasperation to

> these clothes as I spun myself ... And Job Haxey wove'em and brought the piece home on his back, as I remember standing at the door and seeing him come, before I ever though to'marrying your father.[96]

Flax and hemp were grown and processed by all social classes and are found in Benthall Hall *(13)* as well as in some of the poorest households in the Severn Gorge.

Once gathered, a crop of hemp or flax was soaked or *retted*. Roger Evans *(139)* had 'hempe wattered and unwatered', and the stone trough he owned may have been used for soaking. Roger Downes *(172)* also had flax that had been 'watered'. Next it was beaten or *scutched* to separate the long fibres, the line which was made into flaxen yarn and fabrics, from the short fibres, known variously as tow, noggs or hurds, from which hurden yarn and fabrics were made. Roger Evans *(139)* was amongst those who owned hatchells, the combs used for this purposes, and Joseph Reynolds *(10)* had three dozen of *hatchelled* flax. Hemp and flax were usually measured in stones *(120, 122, 174, 180, 183, 187)* or pounds *(28, 30, 118)*, but John Goodman *(183)* had a dozen of hemp, perhaps meaning 12 bundles, and William Benbow *(30)* had six *kinchings* of hemp. A 'kinching' is a loop, and in this context probably means a bundle. Values for a stone of hemp varied between 1s. and 6d. Hemp and flax were probably spun on the small, little or short wheels listed in inventories, while long, large or great wheels were used for spinning wool. Samuel Burrows *(98)* had both a long wheel and a little wheel, while George Wheelwright *(128)* had three little wheels and a long wheel. Spinning wheels were valued between 1s. and 2s. 6d. Spun yarn was accumulated on yarn winds, known variously as 'yarwingles' or 'erwings' *(171)*, a device defined in the inventory of Thomas Beddow *(80)* as 'a pair of blades for winding yarn'. Richard Benthall *(13)* and Hannah Hartshorne *(82)* each had a pair of yarn blades. Yarn was sometimes measured in pounds

(28) but more commonly in *slippings* or skeins *(30, 34, 37, 102, 118, 171)*. Edward Dawley *(37)* had two slippings of flaxen and hempen yarn and 10lbs. of nogs. Hemp, flax and the yarns made from them were stored until a sufficient quantity had been accumulated for particular household needs. There are references *(47, 63)* to storage of dressed hemp and yarn in coffers, and Roger Roe *(171)* had 'two years hemp' worth £1. The hemp owned by William Benbow *(30)* was measured in kinchings, his hurden yarn in slippings, and his woollen yarn in pounds. Linen yarn would be taken to custom weavers (see above) to be woven into cloth. Ann Mullart in 1684 had three ells and half a yard of hurden cloth, probably just woven, which she kept with a slipping of noggen yarn. Joan Harris *(42)* had hemp seed which was itemised with her dressed and undressed hemp.

Some stages of linen processing might be undertaken by specialist dressers. The Smith family of Goose Hill (or Geese Pit) on the Calcutts estate in Broseley were a family of flax dressers. Richard Smith, tow dresser, who died in 1771, had two brothers who followed the same trade. Richard Smith of the same address, flax dresser, was probably his son. This Richard Smith's son was a soldier fighting abroad in 1810, but his nephew, Thomas Smith, was working as a flax dresser. The work of dressing might also be undertaken by itinerant tradesmen like Richard Rhodes, hemp dresser, who died in 1715 while a sojourner in the parish of Willey.[97]

Wool is listed on 11 inventories, and the presence of great wheels, and of 'woollen' as well as linen gears in weavers' inventories *(174)*, show that it was spun and woven in the Severn Gorge, although only on a small scale and for local use. William Benbow *(30)* had 18lbs. of woollen yarn worth 10s. and 5lbs. of wool worth 2s. 6d.

Many cottages in the Severn Gorge retain their brewhouses, sometimes detached, sometimes semi-detached, and usually single-storey buildings. They were an essential feature of the domestic culture of the Coalbrookdale Coalfield well into the 20th century. They can most readily be recognised as parts of 17th-century and early 18th-century cottages, but they were also incorporated into terraces like Carpenters Row, Coalbrookdale, built by the ironworking companies from the 1750s. Miriam McDonald showed in 1988 that this kind of accommodation is found in many societies,[98] in Clydeside tenements, in the Scottish Highlands and further afield, and that it is characteristically 'a reserved part of the domestic space used by women ... an easily slopped-out area'. Activities in brewhouses required 'access to water, a boiler and an area big enough to take the array of wooden tubs and vessels needed'. By the 19th century it was customary to build a setless in a brewhouse, which provided a resting place for heavy loads, a cold surface and storage space beneath. The probate records of the Severn Gorge were the starting points of McDonald's study, and they help to illuminate technological processes, the extent of self-sufficiency in the society which had grown up around mining and working the river, and the role of women in that society. Wills show that testators dividing up residential property were concerned that access to brewhouses should be maintained for all who shared the inheritance.[99]

Brewing equipment is listed on 22 inventories, a higher proportion than in the parishes to the north where it appears on only 25 per cent. The proportion of inventories with brewing equipment increased over time—32 per cent before 1700, 48 per cent between 1700 and 1739, and 50 per cent between 1740 and 1764.

The raw material of beer was malt, specifically mentioned on 20 inventories. Much of the barley grown locally was doubtless used for brewing, but the inventories provide little information about how barley was converted to malt, and there are no records of any full-time maltster. Several inventories show that malting was carried out in the district. The appraisers of William Green *(116)* and Andrew Langley *(47)* listed 'weeting' (i.e. wetting) 'fats' or vats, that would have been used for soaking barley before it was laid out on a malting floor to enable it to start sprouting. Once sprouting had commenced it would, according to the judgement of the maltster, be stopped by heating it in a malt kiln, fired with a smokeless fuel, thus stabilising the sugars which had formed within the grain. John Goodman *(183)* had a malt chamber in which he stored the screen and the hair cloth which would be placed over it to hold the barley when it was placed in the kiln. William Roe *(168)* had a malt house in which he kept both a wetting vat and a stock of charcoal. Other malt rooms and malt houses were used for the storage of cheese, grain or parts for agricultural implements *(10, 80, 171)*. Malt from a kiln might be sifted on a screen called a tray or 'trea' *(79, 80, 124)* to dispense with the remnants of the sprouts. Some malthouses remain in the Severn Gorge, particularly in Ironbridge, and malting was a significant part of the local economy in the 19th century. Several householders had malt stored in bags *(42)*, which suggests that it had been bought from a maltster. A bag of malt in 1667 was valued at 10s. Malt was sometimes measured in stones and quarters *(73, 139)* but more commonly in strikes. The five values given for a strike of malt are reasonably consistent, ranging from 3s. 2d. to 4s. 6d. *(68, 80, 169)*. The largest quantity of malt was held by Edward Edwards *(68)* who had 250 strikes worth £40, the next largest being that at Benthall Hall *(13)* valued at £10. Several inventories list vessels for measuring malt, like John

Leadbeater's *(103)* strike measure or Thomas Beddows's *(80)* peck and half strike.

The process of brewing beer began with the crushing of malt grain in a malt mill, the hand-operated machine the manufacture of which had been learned by Abraham Darby I as an apprentice in Birmingham. Malt mills are listed on 31 inventories, and were valued between 5s. and £2. One inventory reveals that a malt mill was also called a hand mill, one shows that steel mill was also an alternative description *(57)*, while a third refers to 'steel mills to grind malt' *(54)*.

Milled malt was placed in a receptacle in which it would be boiled in water, and then transferred to a vat where more malt would be added. In a brewery such vessels are called mash tuns (or tubs) and they are named on numerous inventories *(21, 94, 95, 102, 103, 113, 135, 182, 190)*. One inventory records a mashing staff *(94)* which was used to stir malt into the liquor. After some hours in the mash tun, water was percolated through the malt and the liquid, by now called the wort, passed into a vessel where it was boiled with hops, which might be called a brewing furnace *(54, 56, 94)*, a brewing vessel, a brewing kettle *(42)*, an old copper furnace *(187)*, a brass furnace in the brewhouse *(164)* or an iron furnace boiler. Several brewhouses were equipped with both iron and brass furnaces *(103)*. Brass furnaces were set in the walls of some brewhouses *(16, 98)* but seem to have been regarded by appraisers as moveables.

Hops are listed on 11 inventories. Mary Guest in 1667 had a sack of hops worth £2 and William Wright in 1720 had two worth £4 14s. 0d. each, but most hops are recorded as 'parcels', an imprecise measurement since values varied from 3s. to £3 *(140)*. The hops on the inventory of Ann Richards *(156)* were worth only 6d.

When the wort and hops had been boiled, the liquor was drained into other receptacles for cooling—coolers are mentioned on many inventories—and then into containers where yeast was added to bring about fermentation. Such vessels might be simple tubs, brewing tubs, barm tubs *(94)*, brewing stunds *(42)* or brewing mitts, or ale vats, a term which might be rendered as 'ill vat' *(94)* or 'elfate' *(58)*. Most inventories which give details of the contents of brewhouses list tundishes, the funnels used in transferring liquor between different containers. When fermentation was sufficiently advanced the beer would be drawn into casks of various sizes. Inventories mention pipes *(36, 139)* which might contain 126 gallons, hogsheads *(26, 36, 101)* holding 48 gallons, half hogsheads *(85, 101)*, kilderkins *(80)* holding 16 gallons and firkins holding eight gallons. Beer might be measured by a gaun or the kind of gallon measure held by George Buttery *(120)*, or by the measuring hoop (i.e. tub) owned by John Goodman *(183)*. Ann Simpson *(102)* had about 80 gallons of ale stored in nine barrels of different sorts. Barrels were placed on racks called stillings *(135, 196)*, or on wooden horses *(94, 195)*. Several inventories mention the strainers used in brewing, like the cleansing sieve in the brewhouse of Richard Cox *(179)*. Inventories which illustrate the brewing process particularly well are those of Richard Aston *(21)*, Silvanus Ball *(95)* and John Leadbeater *(103)*, while that of Richard Benthall *(13)* provides insights into the world of country-house brewing that has been described by Sambrook.[100]

Brewhouses were also used for making butter and cheese. Dairy equipment is most common in Little Wenlock where several farms produced cheese as a cash product (see above). Many other families who made their livings by other means also practised dairying. Richard Barker, a collier who died in 1731 with possessions worth only £14 14s. 2d., had three cows, together with a cheese press, a cheese tub, a milking pan and a gaun. John Harper *(187)* owned only two cows, but had a churn and churn staff, a cheese tub, cheese press, milk bowls, butter scales and a kneading tub. Thomas Hartshorne *(19)*, tobacco pipe maker, owned two milking cows, and had a churn, milking cans and milking gauns. The house of Samuel Burrows *(98)*, carpenter, included a brewhouse, and an adjacent pantry where there was dairy equipment including a milking gaun to deal with the milk from his one cow, a cooler, two slob benches, two spinning wheels and two flitches of pork. Some people who owned no cows had equipment like milk pans, butter tubs and churns, and perhaps bought in milk to make butter or cheese. The inventory of Joseph Whitefoot *(91)*, a mason and apparently a tavern keeper, who kept no cows, shows that his back kitchen and buttery, probably the domain of his wife Elizabeth, included a furnace, a boiler, a selection of barrels and tubs and a horse on which they stood, two iron pots, a brass kettle, a butter tub, a flour tub and two slob benches. Sampson Buckley *(59)* had milk pans and steans, William Whyston *(124)* a butter tub, George Parton *(137)* a churn, but none of them kept cows. It is possible that they were elderly men who had disposed of their cattle as they grew too old to manage them.

The preparation of dough for breadmaking is also likely to have been a female activity undertaken in the brewhouse. Some items of coopery ware, in particular kneading tubs or kneading mitts *(9, 37, 60, 64, 78)*, could have been used either in preparing bread or in dairying. One inventory *(58)* suggests that a kneading tub was different from a kneading mitt.

Laundry work was also undertaken in brewhouses. Washing tubs are mentioned on some inventories *(13, 18, 58, 124, 130)*, and many of the tubs whose functions are not defined were doubtless used for washing clothes. The only reference to soap is in the stock of the shop of George Bayley *(64)* and there is just one reference to ash balls *(104)*, made by moulding together fat, possibly dripping, and wood ash, which provided a crude substitute for soap. Ironing was undertaken with smoothing irons or sad irons, cast iron products of the foundry at Coalbrookdale after 1709, but used in the district at least as early as 1675. Smoothing irons became more sophisticated in the 18th century, due partly to the enterprises of Isaac Wilkinson the ironmaster. Box irons *(171)* which stood on holders, and into which cleats of heated iron could be placed, were coming steadily into use and a Madeley inventory of 1733-34 *(183)* distinguished a box iron from a smoothing iron.

Water was required for almost all the work women did in brewhouses. It was carried in water pails *(13, 21, 108, 110, 131, 180, 182)* or perhaps in leather jacks *(40)*, and stored in the array of tubs found in all brewhouses. Some water doubtless came direct from the Severn, from local streams or from mill or ironworks pools. One of the most celebrated early views of the Iron Bridge shows a woman dipping a container into the river.[101] Water also came from wells and winding apparatus is recorded in the inventories of Francis Evans *(132)*, who had a 'bucket, well rope and barrel', and William Roe *(168)*.

Conclusions

These inventories present a portrait of 'industrial communities' before the 'Industrial Revolution', but it is important to seek out the implications of both terms. The focus of the economy of the Severn Gorge between 1660 and 1764 was the extraction and distribution of coal, the work of miners and mariners. Others used coal to make iron, lead, lime or ceramic objects, and provided the wooden and hempen artefacts required by those who dug and sailed, or by farming supplied food for the rest of the population. Yet to a large extent the members of this society fended for themselves. Many families built their own houses, brewed their own beer, made their own butter, spun yarn for bed-, table- and household-linens and for their clothing, and produced their own bacon and pork. Yet, paradoxically, these were not families isolated from the main currents of 18th-century society. They were linked by trade with the second city of the kingdom, and were well acquainted with clocks, looking glasses and other luxuries. If these were 'industrial communities', what changed with the 'Industrial Revolution'?

It is unfortunate that inventories do not survive after the early 1760s to enable the changes in material culture of the late 18th century to be analysed. The economic changes can be measured through both documentary and archaeological sources. Leases and account books show that, after the opening of the first blast furnace at Horsehay in 1755, the economy of the area came to be focused on large companies, which leased extensive tracts of land for mining and used the iron ore and some of the coal they extracted in blast furnaces to produce iron, and also marketed coal, bricks, lime and sometimes other products. They operated railways and employed sub-contractors to direct their mines. The entrepreneurs who managed the companies were also involved in canals and turnpike roads, but significantly not in the operation of Severn barges. In archaeological terms the change is marked by the increase in the size of colliery spoil tips, and by the building of terraced housing designed for families destined to be permanent employees of the companies. Nevertheless, old cottages remained in use and, as in Holywell Lane in Dawley,[102] when unemployment threatened, families who occupied them were likely to adapt the ways in which they made their livings to the circumstances of the time rather than take their skills elsewhere.

Women came to be employed as wage-earners, picking nodules of iron ore on pit banks, where a sturdy sense of independence seems to have been maintained, and in the manufacture of porcelain, as factory methods of making pottery were applied at Caughley in 1772 and at Coalport in the 1790s. Probate inventories provide scarcely any evidence about the lives of children before 1764, but it is clear that by 1800 the employment of very young children to carry out tasks underground that were hazardous both to themselves and to their fellow miners had become commonplace, and remained so until employers were constrained by legislation in the 1840s.

The Severn Gorge is a UNESCO World Heritage Site because it was the scene of innovations in technology and management that were copied elsewhere and because it was the focus of much scientific interest in the late 18th century. It was also, like other industrialising regions, a place where class divisions became clear-cut, as is evident from the language used in the social crises of 1795, 1800, 1816 and 1821.[103] The probate records show that society in the area before the mid-18th century was rather different. It was also different from 'pre-industrial societies' in other parts of Britain, from the textile communities of the Pennines, the metal craftsmen of the Black Country and the smiths of Hallamshire, as well as from other ironworking settlements like those in South Wales, which grew suddenly rather than evolving from mining communities.[104]

INTRODUCTION

The historian of the early modern coal industry has remarked:

> Historians often display an unhealthy interest in the spectacular and the unique to the neglect of the Promethean forces which can be unleashed by successive generations of skilled practitioners responding on a daily basis to the demands of an eager market.[105]

The probate records of the Severn Gorge illustrate communities which operated in this way before they were transformed by the spectacular growth of capitalist ironmaking in the 1750s. This introduction has concentrated on the two largest occupational groups, the miners and the mariners, and on the changes in material culture for which the analysis of inventories provides evidence. We are conscious that this is only one step towards a deeper understanding of the communities in the Severn Gorge in the early modern period, but it is one that illustrates some features of the whole process of industrialisation. The publication of this volume will doubtless stimulate further investigation. More powerful information technology will make easier the integration of probate evidence with that from other sources, and may stimulate questions unimagined by present generations.

REFERENCES

1. C. Fiennes, *The Journeys of Celia Fiennes* ed. C.Morris (1947), p.228.
2. B. Trinder and J. Cox, *Yeomen and Colliers in Telford: the Probate Inventories of Dawley, Lilleshall, Wellington and Wrockwardine* (1980)—henceforth Trinder & Cox, *YACIT*.
3. B. Trinder, 'La vie d'une région en cours d'industrialisation: le Bassin houiller du Shropshire 1660-1760', in CILAC, *L'étude et la mise en valeur du Patrimoine Industrial* (1985); Trinder, B., *The Industrial Revolution in Shropshire*, 2nd edition (1981); M.D.G. Wanklyn, 'Industrial Development in the Ironbridge Gorge before Abraham Darby', *West Midland Studies*, vol. 15 (1982), pp.3-7; J. Alfrey and K. Clark, *The Landscape of Industry: patterns of change in the Ironbridge Gorge* (1993); *Victoria History of Shropshire, Vol. IV, Agriculture* (1989), pp.43, 84; P. Stamper, *Historic parks of Shropshire* (1995); N. Cox, 'The Distribution of Retailing Tradesmen in North Shropshire 160-1750', *Journal of Regional and Local Studies*, vol. 13 (1993).
4. D.P. Hussey, G.J. Milne, A.P. Wakelin and M.D.G. Wanklyn, *The Gloucester Coastal Port Books 1575-1765: A Summary* (1995); B. Trinder, 'The Archaeology of the British Food Industry 1660-1960: A Preliminary Survey', *Industrial Archaeology Review*, vol.15 (1993); B. Trinder, 'Revolutions in the Food Industry',

in Canadian Society for Industrial Heritage, *From Industry to Industrial Heritage: Proceedings of the Ninth International Conference on the Conservation of the Industrial Heritage, 1994* (1998); N. and J. Cox, 'Probate Inventories: the Legal Background, Part I', *The Local Historian,* vol. 16 (1984), pp.133-45; N. and J. Cox, 'Probate Inventories: the Legal Background, Part II', *The Local Historian,* vol. 16 (1984), pp.217-28; N. and J. Cox, 'Valuations in Probate Inventories: Part I', *The Local Historian,* vol. 16 (1985), pp.467-78; N. and J. Cox, 'Valuations in Probate Inventories: Part II', *The Local Historian,* vol. 17 (1986), pp.85-100; N. and J. Cox, 'Probate 1500-1800: a system in transition' in T. Arkell, N. Evans and N. Goose, *Till Death do us Part* (forthcoming—2000); B. Trinder, 'The Wooden Horse in the Cellar', in *ibid.*

5. M.D.G. Wanklyn, 'Industrial Development in the Ironbridge Gorge before Abraham Darby', *West Midland Studies,* vol. 15 (1982), pp.3-7.
6. *Victoria History of Shropshire, Vol.X, Wenlock, Upper Corvedale and the Stretton Hills* (1999), pp.266-71.(Henceforth *VCH X*).
7. Wanklyn, *op. cit.*, p.4; B. Trinder,, *The Industrial Revolution in Shropshire*, 2nd edition (1981), pp.6-7 (Henceforth: Trinder, *Industrial Revolution);* Alfrey and Clark, *op. cit.,* p.119; *VCH X,* pp.257-62.
8. *VCH X,* pp.247-57; National Trust, *Benthall Hall, Shropshire* (1965).
9. *VCH X,* pp.365-8; S. Bagshaw, *History, Gazetteer and Directory of Shropshire* (1851), p.55.
10. *Victoria History of Shropshire, Vol.XI: Telford,* pp.35-6 (Henceforth: *VCH XI).*
11. *VCH XI,* pp.28-9; Alfrey and Clark, *op. cit.,* p.151; G. Muter, *The Buildings of an Industrial Community: Ironbridge and Coalbrookdale* (1979), p.86.
12. S.B. Smith, *A View from the Iron Bridge* (1979), pp.14-16.
13. *VCH XI,* pp.79-85.
14. N. and J. Cox, 'Probate 1500-1800: a system in transition' in T. Arkell, N. Evans and N. Goose, *Till Death do us Part* (forthcoming—2000).
15. Trinder and Cox, *YACIT* .
16. Trinder, *Industrial Revolution,* pp.30-3.
17. G.F. Matthews, *Shropshire probates in the Prerogative Court of Canterbury 1700-49* (1928).
18. N. and J. Cox, 'Valuations in Probate Inventories: Part I', *The Local Historian,* vol. 16 (1985), pp.467-78; N. and J. Cox, 'Valuations in Probate Inventories: Part II', *The Local Historian,* vol. 17 (1986), pp.85-100.
19. Trinder and Cox, *YACIT,* pp.6-10.
20. *Ibid.,* p.10.
21. P. Hudson and S. King, 'Rural Industrialising Township and Urban Links in Eighteenth Century Yorkshire', in P. Clark and P. Corfield, *Industry and Urbanisation in Eighteenth Century England* (1994), pp.41-79.
22. Trinder and Cox, *YACIT,* pp.20-2.
23. B. Trinder, 'The Wooden Horse in the Cellar', in T. Arkell, N. Evans and N. Goose, *Till Death do us Part* (forthcoming—2000).

INTRODUCTION (REFERENCES)

24. Lichfield Record Office, probate, Bridgnorth peculiar, Hannah and Catherine Poyner, 17 August 1765.
25. R. Hayman, ' Lloyds Engine House, Ironbridge', *Transactions of the Shropshire Archaeological Society,* 4th series, vol. 72 (1997), pp.38-51.
26. B. Trinder, 'Coalport Bridge: a Study in Historical Interpretation', *Industrial Archaeology Review*, vol. 3 (1979), pp.153-7.
27. N. Cox, 'Imagination and innovation of an Industrial Pioneer: the First Abraham Darby', *Industrial Archaeology Review*, vol. 12 (1990), pp.127-44.
28. Trinder, *Industrial Revolution,* pp.70-1.
29. B. Trinder, ed., *A Description of Coalbrookdale in 1801 AD*' (1970), p.8.
30. Hereford Record Office, probate, John Thomas, Madeley, 8 June 1760.
31. Hereford Record Office, diocesan records, probates, Walter Parker, 10 June 1770; Thomas Rose, 22 October 1770; Michael Parker, 1 June 1801; Robert Horton, 17 June 1761.
32. N. Cox, 'Imagination and innovation of an Industrial Pioneer: the First Abraham Darby', *Industrial Archaeology Review*, vol. 12 (1990), pp.134-5.
33. S. Simpson, *The Agreeable Historian or the Compleat English Traveller* (1746), quoted in B. Trinder, *The Most Extraordinary District in the World*, 2nd edition (1988), pp.15-17; Trinder, *Industrial Revolution,* pp.8-10.
34. Trinder, *Industrial Revolution*, p.8.
35. B. Trinder, *The Industrial Archaeology of Shropshire* (1996), pp.113-14 (Henceforth: Trinder, *Industrial Archaeology*).
36. *VCH X,* p.87.
37. D.R. Atkinson, *The Tobacco Pipes of Broseley, Shropshire*; D. Higgins, R. Morriss and M. Trueman, *The Broseley Pipeworks: an archaeological and historical evaluation* (1988). We are grateful to Dr. Peter Wakelin and Dr. David Higgins for their advice on tobacco pipe makers.
38. Trinder, *Industrial Archaeology*, pp.174-5.
39. Lichfield Record Office, Bridgnorth peculiar, probate Edward Jefferies, 8 April 1673.
40. E. Le Roy Ladurie, *Montaillou: Cathars and Catholics in a French village 1294-1324* (1980), pp.270-301.
41. University of Wolverhampton, Gloucester Portbooks Database.
42. The most recent account of the history of commercial navigation on the Upper Severn is in Trinder, *Industrial Archaeology*, pp.168-75. Material relating to barge-owning families is drawn from the account books of the Coalbrookdale Company (fully listed in Trinder, *Industrial Revolution*, pp.276-8; a list of bargemen owing money to George Weld in 1748 in Shropshire Records & Research 1224/71; accounts of coal taken by bargemen from the wharf of the Madeley Wood Company in the 1790s in Shropshire Records and Research 271/1; the Commonplace Books of Thomas Beard in Alderman Jones's Collection, Shropshire Records & Research 1649; census enumerator's returns.

43. Hereford Record Office, Diocesan Records, probate, Ann Onions, 21 July 1757; *Shrewsbury Chronicle*, 23 January 1796.
44. H.E. Forest, *The Old Houses of Wenlock* (1914), p.89.
45. *Shrewsbury Chronicle*, 23 December 1786.
46. N. Cox, 'Imagination and innovation of an Industrial Pioneer: the First Abraham Darby', *Industrial Archaeology Review*, vol. 12 (1990), pp.137-8; University of Wolverhampton, Gloucester Portbooks Database.
47. Trinder, *Industrial Revolution*, p.64.
48. Trinder, *Industrial Archaeology*, pp.168-9.
49. N. Cox, 'Imagination and innovation of an Industrial Pioneer: the First Abraham Darby', *Industrial Archaeology Review*, vol. 12 (1990), pp. 137-9.
50. Hereford Record Office, Diocesan Records, probate, John Oswell, 5 July 1786.
51. *Shrewsbury Chronicle*, 5 November 1802.
52. *Ironbridge and Wenlock Journal*, 30 October 1869.
53. M. Prior, *Fisher Row: Fishermen, Bargemen and Canal Boatmen in Oxford 1500-1900* (1982), pp.64-7, 70, 87.
54. N. Hemming, 'A Provincial Carpenter and Joiner in the eighteenth century: a case study of John Clifton of Oundle 1717-84', MA dissertation, University College Northampton, 1997.
55. Hereford Record Office, Diocesan Records, probate, Charles Gwyn, 28 January 1799.
56. National Trust, *Benthall Hall, Shropshire* (1965).
57. *VCH XI*, p.60.
58. R.R. James, 'Two Celebrated Salopian Surgeons', *Transactions of the Shropshire Archaeological Society*, 4th series, vol. 6 (1916-17), pp.205-20. We are grateful to David Lloyd of Ludlow for further information on the Hawkins family.
59. Hereford Record Office, Diocesan Records, probates, Isaac Wyke, 1 July 1755; Jacob Wyke, 10 November 1780.
60. N. Cossons and B. Trinder, *The Iron Bridge: Symbol of the Industrial Revolution* (1979), p.20; Hereford Record Office, Diocesan Records, probate, Jacob Kitchen, 30 June 1780.
61. Trinder and Cox, *YACIT*, pp.10-41.
62. Trinder, *Industrial Archaeology*, pp.240-2.
63. *Ibid.*, pp.134-6.
64. Trinder and Cox, *YACIT*, pp.47-61; Trinder, *Industrial Archaeology*, p.137.
65. Lichfield Record Office, Diocesan Records, probates, Caleb Higgins I, 19 April 1710; Caleb Higgins II, 13 June 1727, both of Shifnal.
66. Smith, *op. cit.*, p.15; J. Randall, *A History of Madeley* (1880), p.290.
67. Trinder and Cox, *YACIT*, pp.72-5.
68. Shropshire Records and Research 2280/2/1-9.
69. *Ibid.*

INTRODUCTION (REFERENCES)

70. Trinder and Cox, *YACIT*, pp.83-4.
71. *Victoria History of Shropshire, Vol. IV, Agriculture* (1989), pp.141-9; P. Stamper, *The Farmer feeds us all* (1989), pp.25-39.
72. P. Stamper, *The Farmer feeds us all* (1989), p.37; Trinder & Cox, *YACIT*, pp.1-62, 452-5.
73. P. Stamper, *The Farmer feeds us all* (1989), pp.37-8.
74. *VCH XI*, p.80.
75. Hereford Record Office, Diocesan Records, probate, John Dyer, 6 May 1806.
76. Alfrey and Clark, *op. cit.,* pp.115-19; G. Muter, *op. cit.,* p.26, plates 46, 55; Trinder, *Industrial Revolution*, pp.187-8; J. Powell and M. Vanns, *Archive Photograph Series: South Telford* (1995), p.15.
77. H.D. Roberts, *Downhearth to Bar Grate; an illustrated account of the evolution in cooking due to the use of coal instead of wood* (1987), in which sets of skewers are illustrated on p.77, basting spoons on p.28, and brandreths on p.29.
78. Lichfield Record Office, Diocesan Records, probate, Priscilla Pugh, Shrewsbury, 1724.
79. Roberts, *op. cit.,* p.55.
80. Trinder and Cox, *YACIT*, p.103.
81. Roberts, *op. cit.,* pp.36-7.
82. Trinder and Cox, *YACIT*, p.91.
83. *Ibid.*, pp.93-5.
84. *Ibid.*, pp.98-9.
85. *Ibid.*, pp.36-8.
86. R. Holme, *The Academy of Armoury* (1688), book 14, p.11.
87. J. Hatcher and T.C. Barker, *A History of British Pewter* (1974), pp.91, 121-3, 127-8; R.F. Homer and D.W. Hall, *Provincial Pewterers: a study of the craft in the West Midlands and Wales* (1985); Trinder and Cox, *YACIT*, p.106; Lichfield Record Office, Diocesan Records, probates, John Pool, 28 February 1667/8, William Dickinson, 26 January 1691/2, John Poyner, 19 October 1705, all of Newport.
88. A. Jones, *Finds Typologies; Pottery I: The Coarse Earthenwares* (1988); A. Jones, D. Higgins and M. Truman, *11 Benthall Lane* (1987); Hatcher and Barker, *op. cit.,* p.132.
89. F.H. Garner and M. Archer, *English Delftware*, 2nd edition (1972), pp.1, 52; W.J. Pountney, *The Old Bristol Potters* (1920); H. Owen, *Two Centuries of Ceramic Art in Bristol* (1873).
90. B. Trinder, 'The Wooden Horse in the Cellar', in T. Arkell, N. Evans and N. Goose, *Till Death do us Part* (forthcoming—2000).
91. Trinder and Cox, *YACIT*, p.100.
92. E.P. Thompson, 'Time Work-Discipline and Industrial Capitalism', *Past and Present*, vol. 38 (1968), reprinted in E.P. Thompson, *Customs in Common* (1993), pp.352-403.
93. D.J. Elliott, *Shropshire Clock and Watchmakers* (1979), pp.9-23, 82.

94. Hereford Record Office, Diocesan Records, probate, Ralph Seward, Stottesdon, 20 March 1667/8.
95. *VCH XI*, p.83.
96. George Eliot, *The Mill on the Floss,* Nelson edition (n.d.), London: Nelson, p.225.
97. Hereford Record Office, Diocesan Records, probates, Richard Smith I, 10 July 1771, Richard Smith II, 9 April 1810, both of Broseley; Richard Rhodes, 20 July 1715, of Willey.
98. M.R. McDonald, 'The wash-house: an archaeological and functional evaluation, with special references to the "brew-us" of the Ironbridge/Coalbrookdale area', Ironbridge Institute, Master's dissertation, 1987-88.
99. Hereford Record Office, Diocesan Records, probates, John Bailey, 24 June 1774, John Brook, 5 June 1799, Michael Parker, 1 June 1801.
100. Trinder and Cox, *YACIT*, p.111; P. Sambrook, *Country House Brewing in England 1500-1900* (1996).
101. Smith, *op. cit.,* pp.18-24.
102. K. Jones, M.W. Hunt, J. Malam and B. Trinder, 'Holywell Lane; A Squatter Community in the Shropshire Coalfield', *Industrial Archaeology Review*, vol. 6 1982), pp.163-85.
103. Trinder, *Industrial Revolution*, pp.227-34.
104. P. Hudson and S. King, 'Rural Industrialising Township and Urban Links in Eighteenth Century Yorkshire', in P. Clark and P. Corfield, *Industry and Urbanisation in Eighteenth Century England* (1994), Leicester: Centre for Urban History, University of Leicester, pp.41-79; M. Rowlands, *Masters and Men in the Small Metalware Trades of the West Midlands* (1975); D. Hey, *The Fiery Blades of Hallamshire: Sheffield and its Neighbours 1660-1740* (1991), Leicester: Leicester University Press; C. Evans, *Labyrinth of Flames: Work and Social Conflict in early industrial Merthyr Tydfil* (1993), Cardiff: University of Wales Press.
105. J. Hatcher, *The History of the British Coal Industry I, Before 1700* (1993), p.552.

A LIST OF PEOPLE

A list of people from the parishes of Benthall, Broseley, Little Wenlock and Madeley, whose wills or administration bonds are recorded in the Calendar of Wills provied in the Bishop's Constitory Courts of the Diocese of Hereford between 1662 and 1764.

NOTES

The date in volumn five in that which appears on the invent9ory. That in column six is the date of exhibition or probate. It is by this date that the document is located. In a very few cases the date of exhibition may be earlier than the date of the inventory. All such examples have been found to be correctly transcribed.

An asterisk (*) in column four indicates that the occupation of the persons concerned has been deduced from the contents of the inventory, or that it is known from the will or other sources.

ABBREVIATIONS

nd = no date   no inv. = no inventory

Name	Parish	Township etc.	Occupation	Inventory Date	Date of Exhibition or Probate	Value	Number (if published)
Acton, Eliza	Bro	—	Widow	—	30 July 1745	no inv.	
Acton, Thomas	Bro	—	—	15 Jan. 1728-9	22 April 1729	18 16 00	
Adams, Francis	Bro	—	Gent	27 Mar. 1668	22 April 1668	488 06 04	22
Adams, Francis	Bro	—	Collier	10 May 1728	4 Mar. 1728-9	04 05 06	
Adams, Francis	Bro	—	Victualler	—	13 April 1763	no inv.	
Adams, John	Bro	—	—	3 Aug. 1671	3 Aug. 1671	04 00 00	27
Adams, John	Bro	—	Ground Collier	n.d.	22 Sept.1756	02 07 03	
Adams, Maurice	Bro	—	Coal miner	24 July 1754	30 July 1754	13 08 06	
Adams, William	Bro	—	—	—	3 June 1729	no inv.	
Aierley, Sarah	Bro	—	—	—	28 Oct. 1745	no inv.	
Amis, Edward	Bro	—	Blacksmith*	28 Feb. 1692-3	18 May 1693	74 03 00	52
Amphlett, William	Bro	—	—	18 Dec. 1717	4 Mar. 1717-8	60 02 11	
Andrews, John	Ben	—	Carpenter*	30 Jan. 1691-2	4 July 1692	07 00 00	
Andrews, Laurence	Ben	—	Carpenter*	17 April 1667	6 May 1667	42 08 06	1
Armstrong, George	Bro	—	Trowman*	30 May 1740	3 June 1740	18 14 06	
Ashwood, John	Mad	—	Yeoman	9 Oct. 1674	19 Nov. 1674	165 10 00	
Ashwood, William	Mad	Madeley Wood	Nailer	7 Sept. 1667	10 Sept. 1667	08 16 03	141
Ashwood, William	Mad	Madeley Wood	Blacksmith*/ Trowman*	30 Nov. 1681	17 May 1682	38 10 00	152
Ashwood, William	Mad	Madeley Wood	Blacksmith*/ Trowman*	4 May 1696	4 May 1696	35 01 06	160
Aston, Armilla	Mad	Madeley Wood	Widow	17 Oct. 1662	—	16 03 04	
Aston, John	Ben	—	Collier*	15 Oct. 1690	21 Oct. 1690	17 18 00	5
Aston, Richard	Ben	—	—	n.d.	21 Sept. 1756	09 02 06	21
Aston, Thomas	Bro	—	—	6 April 1754	6 May 1754	04 15 02	
Aston, William	Bro	Linley	—	—	5 May 1675	no inv.	

… A LIST OF PEOPLE

Name	Parish	Township etc.	Occupation	Inventory Date	Date of Exhibition or Probate	Value	Number (if published)
Atherton, James	Ben	—	—	31 Jan. 1689-90	18 Feb. 1689-90	13 08 04	
Ball, John	Bro	—	Collier	15 Aug. 1699	22 Aug. 1699	18 00 02	56
Ball, Samuel	Bro	—	Collier	22 Aug. 1728	16 Sept. 1728	17 10 00	
Ball, Silvanus	Bro	—	Trowman*	31 May 1743	12 July 1743	84 11 06	95
Ball, William	Bro	—	Trowman	—	1 Aug. 1758	no inv.	
Banks, Bridget	LW	—	Widow	13 June 1724	21 July 1724	04 13 00	
Banks, Richard	LW	—		2 Sept. 1718	9 Sept. 1718	04 08 06	
Barker, John	Bro	—	Yeoman	—	8 July 1760	no inv.	
Barker, Richard	Mad	—	Collier	18 Nov. 1729	3 May 1731	14 14 02	
Barnett, Samuel	Bro	—		16 Nov. 1752	24 Sept. 1753	12 02 06	
Barrett, Henry	Bro	—	Carpenter*	20 Oct. 1676	12 Jan. 1676-7	17 11 04	35
Baugh, William	LW	—		21 May 1755	22 May 1755	03 10 00	134
Baugh, William	Mad	—		19 Oct. 1759	3 Dec. 1759	19 09 01	
Baxter, Frances	LW	—	Widow of clergyman	23 Mar. 1663	26 April 1664	19 19 02	115
Bayley, George	Bro	—	Shopkeeper*	28 Feb. 1717-8	9 Feb. 1718-9	09 15 05	64
Bayley, John	Mad	Madeley Wood	Ground Collier	8 Feb. 1711-2	8 April 1712	02 05 00	167
Bayley, Thomas	Bro	—		20 April 1724	21 April 1724	10 10 02	
Bayliss, John	Mad	—	Ground Collier	27 Jan. 1710-1	25 Feb. 1710-1	01 15 06	
Beard, Eustace	Ben	—	Waterman	30 May 1726	14 June 1726	19 13 10	14
Beard, Eustace	Ben	—	Trowman	—	11 Oct. 1762	no inv.	
Beard, Jane	Bro	—		—	28 May 1745	no inv.	
Beard, Richard	Mad	—	Mariner	—	21 April 1764	no inv.	
Beard, Thomas	Bro	—		16 Aug. 1681	27 Sept. 1681	18 00 00	
Beard, Thomas	Ben	—	Trowman	9 Sept. 1706	11 June 1707	115 06 08	7

Name	Parish	Township etc.	Occupation	Inventory Date	Date of Exhibition or Probate	Value	Number (if published)
Beddoe, *see* Beddow							
Beddow, Henry	Bro	—	—	1 Nov. 1754	30 June 1755	02 15 00	
Beddow, John	Bro	—	—	—	9 Oct. 1694	no inv.	
Beddow, John	Bro	—	Collier	15 Jan. 1736-7	18 Jan. 1736-7	09 04 06	
Beddow, John	Bro	—	Butcher	n.d.	25 Sept. 1739	16 16 06	
Beddow, Mary	Bro	—	Single woman	15 Aug. 1733	15 Aug. 1733	07 07 00	
Beddow, Mary	Bro	—	Widow	n.d.	22 June 1762	05 07 00	112
Beddow, Thomas	Bro	Swinbatch	Yeoman	26 Mar. 1733	10 April 1733	130 03 10	80
Beddow, William	Bro	—	—	n.d.	17 July 1761	10 03 00	
Bedward, John	Mad	Madeley Wood	Carpenter	—	14 Sept. 1761	no inv.	
Bedware, *see* Bedward							
Beech, Richard	Mad	—	Labourer/Collier	20 Dec. 1686	21 April 1687	12 07 05	155
Bell, John	Bro	—	—	12 June 1755	3 July 1755	08 05 06	
Benbow, Francis	Bro	—	Trowman	n.d.	7 Aug. 1710	17 17 04	
Benbow, Francis	Bro	—	—	18 April 1752	27 April 1752	09 09 00	
Benbow, Margery	Bro	—	Widow	13 Dec. 1684	20 Jan. 1684-5	04 13 11	
Benbow, Robert	Bro	—	Yeoman*	9 July 1672	3 Sept. 1672	23 16 02	28
Benbow, William	Bro	—	Trowman	4 April 1673	8 April 1673	67 15 04	30
Benthall, Richard	Ben	Benthall Hall	Esquire	26 May 1720	26 Sept. 1720	502 05 03	13
Biddle, William	Bro	—	Collier*	7 April 1671	7 May 1672	35 15 00	
Biddle, William	Bro	—	—	—	14 April 1674	no inv.	
Birch, Thomas	Mad	—	Husbandman	6 June 1699	25 May 1699	50 18 02	
Bird, William	Bro	—	—	19 May 1740	21 May 1740	16 10 04	
Blest, John	Mad	—	—	25 April 1694	27 April 1694	16 04 06	
Blocksidge, Thomas	Mad	—	Butcher	—	26 Aug. 1761	no inv.	
Boarder, James	LW	—	Blacksmith	27 July 1665	25 April 1666	50 50 03	

A LIST OF PEOPLE

Name	Parish	Township etc.	Occupation	Inventory Date	Date of Exhibition or Probate	Value	Number (if published)
Boden, Edward	Mad	Lloyds	Collier	25 July 1691	15 Sept. 1691	44 02 02	159
Boden, Edward	Mad	—	Coal Miner	—	17 July 1761	no inv.	
Boden, Elizabeth	Mad	—	Widow	n.d.	2 Oct. 1716	18 15 00	
Boden, John	Mad	—	—	24 Aug. 1706	27 Aug. 1706	02 14 10	
Boden, John	Mad	—	Collier	11 May 1713	19 May 1713	04 09 08	
Boden, John	Mad	Madeley Wood	Coal Miner	15 Nov. 1746	9 Sept. 1747	04 07 04	185
Boden, Richard	Mad	Madeley Wood	Yeoman	20 July 1724	21 July 1724	04 19 00	
Boden, Thomas	Mad	—	Collier	20 Nov. 1750	30 July 1751	13 10 02	188
Botteley, William	Mad	—	—	12 Oct. 1725	3 May 1726	01 18 00	
Botteley, William	Mad	Madeley Wood	Collier/Publican	n.d.	23 June 1762	18 05 00	196
Bowdler, Audley	Mad	—	Yeoman	1 June 1715	12 July 1715	306 04 02	169
Bowdler, Henry	Mad	Madeley Wood	Chandler	24 Aug. 1719	1 Oct. 1719	48 09 06	
Bowdler, Humphrey	Mad	—	Gent	18 Sept. 1666	8 Oct. 1666	582 11 00	140
Bowdler, Samuel	Mad	—	—	—	18 May 1742	no inv.	
Bowdler, Samuel	Mad	—	—	—	3 Jan. 1744-5	no inv.	
Bowen, Thomas	Mad	—	—	8 Mar. 1665-6	10 April 1666	179 11 08	
Bowen, William	Bro	—	Collier*/Yeoman	27 July 1676	18 Jan. 1676-7	08 03 11	
Boycott, Thomas	LW	—	Butcher*	n.d.	15 April 1755	16 01 09	
Boycott, William	LW	—	Butcher	13 June 1709	21 June 1709	57 05 00	
Bradley, Andrew	Ben	—	Labourer	4 July 1689	18 July 1689	09 02 08	135
Bradley, George	Ben	—	Trowman	7 Jan. 1719-20	9 Feb. 1719-20	123 03 00	12
Bradley, Ralph	Ben	—	—	9 Mar. 1671-2	18 Mar. 1672-3	03 12 02	2
Bradley, William	Ben	—	Trowman	—	3 Nov. 1702	no inv.	
Briscoe, George	Mad	Coalbrookdale	—	—	6 July 1758	no inv.	
Briscoe, Thomas	LW	—	—	1 Oct. 1684	23 Sept. 1684	63 05 00	
Briscoe, Thomas	LW	—	Yeoman	—	12 May 1730	no inv.	

Name	Parish	Township etc.	Occupation	Inventory Date	Date of Exhibition or Probate	Value	Number (if published)
Brook, Adam	Mad	—	—	1 July 1758	4 July 1758	16 11 06	
Brook, John	Mad	Madeley Wood	Yeoman	27 Feb. 1720-1	27 Mar. 1721	07 11 09	
Brook, John	Mad	Madeley Wood	Ground Collier	—	3 July 1744	no inv.	
Brook, Richard	Mad	—	Trowman*	13 April 1669	25 April 1670	99 10 00	142
Brook, Thomas	Ben	—	Trowman*	6 Oct. 1683	4 Mar. 1683-4	18 10 00	
Brown, Elizabeth	Ben	—	Spinster	—	15 Nov. 1738	no inv.	
Brown, John	Bro	—	—	—	6 June 1732	no inv.	
Brown, Richard	Bro	—	—	19 Feb. 1721-2	8 May 1722	15 10 00	
Buckley, Ambrose	Bro	—	Trowman*	n.d.	6 July 1758	50 00 07	109
Buckley, Andrew	Bro	Holly	Trowman	—	3 June 1740	no inv.	
Buckley, Benjamin	Bro	—	Trowman*	28 May 1740	3 June 1740	127 06 00	85
Buckley, George	Bro	—	Trowman	—	18 May 1742	no inv.	
Buckley, John	Bro	—	Trowman*	10 Mar. 1681-2	14 Feb. 1681-2	50 03 00	
Buckley, John	Bro	—	—	—	23 Aug. 1683	no inv.	
Buckley, Maria	Bro	—	—	—	7 May 1750	no inv.	
Buckley, Sampson	Bro	—	Dyer	23 June 1711	30 Oct. 1711	84 17 04	59
Bulkley, see Buckley							
Burgwyn, Edward	LW	—	Yeoman	7 May 1691	8 May 1691	11 06 04	121
Burgwyn, John	LW	—	—	13 Feb. 1682-3	14 Oct. 1684	10 03 06	
Burrows, Samuel	Bro	—	Carpenter & Joiner	22 Feb. 1744-5	1 July 1745	38 06 02	98
Buttery, George	LW	Huntington	—	19 Oct. 1691	22 Oct. 1691	18 09 08	120
Carrington, Henry	Bro	—	Glover	29 July 1740	5 Aug. 1740	37 09 00	86
Carrington, Joseph	Bro	—	Glover	n.d.	27 May 1746	15 00 00	
Cartledge, Thomas	LW	—	Potter	n.d.	8 July 1760	18 17 06	136

A LIST OF PEOPLE

Name	Parish	Township etc.	Occupation	Inventory Date	Date of Exhibition or Probate	Value	Number (if published)
Cartwright, Henry	LW	—	Yeoman	—	5 Aug. 1746	no inv.	
Clemson, Mary	Mad	—	Widow/Ropier	30 April 1753	7 May 1753	55 11 10	*189*
Clibbury, John	Bro	—	Corvisor	17 July 1688	21 Nov. 1688	07 09 04	
Clibbury, John	Bro	—	Corvisor	27 May 1740	18 July 1740	107 06 00	
Clibbury, Joshua	Bro	—	Collier	5 Sept. 1732	12 Sept. 1732	08 17 06	
Cludd, Edward	Mad	—	Collier	10 April 1732	11 July 1732	04 09 02	*180*
Cludd, William	Mad	—	Weaver	16 June 1726	4 July 1727	14 12 07	*174*
Colley, James	Mad	Coalbrookdale	Yeoman	29 June 1709	2 June 1710	160 01 00	
Colley, Joyce	Bro	—	Widow	n.d.	24 Oct. 1698	no inv.	
Cookson, Thomas	Mad	—	Weaver*	n.d.	14 Dec. 1725	07 10 00	
Cope, Henry	Bro	—	—	1 June 1682	10 Mar. 1684-5	13 19 05	
Cope, John	Mad	—	Tailor	26 July 1734	27 Feb. 1682-3	98 14 06	
Cope, John	Bro	—	Spinster	17 Sept. 1759	24 Sept. 1734	17 05 00	
Corbett, Elizabeth	Bro	—	Labourer	7 Feb. 1718-9	18 Sept. 1759	323 16 02½	
Corbett, Thomas	Bro	—	Weaver	29 June 1680	14 April 1719	18 18 06	
Cowper, John	Mad	Madeley Wood	Carrier	n.d.	19 May 1681	23 10 00	*150*
Cox, Benjamin	Mad	—	Widow of Collier	8 Mar. 1714-5	9 Feb. 1719-20	04 00 00	
Cox, Edward	Bro	—		2 Mar. 1684-5	8 Mar. 1714-5	25 11 00	*61*
Cox, Elizabeth	Mad	Madeley Wood			10 Mar. 1684-5	07 07 08	
Cox, John	Mad	Madeley Wood	Collier	29 Sept. 1682	13 Jan. 1682-3	11 09 04	
Cox, John	Bro	—	—	16 May 1683	4 Mar. 1683-4	10 16 06	
Cox, Richard	Mad	Madeley Wood	Collier	24 Nov. 1731	12 Sept. 1732	06 16 10	*179*
Cox, Robert	Mad	Stone Head	Collier	20 June 1737	18 July 1738	03 13 00	
Cranage, John	Ben	—	Collier	29 June 1753	9 July 1753	31 16 00	
Crew, Thomas	Bro	—	Pedlar	29 April 1668	19 May 1668	34 09 02	*23*

Name	Parish	Township etc.	Occupation	Inventory Date	Date of Exhibition or Probate	Value	Number (if published)
Crompton, Adam	Mad	—	Coal Miner	5 April 1723	18 June 1723	07 12 06	173
Crompton, John	Bro	—	Trowman	9 June 1735	21 June 1736	10 12 06	
Crompton, Oliver	Mad	Madeley Wood	—	18 July 1667	10 Sept. 1667	17 16 08	
Crompton, Richard	Bro	—	—	28 Sept. 1719	1 Oct. 1719	18 08 00	
Crompton, Timothy	Bro	—	Collier	5 Nov. 1672	11 Mar. 1672-3	100 12 04	29
Crow, John	Bro	—	Clerk	—	2 July 1689	no inv.	
Crowther, Thomas	Bro	—	Glazier	29 May 1741	2 June 1741	09 03 08	89
Crumpton, *see* Crompton							
Cullis, Hugh	Ben	—	Trowman	9 Feb. 1729-30	3 Mar. 1729-30	12 05 00	16
Cullis, Richard	Ben	—	—	6 Oct. 1762	11 Oct. 1762	09 08 06	
Cumbersom, Samuel	Bro	—	Mariner	—	10 Oct. 1749	no inv.	
Danks, John	Bro	—	—	n.d.	9 July 1760	17 05 06	
Danks, Thomas	Mad	Madeley Wood	Collier	—	10 Dec. 1745	no inv.	
Darby, William	Bro	—	—	n.d.	2 April 1723	14 05 00	
Darby, Mary	Mad	—	—	—	8 July 1718	no inv.	
Davies, Anne	Bro	—	Widow	19 May 1742	7 June 1742	10 01 10	
Davies, Ann	Bro	—	—	12 April 1745	12 April 1745	12 10 00	
Davies, Charles	Bro	—	Blacksmith	22 Jan. 1671-2	27 Feb. 1671-2	09 12 08	
Davies, John	Bro	—	Blacksmith	—	1 July 1729	no inv.	
Davies, Margaret	Bro	—	—	n.d.	23 Mar. 1730-1	15 03 00	
Davies, Mary	Bro	—	Widow	12 May 1742	12 May 1742	01 03 06	
Davies, Owen	Bro	—	Tailor	23 Feb. 1729-30	3 Mar. 1729-30	12 15 10	
Davies, Richard	Mad	—	Ground Collier	n.d.	19 Oct. 1757	02 01 00	
Davies, Roger	Bro	—	—	29 May 1672	4 June 1672	12 14 10	
Davies, Thomas	Bro	—	Collier	25 Oct. 1716	2 April 1717	13 12 02	

A LIST OF PEOPLE

Name	Parish	Township etc.	Occupation	Inventory Date	Date of Exhibition or Probate	Value	Number (if published)
Davies, William	Mad	Madeley Wood	Waterman	11 April 1695	16 April 1695	17 11 06	
Dawley, Ann	Bro	—	Widow/Barge Owner*	16 Aug. 1684	2 Sept. 1684	28 02 04	45
Dawley, Edward	Bro	Broseley Wood	Barge Owner*	22 April 1679	1 July 1680	12 09 00	37
Dawley, Edward	Ben	—	Barge Owner*	20 Aug. 1689	1 Oct. 1689	51 04 00	
Dawley, John	Bro	—	—	4 Aug. 1689	3 Sept. 1689	06 10 10	49
Dawley, Naboth	Ben	—	—	4 June 1677	30 May 1678	29 08 04	
Day, Daniel	Ben	—	Yeoman/Barge Owner*	29 June 1743	12 July 1743	08 05 00	18
Day, William	Ben	—	Trowman	4 Aug. 1742	7 Sept. 1742	17 15 00	17
Dea, see Day							
Deuksell, George	Mad	Furnace Bank	Yeoman	28 May 1717	30 July 1717	122 08 04	170
Deuksell, George	Mad	—	Yeoman	—	22 April 1760	no inv.	
Dodson, Andrew	Ben	—	Trowman	25 Nov. 1708	8 Nov. 1709	169 12 06	8
Dorral, Robert	LW	Huntington	Yeoman	3 Mar. 1729-30	16 June 1730	15 09 00	
Doughty, John	Mad	Madeley Wood	Carpenter	24 April 1728	14 May 1728	36 10 11	178
Downes, Roger	Mad	Madeley Wood	Brass Founder	28 Oct. 1719	1 May 1720	18 04 00	172
Duppa, Mary	Mad	—	—	—	28 May 1740	no inv.	
Eardley, William	Mad	Madeley Wood	Engineer	27 Mar. 1729	2 June 1729	11 12 00	177
Easthope, Francis	Ben	—	Trowman	n.d.	4 May 1697	19 02 06	
Easthope, Francis	Mad	Madeley Wood	—	4 Nov. 1741	6 April 1742	12 07 00	
Easthope, Francis	Mad	—	—	n.d.	9 Sept. 1747	11 16 00	
Easthope, George	Mad	Madeley Wood	Shipwright	2 Mar. 1681-2	8 Aug. 1682	04 09 08	153
Easthope, John	Bro	—	Yeoman	n.d.	22 Sept. 1741	11 05 06	
Easthope, John	Mad	Madeley Wood	Yeoman	30 July 1746	5 Aug. 1746	07 12 06	186

Name	Parish	Township etc.	Occupation	Inventory Date	Date of Exhibition or Probate	Value	Number (if published)
Easthope, Oliver	Ben	—	Trowman	13 April 1680	1 July 1680	29 10 08	
Easthope, Thomas	Ben	—	Trowman	2 Nov. 1673	23 Mar. 1673-4	03 16 00	
Easthope, Thomas	Ben	—	—	4 Dec. 1675	2 Mar. 1675-6	07 05 00	
Easthope, Thomas	Ben	—	—	—	10 April 1677	no inv.	
Easthope, Thomas	Mad	—	—	n.d.	22 June 1762	05 09 00	
Easthope, William	Mad	Madeley Wood	Labourer/Ground Collier	28 Dec. 1743	3 July 1744	19 06 06	184
Eaves, Edward	Bro	—	Yeoman	7 Sept. 1664	20 Sept. 1664	136 04 03	
Eaves, Edward	Bro	—	—	1 July 1710	7 Aug. 1710	04 17 07	
Eaves, Francis	Bro	—	—	1 April 1673	30 April 1673	04 09 04	
Eaves, Francis	Bro	—	—	16 Mar. 1752	27 April 1752	09 08 00	
Eaves, John	Bro	—	Trowman	4 Nov. 1691	17 Nov. 1691	19 05 00	
Eaves, John	Bro	—	Collier	17 May 1740	21 May 1740	03 08 00	
Eaves, Richard	Bro	—	Trowman	28 Dec. 1692	18 May 1693	36 16 08	
Edmunds, John	Mad	—	Weaver*	15 June 1743	13 Sept. 1743	14 12 01	
Edwards, Christopher	Ben	—	—	20 Sept. 1689	29 Oct. 1689	14 13 04	
Edwards, Edward	Bro	—	—	15 May 1723	18 June 1723	233 10 00	68
Edwards, Francis	Bro	—	—	—	5 Aug. 1746	no inv.	
Edwards, Joyce	Bro	—	Widow	n.d.	1 April 1765	34 10 00	
Edwards, Noel	Bro	—	Yeoman	17 April 1730	14 April 1730	153 04 00	77
Edwards, Noel/Nevill	Bro	—	—	n.d.	4 May 1756	19 05 00	
Edwards, Richard	Bro	—	Shoemaker	3 Feb. 1752	11 Feb. 1752	25 09 00	105
Edwards, Thomas	Bro	Rowton	—	—	19 July 1737	no inv.	
Eele, Eleanor	Bro	—	Wife	4 June 1701	4 June 1701	18 00 00	
Evans, Francis	Bro	—	—	29 April 1732	2 May 1732	02 05 03	78
Evans, Francis	LW	Huntington Heath	Collier	15 July 1736	27 July 1736	03 19 11	132

A LIST OF PEOPLE

Name	Parish	Township etc.	Occupation	Inventory Date	Date of Exhibition or Probate	Value	Number (if published)
Evans, George	Bro	—	Clerk*	—	5 Aug. 1710	no inv.	
Evans, John	Bro	—	Tailor	n.d.	20 May 1684	12 12 06	*44*
Evans, John	Bro	—	Trowman	19 May 1736	25 May 1736	18 03 06	
Evans, Margaret	Mad	—	Widow	27 Jan. 1676-7	27 Mar. 1677	27 09 10	*149*
Evans, Richard	Bro	—	—	n.d.	2 July 1700	09 05 02	
Evans, Roger	Mad	—	—	9 Sept. 1665	2 Nov. 1665	96 18 06	*139*
Evans, Roger	Mad	—	—	—	10 Sept. 1667	no inv.	
Evans, Samuel	Bro	—	Collier	30 May 1687	21 June 1687	36 17 08	*46*
Evans, Samuel	Bro	—	Master Collier	18 Sept. 1733	3 Oct. 1733	172 16 06	*81*
Evans, Sarah	Bro	—	Spinster	n.d.	25 Feb. 1723-4	03 10 00	
Evans, Thomas	Bro	—	Corviser	3 Feb. 1772-3	2 April 1723	18 09 06	
Evans, William	Ben	Posenhall	Yeoman	20 July 1680	26 Mar. 1683	24 10 08	*4*
Evans, William	Bro	—	Collier	16 April 1699	18 April 1699	19 00 06	
Evans, William	Ben	Posenhall	Wheelwright	9 Mar. 1723-4	21 April 1724	15 17 06	
Everall, *see* Garbett							
Eves, *see* Eaves							
Farmer, John	Mad	—	—	—	26 Aug. 1707	no inv.	
Fletcher, Elizabeth	LW	—	—	—	13 Oct. 1725	no inv.	
Fletcher, George	LW	—	Ropemaker	22 May 1730	16 June 1730	12 00 00	*131*
Fletcher, John	LW	—	Yeoman/ Blacksmith	17 Mar. 1714-5	20 Sept. 1715	105 11 08	*126*
Fletcher, Joseph	LW	—	Ropemaker	—	28 June 1759	no inv.	
Forsbrook, *see* Fosbrook							
Fosbrooke, Jane	Mad	—	Widow	23 May 1681	28 Oct. 1681	64 16 04	
Fosbrooke, John	Mad	—	Yeoman	29 Mar. 1676	19 April 1676	70 04 06	

Name	Parish	Township etc.	Occupation	Inventory Date	Date of Exhibition or Probate	Value	Number (if published)
Fox, Nicholas	Mad	—	Yeoman	—	2 June 1729	no inv.	
Francis, Francis	Ben	—	—	n.d.	13 June 1693	03 00 00	
Francis, John	Ben	—	—	28 Mar. 1721	28 Mar. 1721	19 03 00	
Freeman, Deborah	Bro	—	Widow	—	11 Dec. 1759	no inv.	
Freeman, James	Bro	—	Gentleman	15 Mar. 1722-3	2 April 1723	575 14 06	67
Frisby, Maria	Bro	—	Widow	—	20 Sept. 1709	no inv.	
Garbett, Martha (*als*. Everall)	Mad	—	—	24 Aug. 1723	16 Feb. 1724-5	12 15 00	
Garmson, Henry	Bro	—	Carpenter	19 May 1709	21 June 1709	19 07 08	
Garmson, James	Bro	—	—	24 May 1745	27 May 1746	11 01 02	99
Gears, Beatrice	Ben	—	Widow	2 May 1728	4 June 1728	19 09 00	15
Gears, Francis	Bro	—	Tailor	4 May 1692	23 Aug. 1692	11 15 08	50
Gears, Richard	Bro	—	—	1 May 1666	15 May 1666	04 18 06	
Gears, Richard	Bro	—	Tallow Chandler	10 May 1720	27 Sept. 1720	158 19 05	66
Gears, Thomas	Bro	—	Servant Man	19 April 1715	10 May 1715	16 03 06	
Gething, Thomas	Ben	—	—	29 June 1758	4 July 1758	04 15 06	
Gifford, Rose	Mad	—	—	—	2 Mar. 1763	no inv.	
Gittins, Matthew	Ben	—	—	14 Sept. 1759	17 Sept. 1759	17 12 06	
Glassbrooke, George	Mad	Furnace Bank	Carpenter	15 June 1709	26 July 1709	16 16 08	163
Glassbrooke, Thomas	Mad	Madeley Wood	Blacksmith	2 July 1694	16 April 1695	18 15 00	
Goodman, John	Mad	—	—	9 Jan. 1733-4	15 Jan. 1733-4	146 17 02	183
Goodman, Mary	Bro	Swinney	Widow	25 July 1671	15 Aug. 1671	10 08 04	
Goodman, William	Mad	—	Cordwainer	—	1 June 1763	no inv.	
Gough, Ann	Bro	—	Widow	22 Jan. 1741	12 May 1741	11 08 08	88
Gough, Susanna	Bro	—	—	—	26 April 1737	no inv.	

A LIST OF PEOPLE

Name	Parish	Township etc.	Occupation	Inventory Date	Date of Exhibition or Probate	Value	Number (if published)
Gough, Richard	Bro	—	—	29 Dec. 1724	1 Mar. 1724-5	04 16 08	
Gower, Thomas	Bro	—	Trowman	28 Feb. 1728-9	4 Mar. 1728-9	143 07 00	75
Granger, Elizabeth	Mad	—	Widow	22 Mar. 1757	21 July 1757	03 02 06	
Gray, Edmund	LW	Huntington	Yeoman	22 Jan. 1729-30	16 June 1730	110 08 00	130
Green, Samuel	LW	—	—	n.d.	14 Sept. 1719	17 18 00	
Green, William	LW	—	Yeoman	17 Feb. 1667-8	3 Mar. 1667-8	193 14 04	116
Green, William	LW	—	—	—	19 Jan. 1668-9	no inv.	
Grice, George	LW	Huntington	Mason	12 Mar. 1665-6	10 Sept. 1667	52 00 00	
Griffiths, Thomas	Bro	—	—	19 Jan. 1684-5	10 Mar. 1684-5	14 11 08	
Griffiths, Thomas	Bro	—	—	30 Aug. 1745	27 May 1746	14 07 03	
Guest, George	Bro	—	Collier	24 Aug. 1674	19 Aug. 1674	33 02 10	33
Guest, Mary	Bro	—	Widow	26 April 1667	29 April 1667	63 05 06	
Guest, Richard (*als.* Guist)	LW	Smalley Hill	Yeoman	n.d.	5 Sept. 1737	18 30 06	
Haddon, Francis (*als.* Hatton)	Bro	Gitchfield	—	13 Mar. 1676-7	10 April 1677	10 09 08	
Haddon, Francis	Bro	—	Trowman*	9 Oct. 1682	10 Oct. 1682	08 10 00	
Haddon, Thomas	Bro	—	Yeoman	3 Feb. 1681-2	14 Feb. 1681-2	25 07 00	
Hagar, John	Mad	Strethill	Trowman	3 Jan. 1672-3	18 Mar. 1672-3	230 10 00	144
Hagar, Richard	Mad	—	Yeoman	—	5 Mar. 1682-3	no inv.	
Hall, William	Bro	—	Weaver*	5 Aug. 1758	7 Aug. 1758	13 04 00	110
Hallen, Ann	Mad	—	Widow	n.d.	27 Mar. 1756	15 00 00	
Hallen, Cornelius	Mad	Coalbrookdale	Plater	—	27 May 1746	no inv.	
Hammond, Samuel	LW	—	Clerk	—	20 April 1763	no inv.	
Hanley, Thomas	Bro	—	—	1 Nov. 1721	17 Dec. 1721	09 17 06	

Name	Parish	Township etc.	Occupation	Inventory Date	Date of Exhibition or Probate	Value	Number (if published)
Harper, John	Mad	—	Yeoman	7 April 1749	19 Sept. 1749	31 14 03	187
Harriotts, John	Bro	—	Blacksmith	14 Jan. 1690-1	27 April 1691	39 17 00	
Harris, Elizabeth	Bro	—	Widow	n.d.	20 Jan. 1684-5	02 17 06	
Harris, Humphrey	Bro	—	—	2 Mar. 1672-3	8 April 1673	11 14 04	
Harris, Joan	Bro	—	Widow*	n.d.	8 Aug. 1682	17 00 06	42
Harris, John	Bro	—	Coal Miner	26 Mar. 1674	14 April 1674	22 17 01	32
Harris, William	Bro	—	—	n.d.	1 July 1680	04 12 09	
Harrison, James	Bro	—	Coal Miner*	7 Sept. 1677	25 Sept. 1677	59 01 04	36
Harrison, Thomas	Bro	—	Gentleman	—	3 Aug. 1731	no inv.	
Hartshorne, Catherine	Ben	—	Spinster/Servant maid	1 Dec. 1712	23 June 1713	25 05 06	11
Hartshorne, Charles	Ben	—	Shoemaker	—	5 Aug. 1746	no inv.	
Hartshorne, Dorothy	Ben	—	Widow/Innkeeper	13 Oct. 1682	6 Nov. 1683	20 12 04	
Hartshorne, Edward	Ben	—	Blacksmith*	24 April 1694	27 April 1694	60 19 04	6
Hartshorne, Eleanor	Ben	—	Widow	n.d.	16 Nov. 1714	03 08 00	
Hartshorne, Hannah	Bro	—	Weaver*	15 Jan. 1736-7	29 Mar. 1737	04 13 00	82
Hartshorne, Jane	Ben	—	—	—	25 Sept. 1739	no inv.	
Hartshorne, John	Ben	—	—	n.d.	21 Nov. 1688	04 11 06	
Hartshorne, John	Ben	—	Tailor	n.d.	7 June 1737	03 17 06	
Hartshorne, Joyce	Bro	—	Widow	—	18 July 1763	no inv.	
Hartshorne, Margaret	Ben	—	Widow	n.d.	5 June 1753	17 00 00	
Hartshorne, Maurice	Ben	—	Innkeeper*	24 Aug. 1682	14 Sept. 1682	20 15 00	
Hartshorne, Rebecca	Ben	—	Widow	30 May 1716	15 Jan. 1716-7	19 05 00	
Hartshorne, Richard	Bro	—	Carpenter	17 Nov. 1760	17 July 1761	07 11 03	111
Hartshorne, Samuel	Bro	—	Weaver	—	28 Mar. 1732	no inv.	

A LIST OF PEOPLE

Name	Parish	Township etc.	Occupation	Inventory Date	Date of Exhibition or Probate	Value	Number (if published)
Hartshorne, Thomas	Ben	—	Labourer*	n.d.	13 June 1676	05 14 08	
Hartshorne, Thomas	Ben	—	Master Collier	n.d.	12 Dec. 1682	66 02 00	
Hartshorne, Thomas	Ben	—	Labourer/Yeoman	20 Dec. 1686	21 April 1687	04 05 00	
Hartshorne, Thomas	Ben	Hill top	Tobacco Pipe Maker	10 Sept. 1743	12 Sept. 1743	35 08 00	*19*
Hartshorne, William	Bro	—	—	—	1 June 1763	no inv.	
Haslewood, Ann	Mad	—	Widow	—	18 Aug. 1763	no inv.	
Haslewood, William	Mad	—	Tailor	20 Jan. 1759	28 June 1759	04 15 00	
Hatton, Edward	Mad	Madeley Wood	Collier	2 Feb. 1725	12 Oct. 1725	01 19 11	
Hatton, John	Mad	—	Carpenter	7 Oct. 1695	4 May 1697	07 06 07	
Hatton, Joseph	Mad	—	Writing Master	—	7 May 1764	no inv.	
Hawkins, Caesar	Bro	(also of Ludlow)	Chirurgion	1 Oct. 1707	11 July 1708	105 19 00	
Haynes, Dorothy	Ben	—	Widow	n.d.	18 April 1738	11 14 10	
Haynes, Richard (*als.* Hines)	Bro	—	—	—	1 June 1763	no inv.	
Hayward, Maurice	LW	—	Yeoman	1 Sept. 1746	4 May 1747	16 10 00	
Head, Samuel	Bro	—	Trowman	14 April 1697	4 May 1697	16 16 06	
Head, Samuel	Bro	—	—	12 June 1744	25 Sept. 1744	07 03 06	*97*
Heatherley, John (*als.* Adderley)	Mad	—	Gentleman	—	27 Nov. 1761	no inv.	
Heatherley, Maria	Mad	—	Widow	—	27 June 1733	no inv.	
Hemlock, John	Bro	—	Locksmith	n.d.	8 April 1673	08 02 00	
Henworth, Mark	Mad	—	Miller	29 Sept. 1729	19 July 1732	08 19 00	
Herbage, Edward	Mad	—	Yeoman	2 Nov. 1724	19 Jan. 1724-5	09 19 10	*181*
Hern, James (*als.* Horn)	Bro	—	—	12 Jan. 1742-3	18 Jan. 1742-3	04 03 06	
Highway, Richard	Mad	—	Yeoman	—	28 Sept. 1763	no inv.	

Name	Parish	Township etc.	Occupation	Inventory Date	Date of Exhibition or Probate	Value	Number (if published)
Hill, Richard	Bro	—	Cordwainer	23 Jan. 1748-9	31 Jan. 1748-9	04 05 00	
Hill, Robert	Bro	—	Mercer	3 Oct. 1679	22 Oct. 1679	139 02 07¾	39
Hinds, see Haynes							
Hodgkiss, Cornelius	Mad	—	—	29 May 1724	9 Mar. 1724-5	03 19 06	
Hodgkiss, George	Mad	Madeley Wood	Ground Collier	—	27 May 1746	no inv.	
Hodgkiss, John	Ben	—	Labourer	1 Sept. 1737	6 Sept. 1737	06 12 06	
Hodgkiss, Michael	Mad	—	Collier	5 April 1711	—	50 05 00	
Hodgkiss, Thomas	Mad	—	—	21 June 1753	9 July 1753	03 12 10	
Holbrook, Ralph	Mad	—	Yeoman	—	22 April 1760	no inv.	
Holland, Edward	Mad	Madeley Wood	Coal Miner	5 Dec. 1750	26 Feb. 1750-1	03 10 00	
Holland, George	Mad	—	Collier	17 Jan. 1763	1 June 1763	21 08 06	
Holland, John	Mad	Madeley Wood	Yeoman/Barge Owner*	20 May 1690	22 May 1690	374 18 02	158
Holland, Mary	Mad	—	—	—	25 Sept. 1722	no inv.	
Holland, Robert	Mad	—	—	2 April 1711	24 April 1711	10 15 00	
Holland, Robert	Mad	Madeley Wood	Miner	n.d.	13 Nov. 1727	14 05 06	
Hollingshead, Edward	Bro	—	Yeoman	27 Feb. 1717-8	3 Mar. 1717-8	06 10 04	
Holmes, Judith	Bro	—	Widow	17 July 1708	20 July 1708	82 08 01	57
Holmes, Thomas	Bro	—	Trowman	18 May 1702	21 May 1702	94 17 00	
Holmes, William	Bro	—	—	17 Sept. 1741	22 Sept. 1741	18 09 06	90
Horbage, see Herbage							
Howle, Mary	LW	—	—	—	3 July 1744	no inv.	
Hughes, Thomas	Bro	—	Tobbaco Pipe Maker	18 July 1735	25 May 1736	13 04 00	
Humphries, Rowland	Bro	—	Weaver	—	21 July 1759	no inv.	
Hutchinson, Alice	Mad	—	Widow	5 May 1664	8 May 1664	24 05 00	

A LIST OF PEOPLE

Name	Parish	Township etc.	Occupation	Inventory Date	Date of Exhibition or Probate	Value	Number (if published)
Hutchinson, John	Mad	—	Yeoman	17 May 1714	1 Sept. 1714	14 10 03	
Huxley, John	Bro	—	Gentleman	2 May 1671	4 Mar. 1671-2	347 00 00	
Huxley, John	Mad	—	—	n.d.	11 Oct. 1757	08 10 06	
Instone, John	Ben	—	Blacksmith	—	29 June 1759	no inv.	148
Jackson, Lydia	Bro	—	Spinster	n.d.	24 Sept. 1739	19 00 00	
James, Henry	Mad	—	Bowyer	n.d.	4 May 1676	07 08 07	
James, James	Bro	—	—	7 Mar. 1759	19 Mar. 1759	04 13 06	
James, John	Ben	—	—	22 May 1679	1 June 1680	14 05 10	
James, John	Ben	—	—	—	13 June 1682	no inv.	
Jaundrell, John	Mad	—	Vicar of Madeley	—	3 Nov. 1753	no inv.	
Jefferies, John	Bro	—	Yeoman	17 Jan. 1717-8	21 Jan. 1717-8	18 13 00	
Jerman, Thomas	Bro	—	Husbandman	24 June 1689	18 July 1689	21 19 08	
Jervis, Richard	LW	Huntington	Yeoman	23 April 1715	20 Sept. 1715	55 05 00	123
Johnson, Robert	Bro	—	—	n.d.	3 Mar. 1714-5	03 10 00	
Jones, Edward	Bro	—	—	14 May 1668	19 May 1668	08 13 10	24
Jones, Edward	Bro	—	—	18 April 1671	22 May 1671	04 08 04	
Jones, Edward	Bro	—	Collier	9 Dec. 1684	20 Jan. 1684-5	06 06 02	
Jones, Edward	Bro	—	Collier	6 Aug. 1742	23 Nov. 1742	10 02 06	92
Jones, Elizabeth	Bro	—	Widow	8 May 1677	12 June 1677	04 15 10	
Jones, Elizabeth	Bro	—	—	—	6 Nov. 1683	no inv.	
Jones, Francis	Bro	—	Trowman	15 Sept. 1728	28 Jan. 1728-9	09 19 11	
Jones, Hugh (*als.* James)	Bro	—	Trowman	22 April 1689	30 Oct. 1689	39 08 06	48

Name	Parish	Township etc.	Occupation	Inventory Date	Date of Exhibition or Probate	Value	Number (if published)
Jones Jonathan	Bro	—	Trowman	6 Mar. 1716-7	12 April 1717	16 03 06	
Jones, John	Mad	Coalbrookdale	Forgeman	21 June 1754	24 June 1754	16 12 00	190
Jones, Richard (*als.* Hughes)	Bro	—	Labourer/Trowman	13 June 1684	8 July 1684	04 02 04	
Jones, Roger	Bro	—	Weaver	12 May 1668	19 May 1668	09 10 08	
Jones, Thomas	Bro	—	—	28 Jan. 1672-3	1 July 1673	01 18 00	
Jones, Thomas	Bro	—	Yeoman	n.d.	3 May 1726	59 01 00	
King, Henry	LW	—	—	23 Mar. 1730-1	23 Mar. 1730-1	30 15 00	
Lacon, Richard	Bro	—	—	—	2 May 1676	no inv.	
Lacon, Walter	Ben	—	—	n.d.	1 May 1749	19 19 00	
Langley, Andrew	Bro	Woodhouse	Gentleman	7 Oct. 1687	24 Oct. 1687	456 00 00	47
Langley, Francis	Bro	—	Gentleman	24 May 1687	24 May 1687	30 00 00	
Langley, John	Bro	Swinbatch	Gentleman	8 Nov. 1693	21 Nov. 1693	85 00 06	53
Langley, John	Bro	Swinbatch	Gentleman	15 May 1702	30 May 1702	13 13 06	
Langley, John	Bro	—	—	—	18 Aug. 1710	no inv.	
Langley, John	Bro	Swinbatch	Gentleman	—	4 Aug. 1730	no inv.	
Langley, Mennes	Bro	—	Gentleman	11 April 1699	18 April 1699	35 19 10	55
Langley, Samuel	Bro	—	—	—	16 Nov. 1697	no inv.	
Langley, Samuel	Bro	—	Gentleman	n.d.	6 June 1698	239 15 00	
Leadbeater, John	Bro	—	Gentleman	27 Sept. 1753	11 Aug. 1755	66 02 07	103
Lee, Thomas	Bro	—	Nailer	27 Sept. 1694	9 Oct. 1694	80 05 00	54
Legg, John	Bro	—	—	n.d.	9 Feb. 1719-20	11 03 06	
Lewis, John	Mad	Madeley Wood	—	26 Feb. 1694-5	16 April 1695	07 08 06	
Lewis, Robert (*als.* Davies)	Mad	—	—	6 May 1676	13 June 1676	01 16 06	

A LIST OF PEOPLE

Name	Parish	Township etc.	Occupation	Inventory Date	Date of Exhibition or Probate	Value	Number (if published)
Lewis, Thomas	Mad	—	—	n.d.	25 June 1763	no inv.	
Lewis, William	Bro	—	Trowman	1 Dec. 1670	7 Dec. 1670	32 07 10	26
Lewis, William	Bro	—	—	—	19 Aug. 1674	no inv.	
Lewis, William	Bro	—	Wheel Turner	—	3 July 1755	no inv.	
Littleford, John	Bro	—	Cooper	—	9 May 1721	no inv.	
Littleford, Vincent	Bro	—	Carpenter	—	26 Feb. 1733-4	no inv.	
Lloyd, Edward	Mad	—	Trowman*	29 Oct. 1709	8 Nov. 1709	74 19 04	164
Lloyd, Edward	Mad	—	Trowman*	10 April 1746	5 Aug. 1746	18 17 06	
Lloyd, George	Bro	—	—	25 Mar. 1755	28 Feb. 1755	16 12 00	
Lloyd, John	Mad	Madeley Wood	Trowman/Innkeeper	17 Mar. 1675-6	18 April 1676	76 13 02	146
Lloyd, John	Mad	—	—	—	7 May 1677	no inv.	
Lloyd, William	Bro	—	Collier	30 May 1732	12 Sept. 1732	03 10 06	
Lloyd, William	Bro	—	Collier	n.d. 1728-9	22 April 1729	07 13 00	
Lloyd, William	Bro	—	Trowman	16 Oct. 1756	13 Nov. 1756	34 03 00	
Love, Robert	Bro	—	Ground Collier	27 Feb. 1754	6 May 1754	16 18 06	104
Madelin, Benjamin	Bro	—	Trowman*	26 May 1763	1 June 1763	35 01 00	
Mann, John	Bro	—	—	23 May 1663	30 Aug. 1664	24 14 08	
Martin, Joseph	Bro	—	Waterman	2 May 1726	14 Sept. 1726	16 17 00	
Martin, Joseph	Bro	—	—	n.d.	4 July 1752	03 10 00	
Mason, Richard	Bro	—	Innholder	22 Aug. 1727	19 Sept. 1727	19 05 00	72
Matthews, John	Bro	—	—	—	4 July 1727	no inv.	
Maybury, William	Mad	—	—	20 Oct. 1703	22 Aug. 1704	14 12 11	161
Mayor, Henry	Bro	—	Yeoman*	9 Oct. 1708	14 Dec. 1708	15 18 04	
Mayor, Henry	Bro	—	Collier	—	8 May 1753	no inv.	

Name	Parish	Township etc.	Occupation	Inventory Date	Date of Exhibition or Probate	Value	Number (if published)
Mayor, John	Bro	—	—	29 Sept. 1719	1 Oct. 1719	18 15 00	65
Mayor, William	Bro	—	—	25 Feb. 1690-1	28 April 1691	58 00 06	
Mecham, John	Mad	Coalbrookdale	—	—	29 July 1754	no inv.	
Miles, Elizabeth	Bro	—	—	—	28 July 1741	no inv.	
Millington, Roger	Ben	—	Collier	7 Nov. 1673	10 Dec. 1673	03 12 11	
Millner, William	Bro	—	Stone Mason and Bricklayer	—	2 May 1773	no inv.	
Mivart, Sarah (als. Grey)	Bro	—	Spinster	—	12 Sept. 1665	no inv.	
Morgan, Silvanus	Bro	—	Yeoman	—	17 July 1761	no inv.	
Morris, John (als. Davies)	Mad	—	—	30 July 1680	31 July 1683	04 10 06	
Morris, John	Bro	—	—	—	7 June 1737	no inv.	
Morris, William	Bro	—	Tobacco Pipe Maker	5 July 1756	5 July 1756	09 18 06	106
Mullart, Anne	Mad	—	Spinster	8 Dec. 1684	22 Jan. 1684-5	15 14 08	
Munday, George	Ben	—	Yeoman	20 June 1759	25 June 1759	17 11 06	
Nash, Edward	Bro	—	Collier*	29 Sept. 1713	10 Sept. 1717	18 12 08	60
Nash, John	Bro	—	Collier*	4 Mar. 1667-8	22 April 1668	04 17 00	
Nevitt, Joseph	Ben	—	Waterman	—	17 July 1761	no inv.	
Nott, Thomas	Bro	—	—	10 June 1664	13 Dec. 1664	04 12 00	
Oakes, Francis	Bro	—	Collier*	5 June 1671	10 July 1671	212 03 08	
Oakes, Francis (als. Stukly Oakes)	Bro	—	Trowman	27 Dec. 1721	28 April 1721	17 19 00	

A LIST OF PEOPLE

Name	Parish	Township etc.	Occupation	Inventory Date	Date of Exhibition or Probate	Value	Number (if published)
Oakes, Francis	Bro	—	Trowman*	14 Feb. 1734-5	13 Mar. 1734-5	39 00 00	
Oakes, John	Bro	—	Trowman	16 May 1744	22 May 1744	08 11 09	96
Oakes, John (*als.* Jackathin Oakes)	Bro	—	Trowman	—	20 Dec. 1755	no inv.	
Oakes, Jonathan	Bro	—	Waterman*	n.d.	26 June 1764	29 13 02	114
Oakes, Mary	Bro	—	Widow/Barge Owner	n.d.	15 Nov. 1726	18 00 00	
Oakes, Roger	Bro	—	Trowman	18 June 1669	25 June 1669	08 05 04	
Oakes, Roger	Bro	—	—	12 Mar. 1693-4	27 April 1694	55 01 08	
Oakes, William	Bro	—	Collier*	2 Dec. 1669	23 Sept. 1670	167 07 00	25
Ogden, Mary	Bro	—	—	31 July 1717	28 Oct. 1717	116 05 00	62
Ogden, Robert	Bro	—	Clerk	18 Mar. 1679-80	22 Mar. 1679-80	392 18 06	41
Oliver, Thomas	Bro	—	Mercer	4 Aug. 1692	22 Aug. 1692	266 140 1½	51
Onions, Ann	Bro	—	Widow	—	21 July 1757	no inv.	
Onions, John	Bro	—	Collier	—	22 July 1735	no inv.	
Oswald, John	Bro	—	Trowman*	14 Jan. 1728-9	4 Mar. 1728-9	18 16 02	
Owen, Edward	Mad	Madeley Wood	Waterman	1 June 1728	16 July 1728	93 07 00	176
Owen, Edward	Mad	—	Trowman*	21 June 1732	25 Sept. 1734	213 12 07	182
Owen, James	Mad	Madeley Wood	Waterman	—	1 June 1763	no inv.	
Owen, Timothy	Bro	—	—	30 Aug. 1727	3 Sept. 1728	51 00 00	
Owsley, Elizabeth	LW	—	Widow	n.d.	15 April 1755	18 02 06	
Owsley, John	LW	—	Yeoman	27 Sept. 1731	9 Nov. 1731	37 01 00	
Oxenboles, Sarah	Mad	—	Widow	30 Nov. 1681	2 May 1682	04 18 06	
Palmer, John	Mad	Madeley Wood	Master Collier	4 June 1759	28 June 1759	96 09 09	193
Palmer, Richard	Mad	—	Coal Miner	4 Oct. 1756	21 July 1757	12 09 00	

Name	Parish	Township etc.	Occupation	Inventory Date	Date of Exhibition or Probate	Value	Number (if published)
Palmer, Thomas	Bro	—	—	—	10 Oct. 1704	no inv.	
Parks, Alexander	Mad	—	—	1 Feb. 1680-1	25 Oct. 1681	02 13 06	
Parton, Francis	LW	—	Yeoman	12 Nov. 1728	3 June 1729	169 03 04	129
Parton, George	LW	—	—	n.d.	4 May 1761	03 05 07	137
Parton, Richard	LW	—	—	n.d.	14 Mar. 1670-1	17 18 02	118
Parton, William	LW	—	—	22 Sept. 1691	22 Oct. 1691	58 12 06	
Pearce, John	Bro	—	Trowman*	16 Aug. 1707	3 Dec. 1707	17 05 00	
Pearce, John	Bro	—	Master Collier	25 July 1709	26 July 1709	318 03 11	58
Pearce, Richard	Bro	—	Master Collier	14 July 1732	11 July 1732	483 06 08½	79
Pearce, William	Bro	—	Collier*	28 May 1672	4 June 1672	08 04 08	
Pearce, William	Bro	—	Master Collier	8 Dec. 1742	26 April 1743	35 04 04	94
Pearce, William	Bro	—	—	n.d.	14 Feb. 1757	29 18 06	
Penn, Mary	Bro	—	Widow/Shopkeeper	9 Mar. 1740-1	5 April 1742	105 10 01	87
Penn, Richard	Ben	—	—	—	30 June 1740	no inv.	
Penny, Timothy	LW	(Late of Bayton, Worcs.)	Gentleman	—	7 Mar. 1763	no inv.	
Perks, see Parks							
Pew, see Pugh							
Phillips, George (*als.* Reynolds)	Bro	—	Trowman*	17 Jan. 1705-6	19 Feb. 1705-6	19 03 00	
Phillips, Rebecca (*als.* Reynolds)	Bro	—	Widow	n.d.	9 May 1676	02 13 00	
Phillips, Thomas	Bro	—	Waterman	—	25 Oct. 1743	no inv.	
Picking, John (*als.* Pirkins)	Mad	—	Labourer	8 Dec. 1709	1 June 1710	07 13 08	

… A LIST OF PEOPLE

Name	Parish	Township etc.	Occupation	Inventory Date	Date of Exhibition or Probate	Value	Number (if published)
Poole, John	Bro	—	Labouring Waterman	15 July 1724	21 July 1724	01 18 06	70
Poole, John	Bro	—	Trowman	7 Nov. 1739	10 Dec. 1739	84 14 00	83
Potts, Alice	Bro	—	Widow	1 April 1707	1 April 1707	31 00 00	
Potts, Thomas	Bro	—	Yeoman/Master Collier	4 June 1692	27 Sept. 1692	24 18 08	
Potts, Thomas	Bro	—	Waterman*	27 May 1707	27 May 1707	30 00 00	
Potts, Thomas	Bro	—	—	10 June 1746	5 Aug. 1746	11 15 00	
Powell, Daniel	Bro	—	Day Labourer	8 Feb. 1733-4	28 Sept. 1736	10 07 06	
Powis, Ann	Bro	—	Widow	n.d.	16 Feb. 1736-7	06 00 00	
Preen, Thomas	Ben	—	—	26 Feb. 1746-7	25 June 1756	09 00 00	
Price, David (*als.* Trickels)	Mad	—	Yeoman*	15 Oct. 1680	15 Dec. 1680	17 03 06	
Price, Humphrey	Mad	—	Yeoman	31 Mar. 1729	20 Oct. 1747	03 14 00	
Price, Humphrey	Mad	—	—	n.d.	7 Aug. 1758	02 08 06	
Price, Thomas	Bro	—	—	27 Mar. 1682	2 May 1682	17 16 08	
Pritchard, Christopher	Mad	Coalbrookdale	Smelter or Lead Man	—	8 May 1753	no inv.	
Pritchard, Richard	Mad	Coalbrookdale	Yeoman/ Shopkeeper	24 Mar. 1759	27 June 1759	15 13 00	194
Pugh, Andrew	Bro	—	Chandler	20 July 1696	22 Sept. 1696	17 15 10	
Pugh, John	Bro	—	Trowman*	29 July 1698	11 Oct. 1698	158 05 00	
Pugh, Thomas	Bro	—	Trowman	—	1 Oct. 1719	no inv.	
Rainford, Francis	Mad	—	—	—	12 Sept. 1732	no inv.	
Reynolds, Edward	Bro	—	Dyer/Ferryman	10 Nov. 1742	25 Oct. 1743	02 08 00	93

Name	Parish	Township etc.	Occupation	Inventory Date	Date of Exhibition or Probate	Value	Number (if published)
Reynolds, Joseph	Ben	Posenhall	Yeoman	19 April 1693	19 July 1693	12 00 00	
Reynolds, Joseph	Ben	Posenhall	—	18 July 1712	23 Sept. 1712	142 04 10	10
Reynolds, William	Ben	—	—	—	28 Mar. 1732	no inv.	
Rhoden, see Roden							
Rhodes, Margaret	Bro	—	Widow	n.d.	10 Feb. 1673-4	02 11 06	
Rhodes, Robert	Bro	—	—	n.d.	20 April 1697	03 02 09	
Richards, Ann	Mad	—	Widow	4 Mar. 1688-9	15 July 1689	23 05 02	156
Richards, John	Mad	—	—	n.d.	13 Mar. 1755	04 17 00	
Richards, Michael	Mad	—	Vicar of Madeley	25 May 1671	10 July 1671	37 14 00	
Roberts, Henry	Bro	—	—	26 Feb. 1714-5	8 Mar. 1714-5	01 18 09	
Roberts, John (*als.* Belcham)	Bro	—	—	9 Jan. 1683-4	15 April 1684	04 02 04	43
Roberts, John	Mad	—	Husbandman	28 Mar. 1701	24 May 1701	37 15 00	
Roberts, Peter	Mad	—	—	—	21 May 1764	no inv.	
Roberts, Richard	Bro	—	—	n.d.	22 Feb. 1698-9	47 10 06	
Roberts, Thomas	Mad	—	Yeoman	n.d.	7 Aug. 1758	06 19 00	
Roberts, William	Mad	—	Miller	—	20 Feb. 1764	no inv.	
Roden, James	Bro	—	Collier	17 May 1683	4 Mar. 1683-4	03 07 09	
Roden, Richard	Bro	—	Yeoman/Shopkeeper	12 Feb. 1723-4	21 April 1724	37 00 00	69
Roden, Samuel	Bro	—	Coal Miner	23 July 1725	9 Oct. 1725	04 11 06	
Roden, Samuel	Mad	Coalbrookdale	Carpenter	—	20 Mar. 1762	no inv.	
Roden, Thomas	Bro	—	Tobacco Pipe Maker	n.d.	19 Jan. 1723-4	12 12 07	71
Rodes, *see* Rhodes							

A LIST OF PEOPLE

Name	Parish	Township etc.	Occupation	Inventory Date	Date of Exhibition or Probate	Value	Number (if published)
Roe, Roger	Mad	—	Yeoman*	19 Jan. 1718-9	10 Feb. 1718-9	229 12 08	*171*
Roe, William	Mad	—	Yeoman	26 July 1714	1 Sept. 1714	181 00 10	*168*
Rogers, Daniel	LW	—	—	6 Feb. 1738-9	25 Sept. 1739	37 19 06	
Rogers, John	LW	Wrekin	—	n.d.	24 June 1754	19 05 00	
Roper, Sarah	Bro	—	Widow	22 May 1736	22 June 1736	04 16 00	
Roper, Timothy	Bro	—	—	3 April 1724	21 April 1724	17 08 09	
Rowlands, John	Mad	—	Trowman*	16 Jan. 1753	27 Jan. 1753	35 09 00	
Rowlands, John	Mad	—	Yeoman	—	6 July 1758	no inv.	
Rowley, John	Bro	—	Trowman*	25 June 1736	27 July 1736	18 15 00	
Rowley, John	Bro	—	Trowman*	17 Mar. 1749-50	2 April 1750	16 17 06	
Rowley, Mary	Bro	—	—	—	6 May 1754	no inv.	
Rowley, Milborough	Mad	—	Widow*	2 July 1699	22 Aug. 1699	01 19 04	
Rowley, Thomas	Bro	—	Waterman	—	11 Dec. 1745	no inv.	
Rowley, Thomas	Mad	—	Blacksmith*	n.d.	23 Sept. 1755	13 07 00½	*192*
Rowley, William	Ben	—	Trowman	—	30 July 1745	no inv.	
Rushon, Francis	Mad	—	Husbandman/Cooper	27 April 1665	14 Nov. 1665	43 09 08	*138*
Russell, Edward	Bro	—	Trowman	12 Aug. 1670	20 Sept. 1670	81 13 04	
Russell, Elizabeth	Bro	—	Widow	8 Dec. 1679	23 Mar. 1679-80	11 15 08	*40*
Russell, John	Bro	—	Yeoman	13 Oct. 1727	3 Sept. 1728	09 17 00	
Rutter, John	Ben	—	Yeoman*	7 Jan. 1708-9	22 Mar. 1708-9	78 19 07	*9*
Rutter, Richard	Bro	—	—	n.d.	25 July 1673	02 06 06	*31*
Rutter, William	Ben	—	Collier*	26 Aug. 1679	15 Sept. 1679	87 16 00	*3*
Sandells, William	Bro	—	—	n.d.	5 June 1706	17 00 00	
Sansom, Edward	Bro	—	—	7 July 1753	11 July 1753	17 02 04	

Name	Parish	Township etc.	Occupation	Inventory Date	Date of Exhibition or Probate	Value	Number (if published)
Sansom, William	Bro	—	Yeoman	17 April 1688	10 May 1688	23 03 00	
Search, William	LW	—	Gentleman	—	25 Sept. 1722	no inv.	
Shaw, Morris	Bro	—	Weaver*	1 Oct. 1717	28 Oct. 1717	17 18 06	
Sheinton, see Sherrington							
Shepherd, Ann	LW	—	—	—	17 May 1762	no inv.	
Sherbrook, Amos	Bro	—	—	n.d.	12 Nov. 1753	04 00 00	
Sherbrook, Mary	Bro	Madeley Wood	Widow	20 Nov. 1753	1 Oct. 1753	16 11 00	
Sherratt, John	Mad	—	Tallow Chandler	21 June 1676	6 July 1676	290 00 00	147
Sherrington, William (als. Sheinton)	LW	—	Yeoman	25 April 1698	28 Feb. 1698-9	44 03 06	
Shrigsley, William	Mad	—	Husbandman	10 Sept. 1668	2 Jan. 1668-69	14 16 02	
Signer, see Syrer							
Simmonds, John	LW	Huntington	Yeoman	7 Sept. 1715	8 Sept. 1715	84 00 00	
Simmonds see Symonds							
Simpson, Ann	Bro	—	Widow	25 April 1750	15 May 1750	18 14 06	102
Slicer, John	Mad	—	Iron Pot Founder	—	17 July 1761	no inv.	
Smith, Charles	Bro	—	—	21 Jan. 1737-8	24 Jan. 1737-8	07 09 05	
Smith, Joyce	Bro	—	Widow	13 Mar. 1749-50	13 Mar. 1749-50	11 00 00	
Smith, Mary	Ben	—	Widow*	6 May 1721	9 May 1721	95 11 06	
Smith, Richard	Ben	—	Collier*	22 June 1713	23 June 1713	38 01 05	
Smith, Richard	Bro	—	—	12 Dec. 1739	12 Dec. 1739	04 12 00	
Smith, Richard	Ben	—	—	—	2 June 1741	no inv.	
Smith, Samuel	Ben	—	Shoemaker	n.d.	1 Aug. 1698	09 14 10	
Smith, William	Ben	—	Collier*	22 April 1752	27 April 1752	13 05 06	20
Smitheman, James	Mad	—	Gunsmith	16 Nov. 1709	1 June 1710	18 06 04	165
Smitheman, John	LW	—	Yeoman	9 Oct. 1689	29 Oct. 1689	178 18 00	119

A LIST OF PEOPLE

Name	Parish	Township etc.	Occupation	Inventory Date	Date of Exhibition or Probate	Value	Number (if published)
Smitheman, Richard	Mad	—	—	—	25 Sept. 1722	no inv.	
Smitheman, Thomas	Mad	—	Tailor	1 Dec. 1722	10 Dec. 1722	10 01 00	
Spencer, Joan	Mad	Madeley Wood	Widow	6 Mar. 1673-4	31 Mar. 1673-4	11 10 00	145
Spruce, Edward	Mad	—	—	—	22 Sept. 1763	no inv.	
Squire, John	Bro	—	—	—	3 June 1752	no inv.	
Stanley, Elizabeth	Mad	—	Wife	8 May 1721	9 May 1721	10 00 00	
Stanley, Thomas	Mad	—	Yeoman*	n.d.	23 May 1672	89 10 04	
Starkey, Dorothy	Mad	—	—	16 Feb. 1667-8	13 Oct. 1668	357 03 11	
Steventon, Thomas	Mad	—	—	n.d.	14 Feb 1670	110 05 00	
Stockton, John	Mad	—	—	3 June 1701	3 June 1701	04 09 06	
Stokes, Adam	Bro	—	Trowman	27 Dec. 1675	26 Jan. 1675-6	58 03 06	34
Stratton, Richard	Mad	—	Butcher	13 Dec. 1739	3 June 1740	18 01 00	
Styche, Richard	Mad	—	—	17 June 1740	1 July 1740	47 00 00	
Swift, John	LW	—	Yeoman/ Husbandman	4 May 1682	11 July 1682	71 11 00	
Swift, Margery	LW	—	Widow	30 Aug. 1726	14 Nov. 1727	32 13 06	
Symonds, John	Bro	—	Trowman*	15 July 1706	27 Aug. 1706	62 03 00	
Symonds, *see* Simmonds							
Syrer/Syner, Cornelius (*als.* Taylor)	Bro	—	—	n.d.	15 July 1718	01 18 08	
Taylor, Benjamin	Mad	—	Vicar of Madeley	9 Nov. 1704	9 Feb. 1704-5	240 18 00	162
Taylor, Henry	Mad	—	—	20 July 1705	13 Nov. 1705	65 19 02	
Taylor, Richard	LW	—	Butcher	8 Jan. 1744-5	23 April 1745	41 15 00	
Taylor, Robert	LW	—	—	n.d.	10 July 1760	13 14 00	

Name	Parish	Township etc.	Occupation	Inventory Date	Date of Exhibition or Probate	Value	Number (if published)
Taylor, Thomas	Bro	—	Tobacco Pipe Maker	21 Jan. 1739-40	3 June 1740	15 09 08	84
Taylor, see Syrer							
Teece, Thomas	Bro	—	Locksmith	20 Feb. 1727-8	9 April 1728	45 16 05	73
Teece, William	Bro	—	Waterman	20 Oct. 1757	24 Aug. 1758	04 05 00	
Thomas, Edward	Mad	—	Collier	6 Sept. 1715	8 Sept. 1715	01 19 00	
Thomas, Edward	Mad	Madeley Wood	Coal Miner	n.d.	3 July 1755	10 09 03	191
Thomas, George	Mad	Coalbrookdale	—	n.d.	8 July 1760	10 06 06	195
Thomas, John	Mad	Coalbrookdale	Pot Founder	—	8 July 1760	no inv.	
Thresslecock, Roger	LW	Leasows	Yeoman	6 Sept. 1742	7 Sept. 1742	81 16 06	133
Thursfield, John	Bro	—	Potter	—	10 July 1760	no inv.	
Tilbroom, Thomas	Ben	—	Yeoman	5 April 1712	17 June 1712	35 19 00	
Tomson, Richard	LW	Coalmoor	Collier	1 April 1726	14 June 1726	04 19 01	
Transome, Edward	Mad	—	Trowman*	13 April 1687	21 June 1687	09 17 00	
Tranter, Roger	Mad	—	Labourer	10 Dec. 1689	18 Feb. 1689-90	10 07 02	157
Trickels, see Price							
Trusham, Thomas	Bro	—	Gardener	—	12 Mar. 1763	no inv.	
Tudge, Margaret	Bro	(als. of Hughley)	—	—	14 Oct. 1725	—	
Turner, Frances	Mad	—	Widow	1 May 1671	22 May 1671	53 10 00	
Turner, Timothy	Mad	—	—	11 May 1691	14 May 1691	84 00 08	
Twyford, Luke	Mad	The Lodge	Gentleman	28 Nov. 1711	22. Jan. 1711-2	137 03 10	166
Twyford, Richard	Mad	Madeley Wood	Yeoman	30 Nov. 1681	22 May 1682	204 18 06	151
Unwyn, Edward	Ben	—	Yeoman	3 June 1706	23 July 1706	63 15 00	
Walker, George	LW	—	Collier	—	10 July 1760	no inv.	
Walton, Charles	Bro	Swinney	Husbandman*	18 Jan. 1688-9	1 July 1690	54 10 00	

A LIST OF PEOPLE

Name	Parish	Township etc.	Occupation	Inventory Date	Date of Exhibition or Probate	Value	Number (if published)
Walton, John	Bro	—	Miller*	29 Aug. 1699	19 Sept. 1699	19 00 00	
Ward, Edward	Bro	—			15 April 1745	no inv.	
Ward, William	Bro	The Ridding	Yeoman		11 July 1732	no inv.	
Warren, John	Mad	—			29 Oct. 1717	no inv.	
Wase, John	Bro	Whitehall	Gentleman		30 Dec. 1758	no inv.	
Watkiss, Moses	Bro	—	Collier	n.d.	22 June 1762	14 01 00	113
Watkiss, Thomas	Bro	—	Ground Collier	n.d.	15 April 1684	06 11 10	
Weaver, James	Bro	—		22 Feb. 1734-5	2 June 1735	16 17 11	
Weaver, Richard	Bro	—		n.d.	12 July 1743	12 05 06	
Wheale, Thomas	Ben	Posenhall	Glover	6 Dec. 1686	21 April 1687	33 10 00	
Wheeler, John	Mad	—	Yeoman	n.d.	18 July 1750	12 16 00	
Wheelwright, George	LW	—	Yeoman	15 Mar. 1713-4	1 Sept. 1714	243 12 06	125
Wheelwright, Richard	LW	—	Yeoman	2 Mar. 1708-9	21 June 1709	42 16 00	122
Wheelwright, William	LW	—	Yeoman	24 Sept. 1714	20 Sept. 1715	116 01 06	127
Wheelwright, William	LW	—	Yeoman	23 July 1717	30 July 1717	97 16 00	128
Whitefoot, Eliza	Bro	—			7 June 1749	no inv.	
Whitefoot, Joseph	Bro	—	Mason	15 Mar. 1741-2	5 April 1742	19 03 00	91
Whitemoor, Ann	Bro	—	Single woman	—	17 Oct. 1747	no inv.	
Whitemore, John	Bro	—	Chandler	19 Aug. 1679	27 Aug. 1679	70 13 10	38
Whitemore, Maria	Bro	—		—	5 Aug. 1740	no inv.	
Whitmore, Robert	Bro	—	Tallow Chandler*	20 Jan. 1717-8	4 Mar. 1717-8	1220 18 02	63
Whitmore, Robert	Bro	—	Tallow Chandler*	4 July 1727	19 Sept. 1727	33 09 06	
Whitmore, William	Bro	—	Tallow Chandler*	25 April 1728	16 June 1728	70 02 00	74
Whittall, Francis	Bro	—	—	2 May 1729	28 April 1730	17 07 00	

Name	Parish	Township etc.	Occupation	Inventory Date	Date of Exhibition or Probate	Value	Number (if published)
Whyston, William	LW	—	Rector of Little Wenlock	26 May 1713	23 June 1713	51 11 00	*124*
Wild, Francis	Bro	—	Collier	—	1 June 1763	no inv.	
Wild, John	Bro	—	Trowman	13 June 1747	10 July 1747	47 00 02	*100*
Wild, Mary	Bro	—	—	—	30 Aug. 1729	no inv.	
Wild, Thomas	Bro	—	—	—	8 July 1760	no inv.	
Wilkinson, Thomas	Bro	—	—	—	7 June 1749	no inv.	
Wilks, Francis	Bro	—	Collier	7 Nov. 1757	15 Nov. 1757	06 03 10	*108*
Williams, Ann (*als.* Hypkes)	Bro	—	—	13 Feb. 1673-4	23 Mar. 1673-4	02 14 00	
Williams, Francis	Bro	—	—	8 April 1720	26 April 1720	02 10 11	
Williams, Joan	Bro	—	Widow	—	15 April 1680	00 19 00	
Williams, Robert	Bro	—	—	—	23 Sept. 1745	no inv.	
Williams, Thomas	Bro	—	—	19 May 1729	1 July 1729	35 02 10	*76*
Williams, Thomas	Bro	—	Waterman	—	27 April 1752	no inv.	
Williams, William	Bro	—	Collier	29 Sept. 1733	1 Oct. 1733	05 15 00	
Wood, Richard	LW	—	Collier	10 Mar. 1665-6	27 Mar. 1666	16 19 04	
Woseley, Francis	LQ	—	Mason	7 April 1673	8 April 1673	12 17 00	*117*
Wright, William	LW	—	Yeoman	n.d.	31 May 1720	90 12 00	
Wyke, Isaac	Bro	—	Surgeon	—	1 July 1755	no inv.	
Yardley, *see* Bardley							
Yates, Edward	Mad	—	Trowman*	16 June 1673	24 June 1673	92 15 00	
Yates, Edward	Mad	—	Waterman	12 June 1724	8 Dec. 1724	24 00 00	
Yates, Edward	Mad	—	—	n.d.	15 Feb. 1757	11 02 04	
Yates, John	Mad	Madeley Wood	Fisherman*	25 April 1670	25 April 1670	25 05 02	*143*

Name	Parish	Township etc.	Occupation	Inventory Date	Date of Exhibition or Probate	Value	Number (if published)
Yates, John	Bro	—	Trowman*	n.d.	25 Nov. 1757	43 05 00	*107*
Yates, John	Mad	—	Owner	n.d.	8 June 1761	04 10 00	
Yates, Mary	Mad	—	Widow	n.d.	13 Mar. 1687-8	18 11 06	*175*
Yates, Mary	Mad	—	Widow	19 June 1727	4 July 1727	73 05 00	
Yates, Robert	Mad	—	Trowman	12 Dec. 1677	24 April 1683	38 11 06	*154*
Yates, William	Bro	—	Trowman	3 June 1748	4 July 1748	124 17 06	*101*
York, Thomas	Mad	Madeley Wood	Ground Collier	20 June 1759	27 June 1759	09 02 10	

THE INVENTORIES, 1660-1750

The Inventories of Bentall, Broseley, Little Wenlock and Madeley

(The transcripts of the probate inventories in the Herefordshire Record Office appear by courtesy of the County Archivist.)

THE INVENTORIES are printed parish by parish in alphabetical order, and within each parish chronologically according to the date of appraisal. Each inventories has a heading which gives the name of the deceased, his parish or place of residence, his occupation (which may be taken from other sources than the inventory), the date of the inventory, the date of exhibition or probate, the names of the appraisers, and in some cases additional genealogical information. No attempt has been made to explore exhaustively all the possible sources of genealogical information concerning the deceased. In some cases summaries of wills are added.

The List commencing on p. 88 should be consulted for alternative versions of surnames and aliases. Where two names are given in the headings of an inventory they are both quoted on the original, and are wholly different names by both of which, it may be assumed, the deceased was known.

The inventories have been transcribed exactly as written, but all amounts of money have been copied in a standarddised six-digit form, which is used on many of the originals. All roman numerals have been converted to Arabic, and sub-totals on the originals have been omitted. The names of rooms are used as sub-titles even if they are incorporated within the texts of the originals. Dashes indicate gaps on the originals caused by tears, folds or similar causes, but the inventories have been well-kept by their various custodians and such damage is rare. The totals of the inventories are those calculated by the appraisers, but the values of untotalled inventories have been calculated and inserted.

An asterisk (*) by the name of an appraiser indicates that he gave his assent to the inventory with a mrk and not with a signature.

THE INVENTORIES OF BENTHALL

1. Lawrence Andrews

Of Benthall. Inventory 17/IV/1667 by Richard Sheppard and John Gears, exhibited 6 May 1667 for the administrators.

Imprms. Brasse and pewter of all Sortes valued . . .	05	10	00
Iron Ware of all sorts	03	10	00
Linnings and Napery of all sorts valued	03	05	10
All sorts of Joyners are as Beedsteeds Table boards formes Chests chairs & the like.	10	11	00
It. his workinge tooles	03	00	00
Bedding of all sorts valued	05	15	00
It. three Cowes value	06	00	00
It. two Swyne	00	10	00
It. all kinds of woodden ware and utenses value . . .	01	06	08
It. the decedents wearing apparrell	03	00	00
totall . .	42	08	06

2. Ralph Bradley

Of Benthall 'drowned in the River Severn' 20/X/1669 and apparently not buried at Benthall or Broseley. Inventory 9/III/1671 by Ralph Bradley* and John Barnfield* exhibited 18/III/1672 (*sic*) for Jane Bradley relict and administratrix (née Guest m 1667 at Broseley, brother of George Guest *(33)*). Widow Bradley—a pauper discharged from Hearth Tax; Ralph Bradley—1 hearth.

Impr's One Chest	00	05	00
It one Bedsteed	00	03	00
It one fflocke bed one boulster a pillow one coverlid & blanket .	01	00	00
It one Iron grate two wings	00	02	06
It pewter at the price	00	10	00
It one smalle iron poot & one small Cettle . . .	00	03	00
It the wooden ware	00	06	08
It sume Course linings	00	10	00
It one frying pann	00	01	00
It one Tongs & fire shovell	00	01	00
It one Table & Iron pott with other trifells . . .	00	01	00
The sume totall . .	03	12	02

3. William Rutter

Of Benthall. According to his inventory he died 26/VIII/1679 but a William Rutter was buried at Broseley the day before. Inventory 15/IX/1679 by Jo. Matthewes, Tho. Hartshorne senior and Edward Hartshorne (his son in law *(6)*) exhibited the same day for Jane Rutter, relict and administratrix. Samuel and John Rutter yeomen also signed the bond. Presumably his sons (b 1645) and 1652 *(9)*). 4 hearths.

Imprimis. ffour small Bullocks	10	05	00
Item. Eight Cows	19	10	00
Item. four Rearing Calves	02	00	00
Item. Six working Horses and Mares	13	13	04
Item. All sorts of Graine in ye Barne	06	10	00
Item. two small Ricks of Hay	05	05	00

In the Kitchen

Brasse & pewter.	02	00	00
Item. Iron and Iron ware	01	00	00

In the Little Chambr

One table board one fforme & one Chair.	00	13	04

In the Roome over it

One standing Bed and one Truckled Bed with their ffurniture	01	06	00

In the Chambr ovr the Kitchin

One Standing Bed one Chest one Box one ffeather Bed and Bolster two Blanketts and one Coverlett .	03	02	06
Milking Pailes vessels and other Trining Ware belonging to the dayrey .	00	16	00
Linnens and othr Napery Wares .	01	10	00
The decedent's wearing Apparell and money in his pockettt	01	13	04
Earthen Ware	00	01	06
Oweing to the decedent upon Bond	06	12	00
Owing by the pish of Bentall toward the Rebuilding of the Chappell and the Erecting of the pewes .	05	00	00
ffoure swine	01	13	00
One Cart one Tumbrell and othr Implemts of Husbandry .	05	00	00
All things of Lumbr and of small value .	00	04	00
tot sum .	87	16	00

4. William Evans

Yeoman of Posenhall in Benthall but apparently not buried there or in Broseley. Inventory 20/VII/1680 by Richard Colley and William Phillips* exhibited 26/III/1683 by Alice Evans relict and executrix. Will 20/VI/1680 left his wife Alice 4 cows, a mare, the feather bed and furniture in the parlour, table board, frame and benches; his son William a year old heifer and 9 sheep; his son Robert 2 calves and 10 sheep; his daughter Margery Evans a two year old heifer and 10 sheep, the best featherbed and bolster, 3 best flaxen sheets, the best tablecloth, the best pillowbeer, the two biggest pewter dishes, 6 flaxen napkins and one of the best brass kettles; and his son George a pair of flaxen sheets. 2 hearths in Posenhall.

Impr's fowre Welch kine.	08	00	00
It Two yong bease & Two Weaneling Calves	03	00	00
Ite' one Mare & yeareling Coult.	02	10	00
Item one Sow & foure piggs	00	13	04
Item sheepe at	02	18	00
Ite' Beadsteeds beds & bedding.	00	06	00
Item Linnions of all sorts	01	10	00
Ite' Brasse & pewter	02	00	00
Item Table boords & benches & all other wooden ware	01	10	00
Ite' Imployments of husbandry	01	00	00
Ite' the deceaseds weareing Apparrell	01	00	00
Item Al things forgotten & Unaprized	00	03	04
Sume totall	24	10	08

5. John Aston, the elder

Collier of Benthall, buried 17/VII/1690 at Broseley. Inventory 15/X/1690 by John Batley, Samuel Rutter and John Andrews exhibited 21/X/1690 by George Aston son and administrator (b 1666).

Impr'mis Brasse & pewter	03	00	00
Ite' One Joyned bedstead	00	15	00
Ite' One chest three coffers & two cubboards	01	00	00
Ite' two plaine bedsteads.	00	13	04
Ite' Two feather beds & bolsters & the furniture belonging to them.	02	00	00
Ite' Two table boards & two foarms & one dresser	00	16	00
Ite' Two Hogsheads & three barrells one mitt & other Coupery ware	01	00	00

Ite' Six chaires w'th the stooles & ye rest of the wooden ware	00	06	08
Ite' ffoure maundrells one shovell one spade three wedges & other implem'ts belonging to the trade of a Collier	00	10	00
Ite' Two little iron potts & all other iron ware	01	00	00
Ite' Apry ware	03	00	00
Ite' All his wearing apparell & money in his house	03	00	00
Ite' Two swine	00	15	00
Ite' All things omitted	00	02	00
Tot	17	18	00

6. Edward Hartshorne, senior

Blacksmith of Benthall, buried 30/V/1693, two days after he died. Inventory 24/IV/1694 by George and Ralph Hartshorne exhibited 27/IV/1694 by Rebecca Hartshorne relict and administratrix (daughter of William Rutter *(3)*, sister of John Hartshorne (m 1670).

Imprs. In ye Dwelling house
one grate 1 jack one small table one fir sclice & tounges pewter & brass woodware earthenware with other convenient things prized 08 10 04

It. In ye Parlor
3 round small tables 12 chairs a clock a grate 1 payer of tounges a parcell of small books prized to ye value of 3 pounds 15 shill 6 pence 03 15 06

It. In ye Chamber over ye parlor
two feather beds & bedsteads with hangings hillings convenient Six Chaiers one Chest & one looking glass one small table a grate prizd to ye value of 7 pounds 4 shill 4 pence . . . 07 04 04

It. In ye Chamber over ye house
two feather beds & bedsteads with hangings & hillings one press two chests two small trunks six Chaires one side cobbert Prizd to ye value of eight pounds one shilling 08 01 00

It. In ye Cockloft over ye house & Parlour Chamber
five Lodging beds 2 tables & two fourmes one box Prizd to ye value of four pounds & six pence . . . 04 00 06

It. In sheets Napkins table Clothes towels pillows beares & small Linings Prizd to ye Value of eight pounds 17 shill & six pence . 08 17 06

THE INVENTORIES OF BENTHALL

The Wearing Cloths of ye deceased Edw Hartshorne of all sorts prized to ye value of three pounds 14 shillings . . .	03	14	00

It. In ye seller

three barrels two hogeheds 3 tubs 1 Mitt prized to ye Value of 4 pounds	04	00	00

It. In ye shop

one payer of bellyes one Anvell one vice toungs & other convenient tools thereto belonging prized to ye value of seaven pounds five shillings	07	05	00

It. In Chattle

One Cow one Mare one small pigg Prizd to 5 pounds 11 shilling .	05	11	00
The whole sum Amounting to . .	60	19	04

7. Thomas Beard

Trowman of Benthall, buried 'pater fam.' 7/IX/1706. Inventory 9/IX/1706 by Thomas Hughes and Ustas Beard* exhibited 11/VI/1707 by Richard Bartlem trowman of Benthall now husband to Sara relict and administratrix. 6 children all under age.

Item. one middle sized Trowe and one small Barge with their riggin materialls thereunto belonging	60	00	00
Item. one ffeather Bedd and bolster two Pillowes one Rugg two blanketts and bedsteeds and other necessaries thereunto belonging	06	05	00
Item. Two flock bedds two bolsters two pillowes four blanketts one Rugg and bedsteeds and other necessaries thereunto belonging	03	00	00
Item two paire of fflaxen sheetes two paire of hempen sheetes six paire of hurden sheets and ffour pillow beirs . .	03	16	00
Table Linen Two Table clothes one dozen of hurden napkins and other small Towells	00	12	00
Item one Joyned press one small Cupboard Two Joyned Chests one old Trunck Three small boxes one old coffer . . .	01	15	00
Item. Three small Tables one Joyned Chaire one dozen of small segg Chaires and Three Joynd stooles	00	19	00
Item. Ffive small barrells six small stunds one paile and other necessary woodenware belonging thereunto one Joynd cradle .	01	05	00
Item. ffour brass Potts three brass Kettles one brass pann two warmeing pan two Candlesticks Two brass Andirons two small skormers two small brass Ladles	05	09	00

Item. nineteen Pewter dishes sixteen plates Three pewter Canns two candlesticks one small bason halfe a dozen of porringers one small salt one Chamber pott	05	00	00
Item. two small broaches one small Jack one Grate and other necessary Iron worke belonging to the fire . . .	01	00	00
Item. ordinary things unmentioned	00	05	00
one swine	01	00	00
Item. one speriall bond with other goods and lawfull debts amounting to	20	00	00
Item. the deceds wearing Apparrell	05	00	00
Totall . .	115	06	08

8. Andrew Dodson

Trowman of Benthall, buried 19/XI/1708 'pater fam.'. Inventory 25/XI/1708 by Tho. Evans, Tho. Coape and Ustius Beard exhibited 8/XI/1709 by Elizabeth Dodson relict and administratrix. No will.

Imprs. for Wearing Apparell		05	00	00
for Pockitt Mony	(oblit)	00	00	00
for one Trowe		80	00	00
5 ffether Beds and all things belonging to them . . .		30	00	00
2 flock Beds and all things belonging to them . . .		01	10	00
Sixteen Pewter Dishes		02	10	00
9 Plates 3 Pewter Quarts 3 pints 1 Pewter Cann . . .		01	01	06
1 fornis 2 Iron Pots 2 little Marments 1 pasnit . . .		02	00	00
2 Driping Pans		00	10	00
1 Jack and 3 Broaches		01	06	00
1 grate fireshuel and tongs and oather small Iron Ware . .		01	00	00
4 tables and five forms		02	15	00
2 screens 2 Gine stools		01	00	00
2 Gine Presses 1 Dissen of Chears		02	10	00
3 Chests 5 Boxes		02	00	00
4 Hogshits 6 Barrels		03	00	00
3 Coolers and oather Woodden vessels		01	10	00
1 Clock and Clock case		02	10	00
3 Swine		01	10	00
for Stock of Drink		12	00	00
Lining of all sorts		10	00	00
Debts due and desperate		05	00	00
Toto . .		169	12	06

9. John Rutter

Yeoman of Benthall, buried [according to Much Wenlock register at Benthall] 25/XII/1708 'pater fam.' (56y). Inventory 7/I/1708 by Rd. Littlehales, Tho. Green and Rd. Woofe* exhibited for Mr. Richard Benthall executor 13, who took the oath 22/III/1708. Nuncupative will on or about 18/XII/1708 left his brother Samuel all goods wood and timber; his sister Martha Jones (b 1657) £1 and his nephew James Hartshorne, son of his sister Rebecca (b 1647) £1. No provision apparently made for his own children. Probably son of William Rutter (3).

Imprs. in the house

One long Table	00	03 06
One Cupboard	00	05 00
One Skreen	00	02 00
ffive Pewter Dishes	00	12 00
One Brass Pott	00	14 00
One Brass Kettle	00	10 00
One joyned forme & one joyned Chair	00	02 00
Six Wood Chaires	00	03 00
One warming Pann	00	01 00
One Iron Driping Pann	00	03 06
One Iron Jack	00	05 00
A Chees Plate a Tinnen Pann & other lumber	00	02 06

In the Room over the house

Two ffeather Bedds & Blanketts bedsteads & furniture thereto belonging	02	10 00
Two little Tables	00	04 00
One wooden Chair	00	00 09

At the Stair head

One Deske & one Coffer	00	03 04

In the Cockloft

One fflock bedd & steads thereto belonging	00	04 02

In the Parlor

One long Table & other Lumber	00	04 07

In the room over it

One fflock bedd & bedsteads	00	04 08

In the Kitchin

Two ffurnaces	03	10 00

Two barrells & a hogshead	00	06	00
A kneading Mitt	00	02	00
A Cheese Tubb & a Churne	00	04	00
ffour Chees vates & other wooden ware	00	03	00
Two broaches & otherold Iron ware	00	04	00

In the room over the Kitchin

One broken Chest	00	01	06
One Coffer	00	00	09
The deceds wearring apparell	02	00	00
Provision in the house of all sorts	08	00	00
Eight Cows	17	00	00
Eight Oxen	19	00	00
ffour old horses	06	00	00
Two Swine	01	13	04
Implements of husbandry & for wagoning	04	15	00
Wagon wheeles	07	05	00
Corn in the barne unthrashed	00	14	00
Oates unthrashed	00	03	06
Barly unthrashed	01	02	06
hay	10	00	00
	78	19	07

10. Joseph Reynolds

Gent of Posenhall in Benthall, buried 12/VII/1712. Inventory 18/VII/1712 by John Chilton of the Wike and Thomas Wellings of Posenhall exhibited for Francis Reynolds brother and Mr. William Reynolds, Mr. William Icke and Richard Geeres kinsmen. Will 5/III/1712 left his wife Elizabeth a messuage in Posenhall and the personal estate for her life. After his son William was to have the messuage, the half tester bedsteads in the hall chamber, the pantry table and dish bench; William's son Richard the long table and 6 joined stools in the hall adjoining the parlour, the malt mill and the iron furnace hanging in the brewhouse and William's other children, John, Joseph and Elizabeth 20s. each; his granddaughters Elizabeth and Martha Allen one box and the linen therein in the cockloft, Elizabeth to have the shorter chest in the hall chamber as well; and his daughter Mary wife of Amos Hands was residual legatee.

Imprimis In the hall Chamber

One ffeather bed, Two boulsters and six blanketts	05	00	00
Two Chaff beds and one fflock bed	01	00	00
Two pair of bedsteads and one sett of hanings	01	00	10
one Chest and desk	00	15	00

A new peice of fflaxen Cloth	00	15 00
Sheets, Napkins, pillow beers & other Linnen of all sorts in the same Chamber	05	10 00
Three dozen of hatcheled fflax	00	18 00

In the parlour Chamber

one ffeather bed boulster Chaff bed, one pillow & Three blanketts	04	00 00
a Dressing Table.	00	02 06

In the Kittchen and Buttery Chamber

one ffeather bed two Chaff beds, ffive blanketts, Three Coverletts bedsteads and hangings	03	10 00

In the Cheese Chamber

Eleaven pair of hurden sheets and other linnens	02	15 00
Two Coffers, a Candle box, six cheese boards and Eighteen Cheeses	01	10 00

In the Inner and Outwd Cockloft

Old household goods and things of all sorts	02	00 00

In the Brewhouse

Brewing tubbs and vessells of all sorts	01	10 00
A Cheese press & large Iron beam & scales	02	00 00

In the hall

A Joyn'd forme, ffive old Chaires two Cushions & a large Twiggen baskett	00	05 00

In the parlour

a large Ovell Table a Cupboard & nine Joyn'd Chaires	02	00 00

In the Buttery

Three barrells an old hanging Cupboard & a small Twiggen baskett with othr old things	01	00 00

In the Milk house

Two barrels, a Churn, Eight Cheese ffatts, two pailes, two Gawnes, & severall other milk vessells & Wooden Ware	00	17 00

In the Dwelling house

ffifteen pewter Dishes wth some pewter plates	02	05 00
Brass of all sorts	03	10 00
Iron Ware of All sorts (The Jack excepted) with other odde things	02	00 00

In the mault house

ffellyes wth all sorts of Old things belonging to husbandry .	01	00 00

In the Convenient house

Three pair of Stocks & ffellyes	01	10 00
other Implemts of husbandry of all sorts	05	00 00
A Stallion horse, a Mare & two Colts	15	00 00
A Yoake of Oxen	11	10 00
four Cows a two year old heifer & a bull	22	00 00
Tenn Sheep	01	15 00
Three Calves	01	10 00
Two hog swine & three little piggs	01	15 00
Three & Twenty Strike Soweing of Wheate and Measeling. .	14	00 00
Twelve Strike Soweing of Barley	05	08 00
Six Strike Soweing of pease	01	16 00
Eighteen Strike Soweing of Oates	04	10 00
A Strike Soweing of ffetches	00	05 00
his Weareing Apparrell & Money in his purse . . .	10	00 00
Things Omitted & not herein pticulrly mentioned . . .	00	13 04
It. for hay	07	00 00
Tot . .	142	04 10

11. Catherine Hartshorne

Spinster and serving maid of Benthall. In her will she asked to be buried in Benthall church. Inventory 1/XII/1712 by Ralph Harper* and Thomas Hartshorne exhibited 23/VI/1713 by Mary Brian *alias* Hartshorne sister and executrix. Her mother and another sister, both called Elinor Hartshorne, were also executrices. Will 19/V/1712 left £16 of wages due from Philip Benthall Esq. of Benthall to her mother and 3 sisters, Mary Hartshorne *alias* Bryan, Cornelia wife of Francis Oakes and Elinor Maund.

Impr's the Dec'ds wearing apparell with other necessary Linnens belonging to a Servant maid	05	00 00
Item four Sheep, 1 pewter Can 1 pewter Dish & 3 small pewter plates	00	15 06
Item Good & Lawfull wages in the hands of Phillip Benthall Esqr	16	00 00
Item And alsoe in the hands of Rich'd Benthall Esqr . .	02	15 00
Wooll & fflax	00	15 00
Tot . .	25	05 06

12. George Bradley

Trowman of Benthall but not apparently buried there. Inventory 7/I/1719 by John Benbow and Tho. Hartshorne exhibited 9/II/1719 for Jane Bradley relict and administratrix (b 1668 daughter of Adam Stokes *(34)* m 1689). Their 3 sons, George (b 1690), William (b 1694) and John (b 1697) were all trowmen. Bradley used several boats but most often 'the Duchess' working her himself from Montgomery carrying mainly lead.

Goods in the Kitchen

Impris. Iron ware of all sorts for necessary use	01	00	00
Pewter dishes and plates with some other small useful things	02	00	00
One old Press one old screen one small table and two old dressers.	00	11	00
one dozen and three comon chaires belonging to the use of the house	00	15	00
Item. One Clock and two small round Tables in the parlour	02	00	00

Item in the brewing house and buttery

One old fformace one small Boyler five Barrells and four old Coolers.	02	01	06
Item ffive reasonable Lodging Bedds and bedsteeds and all things necessary therunto belonging in the dwelling house.	10	00	00

Item above Staires

one looking Glass three small square tables two Middleing Chests of Drawers one Joyn's chest one small Cupboard.	02	02	06
Item Table Linnen three Tablecloths three dozen of Napkins overworn	00	18	00
Item three indifferent resonable vessells and two old Boats upon the River of Severn and all Implements thereunto belonging	80	00	00
Item the deceds wearing Apparrel	01	10	00
Item debts sperate and desperate.	02	00	00
Item Some old Lumber things not named	00	05	00
Tot	123	03	00

13. Richard Benthall

Esq of Benthall Hall, Benthall, buried 9/V/1720. Inventory 26/V/1720 by Samuel Littlehales, Thomas Hewlett, Richard Pitt and Richard Weaver exhibited 26/IX/1720 by Mrs. Elizabeth Brown spinster, 'beloved friend and kinswoman' and executrix to whom he owed £1,050. Will 28/VI/1717 left all to her for life and then to his nephew Walter Langley gent of Rotherham, Yorkshire.

Imprs. In the little Parlor

The Brewroe at.	05	00	00
Thirteene cane chaires at.	02	00	00
one Repeating Clock at.	03	00	00
one Little Joyn'd Table at	00	02	00
Pictures & Mapps at	00	10	00
One ffire showell, one pair of Tongues one ffender & one poker.	00	05	00

Item. In the Hall

One Long Table & fformes at	01	00	00
Two Ovell Tables at	00	18	00
Six old chaires at	00	04	00
five old Guns & one pair of pistolls	03	05	00
One old Iron Grate at	00	03	00

Item. In the Smoaking Roome

Two tables at	00	04	00
One ffire showell & one pair of Tonges one poker, one Fender & one Plate at	00	05	00
One pair of Tables at	00	01	06

Item. In the Great parlor

Three old Tables at	00	03	00
Two dozen of Bark Hoopes at	00	04	00
A still & Brandard at	00	07	00
Severall Odd things there at	00	05	00
Corn ready threshed & Winnowed at	06	00	00

Item. In the passage leading from the hall to the Great parlor

One old leather Saddle & Bridle at	00	05	00

Item. In the Stair Case

One old Clocke.	00	05	00

Item. In the Testators Roome & Clossett

A Bedstedd ffether Bed Boulsters & Hangings	02	10	00
one Chest of Drawers at.	00	10	00
one Large Box at	00	03	00
one Easy Chair at	00	10	00
Two old Looking Glasses at	00	02	00
one old Dale Box at	00	00	06
one Fireshovel one pair of Tongs one Fender one poker & Brush at some other odd things of small use	00	05	00

THE INVENTORIES OF BENTHALL

Item. In Old Mr.Benthall's Clossett

Some odd Things at	00	02	06

Item. In the Middle Roome

A Red ffeather Bed Boulster pillowes hangings Quilt & Blanketts at	05	00	00
Two Chaires at	00	04	00
One ffireshovel one pair of Tongs & Poker . .	00	02	00
One looking Glass at	00	05	00
One close stool at	00	02	00

Item. in the Red Roome

A Bedstedd ffeather Bedd Hangins Coverlid Quilt Blanketts Boulsters Pillows & window Curtaines at	07	00	00
ffower chaires at.	00	08	00
One ffire showell One pair of Tongs one ffender & one Poker at.	00	04	00
One Table one Stand & one Close Stool . . .	00	05	00

Item. in the Dineing Roome

A Bedstedd Bed Blanketts Boulster & Rugg at . .	00	10	00
Three Tables at	00	04	00
Dale Boards & other Boards at	00	05	00
Eight Stone of wool at	00	00	00
Lumber & other Things of small worth . . .	00	04	00

Item. In the Buttery Chamber

One Bed Bedstedd Hangings Blanketts Boulsters pillow & Coverlidd side Table & Chair at	00	15	00

Item. In the Kitchen Chamber

One Bedstedd ffeather Bedd hangings Blanketts Boulster pillow & Coverlidd	01	05	00
Two Tables & Two chaires at	00	02	00
one ffire shovel one pair of Tongs one Poker & one Bellows .	00	03	06

Item. In the Paistrey Chamber

One Bedstedd ffeather Bedd Hangings Boulster Blanketts & Rugg at	01	10	00
one old chair at	00	00	04

Item. In the passage leding towards ye starching Roome

Linnen & Linnen cloth at	08	00	00
New Blew cloth at	02	00	00
Two Chests & one Close stool at.	00	10	00

One pillion & cloth at	00	08	00
Lumber at	00	01	00

Item. In the starching Roome

A Bed Boulster & Blanketts at	00	10	00
one old chest & ye Hurden Yarn therein	00	05	00
Two pair of Yarn Blades at	00	02	00
Lumber at	00	01	00

Item. In the Mens Garrett

Two Bedstedds with Bedds Boulsters and Blanketts at . .	01	00	00

Item. In the Middle Garrett

One Bedstedd a few feathers a few Ash Boards & other Lumber at	01	05	00

Item. In the Cheese chamber

Three old chests shelves & Benches	00	10	00
hoopes at	01	00	00
Trenchers at	00	04	00

Item. I Mr.Green's Clossett

fflax & hemp dressed & undressed	05	00	00
Candles at	00	05	00

Item. In the Buttery

An old Table & fforme at	00	02	00
A Bing at	00	02	06

Item. In the Inner Butery

One Table & Shelves at	00	02	06
Knives & fforks at	00	07	06
Glass ware wooden ware and Earthen ware there at . .	00	04	00

Item. In the Paistrey

A Dresser Table & a kneading Tubb	00	02	06

Item. In the Kitchen

Pewter plates at	01	10	00
All other Pewter there at.	02	10	00
Tin ware at	00	03	00
Brass ware at	00	15	00
Iron ware there vizt Racks Spitts Dripping Pan an old Jack two Iron potts & other iron things at	03	00	00

A warming pan	00	02	06
A Table a Salt Box & two chaires	00	04	00
A Gun case at	00	05	00
Water Pailes & other Wooden Ware	00	02	00

Item. In the Wett Larder

Three Powdring Tubbs & Benches	00	10	00

Item. In the Brewhouse

One Malt Mill at.	00	10	00
Some old Brewing Vessells at	01	00	00
A Brass Pott & Kettle at.	00	10	00
one old Cheese press & Soapeing Tubb	00	05	00
Two wash Tubbs & Benches at	00	02	00

Item. In the Dairey

One Brass pan at	00	07	00
Wooden ware Belonging to the Dairy	01	00	00
one cooller at	00	06	00
Earthen Ware there at	00	01	00

Item. In the Ale Cellar

Eight old hogshedds at	02	00	00
ffive Barrells & other small Vessells	00	15	00

Item. In the Small Beer Cellar

ffour hogshedds & one Barrell at.	01	00	00
one old Barm Tubb & Tunning Dish at	00	01	06
Glass Bottles there at	00	10	00

Item. In the Court

Two old ffurnaces at	01	00	00

Item. In the Hackney Stable & Chamber over it

One old Saddle one old Bridle one Collar and one Leather Portmanteau	00	05	00
Malt	10	00	00
Oates ready Thrashed & Winnow'd at	03	00	00

Item. In and Belonging to the Gardens

One stone roll at	00	03	00
one Standing Ladder at	00	01	06
one wattering pan	00	00	06
one Garden Sythe one pair of Garden sheares one Rake one Spade one Haugh & one Wyre Riddle at	00	04	06

Two old Mares one young one & three old Horses	15	15	00
one Bull & Eight Cowes at	30	05	00
Eight Oxen at	31	05	00
young Cattle & Calves	31	12	06
sheep of all sorts at	17	05	00
Swine at.	10	05	06
Poultrey at	00	10	00
Wheat muncorn Barley Pease Oates & Vetches growing on ye ground	52	14	00
Corn in the Barn thrash'd & unthrash'd	06	00	00
hay at	05	02	06
Muck at.	02	00	00
Implements of Husbandrey	14	14	04
Coal Waggons & an Iron chain at	11	00	00
one Clamp of Bricks at	10	10	00
Iron Stone ready gott at	24	02	06
Lymestone ready gott	03	17	00
Coles ready gott at	01	16	00
Pipe makers clay at	02	06	10½
Testators Wearing Apparell Two old Swords and money in his Pockett	08	00	00
Six silver Spoons at	02	10	00
one old silver watch at	02	00	00
ffive old Gold Rings at	02	00	00
Money in the House in Gold Silver & Brass	34	09	10½
Debts Sperate	28	14	10
Debts desp'ate	38	18	06
Things omitted & out of sight	02	00	00
	502	05	03

14. Eustace Beard, senior

Waterman/trowman of Benthall, buried 4/I/1725. Inventory 30/V/1726 by Thomas Hughs and Jno. Hartshorne exhibited 14/VI/1726 for James Beard son and one of the executors. Thomas Hughs of Broseley was the other. Presumably his wife Mary (née Armishrew m 1674) was already dead. Will 23/XII/1725 left his son in law Edward Lloyd senior 1s. and his grandson Edward Lloyd junior £10 to be put to use he having the interest until he comes of age; Nephews John and Thomas Beard and their sister 1 guinea each and Richard and Ustas Beard the same. His son James was residual legatee.

Goods in the house and above Stiars belonging to the deed.

Imprs. One long table and form	00	10	00
Itm. One old Cubbert press	00	04	06
Itm Two old brass kettles a larg one and a little one and one old warming pan	00	15	06
Itm. three old small pewter dishes two plates and one small tankard	00	05	10
Itm. two old damnified barrells	00	02	06
Itm. One half headed pair of bedsteads one overworn flock bedd and bedding belonging to the same	00	08	06
Itm. One Middling Joyn Chest One Joyn Chair one old Side Table a lesser Joyn Chair	00	08	10
Itm. One overworn pair of flaxen sheets one old Table Cloth and half a dozen of very much overworn Napkins . . .	00	06	02
Itm. The Deceaseds old Wearing apparell and other Woolen Cloth for to make more apparell so designed	02	00	00
Itm. Ropes and Sails and other materialls being old rigging for a Waterman's use	14	10	00
Itm. all other old Lumbers not worth mentioning . . .	00	02	00
Total . .	19	13	10

15. Beatrice Gears

Widow and sojourner of Benthall, buried 20/III/1727. Inventory 2/V/1728 by John and Morris Hartshorne exhibited 4/VI/1728 for Thomas Hartshorne son in law and one of the executors. Her daughter Joyce Gears was the other. Will 7/III/1727 left her grandchildren Richard Gears of Broseley, William, Richard and Elizabeth Gears all of Much Wenlock 1s. each; her daughter Elizabeth Hartshorne £10, the best suit of clothes, a silver laced petticoat, 2 shifts, 1 silk and 1 laced handkerchief and a white apron; her son in law Thomas Hartshorne 1 guinea of gold 'towards his trouble'; her granddaughter Mary Hartshorne the shift 'which is too long for me', a pair of white holland sleeves and a white laced handkerchief. Her daughter Joyce was residual legatee. The executors were to get the arrears of rent due from her son Richard Gears deceased for her freehold called Stanwell in Kinlet.

Impr's One Joyn Chest	00	05	00
Item One Joyn Chair and Nursing Chair	00	05	00
Item The Deceaseds Wearing Apparrill	02	00	00
Item Money in the Deceaseds Custody	04	05	00
Item One Other Small Joyn Cubbort One Old Coffer One Old Trunk	00	04	00

Item Rents due to the deceased from Margaret Gearse Relect of Richard Gearse Late of Brosley and Sole Executrix to the said Richard Gearse Deceased	12	00	00
Item Some Small Necessary Linings Belonging to the Deceased not worth mentioning	00	10	0
Inventory toto	19	09	00

16. Hugh Cullis

Of Benthall, buried 27/IX/1729. Inventory 9/II/1729 by John Beard and Charles Hartshorne exhibited 3/III/1729 for Thomas Cullis son and executor. Will 23/IX/1729 left his son Thomas all including the house and vessel, excepting only 1s. each to his son Samuel, an unnamed daughter and his grandson Samuel Cullis.

In the Dwelling hous

Impr's Ten pewter dishes & six plates	00	12	00
It' One dresser & drawers, three Tables, One Skreen	01	09	00
It' One Boiler, one pott, One Mortar, one Broach	00	08	00

In the Celler

It' Two Barrels, two Tubbs	00	06	00

In the Chamber over ye Dwelling house

It' Two old pair of Bedsteeds & Bedding thereon and ffurniture thereunto belonging, also one old clock, one Table, one Chest, six old Chaires	02	10	00

In the Chamber over the Celler

It' One Bed & ffurniture one chest	01	00	00

In ye house now in ye possion of Michael Barnett

It' One table, One Jack, two Broches, One Grate, three pewter dishes, One large Cupboard, two Tubbs, One Mitt, One Cask, one Brass ffurnace in the Wall, One large Chest, One hanging press, one pair of Bedsteeds & Hangings.	04	10	00
It' the Deceaseds Wearing Apparrell	00	18	06
Lumber of all sorts unmentioned.	00	10	00
Money in the Deceaseds purse	00	05	00
Tot	12	05	00

17. William Day

Trowman of Benthall, buried 7/VI/1742. Inventory 4/VIII/1742, appraisers not named, exhibited 7/IX/1742 for Mary Day relict and executrix. John Day was also executor. Will 22/V/1742 left his wife the house for life until remarriage then to son Isaac (b 1735). the trow on the Severn was to be sold and £40 of the proceeds to be used to bring up the children.

In the Dwelling House

A Dresser of Drawers and Pewter frame and Pewter thereon	01	01	00
A small fire Grate table and Chairs	00	10	06

In the Chambers Over the House

Three Pair of Bedsteds and Beding thereon with other ffurniture there	02	10	00

In the Buttery

Small Barrils and Brewing Vessells	00	12	06

Upon the River Severn

One Water Vessell called a Trow being Mentioned in the Deceaseds Will is found to be Much Damaged Decay'd and out of repair and is adgudg'd by Experienced Workmen not worth above	12	00	00
The Deceaseds Wearing Apparrill.	01	01	00
totall	17	15	00

18. Daniel Dea or Day, the elder

Yeoman/barge owner of Benthall, buried 29/XII/1742. Inventory 29/VI/1743 by Geo. Rowley and Jno. Hartshorne exhibited 12/VII/1743 by Mary Dea relict and executrix. Will 15/IX/1738 left his wife Mary everything for life then to children. The youngest son Daniel Dea was to have the house.

In the Dwelling house

Pewter of all sorts with two Iron Potts & Brass Kettle	00	17	00
Two Tables A Screen a form and Joyn stool	00	09	00
A ffire Grate fire shovel and tongs	00	03	00
Two spits a Cast Iron fire plate and two Warming Pans	00	05	00
All other Lumber and things Unmentioned therein	00	05	00

In the Chamber over the House

Two Pair of Bedsteds and Beding thereon	02	02	00
A Chest and Linnen therein	00	18	00

In the Garrets

A Pair of Bedsteds and Beding thereon an Old Coffer	00	09	00
The Deceaseds Wearing Apparrill.	00	10	00

Upon the River Severn

Two Boats	01	10	00

In the Cellar

Two Barrils two wash tubs and a Cooler .	00	12	00
All other Lumber and things unmentioned	00	05	00
Totall	08	05	00

19. Thomas Hartshorne

Tobacco pipe maker of the Hilltop in Benthall, buried 6/V/1743. Inventory 10/IX/1743 by Jno. Instone and Thomas Pitt exhibited 12/IX/1743 by Morris Hartshorne executor and 'a good help child to us his aged parents both in duty and assistance ever since he was able to work still using a god conscience'. Will 12/IX/1741 left his son John a 'silver spoon marked with his own name in to letters and bought with my own money' and the vice and materials belonging; his son Robert a silver spoon marked RGB on the back and two bedsteads 'by the fireside in my chamber if he will accept them'; his son Thomas a silver spoon marked RGB on the back, 'my Joyn box, my pewter can & my pewter dish marked with my own name'; 'my poor lame and decriped wife' all the rest for life then to his son Morris.

In the Kitchen

A Brass Pan, two Brass Potts, three Brass Kettles, two Pr. of Candlesticks, A Brass Morter and Pestell	01	10	00
Ten Pewter Dishes, fourteen pewter plates, two pewter tankards, One Pewter Candlestick, a pewter Chamber pot a pewter Salt and Mustard Pott	01	10	00

A fire Grate three pair of Tongs. One fire Shovel a fire plate two spitts A dreeping Pan 2 Cleevers 2 flesh forks . . .	01	01	00
An Iron Morter and pestell	00	05	00
A parcell of Tinn Ware	00	02	00
A Warming Pan and frying Pan	00	04	00
Two tables a fourm and Joyn Stool	00	07	00
Two Joyn Chairs, two Ash bottom'd Chairs, three Segg Chairs and a Chafing Dish	00	08	00
Three Smothing Irons A pair of Bellows & a basting Spoon .	00	03	06
A Pair of Hedge Sheers and a Cast Iron fireplace . . .	00	02	06
A Bible and some other Old Books	00	16	00

In the Scullery

A Small Boyler two Iron Potts and pothooks One Marment .	00	10	00
An Old Vice two pails and Other Lumber . . .	00	05	00

In the little Room and Buttery

A Press Cubbert a fourm a Table and Churn three small measures ffour Old Barrils two Milking Gauns a Tuning dish . .	00	10	00

In the Chambers above stairs

Three feather Beds bolsters and Pillows	04	10	00
A flock bed and bolster one Coverlid	00	07	06
Three Rugs four Blankets	01	10	00
Three pair of Bedsteds one sett of Curtains . . .	01	10	00
A Side table and Glass three chests three Boxes a trunk and Close stool	01	10	00
One Silver Cup and Eight Silver Spoons	03	00	00
Three pair of flaxen sheets 3 pair of hemp sheets 4 pair of Hurden sheets 2 Dozen of Napkins 3 pillow beers . . .	03	00	00
A table a Coffer two Cairs and other odd things . . .	00	12	00
The Deceased Wearing Apparrill	01	01	00

In the Shop

A parcell of Old Tobacco pipe tools	00	12	06
Three Spining Wheels 2 Coolers and two tubs . . .	00	12	00
A parcell of rakes and Pike Evils 2 Dresing rakes an Old Sythe .	00	04	00
A Mathook a hack an Ax, a broomhook & two spades . .	00	06	00
All other Lumber and things not particularly Mentioned . .	00	05	00

In the Ground

Two Milking Cows	06	15	00
A small rick of Hay	01	00	00
Inventory totall . .	35	08	00

20. William Smith

Miner/collier of Benthall but apparently not buried there. (34y). Inventory 22/IV/1752 by Geo. Smith and Jno. Hartshorne exhibited 27/IV/1752 by Abigail Smith mother, executrix and residual legatee. Will 8/V/1750 left his sister Ann Smith (b 1731) £5; his sister Margaret Smith his watch and 1 guinea; and his brother George his share of tools belonging to the Ironstore works but to allow his mother what is reasonable for their use, and all wearing apparel including one 'coat cloth blue coloured'.

Tools & Materials belonging to Iron Stone Works (to whit) five Waggons, 6 Mandrills, 2 Dressors, 2 Basketts, 3 shovels, 6 Iron Wheel Cases: 2 Axes	05	00	00
A Clock and Case	01	15	00
A Silver Watch	02	10	00
A fire Grate	00	10	06
The Deceaseds Wearing Apparrell & Linnens and Money in his purse	03	10	00
	13	05	06

21. Richard Aston

Collier of Benthall, buried 26/IX/1753. Inventory (not dated) by Wm. Gittins and Timothy Price* exhibited 21/IX/1756 by Rebecca Aston relict and John Aston son executors. Will 3/IX/1753 left his wife Rebecca the house then to their son John Aston, he to pay £5 to the other son George.

In the Cellar

One Hogshead one Half Hogshead, 4 Barrells all old ones	00	18	00

In the Brewhouse

Two mashing Tubs, three old Water Tubs	00	10	00
One kneading Tub, two Benches	00	03	00
One Water Pail, one Gawn, one Tunning dish (old ones)	00	01	06
One Boiler	00	03	06

In the Kitchen

Nine Pewter Dishes, sixteen Pewter Plates	01	10	06
One Pewter Chamber Pott, one Tankard, 5 Porringers	00	03	00
Two pewter Quart Measures, one Pewter Cup	00	02	00

THE INVENTORIES OF BENTHALL

Fifteen Wooden Trenchers	00	01	00
One old Dresser and Drawers and Pewter Frame.	00	08	00
One old screen, one old Cupboard	00	04	00
One little Table.	00	01	00
Two Spits, two little Brass Candlesticks, one Little Fire Plate and one little Dripping Pan.	00	03	00
One little old Grate and one Pair of Tongs	00	02	00
One old Frying pan. one old Warming Pan	00	03	00
Two little Iron Potts, one brass Kettle	00	03	00

Over the Kitchen

Two Beds and Bedsteads.	02	10	00
One Hanging Press & one Table (old ones)	00	10	00
One little Chest & one old Trunk	00	05	00
One form one Box, one old Arm Chair.	00	01	06
6 Plain Wood Chairs, 4 segg ones	00	06	00
6 Pair of old Hurden sheets, 1 Table Cloth & 6 Napkins.	00	13	06
	09	02	06

THE INVENTORIES OF BROSELEY

22. Mr. Francis Adams

Gent of Broseley buried 12/III/1667. Inventory 27/III/1668 by Audley Bowdler and Richard Sheppard gent and exhibited 22/IV/1668 for William Jerman a 'faithful and trust servant' and executor. Will and codicil both 20/X/1667. Adam's son John *(27)*.

Imprms. Eight oxen value	25	00	00
Itm. Eleven horses and Coults val.	52	00	00
Itm. Carts Waynes Plowes harrowes and all other Implements of husbandry and Edg tooles value	22	00	00
Ite. Saddles Bridles & all other furniture belonging to the stables value	02	10	00
Itm. All sorts of Corne & graine threshed value	17	00	00
Itm. Corne & graine of all sorts groweing value	21	00	00
Itm. hay in the Barnes value	12	00	00
Itm. Gould PLates & ready mony	140	03	00
Itm. the decedents signett Ring val.	01	10	00
Itm. Linnings & Napy of all sorts val.	25	00	00
Itm. ffether bedds & flockbedes of all sorts value.	30	00	00
Itm. Covletts Blanketts Curtaines valends & Bedhillings value	20	00	00
Itm. Table Boards Chairs Bedsteeds ffurmes Cubbarts Chests Truncks stooles & all other Joyners ware val.	20	00	00
Itm. Carpetts and Cushions value.	02	10	00
Itm. All sorts of Brasse pewter and Iron ware within the house val.	19	00	00
Itm. Cowpy and Turners ware of all sorts withing the house valued	06	00	00
Itm. Bookes of all sorts valued	13	06	08
It. A Clock & a Jack value	02	10	00
Itm. Weapons gunns a Crosse Bowe and other Armory value	04	00	00
Itm. Waggons Ropes Chaines and all other Tooles belonging to ye Coleworks val.	20	00	00
Itm. debts owinge to the decedent without pacialty	08	00	00
Itm. the decedents wearing apparell val.	13	06	08
Itm. Muck or Compost & all other things of small value before omitted.	02	00	00
totall	488	06	04

23. Thomas Crew

(Pedlar in Royal Aid 1661) of Broseley but apparently not buried there. Inventory 29/IV/1668 by Thomas Farmer, Richard Bird, Edward Davis and Fra. Huxly exhibited 26/V/1668 for Elinor Crew relict. A week before, Robert Ogden and Richard Knott clerks had been commissioned to take her oath because she unable to travel to Ludlow. Administration granted on the 21st.

ffor Bond lase ribon & other small comodities	07	00	00
ffor 12 remnants of holland	04	00	00
ffor 14 remnants of Schoch Cloth dimitie & calico	02	00	00
ffor 2 remnants of grene say	00	10	00
ffor tafita ribons & fferrets ribon	02	00	00
ffor 2 dozen of Course Bodies	02	00	00
ffor 4 psells of pins gloves knives & inckle	00	06	08
Several remnants of ribons and blew linen	02	00	00
ffor combes & colored thred	00	05	00
Severall remnants of Cotton tapes & Cadis	00	10	00
ffor one table Burd & Charpett & Chest & other goods below Stayes [trumpery deleted]	01	00	00
ffor 1 table 1 Chest bras & pewter & 2 iron pots in the kichen	02	00	00
ffor 3 ffliches Bacon	01	00	00
ffor 1 ffether bed & 3 Chaff Beds & other necessaries belonginge to the same	04	00	00
ffor wearings reparrell	02	00	00
debts owenge	01	00	00
in money in the house	00	09	06
Item lynnen of all sortes vizt sheetes table clothes and napkins valued at	01	10	00
Itm Iron ware of all sortes valued at	00	12	00
Itm. wooden ware of all sortes	00	10	00
Itm. two store piggs	00	12	00
Itm. two chests above stayres val. at	00	04	00
Sum tot.	34	09	02

24. Jones Edward

Of Broseley but apparently not buried there. Inventory 14/V/1668 by William Adams and Henery Taylor* exhibited 19/V/1668 for Jane Jones relict and administratrix. Young children.

THE INVENTORIES OF BROSELEY

Imprim's Pewter of all sorts value	00	15	06
It'm All sorts of Iron ware value	00	13	06
It'm Bedding of all sorts both wollen & Lininge value	03	07	00
It'm Bedsteds value	00	15	00
It'm Lynnings & Na'y of all sorts value	00	09	00
It' All sorts of Joyned ware & other wodden ware or lumber value	00	18	00
It'm Proviscon in the house value	00	07	06
It' One fishing nett at	00	05	00
It'm the Decedents wearing apparell value	01	00	00
It'm All other the goods unpraised or omitted	00	03	04
totall	08	13	10

25. William Oakes, senior

Collier of Broseley buried 12/XI/1669 (64y). Inventory 2/XII/1669 by Thomas Corbett and John Eaves exhibited 23/IX/1670, the day before the administratrix presented her account. Jane Oakes relict had obtained Administration 30/XI/1669. Francis and William Oakes coalminers of Broseley also signed the bond, probably sons (b 1633 & 1643).

Imprimis in ye Taylers chamber

one bedstead ffether bed & furniture	02	00	00
Itm. one truckel bedd one chest and a litle presse.	01	00	00
Itm. Linnens of all sorts	05	00	00
Itm. one Round table	00	05	00

Itm. in the new house

one table board one forme two presses	02	00	00

Itm. in ye parler

one clocke one table board & forme one skreene 3 chaires one smale table and 6 Cushwins	03	13	04

Itm. in the low chamber

one table board 2 formes one press & Cubburd	02	00	00

Itm. in the hall

one Chest one Cubbard 2 chaires on bench	00	13	04

Itm. in the litle chamber
one ffether bedd one ffether beddsteed & furniture & 2 chaires 02 00 00

Itm. in the litle buttery
one Cubbard 00 05 00
Item. Hogsheads barrells and brewinge vessells & one chest . 02 00 00

Itm. in ye Milkhowse
vessells of all sortes 02 00 00

Itm. in ye garden chamber
one bedd one table 00 10 00

Itm. in ye chamber over the howse
2 ffether bedds steeds & furniture & 2 other small beds . . 05 00 00

Itm. in the midle chamber
one ffether bedd and furniture one presse one chest one chaire 02 10 00

Itm. in the parler chamber
one ffether bedd steed & furniture 2 chests 4 trunckes 3 boxes and one Cubburd 06 00 00
Itm. Linnen cloth 00 02 00
Itm. Linnens of all sorts in the parler Chamber . . 10 00 00
Itm. in silver plate 2 boules 8 cupps & 26 spoones . . 16 10 00
Itm. pewter of all sorts 05 00 00
Itm. brasse of all sortes 06 13 08
Iron Ware of all sortes 01 10 00
Itm. Linnen yarne 01 00 00
Itm. divers small implements in the howse . . 00 13 04
itm. one Nagg & Mare and Colt 07 00 00
Itm. 2 Kyne & 4 younge beasts 06 00 00
Itm. Swine of all sortes 06 00 00
Itm. debts oweinge to the testatr by bond . . 50 00 00

Itm. one boate tooles for the Coleworkes horses for the Ginns & other necessaries. 13 13 04

Itm. the decedents wearinge apparell . . . 05 00 00

Sum . . 167 07 00

26. William Lewis

Trowman of Broseley but apparently not buried there. Inventory 1/XII/1670 by John Walton* and Morrise Hartshorne exhibited 7/XII/1670 for Elizabeth Lewis relict and administratrix (née Roberts *alias* Belcham of Broseley m 1651, probably sister of John Roberts *(43)*). In 1672 Widow Lewis was to be assessed for 4 hearths.

Imprs. two old Barges & all that belongs to them lynes, Roapes & an old Sayle	08	00	00
Itm. in the Seller 3 hogsheads 4 Barrells & some drink	01	10	00
Itm. all Lynnens .	01	04	00
Itm. the decedents Apparrell	01	04	00
Itm. one skimmer one Culliner one pewter dish & a salt .	00	02	00
Earthen dishes 10 in nomber	00	01	08
Itm. 2 old Payles	00	01	06
Itm. 2 Twiggen Chayres .	00	03	04
Itm. all swyne	00	16	08
Itm. an old Barge Chest & small Anker unstocked	00	10	00
Itm. two Iron plates behinde the fyer	00	13	04
Itm. Trenchers spoones & dishes .	00	02	04
Itml 17 Tunns of Allablustr	05	19	00
Itm. a debt oweinge the decedent by Richard Viccars	03	00	00
Itm. 2 Tonns of Coles at Brishill .	01	00	00
Itm. the decedents Intrest in a Barge & the tackles thereof lately Recd of Willm Okes and Thomas Williams	08	00	00
toto	32	07	10

27. John Adams

Of Broseley 'who departed this life abt 18 years since' buried 6/I/1653. Inventory 3/VIII/1671 by William Jarman and John Maire exhibited the same day. At the same time Administration to William Crompton husband of Sara sister and administratrix and to William Jarman. Written at the foot of the inventory is 'an Inventary of ye Goods of John Crumpton'. Presumably the inventory was taken at this late date because it had become necessary to establish a right to the chattel lease, the only item listed. This inventory was not intended to be a complete list of the chattels owned by John Adams at the time of his death. For his father Francis Adams *(22)*.

An Inventary of ye goods Chattills & debts of John Adams of Broseley who dep'ted this life ab't 18 years since.

Impr's a Chattill Lease of 4s per Ann being Rent given for ye obtayninge of a passage way for Karriadge of Coles to ye river of Severne in ye County of Salopp apprized at	04	00	00

28. Robert Benbow, senior

Yeoman of Broseley buried 20/IV/1672 (68y); his relict Newell buried 5/VIII/1672. Inventory 9/VII/1672 by William Jarman and John Bowen exhibited 3/IX/1672 by Newell Millechopp *alias* Benboe daughter and administratrix (wife of John Millechopp of Benthall). Robert Benbow had 8 daughters. The eldest was Margaret (b 1625), followed by Elinor (b 1628). Newell was the youngest (b 1645 and recorded as a son in the register). Not closely related to William Benbow *(30)*.

Imprs. Three Cows one Horse and pigg	09	13	00
& also a load of Hay	00	13	04
It. One Chaff bed & one feather bed wth the appurtances thereunto belongeinge	01	06	06
It. one press and Chest & signe post	00	08	00
It. one Bedstead with 3 stooles and 3 quoffers	00	09	00
It. two breweing vessells four milk vessells	00	03	00
It. one table and frame	00	13	04
It. two Chaiers	00	02	00
It. six pound of Nogin and six pound of hemppon or hurden yearne	00	09	00
It. other Implyments amounting	00	04	04
It. ten dishes of pewter	01	00	00
It. in Iron Comodities as tonges grate and two broaches and Cobbarts & pothangers	01	03	04
It. in Wooden meterialls	01	07	00
It. in lingings	01	00	00
It. a over warn Mallt Mill	00	13	04
It. in Vessells	00	10	06
It. in psent money	00	07	06
It. in depts due	01	03	00
The sume totall of this Inventory	23	16	02

May it please this Honourable Courtt, to take in to your Consideration, yt according to the Comand we brought in the Inventory of all and singuler the goods and Cattells or Chattells yt were in the possession of our father and mother deseased in thayr costody, but the goods underwriten were given unto John Millichop Henry Edge and Eleoner Gough widow, daughters to the sd Robert and Newell Benbow, and grandson to them, In thayr live time give unto the above said John Millichop and Newell his wife and Eliener gough wido & Henry Edgge grand sonne to the above said Benbow gave. unto them and in theyer costodies, and in their possession long before their deseace.

It. one Bed and the apertances	01	00	00
It. fowre sheep	00	08	00
It. one Small brasse pott	00	05	00
It. one flagon pott	00	02	00
The sum totall is . .	01	15	00

And further we certifie yt Richard Angle and Margerat the wife of Rich: Angle did object against the Inventoried, It was by the above said parties John Millichop and the rest of us, did tender the above sd Angle and his wife to have them appraised over againe or at the sight of two honest men if there were any thing under valued of the goods, or to take them in to his sd Angls possession Conditionally to satisfie the depts of the above said Robert Benbowes.

29. Timothy Crompton

Collier of Broseley buried 31/X/1672 (26y). Inventory 5/XI/1672 by Edward Lewis* and Richard Cowpar exhibited 11/III/1672 by Mary Crompton relict and administratrix. 2 hearths.

Impr'is ffor Tables & formes & stooles & one Carpitt there tow belonging	03	02	00
ffor Sillver plate	08	00	00
ffor one Clock	02	00	00
ffor Pewter	08	06	04
ffor Brase Ware	01	00	00
ffor Iron Ware y't is for Grate Tongs fire slice Broches & Racks & Dripen pans & Pots & Pote Galls & other Nescary things there unto Be Longing	05	10	00
ffor Bedstids & Beding With all Things there unto belonging .	14	10	00
ffor Rinde Ware	04	05	00
ffor Joyners Ware	04	00	00
ffor Apry Ware	17	17	00
ffor Catell & ffother	14	02	00
ffor Wood & Tools & Wagons belonging unto ye Cole Worke .	13	00	00
ffor Ould Rigin y't did belong to a Barge	05	00	00
So ye value of ye Goods & Catells do Amount to .	100	12	04

30. William Benbow

Trowman of Broseley but apparently not buried there (48y). Inventory 4/IV/1673 by James Harriesonn and William Jarman exhibited 8/IV/1673 for Isabell Benbow relict and administratrix. 1 hearth. Not closely related to Robert Benbow *(28)*.

Imprimis. his wearing Apparrell	02	10	00
And Six kine	12	00	00
One two yeare ould heifer	(2)1	00	00
Three yearling Calves	02	00	00
And Eleven sheep	02	00	00
one Little Nagg	02	00	00
one Little pigg	00	05	00
Two ould Barges. one at	(2)8	00	00
And the other at	02	00	00
Two middle sized Brass kettles	00	13	04
And fower Little Brass kettles	00	10	00
And three Iron potts	00	10	00
One warming pan and a skimmer	00	04	00
one grate, two small Broaches one fire shovell & tonges & one fring pane two paire of pothooks & one Cleever and a paire of pott hangers & hookes	00	08	00
one paire of Bellows	00	00	06
and a cast Iron Barr	00	00	04
nyne pewter dishes & one Tankart	01	00	00
ffive saucers & fower porengers fower pewter Candlesticks Two little Brass Candlesticks and one Little Brass morter one pewter Chamber pott	00	07	00
one pair of Cobbarts	00	01	04
one Bible & some other small books	00	07	00
Two Little table Boards & one bench	00	13	04
Barrells & payles & all other wooden commodityes valued at	00	13	04
one feather Bed & furniture to it	01	06	08
One flock bed & two Chaff beds and Coverings & Blankets belonging to them	01	05	00
fower Bedsteads	01	05	00
Two Chests and one Coffer one Trunke and two boxes	00	12	00
Seaventeene slippings of hurden yarne	00	08	00
Eyghteen pound of woollen yarne	00	10	00
ffive pound of wooll	00	02	06
ffowerteen payre of sheetes fower Table Vloaths and two towels	02	10	00
Three dozen of Napkins and ffower pillow beeres.	00	16	00
Three pound of flax & 6 kinchings of hemp	00	08	00
Six Strike of Corn	00	13	00
Two Straw Hutches	00	03	00
one press	00	13	00
The summ of this Inventory is	67	15	04

A particular accompt of the debts there were Owing by the within named William Benbow deceased and that are to be payd by his Relct.

Impris. to Henry Barret due	.	.	.	.	.	10	00	00
It. to Sarah Taylor	.	.	.	.	.	06	00	00
It. to Mr. John Dawes	.	.	.	.	.	06	00	00
It. To ffrancis Nash	.	.	.	.	.	00	11	08
			In all	.	.	22	11	08

31. Richard Rutter

Of Broseley buried 25/II/1672. Inventory (not dated) by George Phillips, Humphrey Brookes*, Ralfe Barker* and John Arunshire* exhibited 25/VII/1672 for Elianor Rutter relict and administratrix (d 1685), a pauper discharged from Hearth Tax. Their 3 sons were all under age.

for two overworne beds, one a chaffe bed and the an other a fflocke bed	00	07	00
for his old Closen	00	08	00
for a trunke & a Coffer & a box	00	07	00
for a Table boarde	00	02	06
for a Cubort	00	03	00
for a littell iron pott	00	04	00
for 2 littell old brasse kettells	00	02	06
for 3 pewter dishes & 2 Cunterfitt dishes & 10 sasers . .	00	04	00
for 2 old Stunds & a littell barrell	00	02	00
for a paile & littell bond gaune & an old wheele & an old cheare .	00	02	06
for a Greate a pair of Tongs & a broache . . .	00	02	06
for all other old trumpery things not worth speaking of . .	00	01	06
The whole vallue of these Goodes amount to . . .	02	06	06

And This is a true invitary of all her goods that wee see whose names are subscribed

32. John Harris, senior

Coalminer of Broseley buried 25/III1674 (77y). Inventory 26/III/1674 by Edward Cox and John Davis exhibited 14/IV/1674 for Thomas Booth son in law and executor, probate 18/IV/1674. Harris had married twice but both wives were dead. Will 20/III/1673 left his daughter Mary Morris (b 1632) 1 pair of hempen sheets, the kneading trough and half the hemp and linen yarn; her husband William Morris the lease of the house, the 'Synamond Coulered suite' and the uppermost kneeling in church; their daughter Dorothy one kettle next the biggest and the best joined bedsteads;

their daughter Abigail a bed and all belonging to it; their son William one long coffer in the chamber; their son John one coffer standing in the chamber; his daughter Rebecca Poovey (b 1634) half the hemp and linen yarn, the bedsteads on which he lay and 2 pair of hempen sheets; her husband James Poovey the 'gray suite of cloathes'; their son Richard one coffer standing above stairs; Sarah Preston (probably Rebecca's daughter by an earlier marriage) a brass pot and a coffer standing at the stair head; his daughter Ruth Booth (b 1645) the cow, a table board, a cupboard, a flock bed and all belonging to it; her husband Thomas Booth the green coat, a pair of woollen drawers and the other kneeling in church; their daughter Elizabeth a red rug and a great brass kettle. The 3 daughters were to share 9 pewter dishes, 2 salts, a counterfeit dish and 4 wearing sheets. 1 hearth.

Impris. His wearing Apparrell priced at	01	03	04
Also: Hemp and Linnen yarne	00	05	00
Also 4 coffers	00	05	00
Also: Bedsteads and Beds and all the furniture belonging to them.	03	00	00
all the Iron ware belonging to the house.	00	02	04
Also one Table Board & one Cuboard one Little Shelfe and all other wooden ware	00	09	00
Also Sheets and all ye other sorts of Linnens	01	01	00
Also Brasse & Pewter	01	06	08
Also One Cowe.	01	13	04
Money due upon Bonds.	17	10	00
The Summe of this Inventory is.	26	15	11
The ffunerall expences is.	03	18	10
The summ ye ffunerall expences deducted is	22	17	01

33. George Guest

Collier of Broseley died 13/VIII/1674 and buried the next day (42y). Inventory 24/VIII/1674 by William Rutter* and Thomas Corbett, five days after Probate had been granted to William Bulkley yeoman of Broseley and Peter Yates yeoman of Darley in Barrow executors. His wife Elizabeth d 1672 leaving two small sons, Thomas (b 1669) and George (b 1671). Will 12/VIII/1674 left his now wife Mary 'the part of the dwelling house where I now live left to me in my mothers will and all in it' with power to sell 'all the timber in or near the fold'. 2 hearths. Brother in law of Ralph Bradley *(2)*.

THE INVENTORIES OF BROSELEY 155

Imprimis. in the hall house

one table board two forms	01	06	08
Item. one brass pot one kettle on warming pan and other small imployments of brass	01	00	00
Item. One Iron pot one morter pestel frying pan a spade a shovell an axe a bill	00	17	02
Item. seven pewter dishes three plates two guns two flagons two pewter pots seven porrigers one salt one candlestick with some spoons	01	02	00

Item. In the parlour

one ioyned press.	00	18	00

Item. In the little chamber

one feather bed stead and furniture	02	06	08
Item. Linnings of all sorts	01	06	08

Item. in the little chamber over the parlor

two bed steads flock beds with the furniture	01	10	00
Item. one chest	00	06	00

Item. In another chamber

one bed stead feather bed and furniture one coffer two spinning wheels three covrings	02	00	00

Item. In the buttery

one hogshead five barrells with brewing tubs and other imployments of wood thereto belonging	01	06	00
Item. one trunke two chairs two baskets	00	06	08
Item. A cradle cloath a childs rugg with childs Linnings	00	10	00
Item. Timber of all sorts.	04	10	00
Item. money due by specialty	12	00	00
Item. some other imploymnents not yet valued	00	05	00
Item. The apparell of the deceased	01	10	00
The totall summe	33	02	10

34. Adam Stokes

Trowman of Broseley died 14/XII/1675 but apparently not buried there. Inventory 27/XII/1675 by Richard Beard*, John Eaves* and Thomas Williams exhibited 26/I/1675 by Elizabeth Stokes relict and administratrix. The next year she married John Pugh. Daughter Jane (b 1668) m 1689 George Bradley trowman of Benthall *(12)*. 2 hearths.

Impris: one barge called by the name of the Elizabeth with all materials belonging to her	12	00	00
Item. one barge called by the name of the Primrose and all thinges belonging to her	16	00	00
Item. one Cow	02	00	00

Itm. in the Parlour

one ould table board one mitt two ould barrells . . .	00	01	06

Itm. in the Roome over the parlour

one Joyne bedsteed one fflock & a boulster one blankett one ould Rugg one small wheele one ould coffer	01	00	00

Item. In the Chamber

one Joyne bedsteed one half hedded bedsted one fether bed and two ffether boulsters one fflock bed one flock boulster one truckell bedsted two blancketts two ruggs one presse two Chestes on Cuffer one small table board and ffoarme one trunck . . .	02	10	00

Item. in the Kichin

eight pewter disshes one gun one ffllaggon one quart pott two pewter Chamber potts six porrenger Dishes ffour saucers one salt three bras Cettells two bras potts one Iron pott one Iron marment one table board & fforme one Joyne Chaire & three other small ones one iron grate and one small iron back one ffire shovell and other Iron things necessary one tubb and other wooden materialls	03	00	00
Item. 8 payr of sheetes and other linnens wth nine slippings of noggen yorne	01	10	00
Item. ffor provision	02	00	00
Item. one old saile	00	02	06
Item. the Teatators Apparrell	02	10	00
Item. debts due to the Testators in the hands of Will Fidler of Bewdly	08	02	06
It. in the hands of Rich Jones of Shifnall . . .	02	04	00
It. in the hands of James Davies of Madley . . .	02	02	06
Itm. in the hands of Humphry Tiler of Bewdly . . .	00	15	00
Itm. in the hands of Tho: Everall Junr. . . .	00	12	00
It. in the hands of Joseph wright of Sallop . .	00	13	06
It. more in Severall hands	01	00	00
Total . .	58	03	06

35. Henry Barrett

Carpenter of Broseley buried 6/X/1676. Inventory 20/X/1676 by Thomas Aston*, Thomas Aston and William Phillips exhibited 12/I/1676 by Jane Barrett relict, executrix and sole legatee in the will written 5/XII/1660 but only signed 3/VI/1674. Probate 18/I/1676. She died in 1677. No children baptised in Broseley. 1 hearth.

Impr' one bedsteed & beding belonging to the same	01	10	00
Item one Cubbert & one Chest	00	13	04
Item Brasse and pewter	01	00	06
Item one Table boord Stooles & benches	00	06	08
Item loose boards one the loft	01	00	00
Item All Manner of linnens	00	10	00
Item All Iron Ware	00	02	06
Item Apery ware	00	05	00
Item the deseaseds wearing Apparrell	00	10	00
Item Monny due to the deseased by bonds	10	00	00
Item desperratt debts	01	10	00
Item All things forgotten & not Apprized	00	03	04
Sume totall	17	11	04

36. James Harrison

Coalminer of Broseley buried 25/XI/1676. Inventory 7/IX/1677 by William Buckley and Nicholas Harrison exhibited 25/IX/1677 for Margaret Harrison relict and executrix. Will 23/XI/1676 left his executrix the bargain of coals made in Articles between Mary Bromley, Samuel Langley and himself. In 1677 Francis Langley lord of the Manor of Broseley described Harrison as Master Collier at the Downs in Broseley ref. 2 hearths.
[Ref: SRO Forrester papers MSS Box150.]

Impris. Goods Remaineing in the Hall vizt.

Eighteen pewter dishes four pewter Gunns four fflaggons ffour pewter potts ffour pewter Candlesticks Three pewter plates all at .   03 10 00
Item. Brass Remaineing in the Same Roome three bras potts Eight Cettles one bras Basting Spoon all   01 15 00
Item. Iron ware in the same Roome One Iron pott Two dreeping pans Three broaches one payer of Cobberts one frying pan one morter & one pestell one Cleever & Two Hakinge knives four fleshforks & Two Candlesticks & Two plates & one Basteinge Spoon And one Smoothing Iron & Two Tinen pans all at.   01 06 00

Item. one grate one payer of cheeks & sum other Iron ware nott
yett valleyed at 00 08 00
Item. Woodware in the same Roome. one Standinge press one table
board Three Joynstools five Small Chears one paile Two Cans &
Sum other small wood ware all at 00 16 00

Item. in the parloar

Eleaven pewter Dishes Seaven pottingr Dishes Two Salts Three
Chamber potts one small plate one ffeather bed & Joyn bedsteeds
& furniture at 06 00 00
Itm. one Standinge press one table board one Side table one ffoarm
Two Chayers at 02 02 00
Itm. Three cushings 00 02 00

Itm. In the Citching

one furnace & one boyler at 00 13 04
Itm. wod vessells of all sorts at 00 10 00
Itm. one Grate & one peele & one fier slice & pottlinks at . 00 03 00
Itm. one Jack 00 04 00

Item. in the buttry

woodware at 00 08 00

Itm. An other Little buttry

one spininge wheel one Churne & sum other Small ware . . 00 04 00

Itm. In the Groundseller

Six Hogsheads one pipe & one barrell at 01 10 00
Itm. Two Hogsheads of drinke 02 00 00

Item. in the chamber over the parlor

one flok bed & bedstid & one ffeather bed & the furniture at . 03 00 00
Itm. one quofer & sum Linen yarne at 00 12 00
Itm. one Clock at 01 10 00

Item. in the Roome over the Hall

Two ffeather beds & bed steeds & furniture at . . . 06 00 00
Itm. Two chests & one Trunk And one Hanging press one small
box at 00 10 00
Itm. one Iron grate & one warming pan And Two Small
Chears at 00 05 00
Itm. Linens of all sorts at 05 00 00

Item. in the Chamber over the seller

Two fflock beds & bedsteeds at 03 00 00

THE INVENTORIES OF BROSELEY

Item. one pitt Rope at	01	00 00
Item. Three Horses at	07	10 00
Itm. one Saddle pad & bridle at	00	08 00
Itm. one yeare ould calfe at	01	00 00
Item. one Anvill & Sum other smiths Tooles	03	00 00
Item. Moneys oweinge to the Testator	02	00 00
Itm. Weareing Apparrell	02	10 00
Item. for Things out of Sight omitted or forgotten	00	05 00
Sum totall	59	01 04

37. Edward Dawley

Bargeowner of Broseley Wood buried 21/IV/1679. Inventory 22/IV/1679 by Wm. Rutter, John Hartshorne and Wm. Bradley exhibited 1/VII/1680 for Ann Dawley relict and administratrix *(45)*. Possibly the Edward Dawley discharged as a pauper from Hearth Tax; not to be confused with a contemporary Edward Dawley bargeowner of Benthall d 1686.

Imprimis in the dwelling house

one small Iron grate & tongs one small marment two small broatches one payre of Cobberts one fier slice pott gailes & other small necessaries	00	10 08
Item. four brasse Kettles one old warmeinge pan one scumer & other small necessary things	00	08 10
Item. three pewter dishes three small plates one Candlesticke one flaggon one pollenger spoones & other small necessarie things	00	06 08
Item. one small table board one Chaire one old Chest one old Cupboard one old Coffer four small casks one paile one Kneading Mitt and other small things	00	08 02
Item. one old flocke bed in the Chamber a Joynd bed and all things thereunto belonging	00	11 10

Item. in the upper roome

two old flock bedds lyinge upon nayled boards linnen and woollen thereunto belonginge	00	06 02
Item. two payre of old hempen sheets four payre of hurden sheets one dozen of old hempen napkins one small hempen table cloth one dozen of hurden napkins & a halfe two small towels and other small necessary things Item twenty two slippings of flaxen yarne and hempen ten pounds of noggs	00	19 04
Item. one old Barge and all thereunto belonginge	08	08 08
Item. the deceadents weareing apparrell of all sorts	00	08 08
Tot	12	09 00

38. John Whitmore

Chandler of Broseley died 6/VIII/1679 but apparently not buried there. Inventory 19/VIII/1679 by Thomas Corbett, John Davies and Samuel Barrett exhibited 27/VIII/1679 for Robert Whitmore son, one of the executors *(63)*. A second son William was the other. Will 30/I/1676 reveals that the house was consistent with the four hearths of 1672 and much larger than the inventory suggests. His wife Elizabeth was to have the house, orchard, shop and implements of trade; his son John the upper and lower rooms on the west side of the house and half the garden and yard; his son William the hall and parlour with the butteries and chamber above on the east side; and his son Robert the workshop, outhouses and yard. William Whitmore grandson *(74)*.

Imprmis. In ye Hall house
one table & Forme	00	08	06
Item. One Cobard & one Chaire	00	14	00

It. In ye Chamber
two feather beds & Furnitur	08	06	08
It. Two Chest One Cubart & one Coffer	01	06	08
It. one Littell Table & five Chaires	00	10	00
It. Linnens of all sorts	05	06	00
It. one coffer and some small stooles	00	04	00
It. Cooperies ware of all sorts	00	15	00

It In ye other end of ye house
goods of severall sorts	05	00	00
It. Brasse & pewter of all sorts	01	10	00
It. Iron Ware of all sorts	01	10	00
It. One Band of forty popunds	40	00	00
It. some small things omitted	00	03	00
It. Tooles in ye Shoppe	02	00	00
It. The apparell of ye deceased	03	00	00
Sume total	70	13	10

39. Robert Hill

Mercer of Broseley buried 26/IX/1679. Inventory 3/X/1679 by Ed. Simons and William Cocke exhibited 22/X/1679 for Jane Hill relict and administratrix. Their son Humphrey (b 1675) remained there all his life but there is no evidence that the mercer's shop was maintained after Robert's death. There is no appropriate assessment for Hearth Tax so Hill was possibly a recent incomer.

Ips. His Wearing Apparrill	03	00	00
It. ffor wares in the shope and all other imples. thearein	45	14	02
It. debts by bills and bonds	13	00	00
It. good debts in the shop booke and desperate debts in the shop booke in all	44	07	01 ¾
It. al sorts of brass and pewter	02	10	00

Item. In the dwelling house

3 tables 6 stooles and two Cubbords	01	04	00

It. in the loer Chamber

1 bed & steads and furniture with 2 Cubards & 6 Stooles.	05	00	00
It. on hogshead 2 barrills with other brewing utensells	01	00	00
It. for Iron utensels inthe house and buttry	00	13	04

It. in the Chamber over the loer Chamber

1 bed steads 1 table 1 trunck	00	15	00

It. in the Chamber over the house

on bed steads and furniture 1 Chest 2 quoffers 1 trunck 2 boxes	03	00	00
It. 8 paire of flaxen & Hempton sheetes and 1 doz ½ naptkins 2 table Cloaths and two paire Coarse sheetes	01	15	00
6 greene chaires.	00	04	00
It. on gray horse and on swine	03	10	00
It. reddy monys in the house	12	10	00
It. ffor things forgotten and unseene	01	00	00
Suma totalis	139	02	07 ¾

40. Elizabeth Russell

Relict and executrix of Edward Russell (d 1670) of Broseley buried 25/X/1679. Inventory 8/XII/1679 by Robt. Mathewes, Willm. Buckley, William German and Thomas Teece exhibited 23/III/1679 (the day after probate) by Edward Russell son and executor. Will 4/VIII/1679 referred to a cottage in the possession of her mother, Alice Davies widow, and a meadow called New Tyneing in the possession of John Harris, being on the south side of Coalpit Hill both leased 4/IX/1656 for 99 years and three lives by John gent Langley of the Tuckies and Samuel his son and heir. See Andrew Langley's will *(47)*. Widow Russell—3 hearths, Edward Russell—2 and widow Davies—1.

In the Parlor or new Roome

Seven pewter dishes three pewter Salts two brass Candlesticks one pewter Candilstick and eleven small sausers valued at	00	18	00

In the chamber over the parlor

one joynt bed and furniture	02	10	00

In the middle room

eight small dishes two pewter guns and three pewter flaggons with two chamber potts	00	14	00

In the Chamber over the middle room

two small bedsteads two flock beds two coverlids and one blanket.	01	00	00

In the Kitchin

three small Kettles one small brass pan one warming pan with other small things in the same room	00	13	04

In the chamber over the Kitchin

one bed and bedstead with two old blankets	00	06	08
Three Leatharn Jacks	00	02	00
one paire of bedsteads in the great buttery and one pair is the little room	00	06	08
Linnens of all sorts	02	10	00
ffour stalls of Bees	00	05	00
Things omitted or not prized	00	05	00
Desperate debts .	02	00	00
Totall Sume	11	15	08

41. Robert Ogden

Clerk rector of Broseley buried by his request 2/III/1679 in the chancel under the seat reserved for the rector. Inventory 18/III/1679 by Will. Mathewes, Thomas Corbett and Will. German exhibited 22/III/1679 for Mary Ogden relict and executrix *(62)* and sister of Robert Whitmore *(63)*. She was his second wife; the first Elizabeth d 1664. There were no children. The Rectory was assessed for 6 hearths.

THE INVENTORIES OF BROSELEY

Joyne worke of all sorts	09	00	00
Coopery and Trenin Ware of all sorts	03	00	00
Brass Pewter and Tin ware of all sorts . . .	12	00	00
Beds and Bedsteads of all sorts	36	00	00
Linen of all sorts	50	00	00
Iron ware	06	13	04
Carpetts chairs stooles Cyshions & window curtains . .	03	00	00
Plate Rings & Watches	20	00	00
His study of Bookes	90	10	00
Clock & Jacke	03	00	00
White ware glasses Botteles belonging to the deced. .	05	00	00
Implemts of Husbandry of all sorts	03	00	00
Two Mares	08	00	00
Two kine	06	00	00
One horse litler or Harness	03	00	00
Muck & compost	00	10	00
Hay	05	00	00
Corne on the ground & in ye Barne . . .	10	00	00
Hemp flaxe & yearne of all sorts	10	00	00
Swine	03	00	00
One Chattell Lease	30	00	00
Shelves boards & dressers	01	00	00
Household Provision of all sorts	15	00	00
His Gownes Cassocks & other wearing apparell . .	20	00	00
One bond depts & mony in ye house . . .	37	05	02
Other thinges omitted & unpriced. . . .	00	10	00
ye sume is . .	392	18	06

42. Joan Harris

Relict of Humphrey Harris (d 1672) of Broseley, buried 22/XI/1681. Inventory (not dated) by Richard Benbow and Charles Parton* exhibited 8/VIII/1682 for the administratrix, Elizabeth daughter (m Roger Oakes). Humphrey Harris - 2 hearths.

Imprimas. Six pewter dishes one flagon and one pewter gun with other small pewter	00	12	06
Item one brewing kettell 2 bras banns 2 bras bots with other small brass wares	01	10	04
Item one Grate sclice and tongues spitt and cobborts one driping pan one frying pan and two Iron potts with other Small Iron ware	01	01	02
Item two feather beds and three boulsters one Joyne bedstide and two standing bedstids	03	01	06
Item one rug 3 blanketts one coverlett	01	04	06
Item One payre of hempenn sheetes nine payre of hurden sheetes and two table clothes with other lining	01	06	08

Item One Joyne chest three quoffers	00	13	04
Item three table boards one Joyne forme and one stoole .	01	05	08
Item One hogshed two kinderkins and three litle firkins	01	00	00
Item One Joyne cubbott .	00	06	08
Item One small brewing stonde two litle coolers two payles and two litel stonds with other small woddon wares	00	08	00
Item one bag of mallt	00	00	00
——.parsell of hoppes .	00	00	00
Item hempe drest and undrest with a small parsell of hemp seede .	00	13	00
Item One baken swine and one Store pig.	01	06	08
Item provission for the house	00	12	00
Item All her wearing Apparrill	02	00	00
	17	00	06

43. John Roberts, *alias* Belcham

Trowman of Broseley, buried 28/I/1683. Inventory 9/I/1683 by John Walton* and Tho. Jones* exhibited 15/IV/1684 by Joan Roberts relict and administratrix. In 1677 Administration of John Roberts *alias* Belcham trowman of Bewdley had been granted to his son also John trowman of Broseley. No appropriate entry in the Hearth Tax. Probably brother in law of William Lewis *(26)*. [Inventory badly damaged]

Two Bedsteads and fower Blankets two Beds fower pair of Sheetes .	01	04	00
One pillis beare Six napkins	00	02	00
Two Boxes, two ould coffers	00	02	06
One Goanr of Butter	00	06	00
One Barrell two ould wooden platters	00	01	00
Three flitchins of Bacon .	00	15	06
Six ould Dishes fower porringers and other small pewter .	00	06	00
Two ould pots three small kettles one Grate and other Iron ware .	00	13	04
One ould Table one paile and other wooden ware	00	02	06
The Deceaseds wearing Apparrell.	00	10	00
total	04	02	04

44. John Evans

Tailor of Broseley, buried 6/V/1684. Inventory (not dated) by Francis Nash, Morgan Humphreys* and John Hains exhibited 20/V/1684 for Mary Evans relict and executrix. Will 28/IV/1684 referred to wife Mary, eldest son Amos, son William (born 1669) and daughter Ann (b 1676).

Impr' Two halfe headed bedsteds with the beds and beding thereunto belongeing	01	10	00
Item Two Chests and two tronkes	00	10	00
Item One Tableboard, One Joyne forme and three little Stooles .	00	10	00
Item One Joyne press and cubbort	00	06	08
Item Two little ffirkins two payles two litle milke vessels One kneding trough	00	03	06
Item One Litle Iron pott and kettle	00	06	00
Item One grate sclice and tongues potgailes flesh forke and frying pan and Smothing Iorne and other Small Ironwares . .	00	06	08
Item Bras	01	06	08
Item Pewter	00	10	06
Item Two Cows and twoo Little Earelings . . .	05	10	00
Item His weareing Aparile	01	02	06
Item Things not seene or forgotten	00	10	00
	12	12	06
The Funerall Charges	02	00	00
The depts that are knowne allready are	09	10	03

45. Ann Dawley

Widow of Edward Dawley *(37)* of Broseley and buried 18/VIII/1684. Inventory 16/VIII/1684 by Robert Guest, William Bradley and Edward Trensam exhibited 2/IX/1684 for Edward Dawley son and executor. Will 14/IV/1684 left her daughter Martha Lawrence of Worcester (b 1650) her best petticoat and waistcoat, her hat a pair of coarse sheets and one of the shifts; her daughter Mary Price 1s.; her daughter Ann Dawley (b 1666) £5, 'all linen sett by for her in a pillow beere', 1 great brass pot, 2 of the biggest pewter dishes, a warming pan, a chest 'that stands in my chamber' and the bedsteads by it, a new bed tick and bolster not filled and the rug and blanket on her bed; her son James (b 1665?) £5, the bed he now lies on, 1 pair of hurden and 1 pair of flaxen sheets, 1 iron pot and 2 pewter dishes and the room 'I now live in' and the room above (or John to pay him £3); her son John (b 1654) the rest of the house and 1 pair of hurden sheets; her granddaughter Ann Price £5 and all her mother's goods towards her bringing up. Her son Edward (b 1659) was to care for her.

Impr's One ould Barge with all materialls thereunto Belonginge	20	00	00
Item Pitch Tarr and Okum	00	06	08
Item a parcell of Coales	00	07	06

Item In ye dwelling howse

one table board & frame one joyned chaire and other od things belonging to the same roome	00	08	00
Item Brass and peauter of all sorts	00	15	00
Item Iron ware of all sorts	00	06	08
Item Earthenware of all sorts	00	01	00

It' In ye Chamber Joyning to the howse

One Chest one Cuffer one box a paire of Bedsteeds	00	10	00
It' Linen and Napry of all Sorts	01	15	00
It' Beds and Bedinge of all Sorts	01	10	00

It' In the Roome over the house

one bedsteed	00	01	06
It' All Coopery ware and other wooden utensills	00	05	00
Item p'vision of all Sorts	00	15	00
Item ye Deceaseds wearing Aparell	01	00	00
It' all old Lumber and od things omitted	00	01	00
Toto	28	02	04

46. Samuel Evans

Collier of Broseley, buried in the second month 1687 presumably in the Quaker burial yard. Inventory 30/V/1687 by Sampson Crompton and Thomas Evans exhibited 21/VI/1687 for Mary Evans relict and administratrix. No appropriate entry in Hearth Tax.

Impr's his purse and Apparrell	01	00	00
10 small pewter dishes and 5 Porringers	00	16	00
1 brass Potts 3 small Kettles	00	05	00
2 Iron Potts	00	05	00
1 brass warming Pann	00	02	06
1 Iron Morter and Pestel	00	02	06
1 Grate one ffier shovell and Tongues with a payer of whinges	00	03	06
1 Spitt ffrying Pan and Clever	00	02	00
1 payer of Cobbards	00	01	00
1 Iron Basting spoon & a fletch forke	00	00	06
1 Smoothing Iron & 2 kandelsticks	00	00	06
2 Tin Panns with a Tin Cover	00	00	06
fitherbed bolster Rugg & Blanketts 1 set of Curtans and vallens	01	10	00
1 Joyne Besteed	00	06	08
1 fflock bed and Bolsteer with a Rugg	00	15	00

THE INVENTORIES OF BROSELEY

1 Joyne Cubbord	00	05 00
1 Chest one old Coffer	00	05 00
2 small boxes	00	02 00
4 payer of Hempten sheetes	00	14 00
2 Table Cloths halfe a duzen of Napkins . . .	00	04 00
1 Table bord 3 chaires 2 stooles	00	04 00
1 Barrell 1 Mitt 1 Stun with other small lumber . .	00	02 06
Debtes due to the Intestate by Bond		
Impr's due from Thomas Suthorne	20	00 00
John Preene	03	00 00
due from ffrancis Man	02	00 00
due from George Tomson upon Bill . . .	00	10 00
Due to the Intestate of Desperate debts viz		
Impr's due from Thomas Beddow	01	14 00
due from Edward Smith	00	19 04
due from Ralph Harrison	00	14 08
due from John James	00	03 00
due from Edmund Hill	00	09 00
Suma Totalis huius Inventarii . .	36	17 08
Debts due and owing fron the Intestate		
Impr's To Robt Rodes	04	00 00
To Moses Vahan	01	00 00
To Kester Morrall	00	16 00
To Tho: Wellins	00	09 00
To Tho: Oliver	00	05 06
To Tho: Evans	00	16 07
Sume is . .	07	07 00

47. Andrew Langley

Gent of the Woodhouse in Broseley, buried 26/IX/1687. Inventory 7/X/1687 by Samuel Bowler gent of Arlscott and Richard Jones yeoman of Buildwas exhibited 24/X/1687 for Joyce Langley relict and executrix. Will 16/VIII/1686. 3 hearths.

Impr'is In the Hall
two table boards & one large Standing Cubbard & two little Cubbards
Fower chairs six cushings one joyne forme & a Clock a grate fier
showell & tongs & Iron back & bookes 10 10 00

In the Parlor

one bed bedsteed & furniture to the same a ovell table six chaires a Cubbard with drawers a paire of tables 07 10 00

In the little Roome by the Parlor

a Press with drawers A Chest with dressed hemp in it a Coffer & little table 03 00 00

In the buttry Chamber

one bed bedsteed & furniture A tabel board two Chests two trunks fower coffers fower boxes two Chaires & a close stoole . .   05 00 00

In the Stairehed Chamber

two beds & bedsteeds with furniture two Chests . . .   04 10 00

In the Chamber over the hall

one bed bedsteed & furniture two little side tables & cover cloathes to them six Chaires & cusshons a truckell bedsteed a grate fier shovell & tongs a pair of bellis a Iron back a looking glass .   13 10 00

In the porch Chamber

one bed & bedsteed & furniture one side table & cover cloath fower Chaires three stooles a looking glass a coffer . .   06 10 00

In the Kiching Chamber

two servts beds & bedsteed three Chests & other things of small vallow 02 10 00

In the Chamber over the dayrey

one bed & bedsteeds & furniture two tables one Chaire & forme .   03 00 00

In the Cheese Chamber

Cheese of all sorts 05 00 00

In the Dayry

milk vessells of all sorts & trinning waire of all sorts . .   03 00 00

In the Kiching

a dresser one forme one table a bras bench a Jack & Iron back a Grate fier shovell & tongs a paire of Racks & Iron Waire brass & pewter of all sorts & a birding Gun 17 00 00

In the Clossett

a little table a Glas cage glasses eight joyne stools Chinawaire a Still a Silver tanckard a silver bole two silver Cupps a dozen & halfe of silver spoones a silver tobacco box 16 10 00

THE INVENTORIES OF BROSELEY

In the Seller

hogsheads barrels & brewing vessells & sorts of Coopery waire &c.	05	00	00

In the backhouse

one Weeting fat two kneading troughs a Corne which & other old lumber .	02	00	00
Linnings sheetes pillow beares table cloaths napkins & all other sorts	20	00	00
Corne in the barne of all sorts & hay in & out of the barne	20	00	00
Cattle 4 Oxen eleaven kine & a bull five two yeare old beasts fower yeare old beasts three wenling beasts three old mares one two year old Colt twenty nine sheepe & eleven swine .	87	10	00
One waine two dung carts two ploughs & plough timber & all other implements of husbandry.	12	00	00
Debts by specialty	200	00	00
The deceadants wearing apparill .	10	00	00
Lumber & other goods out of sight	05	00	00
	456	00	00

Kinswomen Abigail Richards of the Hem - £10
Kinsman Stephen Bradely of Barrow - £10
Kingsman Samuel Bradeley of London - £10
Kinsman Thomas Bradley of Stepney, London - £10
Kinsman Edward Bradley of Stepney, London - £10
Kinsman John Marsh & Sarah Marsh his sister of Benthall - £10
John Andenbrook of Little Hales & Nicholas Andenbrook of Haddon & Ann the wife of Andrew Swift of the Wike - £10 apiece
Kinswoman Ann Law of Bridgnorth - £10
Kinsman Andrew Swift of the Wike - £10
Hired servants who are with me at my decease - 5s a piece
Wife Joyce: Messuage farme & tenement Woodhouse, & barns, stables, gardens, orchards &c. & closes called Jackfield Moanwood & Moanwood Meadow & messuage called Salthouse & tenemt in Broseley (John Legg) & garden & backside & tenemt in Jackfield (Edward Russell) & all lands sellions or butts of ground in the Sevrall fields belonging to Broseley For her life if unmarried, I being desirous that my name may contiue at the Woodhouse ... with full liberty to sink..take, carry away, sell..coles, mine, minerals & quarries & timber on my land for sinking & maintaining shafts of pits, & buildings, & ten tons of wood p.a. from my lands in Broseley, plus 2 pieces of land called Broomy Leasow & Addams Leasow held under yease of 60 yrs from Wm Bromley of Holt, Esq.;

& after, to my heir. Minister & Churchwaradens of Broseley - 12s p.a. for poor on St. Andrews Day
Kinsman Richard Richards of Longford, Clerke & his heirs, if none to Thomas Richards his brother & his heirs, if none to use of Andrew Swift of Wike.
At Joyce's death, whoever of the above is alive (but not Andrew Swift) to inherit, to give:
1) to Abigail Richards their mother, £10 & Richard to give Thomas £10 at same time.
2) Stephen Bradley of Barrow & Thos Bradley of Stepney - £20 a piece
3) Edward Bradley of Stepney & Samuel Bradley of London - £10 a piece
4) Andrew Swift the young of Wike - £50
5) Anne Swift mother of Andrew Swift - £50
6) John Marsh of Benthall & Sarah Marsh his sister - £20 a piece
7) Elizabeth Richards & Elianor Richards 2 of the sisters of the said RR - £10 a piece
8) Kinswoman Ann Law of Bridgnorth - £10

If any of these not paid within 12 months of Joyce's decease, then Andrew Swift to enter messuage in possession of Edward Russell of Broseley & those pieces of land called Jackfield Moanwood & Moanwood Meadow, the Cow Leasow, the Woodhouse Meadow, the Orchard meadow & Great Legg being part of my lands Broseley, & to hold it until he has raised the £250 to pay the above Wife Joyce executrix & residual legatee.

48. Hugh Jones

Trowman of Salthouse in Broseley, buried 23/II/1688. Inventory 22/IV/1689 by John Pew* and Thomas Williams exhibited 30/X/1689 by Mary Jones relict and administratix *(157)*.

Imprimus his purse and wearing apparrell.	03	00	00
Item three featherbeds six bousters 3 pillows	06	06	08
It' two flock beds with four bousters	01	06	08
It' Beddings of all sorts .	01	16	08
It' 4 Bedsteeds & one pres	01	13	04
It' Linnens of all sorts .	03	00	00
It' Brass & Pewter of all Sorts	05	00	00
It' 4 tables one chest one trunk 4 Boxes and two ould coffers	01	08	06
It' 6 Buffott stooles & six chaires	00	10	00
It' two hoghsheads 4 Barrells 2 stunds one tub and other Lumber.	01	00	00
It' Too broches 3 dreeping pans one pair of cobbets 4 flesh forks one grate one frinepan 2 pair of tongs one fire shovell	00	13	04
It' hemp & hempen yarns	00	06	08
It' one Barg called by name the Walton with all furniture belonging to her .	09	00	00
It' one ould Barg called the Joyce with all furniture belonging to her .	02	10	00
It' Chees and bacon with other prvison .	01	16	08
Total sum is . .	39	08	06

49. John Dawley

Of Broseley, buried 2/VIII/1689/ Inventory 24/VIII/1689 by James Hartshorne* and Richard Price* exhibited 3/IX/1689 for Eleanor Dawley relict and administratrix (née Hartshorne married 1677). He was probably the son of Edward Dawley *(37)* and Ann *(45)* so both appraisers were probably related to his wife.

Imp: one chatwell lease	05	00	00
It'm 3 Iron Curtain Rods 2 cloth wollen curtains	00	03	00
It'm 2 bedbords 1 sagen matt	00	01	06
It'm 1 joyne cratch 1 joyne foarme	00	08	00
It'm 1 Twill Bedtick filled with flocks and feathers	00	05	00
It'm The deceased wearinge apparrell	00	13	04
Totall	06	10	10

50. Francis Gears

Tailor of Broseley, buried 7/II/1691 (38y). Inventory 4/V/1692 by Thomas Oliver and Edward Cox exhibited 23/VIII/1692 by John Watkis son in law and executor. Will 2/II/1691 referred to 'aged mother' (Eleanor d 1692, widow of Richard Gears d 1678) and sister Ursula (m 1681 John Watkis).

the testators a parrell	02	15	06
2 tables 2 formes a hoshead & a brass bench & wainscot	01	13	00
1 Clock	02	00	00
6 Chaires	00	03	06
1 deske 2 Bed steads	00	16	06
12 Eles at 1s 6d per Ele	00	18	00
3 peare of Sheres & 3 pressing Irons	00	05	04
Linings 5 sheets 4 sherts 12 Carvets & nekcloths	01	02	06
12 bottles	00	01	04
1 bible	00	02	06
	11	15	08

51. Thomas Oliver

Mercer, of Broseley, buried 23/VII/1692. Inventory 4/VIII/1692 by Henry Bowdler and Christopher Morrall (mercer of Much Wenlock) exhibited 22/VIII/1692 by Mary Bowdler 'dear and loving sister in law', executrix and sole legatee in will 30/III/1692. In 1698 Mary Bowdler *alias* Oliver was buried at Madeley. She may have been the Mary Edwards, widow, who married Mr. Audley Bowdler at Linley in 1668 but it seems more likely that she was the sister of Henry and Audley *(156)* and the person referred to here. There is no appropriate entry in the Hearth Tax returns and no evidence that the shop continued after his death. His wife Elizabeth d 1683 in childbirth.

Imprs. Cloaths Stuffs & all other mercery in ye shopp	149	01	02 ¼
Itm. Grocery of all sorts .	27	18	08

In the Chamber over ye Shopp

one high bed wth a truckle bed under it & all thereunto belonging	05	02	06
It. Seaven Chaires one stoole & an ovall Table	00	15	00
Itm. one Trunck wth frame & a pair of tables	00	12	00

in the middle Chamber

one Bed with beding at .	02	12	06
It. one Smalle table 2 chaires one trunk one box one chest & a looking glass wth a standing press at	01	16	00
It. one gold ring with silver pise[?]	04	15	00
It. one Bed hilling at	01	10	00

in ye room over the house

one Bed wth furniture thereunto belonging	01	13	04
It. one small chest a cradle 2 sadles & bridle one padd	01	03	00

In ye Entry to the Shopp

one small press .	00	10	00

In the kitchen

one furnise of Iron 4 Iron potts wth all other utensils of Iron	04	13	04
All sorts of Wooden ware as Barrells &c..	02	00	00

over the kitchen

one old low bed with bedding	00	14	00

In the dwelling house

one jack .	00	09	00
It. one skreen 2 tables two formes one Joyn'd chaire one Cubboard two ould chaires & a stoole with cussions	01	12	00
Itm. Linnings of all Sortes	07	00	00
It. All sorts of Brass and Tinne	00	17	04

It. Pewter of all sorts	02	10	00
It. Bookes	00	05	00
It. his wearing Apparrell	05	00	00
It. moneys in his pockett.	03	17	00
It. moneys due to him in his booke & otherwise .	39	13	11 ¼
all Ould lumber as boxes &c. and things otherwise forgotten or out of sight .	00	13	04
In toto .	266	14	01 ½

52. Edward Amiss

Blacksmith of Broseley, buried 18/II/1692. Inventory 28/II/1692 by Edward Lloyd* and Wm. Harrison exhibited 18/V/1693 by John Amiss brother and executor. Will 13/II/1692 referred to Edward son of Thomas Amiss and the daughters of his sister and Richard Ward. The burial of Amiss is the first entry relating to the family in the parish register.

Impr's Goods Remaineing in ye Hall

vizt Pewter & Brass of all Sorts at	02	11	00
It' Tables & Cheares & other wooden ware at	01	00	00
It' Barr Iron & other Iron ware at	12	00	00

It' Goodes Remaining in the other Lower room

vis. a Bedd & bedsteeds a Chest & wooden ware at	02	15	00

It' Goodes Remaineing in ye Chamber

vis. Two Beds & Bedsteeds & furniture at	06	00	00
It' A Chest & Trunk & Boxes at .	00	18	00
It' Lynen of All sorts at .	04	06	08

It' Goodes Remaineing in ye Shopp

vis. an Anvill & a payer of Bellows & other Smyths Tooles or Implements at	07	13	04

It' Moneys owing to the Testator.	20	00	00
It' Wearing Apparell at	05	00	00
It' Moneys in ye House .	11	15	00
It' Things out of Sight omitted or forgotten	00	04	00
Totall .	74	03	00

53. John Langley, senior

Gent of the Tuckies in Broseley, buried 1/XI/1693. Inventory 8/XI/1693 by Newell Edwards and William Ward exhibited 21/XI/1693 by Mary Nechills, daughter (b 1643) and executrix. Her son John was also executor. Will 2/III/1691 made when he was 'very aged and weak' referred to his daughter Susan (b 1637 m 1682 William Millichop) and her four children, his son Samuel (b 1631) and his four children (including Mennes *(55)*) and son Francis (b 1635) and his four children. 3 hearths.

In the Brew House
One Mitt one Brewing Tubb one Cooleing ffate one Tundish . 00 12 00

In ye Kitching
Seven Chairs two Table Boards too Joyne Stooles. . . 01 01 00
One warmeing pan too Brass Pots one Marment one Brass pan . 01 03 06
Pewter of all sorts 01 00 00
Ironware:
one paire of Racks Three Broches one Grate one ffier Shovel too paire of Tongs one fflesh one Jack two Dreeping pans . 01 01 10

In ye Garrett over ye Hall
One pair of Joyne Bedsteed with Linnen & one Coffer . . 02 03 06

In ye Chamber over ye Hall
One Table Board 00 03 06

In ye Chamber over ye Kitching
One Bed & Bedsteeds One Truckel Bed one paire of Bedsteds . 01 11 00

In ye Kitt Chamber
One Bed & Bedsteeds one coffer 00 11 06
three Rugs & too Blankets 00 18 00

In ye Chamber over ye Brewhouse
One Bed & Bedsteed & fower Blankets 01 00 00
One Morter & Pestel one Coffer one Barrell One Little Coffer . 00 06 06

In ye Buttery
fower Barrels 00 10 00

In ye Hall
One Little Table too Joyne ffurms one Coffer . . . 00 08 02
Plate 12 00 00

THE INVENTORIES OF BROSELEY

In ye Barne

Corne Threshed & unthreshed	00	18	00
Barley threshed & unthreshed	05	00	00
Oates unthreshed	00	05	00
Hay in ye Barne	04	10	00
Implements of Husbandry	01	05	00
Seven Cows	24	10	00
One Oxe on Bull	09	00	00
One two yeare Old heifor	02	06	08
One Calfe	00	18	00
Seven Swine	02	19	00
One Mare	03	06	08
Butter & Cheese	01	10	00
The Deceasants Weareing Apparrel	03	00	00
Money in his Purse	00	06	00
Things forgotten & unappraized	00	05	00
Tot is	85	00	06

54. Thomas Lee

Nailer of Broseley, buried 15/IX/1694. Inventory 27/IX/1694 by William Buckley, Robert Guest and William Phillipps exhibited 9/X/1694 by Elizabeth Lee relict and administratrix (née Guest married 1667, sister of Robert). 1 hearth.

one Mare at	04	00	00
Nine Swyne at	09	00	00
Beds & bedding of all sorts	09	00	00
all sorts of Linnion as sheets table Cloaths & Napkins	06	00	00
All sorts of Brass pewter & tinnin ware	03	00	00
one Brueing ffurnace boylers & all sort of Iron Ware	03	10	00
Table boards benches Chests boxes & all other Wooden Ware	05	00	00
Beere and ale in the Cellare & the Vessells full & empty	20	00	00
Two ould steel Mills to grind Mault & the geares to them belonging	01	10	00
All sorts of Tooles belonging to the employment of A Naylor and Iron in the chopp & Nayles	03	15	00
Desparat debts oweing to the deceased	10	00	00
The deceaseds Weareing Apparrell	05	00	00
All things fforgotten & not Apprised	00	10	00
Totall	80	05	00

55. Mennes Langley

Gent of Broseley, buried 14/IV/1699 (20y). Inventory 11/IV/1699 by Ric. Manning and Ed. Cox exhibited 18/IV/1699 by Thomas Evans corvisor of Broseley cousin and executor. Will 8/IV/1699 left Thomas Evans a messuage called 'the Tuckies' in the possession of Will. Ellis gent, also plate, money, debts on bond, wearing apparel, rings and jewels and all chattels 'in my possession or that of Richard Littlehales the yonger of the Wike'. Two previous wills made respectively at Shrewsbury and Bridgnorth when he was so ill 'that I was not sensible' appointing first Mr. Henry Langley and secondly Richard Littlehales and Thomas Evans as executors were both revoked. Langley stated that he had failed previously to persuade Henry Langley to return the will made in his favour so that it could be revoked. Mennes was the son of Samuel and grandson of John Langley *(53)*.

Impr'is One Bed bedstead Curtaines and Vallanes one Bowlster and two pillowes thereto belonging	03	05	00
One Rugg one Counterpain and three Blanketts	00	15	00
A Chest of Drawers and looking Glasse & Case for Glasses	03	00	00
Six Chairs and three pictures	01	05	00
A Grate fire shovell and tonges	00	03	00
Linnens of all sorts	05	06	08
A hangar sword and belt	01	00	00
Two fenceing Rapiers	00	04	00
A spice Desk	00	02	00
One Saddle and howlsters	00	08	00
Two Ovale tables and fowre square ones	00	17	06
A fflute, an hunting horne and a Dale box with some small things in.	00	05	00
One pewter dish one pewter Basyn and 4 plates	00	05	06
Three Juggs 3 Chamber potts one brasse Candlestick	00	04	06
Eight dozen of bottles	00	12	00
A Mare	04	00	00
Other small things seen and unseene	00	06	08
A Watch and large peice of Gold in the hands of Mr. Richd Littlehales Junr	07	00	00
Two Rings more in his hands	01	00	00
His wearing apparell	06	00	00
Tot	35	19	10

56. John Ball

Collier of Broseley, buried 29/IV/1699, having died three days earlier (46y). Inventory 15/VIII/1699 by Francis Nash and Thomas Williams exhibited 22/VIII/1699 by Ann Ball relict and administratrix. Probably uncle of Sylvanus Ball *(95)*.

Imprimis Three beds with Bedsteeds And Bedding therto Bellonging	03	03	04
Item too table Boords too Joyne presses one Joyn fforme three Joyn stooles six seggen chayres	02	15	06
It' Three Barrells too tubs, too pailes, one mit with other Lumber.	01	03	04
It' Eight pewter dishes, six pewter plates three pewter candlesticks twoo pewter chamber potts, three Dozen of spoons, ffour pewter fflagons, two Salts	01	10	06
Item Too Bras Ketles one Bras pot one Warming pan Too Brass Candlestiks	01	00	00
Item Too Iron pots too Iron Broches one ffrine pan one dreeping pan too Iron Grates one ffire shovell too payre of Tonges with other small Lumber	01	16	08
Item Ten payre of sheets too Tablecloths, three dozen of napkins with Sume other Linnen	01	18	06
Item one Ax with other necessary Tooles	00	06	08
Item one ould Cloke with weight and Line. . . .	00	16	08
Item Too Swine	01	02	06
It' Too Chest one Trunke six Books	00	16	08
Item The Aparrell of the deceased	01	10	00
Toto is . .	18	00	02

57. Judith Holmes

Widow née Mann, m 1667 Thomas Holmes (d 1701) of Broseley, buried 12/I/1707 (66y). Inventory 17/VII/1708 by Thomas Aston and Edward Bradeley* exhibited 20/VII/1708 for Judith Mayor, daughter and executrix. Richard Pearce kinsman was also executor. Will 7/I/1707 left her son in law George Poole and his wife Elizabeth (b 1673) the cottage 'where I now dwell' and six others as well as some land in the possession of Ruth Holmes; her son in law Benjamin Buckley *(85)* and his wife Mary (b 1668) the cottage they occupied and one other and the 'benefit of the rails or wagon way' through Holly Grove; her daughter Judith Mayor widow (b 1675) one cottage; her daughter Frances Holmes (b 1682) £50, the chest and bed in the parlour chamber and the bed in the chamber over the kitchen; her grandchildren Jane Buckley £5 and William Buckley the £5 owed by kinsman Andrew Buckley.

Imprs. In the Kitchen

One Table board & frame & benches	00	07	00
two Iron dreeping panns	00	07	00
one Tinne dripping panne	00	00	06
one Tinne pasty panne	00	00	06
one Joyn'd Skreene	00	10	00
one Iron Grate	00	04	00
Two Iron Broaches	00	02	00
One warmeing panne	00	01	00
One brass Kettle.	00	08	00
One pewter fframe	00	03	00
one Iron Mortar	00	01	00

Item. In the Back Kitchen

Two brass kettles	00	03	00
Two pewter plates & bason	00	01	00
One wooden Tundish 6d, one brewing vessell 2s, one mitt 1s 6d, one payle 6d, one Joyned Stooll 6d, one old table 6d, one Cratch 6d, one brass bench 6d.	00	06	06
One Iron grate links & pothookes	00	06	00
One Iron pudding plate	00	00	03
One payre of Iron Cobberts	00	02	00
One large furnace of brass & Lead	00	15	00
One Iron Pott	00	03	00

Item. In the Palour

One Joyn'd table & frame & benches four Joyn'd stoolls	01	00	00
Six Segg Chairs	00	01	00
one Round table	00	06	08
one Glass Crate	00	02	06
one Joyn'd Cubbert	00	04	00
one little Joyn'd Cubbert	00	02	06
one Iron grate	00	05	00

Item. In the Sellar

One Malt Mill or Steell Mill	00	15	00
Two Hoggsheads	00	10	00

Item. In the Chamber over the Kitchen

one Chest and little Coffer	00	06	08
one hanging presse	00	05	00
fourteen pewter plates	00	07	00
Twelve pewter dishes	03	00	00

THE INVENTORIES OF BROSELEY 179

one Joyn'd bedstead & feather bed two feather bolsters & a Rugg
one othr Rugg 01 00 00

Item. In the Chamber over the Parlour

One Joyn'd table & frame & benche & four joyn'd stolls . .	01 00 00
Two Turkey workt Chairs	00 02 00
One Joyn'd bedstead feather bed one blankett and a green Coverlett	01 00 00
One Joyn'd Chest & things in the same (viz) ten sheets, fifteen napkins three porringers 2 pewter Candlesticks one Salt three old flagons two tankards one table Cloath and Eight trenchers .	01 10 00

Item. In the two Cocklofts

two halfe headed Joyn'd bedsteads and two basketts . .	00 10 00
The Reversion & remainder of two leases from John Huxley Esqr of the Holly Groves	05 00 00
The Deceaseds wearing apparrell	01 00 00
Desperate debts due & oweing to the Testr. . . .	60 00 00

The total is . . 82 08 01

58. John Pearce, senior

Master collier of Broseley, buried 7/V/1709 (66y). Inventory 25/VII/1709 by Samuel Instone and Thomas Aston* exhibited 26/VII/1709 for George Evans Rector of Broseley and Peter Instance of Harley executors. Will 28/III/1709 left his wife 'the part of the house I now dwell in' and the goods in it; his son Richard *(79)* the clock and jack in the kitchen and the long table in the room over, Richard's wife Joyce £5 and their son John (b 1707) £10; his son William *(94)* the wearing apparell and William's son John (b 1704) £10. Richard and William were residual legatees.

Imprs. In the dwelling house

Twenty pewter dishes	02 00 00
A dozen of plates	00 04 00
Siz quartes	00 04 00
Three flaggons	00 02 06
Three pints & a halfe pinte	00 02 00
Two Chamber potts	00 01 00
Two tankards	00 01 00
Six porringer dishes	00 01 06
One salt seller & 2 sawcers	00 00 09
A Close Stoole pan	00 01 06
ffour tinn panns	00 02 00

One tinn Cover .	00	00	04
Six Brass Kettles.	00	08	00
A press .	00	05	00
A warming pann.	00	01	06
Two Tables & frames & Benches	00	06	00
A Jack .	00	08	00
A screene	00	02	00
Two Joyne Stooles	00	01	00
Two Iron Potts .	00	04	00
Three Broches .	00	01	06
A paire of Cobberts	00	01	00
One dreping pan.	00	01	06
A grate two paire of tongs & two fire shovels & two Iron Plates .	00	05	00
Six Candel sticks.	00	01	06

In the room over the house

one ffether Bed & bedsteeds	01	05	00
One flock bed .	00	05	00
Eighteen paire of sheets .	02	00	00
ffour dozen of napkins .	01	00	00
Two Ruggs four blankets & a Coverlid .	00	10	00
Two small tables & a long Table and benches	01	00	00
One Chest, Two small boxes	00	08	00
Two dozen of Chaires .	00	06	04

Over the seller

One larg looking glass .	00	04	00
Two tables & a Clock .	01	05	00

In the Cockloft

Two Beds a large kneading mitt & a Close stoole, Two Spining wheles .	00	12	00

In the Seller

ffour Hodgsheads, ffour barrells a washing tub & a dreper a tray and a tundish .	01	15	00

In the brewhouse

ffive tubs and a Elfate & maltmill	01	00	00
A kneading tub .	00	02	00

At the futtrid

Eight waggains .	01	00	00
A hundred & ffifty pair of waggn wheeles	02	10	00
A hundred of boards .	00	07	00
ffifty yards of waggon railes	00	11	00

A parcell of baskett feet .	00	01	00
A rope & wind on the bank and bloakes &c.	00	05	00
A Chest .	00	01	00
A chaire and some other sorts of stolls	00	04	00
A lading of Ironstone	04	00	00
A parcell of ½ Inch Boards	00	00	09
the mare & Colte	03	00	00
A new halling line	00	14	00
Ready money in the deceaseds possession at the time of his decease & in other psons keeping	84	09	07
Several bonds some whereof are desperate	44	00	00
Debts due to the deceased from severall by book a great part whereof is desperate	156	11	08
The deceaseds wearing Apparell .	03	00	00
Things omitted or forgotten	00	10	00
Summ totall	318	03	11

59. Sampson Buckley

Dyer of Broseley, but apparently not buried there. Inventory 23/VI/1711 by Edward Willis and Michael Stephens exhibited 30/X/1711 for Mary Bulkley, relict and administratrix. Luke (Spencer deleted) Clutterbuck of Ludlow and William Poole waterman of Broseley also signed the bond. The parish register suggests that Bulkley was only sporadically resident in Broseley since it recorded the death of a child not born there.

Imprs. In the Kitchin

One Iron Grate fire Shovell and tongues three Iron broaches one Iron driping pan 2 Smoothing Irons three broches 4 Iron Candlestickes one frying pan one paire of wafer Irons one large paire of tongues one Iron Mortar & pestle	01	04	00
One Iron Jack .	00	10	00
Twelve pewter dishes 24 plates & 2 Salvers six Porringrs 3 Candlestickes & pewter frame .	02	00	00
One brass Chaffing dish Warmeing pan 2 pair of Scales basting Spoone Snuffer & Case and one Copper cann & 3 Candlestickes .	00	12	00
One round Table & foulding skreene 3 segg Chaires one pair of Bellows & a Cradle	00	06	00

In the pantrey

One Table one half hoshead & 18 Trenchers	00	05	00

In the Skullery

three tubbs 2 pailes one Iron pott & one brass pott & 2 Kettles &
a Little boyler   01   10   00

In the Little Hall

One Large Table.	00	15	00
four Chaires	00	05	00
One Iron Grate .	00	05	00
One Spining Wheele	00	02	06

In the Buttrey

two little barrells 2 milk panns & 2 Steans . . .   00   07   00

In the Chambr over the pantrey

one Chest one flock bed one Blanktt & bedstead . . .   00   07   06
Six paire of hempen & 6 paire of hurden sheets one table Clo. &
12 napkins of Diaper one table Clo; & 12 flaxen Napkins 2 dossen
of hurden Napkins & 6 table Clos: 6 pillow beeres of flaxen .   07   00   00

In the Cambr over the Kitchin

One flock bed 2 blanktts 1 Coverlett & two bolsters bedsteed
Green Curtaines & Vallions   01   10   00

In the Best Chambr

Two feather beds 3 bolsters 4 Blanktts 2 Covrlids 2 bedsteeds
Curtains & Vallions to Each   07   00   00

Two Coffers one Chest .	00	15	00
One Chest of Drawrs	01	00	00
One trunk 2 Chaires one Table .	00	07	00
One Large looking glass .	01	00	00
Drinking glasses .	00	05	00
One bible & twelve other Bookes	01	00	00

In the Behoine Chambr

One feather bed 2 blanketts one Coverlett four Chaires 2 Stooles
one dressing table & boxes 2 sconses bedsteed and Yallow Curtaines
and Vallions & Window Curtaines . . .   08   00   00

Implemts of Trade

Two Scribling horses and 4 paire of Scribling Cards 60 pound of
Wooll 50 pound of Woollen Yarne   04   12   00

20 pound of jersey Yarne	02	00	00
One bag of fustick	01	00	00
one bag of Logwood	00	05	00
one bag of Argill	01	00	00
one barrell of Archill	01	00	00

three pound of brasell att 4d p pound	00	01 00
thirty pound of pot ashes att 4d p pound.	00	10 00
Six paire of Clothiers Sheers	08	00 00
One sheer board.	00	05 00
One Dubbing board	00	05 00
One Dyers press plank and paprs and Iron Crow.	04	00 00
One Clothiers Rack	03	00 00
One Snap Reell.	00	10 00
A handle Cratch and 6 dosn of Teazells	00	10 00
One large furnace	10	00 00
One Lesser furnace	02	00 00
One Woad fatt.	03	00 00
Implemts for Combing Jersey	00	06 08
four Tubbs	00	06 08
Two pair of Scales & Weights	00	10 00
Two Looms & the Gares	04	10 00
the Intestates Wareiong Apparrell.	01	00 00
Tot	84	17 04

60. Edward Nash

Coalminer/collier of Broseley, buried 21/VIII/1713 (54y). Inventory 29/IX/1713 by Tho. Hartshorne, Samuel Evans and Rich. Smith exhibited 10/VII/1714 for Mary Nash relict and executrix. Will 19/XII/1707 left mother Mary Nash the part of the cottage she lived in and two pieces of land leased from George Weld for life, then to brothers and sister, Thomas, John and Elizabeth Nash; and wife Mary (née Smith of Benthall m 1696) the part of the cottage Nash had lived in with the garden.

Impr's One Chattell Lease	04	00 00
Pewter of all sorts	01	05 00
Six old brass Kettles one warming Pan & Ladle three Iron Potts two small Broaches with other Small necessaryes Iron ware thereto belonging	01	01 00
Iron Ware belonging to the ffire Hearth one small Grate ffire Shovell Tongs and other necessaryes thereto belonging	00	08 06
Tin ware & Earthen Ware	00	05 00
Item old joynd Goods & Turners ware Seaven Chairs two small Tables two small Sets of Shelves two Spinning Wheels with some small Coop'y ware one small Cratch	00	13 00
Item other Coop'y ware 3 old Barrells one Kneading Mitt one brewing Vessell one old Tub	00	06 08
It' Three pair of Bedsteads two Chests one Coffer one fforme & some small Boxes	00	18 00

It' Two old ffeather Beds one fflock Bed Three over worne Rugs old Blanketts Two setts of over worne Hangings . . .	02	10	00
It' Linnen of all sorts belonging to a poor man's house . .	01	01	06
It' two Swine	01	12	06
Some old Lumber Goods not worth menconing . . .	00	02	06
The dec'eds wearing Apparell	00	10	00
It' Good & Bad Debts	04	00	00
Totall . .	18	12	08

61. Edward Cox

Carrier of Broseley, buried 11/XII/1714. Inventory 8/III/1714 (no appraisers named) but Elizabeth Evans signed by mark. She was his daughter (b 1672) and administratrix through her husband Richard Evans of Broseley (m 1697) exhibited 8/III/1714.

Impr's the dec'ds wearing Apparrell	04	00	00
Item the dec'ds watch	03	00	00
Item ready money in the dec'ds custody at his decease about .	00	11	00
Item six small horses kept for carrying Coles . . .	18	00	00
	25	11	00

62. Mary Ogden

Widow of Robert Ogden *(41)* of Broseley, buried 26/VII/1717 according to her will 'in my dear husband's grave in the chancel of Broseley church'. Inventory 31/VII/1717 by Francis Barrett and Will Corbett exhibited 28/X/1717 by Ann Whitmore (b 1677) niece and executrix. Will 12/III/1716 left her nephew Robert Whitmore (b 1679) £10, his wife 20s. and his daughters Mary and Rachel respectively 40s. and two silver spoons and one silver spoon; her nephew William Whitmore (b 1686) £10 and a silver porringer; and her niece Ann Whitmore £10 and £3 'I borrowed of her', the wrought silver cup, three silver spoons, the house and all goods except the house linens and wearing apparell which she was to share with her sister Mary (b 1675). These four were the children of her brother Robert *(63)*. She also left Elizabeth wife of Peter Young of Westbury £10 and their daughter Mary the watch and ring with a stone, one pair hemp sheets and a pillow beer, one flax tablecloth and 12 flax napkins; her cousin Ann Thomas the gold ring with a red stone.

Impr's two Gold Rings & Silver Plate	10	00 00
Item three Beds & furniture	10	00 00
Item Two Chests & Linnens in them	05	00 00
Item Books	01	00 00
Item One Chest & seven Boxes	00	05 00
Item One Skreen, Table & Chaires	00	15 00
Item Brass Iron & Latten ware	01	00 00
Item Pewter of all sorts	01	05 00
Item One Chattell	80	00 00
Item Earthen ware & Glasses	00	05 00
Item Coopery Turn'd & Tugar ware	01	10 00
Item old Pictures, things out of sight & forgotten	00	05 00
Item wearing Apparell	05	00 00
Total	116	05 00

63. Robert Whitmore, the elder

Tallow chandler of Broseley, buried 15/I/1717. Inventory 20/I/1717 by Isaac Wyke and Tho. Griffiths exhibited 4/III/1717 by William Whitmore son and executor. Mary Whitmore daughter was also executrix. Will 19/VIII/1717 left his son Robert the wearing apparel, the house now building and the yard on the south side of the house he lived in late in the possession of Francis Roper; his son William was to have liberty to turn up clay for one or more clamp of bricks and to burn the same in the yard; his daughter Mary Whitmore £310 and the furniture in the two lower and one upper rooms at the west end of the house and the best bed; his daughter Hannah Whitmore £200 and the right and tithe of the ground on which the house of his late sister Mary Ogden stood and 'the last enclosure I took out of the common adjoining the house'; grandchildren, daughters of Robert Mary (b 1712) £3, Rachel (b 1715) and Ann (b 1717) 20s. each. Whitmore m Rachel Crow in 1674 (d 1698). Brother of Mary Ogden *(62)*, father of William Whitmore *(74)* and son of John Whitmore *(38)*.

Impr's Chattles to the value of	1126	10 00
Six beds & furniture	16	00 00
Wearing apparel & money in his pockett	10	00 00
Tables Cupboards, one Chest of drawers & one Press	03	05 00
Two Chests & Linnen & two Coffers with yarn	03	02 00
Brass, Pewter & Latten Ware	07	10 00
One Clock & Case Barells & other wooden ware	04	01 02

One Jack, driping pans fire Irons & other Iron Ware	02	00	00
Goods for Sale & Utensills belonging to the Shop	30	00	00
One horse one Pigg a Rick of hay	07	15	00
Two Looking Glasses Pictures, other Glasses Earthe turn'd & tugar ware	02	10	00
Chairs, boxes & books	02	12	06
Trumpery & other things out of sight or forgotten	00	12	00
	1220	18	02

64. George Bayley

Shopkeeper of Broseley, buried 19/II/1717 (the only entry to refer to him). Inventory 28/II/1717-8 by Samuel Hartshorne and Richard Crompton exhibited 9/II/1718 for John Blayney executor. Will 25/I/1717 referred to wife Anne and to a Thomas Bayley and his son John. It mentioned 'two spinning wills' and 'wereing cloths & one shurte', presumably handed over before death as they were not listed in the inventory. Thomas Bayley died in 1723 and his inventory was valued by John Blayney at £10 10s. 02d.

Two ffeather Beds & the ffurniture velonging	02	00	00
Sheets and Table Linnen	02	10	00
A Chest 2 Coffers a Box & 3 Small Tables	00	13	06
Six Chairs 3 Stooles and a little Table	00	05	00
Close Stool and Pan, 3 China Dishes, small Covers	00	04	06
Two Pair of Bedsteeds 5 Chairs two Stooles	00	10	00
A Grate Cheeks Shovell Tongs Morter Pestell	00	07	06
Warming Pan, ffrying Pan, a broach & small things	00	06	00
A Press and Cupboard Trenchers and Tin Pans	00	05	00
Pewter 3 Barrells a Neading Mitt a Tub & a Stand	01	00	06
Sope and Tobacco & Small things to sell	01	05	05
A Brass Pot Scales and Iron Waits	00	08	00
Totall	09	15	05

65. John Mayor

Of Broseley, buried 5/VIII/1719 (37y). Inventory 29/IX/1719 by John Littleford and Thomas Hartshorne exhibited 1/X/1719 for Joyce Mayor relict and administratrix (née Davis m 1703, d 1750).

THE INVENTORIES OF BROSELEY   187

Impr's One Small Iron Grate fire shovel & tounges w'th some other necessary Iron Ware belonging to the use of ye fireplace . .	00	09	00
Item one Brass pott with some other brass vessells for necessary use	00	15	09
Item Thirteen Pewter dishes midling and small one Pewter Cann w'th some other small pewter Vessells for necessary use . .	01	11	00
Item Three Small Tables 3 Barrells 3 Small Tubs with all other Wooden ware old Chairs Stools and Benches . . .	02	00	00
Item 2 Indifferent Feather Beds and Bolsters w'th all other necessarys thereunto belonging	03	01	06
Item Four Pair of mean Bedsteds 2 old Lodging Beds, one Chest, 2 Iron potts & some necessary Iron things not mencond by name.	02	02	03
Item One Little Working Mare with Hay intending for her wintering	04	10	06
Item One Midling swine	00	15	00
Item The Deceased's Wearing Apparell with Good and Lawfull debts belonging to him	03	10	00
Tot . .	18	15	00

66. Richard Gears

Tallow chandler of Broseley, buried 12/IV/1720. Inventory 10/V/1720 by Ri. Reynolds and Wm. Bithell exhibited 27/IX/1720 for Margaret Gears relict and executrix. Will 20/III/1719 left his children Richard, William (b 1710) Margaret (b 1711) and Beatrice (b 1717) all free land.

Imprs. In the Kitchin

Copper & Brass of all sorts	02	00	00
Pewter of all sorts	03	00	00
Iron Ware of all sorts	02	10	00
A large Chest, Skreen, Ovall Table five chairs and other Wooden ware	01	10	00

In the Pantry

five chairs and Glass Crate	00	10	00

In the Butterfy & Celler

Eight Barrells, Brewing Vessels Shelves, & Benches . .	01	15	00

In the Brewhouse

a brewing ffurnace, & boiler	00	15	00
A Steel mill wth other old Lumber	01	00	00

In the best Chamber

a Bed & all thereto belonging	02	10	00
Two Chests wth Drawers, Eleven Chaires, a looking Glass, two Ovall Tables, Window Curtains, pictures fire shovell and tonges	03	00	00
Table linnen & Bed linnen of all sorts	10	00	00

In the Cock loft

A small Table, joyned Cradle, Boxes and other Lumber	00	10	00

In the Kitchen Chamber

Two Beds wth the furniture thereto belong	03	00	00
A Cock, Chest and two Chaires	02	10	00

In the Red Chamber

a Bed & all furniture belonging to it	01	10	00
A large Chest, Coffer, & Chair	00	10	00

In the servants Chamber

a bed & bedsteed, wth other lumber	00	10	00
His wearing Apparrell, Book debts, and ready money in his Purse	90	04	05

In the Shopp

half a Tunn of Tallow wrought and unwrought	20	00	00
A Copper furnace, Working Tooles & Implemts belonging to his Trade	04	00	00
Wickyarn	01	19	00
Two Horses	05	00	00
Two Piggs	01	00	00
Sum Tot	158	19	05

67. James Freeman

Gent of Broseley, buried 24/II/1722. Inventory 15/III/1722-3 by Will. Corbett, Fran. Barrett and Tho. Harrison exhibited 2/IV/1723 for Deborah Freeman relict and executrix. Will 18/II/1722 left his son George of the City of London his watch, the largest silver tankard and his wearing apparel and his son James (b 1718) £500.

Imrp's In the Kitchin

Seaven pewter dishes Two dozen & a half of plates	01	10	00
One Kettle one Tea kettle one Chafer two brass Candlesticks six Chairs	00	13	00

One Iron pott one Grate on Jack with other Iron ware & Books . 01 15 00

Item In the Parlour
Two Tables, one looking Glass Eight Chairs . . . 01 09 00

Item In the parlour Chamber
one Bed with ffurniture Eight Chairs 03 00 00
Plate 15 00 00
Bonds Bills & Book debts 530 00 00

Item In the Room over the kitchin
one Bed & ffurniture 04 10 00
Six Chairs one looking Glass 00 10 00

Item In the Garrett
one Box with Linnen 04 00 00
Wearing Apparell 07 15 00
One Sack & a half of hops 02 10 00

Item In the Brewhouse & Cellar
Six Barrells two brewing Tubs 01 05 00
One Malt Mill one Iron ffurnace 01 10 00
Paper Prints & Things forgotten or out of sight . . . 00 07 06

575 14 06

68. Edward Edwards

Of Broseley, buried 6/IV/1723. Inventory 15/V/1723 by John Langley and John Hincksman exhibited 18/VI/1723 for Catherine Edwards relict and administratrix.

Imprimis Eight Cowes	24	00 00
ffour heifors	10	00 00
Two yearlings	02	00 00
ffour horses and one colt	20	00 00
ffive hoggs and Eight stores	05	00 00
Sheep of all sorts	05	00 00
Three Calves	01	10 00
Tenn Acres of groweing Corne	10	00 00
Corn in the Barne	09	00 00
Lent graine of all sorts	09	00 00
Oates in the Barne	04	00 00
ffodder of all sorts	04	00 00
Two hundred and ffifty strike of Mault	40	00 00

Household provision of all sorts vizt Drinke Cheese Beife and Bacon	10	00 00
Implements of husbandry of all sorts	10	00 00
A Clock	02	00 00
Brass and Pewter	04	00 00
Ironware of all sorts	04	10 00
Bedding of all sorts	—	— —
Linnen of all sorts	06	00 00
A Chest of Drawers	02	10 00
Tables of all sorts	02	00 00
Chaires and forms	01	00 00
A Dresser of Drawers and Skreen	01	00 00
Chests and Boxes	01	10 00
Barrells of all sorts	02	10 00
Tubbs and other wooden ware	02	00 00
Lumber out of sight	01	00 00
Wearing Apparrell and money in purse	10	00 00
	233	10 00

69. Richard Roden

Yeoman/shopkeeper of Broseley, buried 16/I/1723. Inventory 12/II/1723 by Nicho. Harrison and Danll. Blackshaw exhibited 21/IV/1724 for Mary relict and executrix. Will 10/I/1723 left to his wife and daughter (b 1710), both called Mary, 'all merchandise goods in the shop and money in the shop book' and leasehold property in the tenure of Thomas Farely leased from Mr. Herbert Langley. Not a close relative of Thomas Roden *(71)*.

Impr's in the Kitchen
a Clock, Jack and other Goods therein value	03	00 00

It' In the Shopp
Goods & Merchandize of the value of	15	00 00

It' in the Cellar
Barrells & Drink	05	10 00

It' in the Brewhouse
a Maltmill and Brewing Vessels	02	00 00

It' in the Brewhouse Chamber
Tickney Ware	00	05 00

It' in the Kitchen Chamber
One Little ffeather Bed with the App'tences and two Boxes & Linnen therein 02 00 00

It' in the Chamber over the Shopp
three Ovall Tables, a doz'n of Chairs, some old Boxes & Little old pictures and some other small Trumpery therein . . . 01 00 00

It' Three Swyne price 02 05 00
It' Wearing Apparrell 05 00 00
It' other Small matters omitted unseen and fforgotten . . 01 00 00

                                                              37 00 00

70. John Poole

Labouring waterman of Broseley, buried 28/VI/1724. Inventory 15/VII/1724 by Eustas Beard and Jonathan Turner exhibited 21/VII/1724 by Priscilla Pool relict and administratrix.

Impr's Two old Lines	00 15 00
one small piece of Hurden Cloth	00 05 06
one old stayfull Rope	00 04 06
Two old Barrows	00 01 04
one old shaft	00 01 02
And a few small trifling things not mentioned . .	00 03 00
Item the Deceaseds wearing apparrell. Very mean . .	00 08 00
Sum tot. .	01 18 06

71. Thomas Roden

Tobacco pipe maker of Broseley, buried 12/XII/1723 (65y). Inventory (not dated) by John Browne, Thomas Hartshorne and Richard Harper exhibited 19/I/1723 by his sons Richard (b 1699) and Samuel* (b 1702) Roden who also signed it. Administration 16/VI/1724. His wife Sarah née Deacon d 1718. Will 10/XII/1723 left the two sons everything including several houses. Not a close relative of Richard Roden *(69)*.

Imp's The dec'ed wearing Apparell 01 00 00
Item Two joint Chests and a Middling Joint Table . . 01 02 06

It' Two indifferent ffeather bedds and bedsteads two old blanketts, One Indifferent Rugge one old Coverlid and two bolsters and other Materialls thereunto belonging 02 10 00
It' Two pair of old hurden Sheets 00 04 00
It' One pair of flaxen Sheets One hempen Sheet and one hempen Table Cloth 00 10 00
It' Ten indifferent pewter dishes and 12 plates . . 01 05 00
It' One old Cupboard one old Skreen Table & one other old Table and joint stool and two drawers 00 16 00
It' One old Warming pann One Iron Spitt a small ffire Grate a Candle box and a Small pair of Tongs and Creeper . . 00 06 00
It' Two old battered Barrells 00 01 00

The Implem'ts and Tooles for ye Art of Tobacco Pipe making belonging to the dec'ed above mentioned
It' One Curricomb Screw and one Cheek Skrew . . . 01 03 00
It' One long pair of peak heel moulds and one long pair of broad heel moulds 00 12 06
It' Two pair of Short moulds one pair of broad heels ye other round heels 00 10 00
It' Two old pair of Short moulds. 00 05 06
It' One pair of hunting Moulds 00 05 00
It' ffour stoppers for the Moulds 00 00 04
It' One old ffire Shovell 00 01 00
It' Working Clay in the Shop 00 07 06
It' One old ffire Grate belonging to the Shop . . . 00 08 06
It' One Dozen of working boards and 14 Wooden Grates for the Pipes &c. 00 10 06
It' Three Slob Benches One old Mitt and Trough two Slob blocks. 00 05 09
It' One Small Marmulet in the Shop 00 03 06
It' Other old Lumbers and Small Usefull Implem'ts elsewhere not in Custody unseen and unmentioned 00 05 00

Total . . 12 12 07

72. Mr. Richard Mason

Innholder of Broseley, buried 14/VIII/1727. Inventory 22/VIII/1727 by Richard Asbury and Tho. Mathews exhibited 19/IX/1727 by Ann Mason relict and administratrix. Two daughters under age.

Impr's in the Kitchen

Brass & Pewter 01 10 00
Iron Ware 00 15 00
Seven Chairs one Little Table & one old skreen . . . 00 04 00

THE INVENTORIES OF BROSELEY

In the Parlour

Two Ovall Tables	00	08	00
A Clock and Case	01	05	00
One Chest and eight Chairs	00	12	00

In the smoaking Room

One small Table & six Chairs	00	05	00

In the Parlour Chamber

One ffeather Bed and ffurniture	02	05	00
Seven Chairs, one Chest of Drawers one little Table one Looking Glass	00	18	00

In the Closet

One Bed, one Chair, one little Table	01	02	00

In the Room over the Kitchen

One Bed and ffurniture	01	12	00
One Table one Chair four Boxes	00	06	00

In the Room over the smoaking room

One Bed two Trunks & one Box	01	03	00

In the Cellar

ffour empty Barrells & three full	02	12	06
Linnen	02	00	00
Two small Piggs	00	18	00
Wearing Apparel	01	00	00
Hay in the stable	00	10	00
Totall	19	05	00

73. Thomas Teece

Locksmith of Broseley, buried 16/II/1727 (46 y). Inventory 20/II/1727 by Thomas Hartshorne, John Instone and Samuel Hartshorne exhibited 9/IV/1728 for John Hartshorne of Hilltop in Bentham and Thomas Hughs junior executors. Will 10/VIII/1727 left Francis Humphrey of Boarton near Wenlock a pair of plush breeches; Thomas and William Teece and Humphrey son of Edward Hill Junior 'my next neighbour' the other clothes; wife Mary the dwelling house and household goods for life or until she marry then to Margaret Hill daughter of Edward Hill junior; the said

Margaret the clock and clock case in the dwelling house; and his father William Teece 6d. a week. Nephew Thomas son of William Teece (b 1715) was to have the shop and shop tools when he is old enough and he was to be apprenticed as a locksmith out of the estate if his own parents could not afford it. Anything left over was to be shared among his own and his first wife's relatives, Nicholas Mellechub of Cleetown, William Teece, Edward Hill senior, Eleanor wife of Robert Malpas, Edward Hill junior and Timothy Cartwright. His first wife Ann d 1722.

Impr's In the dwelling house Pewter of all sorts .	01	10 08
Item One brass pott & kettle & warming pan .	00	16 00
Item One Iron Dripping pan & 2 other Small Iron pans .	00	03 02
Item One Iron Spit & Cobberts .	00	01 04
Item One Small Iron Mortar & Pestell .	00	02 03
Item One Small Iron pot & pothooks, one Marment .	00	02 06
Item One old Marment in the Wall .	00	02 00
Item One old Grate & wings & other Implements belonging to the fire hearth .	00	05 06
Item One Small dresser & drawers much broken .	00	02 06
Item One Small Oval table & two Small Aquare tables .	00	03 00
Item Six old Chairs & 3 Dozen of Trenchers .	00	03 00
Item One old Clock & Clock case .	02	00 00
Item Wooden Vessells of all sorts belonging to the Buttery so called, Three half hogsheads (or better) two barrells two Coolers & 3 other little tubs, all old Vessells. .	00	16 06

Above Stairs

Impr's Three old pair of Bedsteads .	00	04 06
Item Three very olf ffeather beds, two old blankets, three old Coverlids & other Materials thereunto belonging and ten old pairs of hempen & hurden sheets .	03	00 00
Item One Chest 4 Old boxes & One Desk .	00	01 06

In the Working Shop

One old pair of Bellows, One Anvel, 2 bins, 3 hammers ffiles & some other Implements belonging to the Locksmith's trade .	03	00 00
Item Old Iron and Brass .	00	04 00
Item an old Malt Mill in the Shop .	00	08 00
Item An old Gun .	00	02 06
Item a stone of Malt & some other Provision .	04	00 00
Item A small store pigg .	00	05 00
Item Two pair of Scales and Weights .	00	04 00
One Bond debt .	20	00 00
Desparate debts due f Book .	04	18 00
T*he deceased Wearing apparell .	02	00 00

Money in the deced's Custody	00	11	06
More, One old press & other old Lumber unmentioned	00	03	00
Invent"y Tot	45	16	05

74. Mr. William Whitmore

Tallow chandler of Broseley, buried 14/III/1727 (41y). Inventory 25/IV/1728 by Amos Sherborne and John Squire exhibited 16/VII/1728 by Mary Whitmore relict and administratrix (née Squire m 1722). Son Robert Whitmore *(63)*, grandson of John Whitmore *(38)*.

Impr's Coathes to the Value of	00	00	00
Three Beds and ffurniature	08	00	00
Wearing Apparel and Money in his Pockett	07	00	00
Tables Cupboards two Chests of Drawers & one Press	03	10	00
Two Chests & Linnen and Yarne.	08	02	00
Brass Pewter and Latten Ware	07	10	00
One Clock and Case Barrells & other Wooden Ware	03	05	00
One Jack, Dripping pan, fire Irons & other iron ware	02	00	00
Goods for sale & utensills belonging to the Shop	15	00	00
Two horses & one Mare, one Pig & on Rick of Hay	10	00	00
Three Looking Glasses, Pictures, other Glasses, Earth, Turn'd and sugar ware	03	10	00
Chaires, Boxes and Bookes	03	12	06
Trumpery and other things out of sight and forgotten	00	12	00
	70	02	00

75. Thomas Gower

Trowman of Broseley but apparently not buried there. Inventory 28/II/1728-9 by William Poolle and John Hartshorne exhibited 4/III/1728 for Dorothy Gower relict and administratrix. Gower has probably moved from Shrewsbury in 1698. He worked 'the Richard' and 'the Richard and Sarah' from Broseley and Bridgnorth down to Bristol 1699-1712.

In the Hall So Called.

Imp's pewter of all sorts.	01	10	00
It' three Old Ovall Tables & one Old dresser of Drawrs..	00	12	06
It' one ffire Grate & ffurniture thereunto belonging, Two Iron panns, 2 Iron spitts, 4 old Brass Candlesticks, a Skimmer.	00	12	06
It' One Small Hanging Press.	00	05	06

In the Kitchen

It' Old pewter of all sorts	00	05 00
It' Old old ffire Grate & Tons & other old things thereunto belonging	00	03 06
It' Two Small Iron Potts & a Small Brass Kettle	00	03 06
It' One old Joyned Skreen, One ffolding Skreen, two Small Tables, and Six Old Chairs	00	08 00

Above Stayers

It' Three old pair of Bedsteads & 2 old Setts of Curtains	01	06 00
It' three old feather Beds, 3 Old Ruggs, 3 Blanketts	04	00 00
It' 5 pair of old Hurden Sheets, 3 pair of Hempen & fflaxen Sheets, one dozn. of old Napkins, one old Joyned Chest & one Trunk	01	07 06
It' One small Side Table	00	02 06

Over ye Buttery

One old fflock Bed and Bedsteed	00	04 06

In ye Celler

ffour Barrells, 3 Tubbs and a Cooler	00	16 00

Upon the River of Severn

One Trow, One Barge & One ffriggett, wth Ropes, Masts, Sailes, Shafts, Oars, planks and all other Materialls thereunto belonging	130	00 00
The deced's Wearing Apparrell	01	00 00
All other Old Lumber unmentioned	00	10 00
Invt'y Tot.	143	07 00

76. Thomas Williams, the elder

Of Broseley, buried 18/V/1729 (82y). Inventory 19/V/1729 by Richd. Weaver and William Lloyd exhibited 1/VII/1729 for Thomas Williams son and Saml. Hartshorne friend executors. Will 3/IV/1729 left son Thomas (b 1668) the house he and his daughter Elizabeth (m 1718 William Lloyd) lived in during term of lease under John Weld and to allow his daughter 'that part of the house and garden which he thinketh most proper', also first 2y rent of house and ground let to Jos. Carrington in Broseley Wood (purchased from Ed. Pursall gent) but to pay £1 pa to wife Margaret while a widow and £5 pa to grandson John Alcox when 21y, then whole estate to Thomas Williams and his heirs but must not be mortgaged or sold, two pews in Broseley church, one in chancel and one in aisle to go with estate except four seats to wife, son Jonathan Williams, daughter Elizabeth Brooks and grandson John Guest; his son Jonathan (b 1671) the house and garden now in his possession during the term of lease then his eldest daughter Ann the west end of the house and his daughter Kittura the east, the garden being divided; his daughter Elizabeth (m (i) George Guest 1700 (ii) Samuel Brooks) and her sons George and John Guest (b 1708 & 1715) the house she possessed during term of lease and to pay 'my dept' of £2 to Augustine Clibbury for her son's apprenticeship, John to have lesser end of house at end of apprenticeship and half the cattle and swine when 21y, at her death George to have other end, brewhouse and garden to be divided; his wife Margaret house leased under Francis Varley Esq. while a widow, then to grandsons John Guest and Jonathan Williams, but if she married a 'suitably disposed' Broseley man then she was to have quiet possession for 7y (m 1730 Francis Eaves), also half cattle and swine, also the little house near Severn late in possession of Francis Jones while a widow then to daughter Jane Marsh *alias* Alcox during term of lease. Household goods to wife Margaret while a widow but clock and jack and firegrate in the house, purgatory, a large cupboard in the parlour and four large pewter dishes marked IL to the house 'I now live in' during term of lease, and not to be moved from thence. His son Jonathan discharged debts due if he paid funeral expenses and shared costs of probate with wife. Williams was the son of Thomas Williams and Joyce (née Eaves m 1645). Nearly all his family were connected with the river. His two sons Thomas and Jonathan worked trows, the latter moving to Bewdley. Two of his daughters married trowmen, Joyce John Benbow in 1692, and Elizabeth Samuel Brooks. Thomas junior's eldest daughter Elizabeth also married a river man William Lloyd in 1718. The main Williams boat 'the Thomas and Mary' worked regularly from Broseley carrying iron ware from Abraham Darby down to Bristol.

In ye Parlour

Imprs. pewter of all Sorts, 7 Midling Dishes and 15 plates all old pewter	00	14	00
It one Small Dresser of Drawers	00	12	00
It 2 old Brass Kettles	00	11	06
It 4 old 5 Segg Chaires	00	02	06
It One old Small Table & Joyned Stoole	00	03	06
It All other Old Lumber there	00	01	00

In ye Kitchen

It One Joyned Skreen & Small Square Table	00	06	08
It 2 Iron Spitts, & 2 Small Iron panns One Small Clever, & other Small Iron Ware	00	08	00
It Wooden Ware of all Sorts	00	02	00
All other Old Lumber there	00	01	00

In the Celler

It 2 Hogsheads, 2 Barrells, One Kilderkin, 2 Benches & 2 Old Horses so Called.	00	18	06

In the Brewhouse

It One Iron ffurnace, One Iron Marmet both in ye Wall .	00	10	06
It One Cooller, 4 Small Old Tubbs, & 2 Little pailes and One Lading Gaune	00	06	06
It One other Small Iron Marment, One pair of Iron Cobbarts, One Little Wheell, & One Sauce pan also One peck & half peck .	00	04	03
It 2 Old Benches & other Lumber	00	01	06
One old Spade & 3 Hay fforks .	00	01	03

Above Staires

It In ye Room over the parlour

One ffeather Bed, one Blanket, One Coverlid, One Bolster & pillow, One Joyned pair of Bedsteeds and Hangings thereunto .	03	10	00
It One pair of Trukle Bedsteeds, 2 Old fflock Beds One Blanktt & Coverlid, & Hangings & Bolster	01	01	00
It One Joyn'd Chest	00	08	06
It 2 Old Chaires, One old Lumber Trunk.	00	01	00
It Window Curtains	00	00	09

In the Chamber over ye Kitchen

It One pair of half Headed Bedsteads and hangings, One ffeather Bed & Bolster, One pillow, One Blankett, One Spotted Rugg .	03	00	00
It One Joyn'd Chest & 2 old Chaires	00	06	08
Linnens of all Sorts, 3 pair of Hurden Sheets, 4 pair of Hempen Sheets, One pair of fflaxen sheets, 2 fflaxen Table Cloths, 16 old Small fflaxen Napkins	02	15	00
It One Little Box	00	00	06
It One Close Stooll	00	00	09
It The Deceds Wearing Apparrell.	00	16	06

Cattle Belonging to ye Deced

Two Cowes, One Yearling Heifer	07	02	06
Desperate Debts due to the Deced	10	03	00
All other Lumber unmentioned .	00	02	06
Inventory Tot .	35	02	10

77. Noel or Newell Edwards

Yeoman of Broseley, buried 1/I/1729. Inventory 17/IV/1730 by Thos. Beddow and Wm. Pearce exhibited 14/IV/1730 (*sic*) for George Edwards son and executor. Will 7/XII/1729 left children Samuel, Newell, William, John, Edward, Francis, Elizabeth and Mary 1s. each; his daughter Anne 10s. 6d.; his wife Elizabeth and son George the interest for several sums lent at interest, leases of Haddows tenement and of Dean Hill and 'articles of a demise of certain coals' in Broseley under George Weld Esq. His brother in law John Bickerton was to be overseer.

In the Kitchen

Pewter	04	04	00
Iron brass & tinnen Ware	02	10	00
Clock & one Table	02	05	00
half a doz of Chairs	00	06	00

In the Parlour

One feather bed Bedstead & furniture	05	00	00
A Chest of Drawers & two tables	02	10	00
half a doz Chairs	00	09	00
Glass	00	05	00

In the Chamber over the Kichin

Tow bed & bedsteads & furniture	08	00	00
four Chairs	00	10	00
Two Chests & a desk & one Table	01	10	00

In another Chamber

1 bed bedstead & furniture	04	00	00
a Table & three Chairs	00	07	00

In the Cellar

Barrells	01	08	00
Drinks	01	10	00

Brewhouse

Tubs & furnace	02	00	00
Reversion of 2 Leases so long the lives continue five pound each ye anno Proffitt	10	00	00
Money at use & debts	80	00	00
Linnen of all sorts	10	00	00

Silver Tankard & spoons.	10	00	00
yarn & feathers.	01	00	00
The deceds wearing Apparell	05	00	00
Money in purse.	00	10	00
Tot	153	04	00

78. Francis Evans

Of Broseley, buried 27/II/1731. Inventory 29/IV/1732 by Paul Evans and Willm. Jones exhibited 2/V/1732 for Elizabeth Evans relict and administratrix.

Impr's One old bed & the Dec'eds wearing Apparell	00	16	00
It' Two pair of hourden sheets & hillings.	00	04	00
One old Table board	00	02	00
One little Chest.	00	05	00
One little Guinea Box	00	02	06
One old Coffer.	00	01	06
A grate & wings.	00	02	00
A fire shovell & Tongs.	00	01	00
One old Chair.	00	00	06
One frying pann.	00	00	06
One little old dresser	00	00	02
One little Iron pott	00	01	06
One Small Tub.	00	00	06
2 old pewter dishes	00	02	00
One old paile & a piggen	00	00	06
One old barrell.	00	00	09
One old kneeding Mitt.	00	02	00
Six Trenchers.	00	00	06
2 Wooden piggins	00	00	02
Three pewter Spoons	00	00	01
One Small Tin Can	00	00	01
One old boyler.	00	02	00
	02	05	03

79. Richard Pearce

Master collier of Broseley, buried 2/VII/1732. Inventory 14/VII/1732 by Richard Henshaw of Buildwas, Richard Henshaw of Sweeney, Samuel Instone of Wike, John Instone of Wike, John Instone of Benthall and John Houlett joynor. William Pearce also signed. The inventory was apparently never exhibited. Administration 11/VII/1732 for William Pearce principal creditor (and probably brother, see *(58)* and *(94)*).

In the Garrett

One flock Bed, one Chaff Bed, Two Truckle Bedsteads & Two Little wheeles old	00	10	00
Five strikes of Muncorne ordinary	00	10	00
2 Old Mitts .5. Wooden Bottles & some Cheswitts	00	10	00
2 Small Old Tables	00	02	00

In W'm Pearces Chamber

Wheat 31 Strikes.	03	10	00

In the Second Roome over the Kitchen

A Feather Bed w't 60 li very olde much damaged Bedstead & Hangings & 2 Old Blanketts	01	10	00
An Old Chest of Drawers	00	05	00
a Chest & Little Table	00	05	00
An Old Presse and 3 Chairs	00	07	06
An Old Silver Watch	01	00	00
12 paire of Hurden Sheetes, some of them old 1 Table Cloath & 8 Napkins	03	05	00
a small Lookeing Glass & some very little Pictures	00	01	00

In the Little Roome over the Pantry

A Flock Bed a small Bedstead 2 old Chaires & a very Little Table.	00	10	00

In the first Kitchen Chamber

A Parcele of Hemp & some Nogs	01	10	00
2 Chests	00	08	00
4 Small Boxes	00	05	00
some very small Pictures.	00	00	06
A Feather Bolster 2 blanketts & hangins	01	15	00

In the Pantry

some Earthen ware Glasses, & other small things.	00	06	06

In the Kitchen

A Table a Forme & 2 Benches	00	10	00
A Clock Case	00	07	06
An Oval Table and Pewter Frame	00	10	06
An Old Skreen	00	10	00
a Little Oval Table	00	03	06
a Jack & 9 small spitts	00	02	00
An Iron Grate a Pair of Tongues a Paire of stilliards a Clever & other small things ab't the fire place	00	12	00
A Dresser with Drawers.	00	05	00
9 Old Picture Frames	00	01	06
a p'cell of Small Old Bookes & 3 Little Shelves	00	10	06

An Old Glass Frame & six Earthen Plates	00	01	06
6 Large Pewter Dishes w't 50 li att 7d ½ p pound	01	11	03
9 small Pewter Dishes w't 36 li att 7d ½ p pd	01	02	06
26 Pewter Plates w't 17 li att 7d ½	00	10	07 ½
10 Pewter Porringers 4 Pewter Candlesticks 2 salts & 2 small Mustard Potts	00	10	00
a small Lookeing Glass Some Tin Patty Pans & some other Tin Ware	00	03	06

In the Old Parlour

11 Milk Pans 1 Tray 1 Mitt	00	02	00

In the Cellar

1 Old Hogshead	00	06	00

In the Brewhouse

1 Churne 1 Milk Paile 1 Gaune	00	05	00

In the Stable

1 Old Sadle	00	03	00
a Cheese presse	00	05	00
Corne in the Barne unthreshed	00	08	00
Drawed straw	00	07	06
Three Wagon Horses & 5 Mares old	25	02	06
Six Cowes	19	00	00
Corne in the Fields uncutt	05	00	00
a Waggon 2 pair of Harrows 2 Plows & othe Implem'ts of Husbandry & Horses Geares	10	15	00
Some Muck ab't 20 Loads	01	01	00
Ready Money in the house	39	14	10
The dec'ds weareing Apparrele	01	10	00
The Reversion of a Lease of a House from Mr W'm Bromly	01	10	00
Some other small things & Lumber not Mentioned	00	02	06
It'm a Debt due to dec'ed by Bond from Mrs Elizabeth Crompton Spinster	100	00	00
It'm ano'r Debt due f'm the s'd Mrs Crompton to ye dec'd p Bond	30	00	00
It'm ano'r Debt due to the s'd dec'd f'm ye s'd Mrs Crompton p Bond	40	00	00
It'm Due to the s'd dec'd from Thomas Wheeler of Swiney by Bond being a desperate debt	20	00	00
It'm Interest due upon the above mentioned Bonds at the time of the deceaseds Death			
It'm Due by Note of hand from Mrs Eliz' Crompton	03	00	00

It'm Due from Mr Ashwood Mr Pursell & Mrs Crompton being partners in a Coalwork for work done	94	00	00
It'm a Debt supposed to be due fm Rich'd Weaver . .	07	07	00
It'm another Debt supposed to be due fm Edw'd Pursell . .	05	05	00

It'm severall Goods Chattells & Sums of money belonging to the dec'ed which are supposed to be in the hands & poss'ion of Francis Edwards & Joyce his wife Rich'd Weaver & Elizabeth his wife parties in this Suit & also of Elizabeth Edwards widow mother of the s'd francis Edwards of which goods Chattells & sums of money this Exhibitant hath at present no certain account but will be ready to add them to the Inventory by his now exhibited when the same shall come this Ex'hants knowledge & possession.

80. Thomas Beddow

Yeoman of Swinbatch in Broseley, buried 22/III/1732. Inventory 26/III/1733 by Richard Weaver and Richd. Henshaw exhibited 10/IV/1733 for Thomas and Henry Beddow executors. Will 15/III/1732 left his wife Hannah £5 10s., her bed and one pair of the best sheets; his nephew John Beddow collier of Woodland Green in Broseley the cottage in his possession and a half share in the coalworks in Syners Hill, Nashes Leasow and Rodens Yard, all in Broseley; his niece Elinor Wilkes the other half share; the four daughters of his sister Joan Beddow all household goods except the six chairs bought of John Langley which were to go to Mary 'wife of my executor'; and to several other nephews and nieces various cottages.

In the Kitchen

A Table & Joined Bench, Two Joined Stools, a Screen, one Joined Elbow Chair a Salt Box a Pewter fframe and drawers, a Joined Cubbard ffour chairs, a Jack four Iron Spitts, Two Iron dripping pans four Candlesticks a Grate, and cheeks and fender a ffire shovell tongs Gridiron links, 2 Smoothing Irons a warming pan frying pan a Tinn Culender and two Covers a Candlebox, 18 trenchers, Some Earthenware	03	09	00
Eighteen Pewter dishes, 14 pewter plates three Chamber Potts a Porringer a Two Small tankards	03	00	00
Two Large brass Kettles & 2 small Kettles 3 brass potts, and a brass pan a skimmer a skellet a basting spoon . . .	02	10	00
one Cast Iron Pott and Marment	00	05	00

In the Parlour

Three tables Seven chairs	00	15	00
A Clock and Case	01	10	00

In the Parlour chamber and Closet

One ffeather bed bedsted Curtains and Valions three Blanketts and a red rug	05	00	00
Six Chairs	00	06	00
a Close Stool an old trunk and 2 old boxes . . .	00	01	06
one Joyned Chest	00	05	00
Twelve pair of Sheets hempen and Hurden ffive table cloaths 12 napkins	05	00	00

In the Milkhouse Chamber

Two ffeather beds bedsteads Curtains & Valions 3 Coverletts, and four Blanketts, the Better at £5 the other £4 5s. . . .	09	05	00
Two Joined Chests	01	00	00
A Chair a Stool and a Cushion	00	01	06

In the Kitchen Chamber

Two Beds Bedsteads, 6 blankets, 2 ruggs	05	10	00
a Joined Chest	00	04	00
Two Wheels a pair of Blades for winding yarn and 2 churns .	00	06	08

In the Cockloft

Twelve Strike of wheat	02	02	00

In the Milkhouse

one Joyned Cubboard and 2 benches, 1 Tray, 2 cheese fatts, 3 wooden Mitts 3 bowles a mortar a Pestell 2 wooden Bottles 3 Iron Cobberts	01	00	00
Three Milk Panns and some Earthen Ware . . .	00	01	06

In the Cellar

Two half hogsheads 5 Quarter Barrells and a Kilderkin and a Tundish a Pail 2 Gauns 2 old pecks and an half strike . .	01	10	00

In the Brewhouse

one Boyler one furnace	00	15	00
one Kneading mitt 6 tubs	01	00	00

Malthouse

one Malt Mill	01	01	00
15 Strikes of Oates	01	02	06
18 Strike of Malt	03	03	00
13 Strike of Oates sowed on the ground	01	01	00
One Copper furnace very old	00	07	06

THE INVENTORIES OF BROSELEY

In the Barn

Thirty Strike of Wheat	04	15	00
ffive strike of Oats	00	07	06
ffive str Barley	00	10	00
Three Tun and an half of hay	04	07	06

In the Stable

ffive horses and Mares	16	00	00
Two Cows	06	10	00
Two pair of old harrows a Tumbrell and an old Rowl	03	00	00
Two Store Piggs	01	10	00
Poultry of all sorts	00	03	00
Spades Mathooks bill Broomhook rakes and other old Lumber	00	16	08

Att Preens ffarm

ffour Cows	15	00	00
Twelve Tunn of hay	12	12	00
Twenty Load Muck	01	00	00
The Deceased's Wearing apparrell	03	00	00
Money in the house	10	00	00
	130	03	10

81. Samuel Evans, senior

Master collier of Broseley (58y). Presumably buried in the Quaker burying place as requested in his will. Inventory 18/IX/1733 by John Weaver and Richard Savage, never apparently exhibited. Probate 3/X/1733 to Samuel Evans nephew and one of the executors. Mary Pew sister was the other. Will 14/IX/1733. On the same day 'Samuel Evans one of the executors personally appeared ... and being one of the sect commonly called Quakers made his affirmation'. He was the son of Samuel Evans *(46)* and Margaret née Longford.

One pair of Bedsteads & Beding thereupon	01	00	00
One Joyn'd Chest	00	06	00
a parcell of Hops	00	15	00
A parcell of Pitt Augers	00	10	00
One other Pair of Bedsteads	00	08	00
The dec'eds Wearing Apparel	01	10	00

In and about the dwelling below Stairs

One Barrell one Table	00	04	00
One Barrel More And a Cupboard	00	04	06
Five Pewter Dishes	00	10	00
Two Iron Potts one Brass Pott one Morter and Pestell	00	12	00
Two Small Tables	00	02	00
Four Ropes three Tunbarrells	01	10	00
A Parcell of Brich Tile Crests and Gutters	05	00	00
Two Pair of Herden Sheets	00	04	00
All other Odd Lumber	00	01	00
Item Money due the dec'ed ab't	160	00	00
	172	16	06

In the Name of God Amen I Samuell Evans of Brosely in the County of Salop Master Collier being weak in body but of Sound and disposeing mind memory thanks be given to Almighty God for the same doe make this my last Will and Testament in manner following ffirst of all and most chiefly I bequeth my Soul to Almighty God my creator Stedfastly hopeing in and through the merritts and Intercession of my Dear and ever B'd Redeemer Christ Jesus to find a Joyfull resurrection and my body to the Earth to be Decently interred at the discretion of my Executors herein after named in the burying place belonging to the people commonly called Quakers in Brosely aforesaid And for the Enlarging the said buriall place and makeing a more commodious way to the same I give devise and bequeath part of the garden belongeing to the tenem't I lately purchased of John Hawley (viz't) Sixteen feet in breadth from the lane to the said buriall place to the use and behoof of the said people called Quakers for the purpose aforesaid for ever to be by them att their charge inclosed (if they think proper) Item all the rest of the said Tenem't dwelling house and Garden with the appurten'ces I give devise and bequeath to my loveing nephew Samuell Evans Sonn of my brother Timothy Evans his heires and assignes for ever Item I give and bequeath to my sister Mary Pew the Interest of Sixty Pounds to be paid her halfe yearly dureing her naturall life and after her decease my will is that the said Sixty pounds be equally paid amongst her Children Share and Share alike alsoe I do give and bequeath to my said sister Mary Pew the further Sume of fifty=pounds to be paid her within Six Months after my decease Item I give and devise unto my sister in law Elizabeth Evans, the widd of brother William Evans the Sume of Twenty pounds to be paid her att the End of Six Months next after my decease Item I give unto Alice Maud widd the Sume of ffity Shillings to be paid within Six Months after my decease all the rest of my personall Estate of what kind soever I give and devise to my said nephew Samuell Evans sonn of my brother Timothy Evans and I make constitute and appoint the S'd Samuell Evans and my Said Sister Mary Pew Executors Joyntly of this my will desiring that they doe lay out and expend the sume of five pounds in and about my funerall in such manner as they shall think most proper And I do revoak all former wills by me made and declare this to be my last will In Testimony whereof I have hereunto sett my hand and seal this ffourteenth day of September in the year of our Lord 1733.

82. Hannah Hartshorne

Widow (probably of Samuel Hartshorne d 1731) of Broseley, buried 14/I/1736. Inventory 15/I/1736 by Mich. Stephens junior, Jno. Acton and John Patten exhibited 29/III/1737 by John Bill kinsman of Bridgnorth, executor and residual legatee. Will 4/XII/1736 left her servant Josiah Patten 'all looms and shop tools and implements of weaving and the bed where he lieth'.

Impr'is In ye Kitchen

One press 4 pewter Dishes 6 pewter plates one Tankard pewter One Bason pewter One Clock Case and Screan one Table one Joynt Chair 3 Seggen Chairs one Bench A Iron Grate Cheeks fire Shovel and Tongs and plate a Iron Boiler and Fleshfork One Joynt forme One Bend Payle and Buckett One Kneading Tub A Wooden Bason One Brass Potts one Iron Pott One Brass Kettle one frying pan one Forrest Bill

In the Buttery

5 Barrels 2 Brewing Tubs

In ye new shop

3 Looms & Geering belonging to ym one little Wheel

In the Room Over the Old Shop

Two Coffers and one pair of Yarnblads

In the Room Over the Kitchen

One Table & one Chest one box One hanging press One Warming Pan One Joynt Stool 2 Pair of Bedsteads and Bedding thereto Belonging
2 Ladders

                        Appraised all together at.   .   04 13 00

83. John Poole

Trowman of Broseley but apparently not buried there. Inventory 7/XI/1739 By Thomas Williams and Tho Potts exhibited 10/XII/1739 by Sarah Pool (?née Gower 1727) relict and administratrix.

On the river Severn

Two old Barges or Trows with the rigging and Materiall thereunto belonging	60 00 00
Also One old Barge Worn out	06 00 00

One Main mast, one Top mast, one Tarpauling and One Anchor	07	05	00
One Old Barge cut up	02	15	00

In the Deceaseds Kitchen

One Old Screen, One fire Grate One Iron Dripping pann two Spitts	00	10	00

In the Roome over the Kitchen

Two fflock Beds and bedding thereunto belonging	00	15	00

In the parlour

Ten small pewter Dishes Six pewter plates, One pewter Chamber pott, and Six pewter porringers	01	02	06
Also One Old Dresser of Drawers An Old Table an Old Warming pann, and two Old Brass Kettles	00	16	06
Nine Chairs	00	05	00

In the Roome Over the parlour

An Old ffeather Bed and Bedding thereon	01	05	00
Also One Chest with Linnen therein	01	10	00
The Deceaseds Wearing Apparell	01	00	00
Also All other Lumber and things unmentioned	00	10	00
Totall	84	14	00

84. Thomas Taylor, *alias* Syner

Tobacco pie maker of Broseley, buried 19/I/1739. Inventory 21/I/1739 by John Hare and John Hartshorne exhibited 3/VI/1740 for Mary Taylor relict and executrix (née Whitmore m 1718). Thomas Taylor son was also executor though he was only 12y. Will 27/XI/1739 left by his wife Mary the cottage wherein he had dwelt and all goods while single then to his son Thomas except 'one pair of screws of the second best' to his daughter Ann (b 1724) so that she could work at the trade at any time. If Thomas refused to cohabit with his sisters Ann and Mary (b 1732) then they were to have the shop and the new buildings 'lately built'.

In the Kitchen

One Dresser of Drawers and pewter frame	00	04	00
four pewter Dishes Seven pewter plates, Three pewter Quarts, One pewter pint Two pewter porringers	00	10	06
One Tinn Candle Box and Cullinder	00	00	08
A Clock and Clock Case	01	10	00
One fowlding Table	00	01	06

One Small Iron pott	00	01	06
One Small fire grate fire shovel & Tongs .	00	04	00
Three Barrells, One Kneeding Tubb in the Buttery	00	08	00

In the Room over the Kitchen

One feather Bed, Two Blancketts, One Rugg One pair of Bed steads and Curtains	01	15	00
One Chest, One Table Two Small Coffers, 2 Boxes	00	10	00
Six pair of Course Hurden Sheets, One pair of fine Hemp sheets .	00	19	06

In the Roome Over the Shop

One feather Bed, Two Blancketts, One Rugg One pair of Bedsteads	01	15	00
One Small Ovel Table	00	02	06

In the Shop belonging to the Tobacco pipe trade

Three Screws Seven pair of Moults, Twenty Grates, Twenty Boards, three Slob Benches	06	00	00
The Deceased Wearing Apparell .	01	00	00
All other Lumber and things Unmentioned	00	07	06
Inventory Totall .	15	09	08

85. Benjamin Buckley

Trowman of Broseley, buried 21/III/1739. Inventory 28/V/1740 by John Beard, Charles Hartshorne and John Hartshorne exhibited 3/VI/1740 for Mary Buckley relict and administratrix (probably née Holmes m 1669 *(57)*).

In the Kitchen

Twenty seven Pewter Dishes	03	00	00
Three Dozen of Pewter Plates	00	18	00
Nine Pewter Porrengers .	00	04	06
Two Dozen of Trenchers	00	02	00
One Pann, two Kettles, One Pott, three candlesticks one warming Pann, One basting Spoon all of Brass	01	10	00
Tinn Ware of all sorts .	00	05	00
One fire Grate, two fire shovels, two pair of tongs A Purgatory and fire Plate with other furniture	01	00	00
One Driping Pann, four Spitts A Jack and Cobberts	00	18	00
An Old frying pann	00	01	00
Two tables Six Chairs	00	10	00

In the Midle Room

Three Oval tables One Wainscot screen	00	18	06
A Parcell of Old ropes	01	00	00
One Old winlace Barril and winlaces	00	03	00

In the Parlour

One Large Oval table	00	14	00
A Clock and Case	02	10	00
One writeing table with a stone in the Leaf	00	12	06
One Chest of Drawers	00	15	00
One ffeather Bed Bedsteds and hangings with a rugg blanket and Pillows	05	00	00

In the Parlour Chamber

One ffeather Bed Bedsteds & firniture thereunto belongin	05	00	00
One Oval table one Square table	00	18	00
A Chest of Drawers	00	12	00
A Close Stoole, three Chairs and a Looking Glass	00	15	00

In the Kitchen Chamber

One ffeather Bed Bedsteds & ffirniture thereunto	03	00	00
Two Large Chests, one small table	01	16	06
ffour Chairs	00	04	00

Linings in the Chests

Eleven pair of Hurden sheets overworn	01	13	00
Three dozen and a half of Napkins	01	05	00
ffour Pair of fine Sheets & Six Pillow Beers	02	00	00
A Long table Cloth	00	07	06

In the Midle Chamber

Two ffeather beds two Pair of Bedsteds with the Beding and ffirniture thereon	03	00	00
One Chest one hanging Press	00	17	00

In the Brewhouse

two small tubs a small Cooler one Pail	00	06	00

In the Cellar

ffour half hodgsheds	01	00	00

In the ffould

a store Pigg and a Cow	02	10	00

Upon the river Severn

One Trow or Barge with the riging and Materials thereunto belonging also one Mainsail more an old Mast	30	00	00

THE INVENTORIES OF BROSELEY

The reversion of Three Chattle Leases	50	00	00
The Deceaseds wearing Apparill	01	10	00
All other Lumber and things unmentioned . . .	00	10	00
Inventory in the whole totall . .	127	06	00

86. Henry Carrington

Glover of Broseley, buried 8/VII/1740. Inventory 29/VII/1740 By Wm. Carrington and Thomas Mackarell exhibited 5/VIII/11740 for Joanna Carrington relict and administratrix. The burial is the first time the surname appeared in the register. Subsequently two girls were married and there were two burials, suggesting that he arrived with a growing family.

In the Kitchen
Brass and pewter with Iron Ware and other Material thereunto belonging	02	02	00

In the Brewhouse pantry and Scullery
One Iron furnance two Brass Kettles with Brewing Vessells and other Necessaries therein.	01	10	00

In the Cellar
One Hogshead, Two half hogsheads, three quarter Barrells with the Stock of Drink therein	10	00	00

In the Hall or Shop
Leather Washed or unwashed of all Sorts and Gloves made up .	05	00	00
Implyments belonging to the Glovers business . . .	00	05	00

In the parlour
One Ovell Table and Chairs, with one Dresser and Draws and pewter frame	01	00	00

Upon the Stair Case
A parcell of Chalk	00	02	00

In the Chamber Over the parlour
One feather Bed Bedstead & furniture thereunto belonging .	03	00	00
One Dressing Table Glass and Chairs with One Truckle Bed .	00	10	00

In the Brewhouse Chamber
One Chest One Box One Bed	01	00	00

In the Servants Chamber

| One Bed with other old Lumber . . . . . | 00 | 15 | 00 |

In the Closett

| Two peices of Cloth A Small parcell of Wool A Small Chest of Linnon and Linnon Yarn. . . . . . | 03 | 00 | 00 |
| The Deceased Wearing Apparell . . . . . | 02 | 00 | 00 |

In the Workehouse

| Skins undressed . . . . | 00 | 07 | 06 |

In the Barn

| A Small parcell of Hay and Oak Bark . . . . | 01 | 10 | 00 |

In the Stable

| One Horse, sadle, Bridle and pillin . . . . | 03 | 10 | 00 |

In the folde

A sow and pigs & a Store pig	01	00	00
Poultry of all Sorts	00	07	06
All other Lumber and things unmentioned . . .	00	10	00

| Inventory Totall . . | 37 | 09 | 00 |

87. Mary Penn

Widow of Broseley but buried 7/III/1740 at Benthall. She was not the widow of Richard Penn of Benthall d June 1740. Inventory 9/III/1740-1, no appraisers named Thomas Bate signed. It was exhibited 5/IV/1742 by Thomas Bate now or late of the parish of St Swithin in Worcester tallow chandler brother and administrator since her mother Sara wife of Michael Perry had renounced her claim.

In the Writeing Closet

| A Desk and a few Pictures . . . . . | 01 | 05 | 00 |

In the Kitchen

| A Dresser of Drawers and Pewter frame with Pewter thereon and other furniture therein . . . . | 11 | 13 | 03 |

In the Parlour

| A Chest of Drawers A Bofet Tables Chairs and Pictures with other firniture . . . . | 12 | 07 | 10 |

In the Chamber Called the red room

| A Chest of Drawers A feather Bed Bedsteds and Curtains A Table and Chairs | . | . | . | . | . | . | 09 | 17 | 08 |

In the Blew Room

| A ffeather bed, Bedsteds Curtains w'th other firniture | . | . | 06 | 09 | 04 |

In the Green Room

| A ffeather bed, Bedsteds & Curtains w'th other firniture | . | . | 06 | 05 | 04 |
| A chest of Linnen | . | . | . | . | . | . | 05 | 00 | 00 |

In the Servants Chamber

| A Pair of Bedsteds A Bed & Beding thereon | . | . | . | 01 | 00 | 00 |
| Also a Parcel of Old Lumber | . | . | . | . | . | 00 | 10 | 00 |

In the Brewhouse

| Two Iron furnaces w'th Brewing Vessels and other firniture | . | 03 | 06 | 06 |

In the cellar

| Three half Hogsheds w'th other Smaller Vessels &c. | . | . | 01 | 09 | 06 |

In the Buttery & Pantry

| One old Hogshed with Shelves Trenchers and Tin Ware | . | . | 00 | 12 | 02 |

In the Shop

| A Counter boxes Shelves Drawers & Shop Goods | . | . | 38 | 03 | 06 |

| The Deceaseds Wearing Apparrill & Money in her Custody | . | 07 | 00 | 00 |
| All other Lumber and things unmentioned | . | . | . | 00 | 10 | 00 |

| | Inventory totall | . | . | 105 | 10 | 01 |

88. Ann Gough

Widow of Job Gough (née Burgess m 1740) of Broseley, buried 14/I/1740. Inventory 22/I/1740 by Mr. Richard Weaver and Mr. John Morris 'Appraisers in the parish of Broseley', witnessed by Wm. Pearce junior and exhibited 12/V/1741 for Job Gough collier of Broseley son and administrator (b 1711 the year before his father died).

Impr's a breend Cow	.	.	.	.	.	.	02	05	00
A Red Cow	.	.	.	.	.	.	02	00	00
A Earling Heiffer	.	.	.	.	.	.	01	05	00
A Small Sow	.	.	.	.	.	.	01	00	00

In the Kitchen

Six Small pewter Dishes and 9 plates	00	12	00
three pewter porringers, 1 Old Tanchard and 2 Old pewter Spoons	00	01	06
An Old Warming pann	00	01	00
One Grate fire Shovel and Tongs plate flesh fork and spitt an old fryng pann and Cobberts.	00	03	06
An Old Boyler A pott and Marment all old	00	03	00
Two Old Tables, and one Old Screen	00	04	00
One Dozen & half of Trenchers	00	00	08
An Old Brass Kettle	00	01	06

In the Milk house

An Old Cubboard, an Old Churn an Old Barrell and Tundish	00	05	00
Six pair of Old Sheets, and 3 Old Hand Towels	00	10	00
One Bed and One pair of Bedsteds	01	00	00
Wearing Apparell	00	15	00
Old Lumber and things not seen or forgott and not Appraised	00	02	00
Good and Bad Debts	00	10	00
Money in the house	00	09	06
Totall	11	08	08

89. Thomas Crowther

Glazier of Broseley but not apparently buried there. Inventory 29/V/1741. By Jno. Hartshorne exhibited 2/VI/1741 for Elianor Crowther relict and administratrix (née Jones married 1730). In 1750 she married Henry Davis. These are the only Crowthers in Broseley apart from their two daughters Elizabeth (b 1731) and Jane (b 1733).

In the Kitchen

A Dresser and Drawers and pewter fframe	00	15	00
Six pewter Dishes and 6 pewter Plates	00	11	00
A Clock and Clock Case	01	10	00
A Small square Table and four Chairs	00	04	00
A Small ffire Grate and Cheeks fire shovel & Tongs	00	03	00
An Old Small brass Kettle and Brass Candle stick.	00	00	06
An old screen and Iron Spit a pair of Gails	00	03	00

In the Room above Stairs

One pair of Bedsteads & Curtains with the Bed and Bedding thereon	01	00	00
One Chest a Cubboard and Two Boxes	00	12	00

A Table and 2 Chairs a Parcell of Glass & another old Cubboard .	00	08	00
One other pair of Bedsteds with a Bed and Bedding thereunto belonging	01	05	00

In the Shop

A Glasiers Vice a board and a p'cell of old Glass with other Small materials belonging to the Glasiers Calling . . .	02	02	06

A an ? Outhouse

One other old Brass Kettle	00	04	00

More in the house

Two old Barrells & other old Lumber	00	03	00
a parcel of old Pictures	00	01	04
Sixteen Glass Bottles	00	01	04
Totall . .	09	03	08

90. William Holmes, the elder

Of Broseley, buried 10/IX/1741 (probably b 1671 of Robert and Constance Holmes). Inventory 17/IX/1741 by Will. Lewis and Willm. Morris* exhibited 22/IX/1741 for Elianer Holmes relict and administratrix (née Oswald m 1694).

In the Kitchin

A Pewter fframe and pewter thereon	00	15	00
A Smal fire Grate ffire shovell and Tongs . .	00	05	00
Three old Dripping Panns	00	05	00
An old brass Kettle and Warming Pann . . .	00	02	00
A Smal Iron Pott and Kettle	00	01	06

In the Parlor

Two Barrells a Tub and two old Cheirs . . .	00	08	00

Above Stairs

Two pair of Bedsteeds and Bedding thereon . . .	01	10	00
One hanging Press and an old Coffer . . .	00	08	00
The Dec'eds Wearing Apparel	00	15	00

In the hay Bay and Stable

A Smal Quantity of hay	02	10	00

A parcell of Straw		00 05 00
ffive old Horses and their Geering		10 00 00
A Smal parcell of Oates Threshed		01 00 00
All other Lumber and things unmentioned		00 05 00
	Tot'l	18 09 06

91. Joseph Whitefoot

Mason of Brosley, buried 17/II/1741. Inventory 15/III/1741 by Samuel Burrows and John Instone exhibited 5/IV/1742 for Elizabeth Burrows and John Instone exhibited 5/IV/1742 for Elizabeth Whitefoot relict and administratrix d 1748. The first entry in the register relating to this family was in 1717 when two children were buried. Presumably they moved into the district shortly before this with a growing family.

In ye Kitchen

One Clock & Clock Case	01 05 00
a large Oake Oval Table	00 07 00
7 Small Pewter Dishes & 16 Pewter Plates	00 18 00
a dresser & pewter Frame & 2 Doz: of Trenchers	00 06 00
a Chest of Drawers	00 15 00
a small square Table & 6 Chairs	00 06 00
1 Elbow Chairs a joynt stool & 2 other old Chairs	00 01 06
1 Fire grate, a swail & pott Links.	00 04 06
2 Fire shovels, 3 pair of Tongs 3 flesh forks, 1 Cleever	00 02 06
1 Warming pan, a Chopping knife, 2 Spitts	00 06 00
1 Candle box, a dripping pan wth other Tinn Ware	00 02 00
an Old Iron Jack, 3 Smoothing Irons	00 04 00
a Frying pan, a salte box, & a Fender	00 02 00
One Waiter, a Gun, & two Pistolls	00 05 00
2 Pewter Candlesticks & 2 of Iron, a brass Skimmer and Pewter Sauce-pan	00 01 06

In ye Parlour

A Chest of Drawer & round table	00 16 00
1 Square Table & Six Chairs	00 04 00
10 small pictures & Globe	00 01 06
12 Drinking Glasses & 1 Decanter	00 01 00
5 plates, 4 Juggs of Delph Ware	00 01 00

In a Lodging room below stairs

A pair of Redsteads & Hangings, a feather Bed, & Bedding thereon	02 00 00

In ye Little Room

a Spinning Wheels, a maid wth other Lumber	00	02	00
a parcell of Old books	00	02	00

In ye Back Kitchen & Butterys

a small Furnace and Boyler	00	10	00
3 Tubbs a Cooler, 2 pails, & Gaun	00	08	00
2 Iron potts, a small brass kettle	00	04	00
a pair of Racks, & 4 Slobb-benches	00	02	00
a buckett, & other odd Lumber	00	02	06
3 barrels, 3 firkins, a butter-tub, a flower tubb two benches and a Horse	00	07	00
a Lanthorn, & other Lumber	00	01	00
a Dresser & a bench	00	01	00

In the Chumber over ye Lodging Room

a pair of bedsteads, a glock bed & bedding theron	00	08	00
an Old Chest, a Spinning Wheel & a pair of Scales	00	04	00

In the Chamber over the Kitchen

a pair of Bedsteads & Hangings, a feather bed boulster, blanketts & Rugg	01	10	00
a Chest & 3 boxes, & 3 Old Chairs	00	09	00
a Spinning Wheele, a hackney Saddle and Search	00	08	00

In the Chamber over the Parlour

A Cradle, six dozen of glass bottls & Lumber	00	07	00

In the Chamber over the Brewhouse

a pair of Bedsteads & a Chaff bed	00	04	00
3 Pike Evils & 2 Rakes & Lumber	00	02	00

In the Several Rooms above Stairs

6 pair of hurden Sheets, 2 pair of hempen sheets, 2 pillow beers, 4 Table Cloths, 2 Dozen of Napkins & 6 Towels.	01	10	00
The Deceased's Working Tools	00	10	00
also his Wearing apparell	01	00	00

In the Stable

An Old Horse	02	02	00

The Revertion of Two Chattell Leases Worth Nothing

Inventory totall	19	03	00

92. Edward Jones

Collier of Broseley, buried 30/III/1742. Inventory 6/VIII/1742 by William Pearce and Will Lewis apparently never exhibited. Probate 23/XI/1742 to John Jones son and executor. Will 27/III/1742 left his wife (probably Elizabeth née Cullis m 1717) the house and all in it, then to son John. If she remarried she was 'to go down to that little house where my sister now dwells'. His son John to have all stock, all other houses and gardens and the wearing apparel.

In the Kitchen			
Seven Pewter Dishes one Dozen of Pewter Plates one Press two Dripping Pans one Warming Pan.	00	17	00
In the room next to the Kitchen			
A old Grate & Cheeks a old Dresser a Old pott.	00	07	00
In the room over the Kitchen			
A Old Feather Bed a Old Chest and a old Table.	02	10	00
In the Cellar			
One old Barrel.	00	02	06
In Another room over head			
A old fflock Bed	00	10	00
His Implements of his Working Tools			
One Dozen of Mandrells and Nine Shovels two furnished pitt Waggons Seven Basketts Wood and Waggon Rayles	03	06	00
The Testators Wearing apparel value	03	10	00
	10	02	06

93. Edward Reynolds

Dyer of Broseley, buried 12/X/1742. Inventory 10/XI/1742, no appraisers named but the administratrix signed*. She was Catherine Reynolds (née Harnidge m 1718) who exhibited 25/X/1743.

Upon the River Severn			
an Old passage Boat and Materialls thereunto belonging	01	03	00
An Old plank	00	05	00
A Store Pigg	00	10	00
The Deceaseds Wearing Apparrell	00	10	00
Totall	02	08	00

94. William Pearce, the elder

Master collier of Broseley, buried 28/X/1742. Inventory 8/XII/1742 by Saml Burrows and Jno Hartshorne exhibited 26/IV/1743 by George and John Pearce sons and executors. Will 5/IV/1743. Pearce m (i) 1699 Elizabeth Hartshorne of Linley d 1720 and by whom he had surviving children George (b 1700), William (b 1702), Elizabeth (b 1706), John (b 1708) and Ann (b 1713), and (ii) Joyce by whom he had Richard (b 1724), Jane (b 1726) and Margaret (b 1730). Son of John Pearce *(58)* and probably brother of Richard Pearce *(79)*.

In the kitchen

Two Dressors of Drawers and Pewter frame	00	18	00
An Old screen and a Small Oval Table	00	07	00
A Cubboard and Bacon Cratch	00	07	06
A ffire Grate and Wings Fire Shovel & Tonges two fire Plates and Links a pr of Cobberts	00	09	06
A Jack two Spitts a tin Driping pan a Flesh fork a plate and 3 Skurers	00	12	00
Three pewter Quarts	00	02	06
An old Warming pan and ffrying pan 4 old Iron Candlesticks Box Iron	00	06	00
ffour Boarded Bottom Chairs One Seg Chair	00	03	04
Twenty two pewter Dishes 126 lb. at 6d per li'	03	03	00
Thirty one pewter plates a pewter Salver a pewter Mustard pot and six pewter Candlesticks	01	00	00
Two Brass Candlesticks and two old Bibles	00	02	06

In the Parlour

A Clock and a Clock Case	01	01	00
An Oak Oval Table Nine Boarded Bottom Chairs and a Stool	00	12	00
A Cubboard with Drawers and 12 Pictures	00	10	00
Glasses and Earthen Ware on the Chimney peice	00	00	09

In the Brewhouse and old Kitchen

One Brewing ffurnace Broke	00	00	06
Two Mash Tubbs 2 Coolers	00	11	00
Two Slobb Benches & An Old Malt Mill	00	06	00
A Mashing Staff Clenseing Sive & Ladder	00	00	09
ffour old Iron Potts a Brass Kettle and Tinn Culliner	00	05	00

In the Cellar

ffive Hogsheads 2 Half Hogsheads Nine other Barrels One Ill vatt a Barm Tubb a pail and Tun Dish	02	10	00
ffive Horse for Drink to Stand upon	00	05	00

In the Chamber over the Kitchen

Two Oval Tables one Chest	00	15	00
A pair of Bedsteads one Curtean a feather Bed and 2 ffeather Bolsters a Quilt & Blankett	01	08	00
Two Boxes and 5 Chairs	00	03	00

In the parlour Chamber

A ffeather Bed and Bolster a pair of Bedsteads with old Hanging an old Quilt	01	10	00
A Chest of Drawers a Chest two Tables and three Chairs . .	01	04	00
A Large looking Glass	00	08	00

In the little room above Stairs

A pair of Bedsteads a ffeather Bed Boulster and two pillows 2 rugg and two Blanketts	01	05	00
A Chest of Drawers a table and Box	00	05	00

In the Garrott over the Kitchen

Two ffeather Beds Two Bolsters one Blankett and a pair of Bedsteads	02	00	00
One Oval Table a a Tble wth a Slate in ye Leafe . . .	00	08	00
Part of a Sack of Hops	00	14	00
An Old Chest wth other Lumber	00	05	06

On the Stair Case

A Wire Riddle and an old Pad & Search	00	02	00

In the Garrott over the parlour

About 60 foot of Board with other Lumber . . .	00	08	00

Upon the s'ral Lodging Bedds and in a Chest

five pair of Hemp sheets One pair of flax 2 Hurden Table Cloths 2 fflaxen Pillow Beers 3 pair of Hurden Sheets 4 Hurden Towells one Dammask Table Cloth and 2 fflaxen Table Clothes . .	02	02	00
The deced Wearing Aparrel	01	00	00
The reversion of a Chattle Lease	00	05	00

In the Stable

One Pack Saddle a apir of Hampots one Girth 2 Old Hackney Sadles one Bridle	00	06	00

In the Fold

one Large Store pigg & one Lesser	02	00	00
Alsor the revertion of a Morgage about	05	00	00
All other Lumber Unmentioned	00	02	06
. . . .	35	04	04

Wife: house & ground occ. Thomas Moan, & ho & ground occ. Alice Moan, - income for life then to Son Richard & heirs, if none to Wm. Pearch. Not to be mortaged or sold.
Wife: 3 house that were Gouldens for the rest of the term I have them.
Wife: debts owing for butchers meat.
Wife: goods that were brought up here when we shifted house here.

Son George. House & ground wherein I now dwell except that part which is brother William has in his possession. George to pay £21 to my Dau. Ann.
Son George: House wherein he now dwells lasting the time we have therein or the partners of the Tichfield coalwork. If they dispose of it otherwise to pay him £30. Because it cost me soe much money & them not one farthing.
Son William: Part of that house wherein I now dwell for his life, then to George & heirs male, if none to William & heirs male. Not to be mortgaged or sold.
Son William: 2s per week out of my share of Gitchfield coalwork, if my share bring in so much...or else to have what profit it yeilds. Not to be mortgaged or sold if the work continues soe long.
Son John: House and Ground (late Timothy Pryce) & that butcher's shop that is now used by him.
Son Richard: House & ground (now occ.Francis Blakemore) & that butcher's shop now used by him.

Dau. Jane: House & ground now used by Samuel Lewes.
Dau. Ann: house & ground occ. Thos.Griffiths.
dau. Elizabeth: House lately occ. William Bembow.
son William: wearing apparell.
sons George & John. Any more of my share in the Gitchfield coalworks after Wm had his 2s per week.

95. Sylvanus Ball

Trowman of Broseley, buried 21/V/1743 (55y). Inventory 31/V/1743 by John and Richard Beard and John Hartshorne exhibited 12/VII/1743 by William and Sylvanus Ball sons and administrators, born respectively in 1708 and 1715. His wife Mary had died in 1740. Probably nephew of John Ball *(56)*.

In the Kitchen

A Large fier Grate a fier plate a pair of Tongs A Skimmer & plate of skewers with all other Iron ware	00	12	00
An Ovel Table A press Cubboard and a Square Table . .	00	12	00

In the parlour

A Dresser of Drawers and pewter frame	00	16	00
11 pewter Dishes A pewter Cullender	01	02	00

18 pewter plates and pewter Salver	00	08	00
3 Old pewter quarts, 2 Delph ware Basons	00	02	00
2 Iron potts & a Small Brass Kettle & a frying pan	00	05	06
2 Dozen of Trenchers, A Square Table & a Joint Stoole	00	05	00
A Clock and a Clock Case	02	00	00
A fier Grate three Spitts 2 tinn pans & a pair of Cobberts	00	15	00
Nine Chairs with Boarded Bottoms & 3 with Segg Bottoms	00	10	00

In the Brewhouse and Cellar

Three Mashing Tubs, One Cooler, One Kneding Tub and 5 half Hogsheads	01	13	00

In the Chamber over the Kitchen

Two pair of Bedsteads & Curtains, One feather Bed & bolster and a Bed and Bolster flocks and feathers & Beding thereon	02	10	00
A Chest and Linnen therein	01	00	00

In the Chamber Over the parlour

A pair of Bedsteads & hangings	00	15	00
A feather Bed & Bolster A Quilt & Blankett	01	15	00
A Chest and a Cubboard	00	08	00
A Quantity of Corn for Bread	03	00	00
The Deceaseds Waring Apparel	01	00	00

Two Vessells upon the river Severn with the Riggin and Materials thereunto belonging	60	00	00
Good and bed Debts about	05	00	00
All other Lumber and things unmentioned	00	03	00
	84	11	06

96. John Oakes

Trowman of Broseley, buried 22/XII/1743. Inventory 16/V/1744 of 'the household goods and Firniture' (and by implication not the share of the barge) by Jno Bell and Jno Hartshorne. Sarah Oakes relict (née Doughty m 1740) also signed*. Exhibited for her 22/V/1744. Their only child Francis b 1741.

In the Kitchen

A Dresser of Drawers and Pewter frame	00	12	06
ffour Pewter Dishes and Six Pewter plates	00	10	00
A Dozen and half of trenchers and some delph ware	00	02	06

THE INVENTORIES OF BROSELEY

A Cubbert and folding screen	00	03	06
A ffire shovel and tongs and two Candlesticks	00	01	09
Six Chairs One Water Pail	00	04	00
A Tinn Candle Box and a frying Pann	00	01	00

In the Buttery

One Old Barrill	00	02	00

Above Stairs

A pair of Bedsteds Mat and Cord	00	05	00
A Small ffeather Bed bolster and rug	01	00	00
Two pair of Old Hurden Sheets & two towels	00	04	06
A Barge Chest and a Box	00	05	00
Part or share of A Barge Lying upon the River Severn with the Rigin and Materials thereunto belonging	05	00	00
Totall	08	11	09

97. Samuel Head

Of Broseley, buried 13/IV/1744 (46y). Inventory 12/VI/1744 by William Ball* and John Hartshorne. Elizabeth Head relict and administratrix (née More m 1722) also signed* and she exhibited it 25/IX/1744.

In the Dwelling house

five small pewter dishes 14 pewter plates four pewter porringers	00	14	06
A Dresser with Drawers & Shelves A Dozen of Trenchers	00	04	00
2 Small Iron potts a Small Brass Kettle	00	05	00
A Fire Grate fire Shovell and Tongs	00	07	06
2 Spitts 3 Iron Candlesticks a Tin pan 2 Drudgers	00	03	00
An Oval Table 4 Chairs one Warming pan	00	08	06
Six Delf ware Dishes	00	01	00

In the Shop

A Slob Bench and Shelves & Lumber	00	05	00

In the Buttrey

2 Tubs a Small Barrill & Lumber.	00	06	00

In the Chamber over the Kitchen

One Bedstead one feather Bed & Bolster one Rug two Blanquetts.	01	10	00
One Chest an Old Chest of Drawers one Box an old Oval Table one Chair	00	15	00

In the Little room

one Bedstead with Bedding thereon	.	.	.	00 15 00
Linnens of all Sorts Bad and Good	.	.	.	00 17 06
the Deceased's Wearing Apparrell very Ordinary	.	.	.	00 10 00
All other Lumber and things not worth naming	.	.	.	00 01 06
	Inventory Total .		.	07 03 06

98. Samuel Burrows

Joiner and carpenter of Broseley, buried 26/X/1744. Inventory 22/II/1744 by John Hartshorne and Richard Corbett exhibited 1/VII/1745 for Mary Burrows relict and administratrix (née Emery m 1734). The only entries for this surname in the parish register relate to these two and their four children.

In the Kitchen

A Dresser of Drawers and Shelves	.	.	.	00 16 00
Ten old Pewter Dishes and 15 Do Plate	.	.	.	01 10 00
A ffire Grate Wings and ffender Shovel and Tongs	.	.	.	01 00 00
A Jack and Spitt and Cobbarts	.	.	.	00 09 06
A Crane over the fire	.	.	.	00 03 06
An Oval Table a Square Table	.	.	.	00 04 06
Five Ash Chairs .	.	.	.	00 05 00
Two Segg bottomed Chairs	.	.	.	00 02 00
Twelve Tinn Patty panns a Salt Box	.	.	.	00 01 04
Four old Pistolls a Cradle	.	.	.	00 10 00
Two ffliches of Bacon	.	.	.	01 00 00

In the Parlour

A Chest upon a Chest and Drawers	.	.	.	02 10 00
A Writing Desk £1 six Chairs £1.10s	.	.	.	02 10 00
A Clock and Case	.	.	.	02 10 00
A Table three Boxes one Picture one Map	.	.	.	00 09 00

In the Brewhouse

A Brass ffurnace in the Wall	.	.	.	01 00 00
A Tub a Pail two Gauns & two Lumber Benches	.	.	.	00 03 10
A Brass Pott and an Iron Pott	.	.	.	00 12 00
A Spade .	.	.	.	00 02 00

In the Pantry

A Cooler & a Churn	.	.	.	00 05 00

Two old Chairs a Maid a Milking Gaun & Bowl .	00	01	06
A Dresser two Slobs a pair of Scales	00	02	00
Two fflitches of Pork	00	15	00
A Long wheel and little Wheel	00	03	06
Three old Pewter Porringers 3 Spoons six Trenchers	00	01	06
A Walnut Plank .	00	01	06

In the Cellar

Two Hogsheads four quarter Barrells	01	00	00
A Tuning Dish and Shelves	00	01	06

In the Chamber over the Kitchen

A Bedstead and Hangings ffeather Bed Bolster a quilt three Blanketts	05	00	00
One other ffeather Bed and Bolster Bedstead & Beding thereon .	01	10	00
Linns of all sorts Much worn	00	15	00
Two Chests of Drawers not finished	00	10	00
A Close Stool	00	02	06

In the Parlour Chamber

A Bedstead & Hangings a ffeather Bed Bolster and Pillow and Beding thereon & a little Table .	02	10	00

In the Brewhouse Chamber

a parcel of Cheese	02	10	00
A Chest and Box without lids	00	05	00
Four Boards and a spinning Wheel	00	03	06
A Bad parcel of fenering Stuff .	—	—	—

In the Servants Chamber

a pair of Lumber Bedsteads and Beding thereon .	00	10	00
Working Tools in the Shop and belonging thereunto	02	00	00
A Boreing Rodd and Bitts	00	10	00
Old and new Stuff in the Shop and the ffold with all other Lumber .	01	10	00

In the Yard

an old cow	02	00	00
Total .	38	06	02

Sundry Book debts due to the deceased at his decease as appears by his Book and it is not a at present known what is paid and what is unpaid but will be accounted fore when known By me Mary Burrows, Widow of the deceased.

99. James Garmson

Of Broseley, buried 27/IV/1745 (60y). Inventory 24/V/1745 by Charles Bullock and Jon Hartshorne exhibited 27/V/1746 (*sic*) for Elizabeth Garmson relict and administratrix.

One oval Table & one dresser frame	00	05	00
ffour iron pots an old warming pan & two Candlesticks	00	10	00
One old fire Grate & purgatory one spit & fire plate	00	04	00
One Water pail & bowl & 2 old Chairs	00	01	02
One old long Table & a press Cupboard	00	06	00
One Cooler one old Cheese Tub one old wainscot Chair	00	07	00
A pair of bedsteads & beding thereon	00	10	00
Two spinning wheels one Chair & other Lumber	00	05	00
An old parcell of Carpenters Tools	00	07	06
A pair of bedsteads & blew hangings & beding thereon	01	01	00
A hanging press & four old boxes	00	10	00
Six small pewter Dishes 4 Pewter plates & 2 pewter Salts	00	12	00
An old brass Kettle & Tin ware	00	01	06
A Chest four lumber Coffers a Cupboard & three boxes	00	14	00
A pair of bedsteads & beding thereon	00	07	06
A pair of Cobberts & some old iron	00	02	00

In the Buttery

Two old Tubs one Barrell one Cheese press a Slob Dresser & Shelves a tunning Dish & other old Lumber	00	10	00
The dec'ed wearing apparell	00	10	00
One milking Cow	03	10	00
All other odd Lumber & things unmentioned	00	02	06
Total	11	01	02

100. John Wilde

Trowman of Broseley, according to his will living in Gloucester, buried 17/XII/1746 at Broseley. Inventory 13/VI/1747 by Jno. Hartshorne and William Simmons exhibited 10/VII/1747 for Mary Wilde relict and executrix. Will 13/X/1746 left wife Mary a messuage and garden in Broseley for life then to his son Charles (b 1719), also the use of the two vessels or trows on the Severn and the use of all household goods for life then to be divided among three daughters Joyce (m Christopher Simpson 1745), Mary (b 1712 m Isaac Hatton) and Susanna (b 1724 m George Oakes). His son John Wilde 1s.

A Dresser of Drawers and Pewter fframe.	00	18	00
Three small pewter Dishes and six pewter Plates .	00	08	00
A Fire Grate Wing and plate one fire shovel & two pair Tongs and one Iron Dripping pann .	00	12	00
One old Warming pann and one Brass basting spoon	00	02	06
A Box Iron and Heaters one Iron Candlestick	00	01	04
An old Wainscott press and a Square Table	00	10	00
One Iron pott one Brass Kettle .	00	02	00
One Kneeding Tubb and a Gaun.	00	03	00
Two ffirkins and one Brewing Tubb	00	03	06
One Chopping Knife and a fflesh fork	00	00	10
A Tin Drippin pann and a Tin Cover	00	02	00
One Chest one Coffer .	00	08	00
Two pair of old Bedsteads	00	06	06
One old ffeather Bed and Bolster	01	00	00
One Blankett one Rugg .	00	07	06
One fflock Bed & Bolster one Blankett one Rugg.	00	13	00
Three pair of Hemp sheets & some old Towels .	00	12	00
Five old Pictures with other Lumber	00	05	00
The deceased's Wearing Apparrell	00	05	00
An old Trow and a Barge on the River Severn with the Rigging and Materials thereunto belonging	40	00	00
Total	47	00	02

101. William Yates

Trowman of the Bowling Green in Broseley, buried 10/II/1747. Inventory 3/VI/1748 by Richd. Beard* and Jno. Hare exhibited 4/VII/1748 by Mary Yates relict and John Yates son *(107)* executors. Will 19/I/1747 left his wife Mary a vessel on the Severn called 'the John', another trow called 'the Francis' and a boat, the house wherein he lived called the Bowling Green and its furniture for life and then to his son John (b 1721); his son Francis (b 1717?) the other house and garden now under lease called Ladywood which was to go to the children of his son Edward if Francis has no issue; and his son Edward (b 1715) 1s. and no more.

In the Kitchen

A Dresser of Drawers and pewter frame and pewter thereon	03	00	00
A Grate purgatory and fender with other furniture belonging to fire place	01	10	00
A Brass Jack and Brass and Copper furniture upon the Chimney peice and other parts of the Kitchen	02	00	00
Tables and Chairs in the Kitchen.	00	07	06
Tin Ware and Earthen Ware of all sorts .	00	06	00

In the parlour
One Ovel Table, One Square Table, three Chairs, one fier Grate and
Some Old prints. 00 10 00

In the Brewhouse
A Small Iron furnace and Brewing Vessells One Brass pott one
Copper pott and One Iron pott 02 02 00

In the Cellar
One Old Hogshead three Old Hogsheads and some other
Lumber 01 02 00

Upon the Stair Case
A Clock and Clock case and some Old pictures . . . 01 10 00

In the Kitchen Chamber
Two pair of Bedsteads and Hangings Beds Bolsters and Beding
thereon 05 00 00
A Chest with Some Linnen therein 01 05 00
An Old Hanging press A Close stool 3 Old Chairs . . 00 10 00

In the parlour Chamber
Two pair of Bedsteads and Hangings with Beding thereon. . 03 10 00
A Chest of Drawers a Small Table, two Old Chairs and a Looking
Glass 00 14 00
Six Old pictures 00 01 00

In the Garretts
A parcell of Lumber 00 05 00
The Deceaseds Wearing Apparrell . . . 01 00 00

Upon the River Severn
Two Trows much worn with the Riggin and furniture therein and
thereunto belonging 100 00 00
One Old Boate 00 05 00

Inventory Totall . . 124 17 06

Wife Mary - my vessell lying on the Severn called the John with all the rigging & furniture
- another Trow called the Frances with all the rigging and one boat - the house wherein I
now live called the Bowling Green & furniture for life, provided she does not marry, then:
Son John - my house & furniture
Son Francis - other house & garden now under lease, called Ladywood
Son Edward's children - to have Ladywood at death of Francis if no issue
Son Edward - 1s & no more
Wife Mary & son John residual legatees & executors, to use towards paying my debts.

102. Ann Simpson

Widow of Christopher Simpson (d 1742) of Broseley, buried 23/IV/1750. Inventory 25/IV/1750 by J. Wyke and J. Hartshorne exhibited 15/V/1750 by Francis Simpson son and executor. Will 3/IV/1750 left her children Christopher Simpson and Elizabeth Hales 5s. each; her daughter Jane Simpson (b 1736) £5; and her three children the said Jane, Mary Teece (b 1717) and Francis Simpson (b 1728) to share the rest.

In the Kitchen

A Dresser of Drawers & Pewter Frame & Pewter of all sorts	01	01	00
A Fire Grate & Fender & other Iron Ware abt ye Fire Place	00	16	06
Tine ware of All sorts	00	01	00
A Skreen, 3 Tables & Chairs	00	04	00
An Iron dripping Pan & Spits	00	02	00
A Warming Pan Skimmer & Baster Brass	00	02	00
An Iron Mortar & Pestal, 2 sad Irons	00	02	06
A Clock & Clock Case	01	01	00
A Slop Dresser & Shelves	00	00	09
A Small Looking Glass & Glass Ware	00	00	09
A parcel of Delph Ware & Lumber & things unmenconed	00	02	06

In the Parlour

An Oval Table & 6 Chairs 1 Form	00	06	00
An old Press Cupboard & Lumber	00	02	06
17 Slippings of Linnen Yarn & some Hemp & Flax Tow	00	07	06

In the Brewhouse

One Iron Furnace	00	05	00
2 Small Mash Tubs 1 Cooler & Other Brewing Vessells	00	10	00
3 Iron Pots, 2 Brass Kettles 1 Sauce Pan	00	07	06
All other Lumber & things there	00	01	00

In the Cellar

9 Barrels of different Sorts	01	00	00
Abt. 80 gall. of Ale therein	02	00	00
A Parcel of Lumber & other small Vessells	00	05	00

In the Garret

An old Feather Bed & Bedding thereon	00	10	00
A Small Parcel of Hops	00	05	00
2 Spinning Wheels & Lumber	00	03	06

In the Chamber over the Kitchen

2 pair of Bedsteads	00	04	06
2 Small Feather Beds Bolster & Pillows & Beding thereon	02	00	00

1 Table 1 Chest, Coffer & 2 old Boxes	00	10	00
Linnen in the Chest of All Sorts	00	15	00

In the Chanber over the Parlour

a Bedsted & Hangings	00	10	06
A Feather Bolster & Pillow & Bedding thereon	01	10	00
1 Small Table, 3 Chairs	00	07	06
2 old Window Curtains 1 Picture	00	01	00
The Deceds Wearing Apparel of All Sorts	01	01	00
A Small Gold Ring & Money in her Pocket	00	17	06
Bacon & other Provision belonging to the House	00	12	06
One Store Pigg & Lumber in the Stable	00	07	06
	18	14	06

103. John Leadbeater

Gent of Broseley, buried 30/VIII/1753. Inventory 27/IX/1753 by Jno. Hartshorne and Thos. Shaw exhibited 11/VIII/1755 when administration granted to Thomas Shaw weaver of Broseley brother in law and guardian of Thomas Leadbeater minor son (b 1741). In 1735 Leadbeater m Mary Shaw. Probate documents suggest that administration was delayed until Thomas was 13y.

In the Kitchen

A fire Grate & Wings fire shovel & Tongs Purgatory & fenders and other furniture abt the Chimney place	01	15	06
A Box Iron & Heaters and two Cast Mettle Irons	00	04	06
A Brass Jack with the weight Line & Pulleys	01	01	00
four Brass Candlesticks and other Brass furniture	00	05	06
Three spitts a pair of Hand Irons an Iron fender & Candlestick	00	09	03
Tin Ware of all sorts and a Brass Warming Pan	00	08	04
A Dresser of Drawers & Pewter frame	00	10	00
Eleven Pewter Dishes 14 pewter plates 3 Porrengers a pewter Tankard a Candlestick Mustard Pott & Salt	02	00	00
A Pewter Salver 2 pewter Quarts 1 Do. pint	00	04	00
A small square Table and six chairs	00	07	00
One Dish 4 plates 2 Basons Delph Wares 4 Glasses 3 Cups	00	04	06

In the Parlour

An old Table and Nine Chairs	00	11	00

In the Brewhouse

An old Table and frame 1 Chair a Spining Wheel a Cooler a Strike Measure 6 Trenchers two pails 2 Gauns 1 Bowle	00	12	06

Two Brass Kettles & a Brass pott a Copper Sauce pan	00	12	00
A frying pan and an Iron Marment an Iron Mortar & Pestle	00	05	00
A large old Iron furnace a small Brass furnace	01	00	00
four old Mashing Tubbs 1 Cooler with other Lumber	01	00	00

In the Cellar

One old Hogshead 5 half Hogsheads 2 Quarter Barrells	02	04	06
A Yearling Vate & 4 other Barrells & a tuning Dish	00	10	06
Eighteen Glass Bottles	00	02	06

In the Brewhouse Chamber

A Bedstead with Green Curtains a feather bed & Bolster two Pillows	03	05	00
A Spotted Rugg and two Blanketts 1 little Table	00	10	00

In the Parlour Chamber

An old feather Bed & Bolster Rug and Blankett	01	00	00
An old Bedstead Matt & Cord	00	03	00

In the Kitchen Chamber

A bedstead with Blew Hangings	00	15	00
A feather Bed Bolster & Pillow a Rug & two Blanketts	02	00	00
A Chest of Drawers and one other Chest	00	13	00
One Trunk one Box and four Chairs	00	07	00

Linnens

Two pair of old Hurden Sheets 5 Hemp Sheets 9 Napkins two Table Cloths 5 Pillow Cases	02	14	00
The Deceased's Dwelling House upon Lease valued at	40	00	00
Inventory in the whole	66	02	07

104. Robert Love

Ground collier of Broseley, buried 25/II/1754. Inventory 27/II/1754 by J. Hartshorne exhibited by Lawrence Hill son in law and executor. Thomas Love son was also executor. His wife Mary d 1748. Will 16/II/1754 left his daughter Elinor (b 1718 m Lawrence Hill 1741) an oval table, the best bed, a little chest, three pairs of common sheets and one fine one, four napkins, half the pewter, the broach and cobberts, the largest pot, a quarter vessel, the hacking knife, knife, mortar and pestle, box iron and headters, bellows, candlebox, firegate, 3 chairs and half the china plates; his daughter Elizabeth (b 1720 m Roger Wilkes 1748) half the pewter, the other bed, three pairs of sheets and one single, a chest, two boxes, two barrels, a little pot and manment, a kettle, the brewing tub and kneading mitt, firegrate, frying pan and chafing dish, tin pan, two iron candlesticks, the looking glass, half the china plates and two chairs; his son in law Roger Wilkes a piece of new blue cloth in the chest and a piece of new linen cloth about eight ells; his granddaughter Sarah Wilks one little box; and his granddaughter Sidonia Wilks a little spinning wheel and the warming pan. His son Thomas Love was to share the rest equally among all the children.

A Dresser and Drawers and Pewter Frame and Pewter thereon	01	10	00
A Clock and Clock Case	02	00	00
One Oval Table, two other Tables, and Chairs	00	18	00
A Press, Cubbard and Lumber	00	07	06
A small ffire Grate and Pair of Tongues	00	04	00
Two iron Pots, two little Tubs, two Barrels	00	12	00
A warming and Kettle a Marment	00	06	00
two Pair of Bedsteads with the Beds and Bedcloaths belonging thereunto	02	02	00
two Chests, three Boxes, six Delph Plates.	00	17	06
Seven Pair of course Sheets and 3 Napkins	01	01	00
A small Piece of Woollen Cloth and another Piece of Linnen Cloth	01	15	00
A parcel of Ashes in Balls and other Lumber	00	05	00
The Deceased's Wearing Apparel of all sorts	01	10	00
Debts good and bad due to the Deceased about	04	00	00
Total	16	18	06

105. Noel or Nevill Edwards

Of Broseley, buried 20/I/1756 (42y). Inventory (not dated) by Wm. Hall and Richard Pearce exhibited 4/V/1756 by Judith Edwards mother and administratrix. Samuel Edwards chandler of Broseley brother (b 1722) also signed the bond.

Four old lame Horses and an old blind lame mare & the Geering belonging to them valued at	10	00	00
Two old cows	01	00	00
an old Bed & Bedcloths	00	05	00
an old chest of drawers	00	05	00
Wearing apparrell	02	00	00
Stock of Tallow	01	00	00
a small parcell of hay	01	00	00
	19	05	00

106. William Morris

Tobacco pipe maker of Broseley, possibly buried 11/IX/1756. Inventory 5/VII/1756 by M. Stephens and Jno. Hartshorne exhibited 5/VII/1756 by Mary Morris relict and executrix. Will 4/XII/1755 left his brother Samuel Morris the wearing apparel and his wife Mary everything else for life and then to his sisters (unnamed).

In the Kitchen

one Dresser of Drawers a pewter frame and the Pewter thereon .	01	10	00
Three old tables & Three Chairs .	00	10	00
A Fire Grate fire shovel & Tongs	00	06	00
A pair of Steel Irons & some other iron work of the fire place .	00	04	06
A Little Cupboard & other Lumber	00	03	00

In the Pantry

One Salting Bench & shelves	00	02	06
One little firkin & ab't 12 Glass Bottles .	00	02	06
One little Brass pott on Iron pott & one Marment	00	05	00

In the Kitchen Chamber

One p'r of Bedsteads one Curtain a feather Bed Bolster & Bed Cloathes .	01	10	00
One Chest and one table.	00	06	00

The Chamber over the House

One pair of Bedsteads one Curtain one ffeather Bed & Bed Cloaths & skereen	02	00	00
One Chest with two Drawers & a Coffer.	00	10	00

In the Backhouse

Two Kneading Tubs a Meal Tub & two cast metal Iron Boylers & one Dresser	00	13	06

In the Buttery

One Dresser & Shelves & other Lumber .	00	02	06

In the Shop

Tobacco Pipe Tools of all sorts .	01	01	00
Linen of all sorts pretty much overworn .	00	12	00
Tot	09	18	06

107. John Yates

Trowman of Broseley but probably buried at Gloucester (36y). Inventory (not dated and no appraisers named) exhibited 25/XI/1757 by Jane Yeates relict and executrix. Will 8/IX/1757 'being now in the City of Gloucester' left all to his wive Jane including a leasehold house in Broseley occupied by his mother Mary Yates (relict of William Yates *(101)*) and a vessel or trow called 'the John'.

A Trow and Riggin	25	00	00
Wearing Aparel	02	00	00
A Bedstead with blue Hangings Feather Bed, Bolster, Blanket and Rugg	01	10	00
3 Chairs	00	03	00
8 Pair of Sheets	01	10	00
A Bed Quilt	00	06	00
2 Corse Table Cloaths and 6 Napkins	00	05	00
An old Chest & an old Press	00	10	00
A Peice of Corse Cloath for Hangings	01	00	00
A small Looking glass & six Prints	00	10	00
An old Feather Bed & Bolster and old Flocke Bed & Bedstead, Hanings & a Coverlid	01	15	00
5 old chairs and a little Table	00	05	00
A Chest	00	05	00
10 Prints and an old Looking Glass	00	03	00
An old Bedsted	00	01	06
An old Clock	01	05	00
A Jack 5 Candlesticks Coffee Pott and Cann a Skimmer and Skillet	01	01	00
A Grate Purgatory Sway and Fender 2 Spitts Fire Shovel Tongues and Plate	01	05	00
A Warming pan	00	01	06
A Dripping Pan Cullender Cheese Toaster and 11 Patty pans	00	03	00
19 Pewter Dishes & 18 Plates	01	12	00
a Dresser Beaufet 4 Tables and 5 Chairs	01	05	00
A half Hogshead and 2 Quorter Barrels 4 Brewing Vessels a Pail and a Tunning dish	01	00	00
a Furnace	00	09	00
	43	05	00

108. Francis Wilkes

Collier of Broseley, buried 5/X/1757. Inventory 7/XI/1757 by John Cleobury and Thos Bryan exhibited 15/XI/1757 by John Wilkes locksmith of Monmore Green in Staffordshire son and executor. Will

1/VIII/1757 left his daughter Mirron Wilkes (b 1727 Tomirah); his son John (b 1720) the chest and clothes; and his sons William (b 1732) and Richard (b 1737) the house. Both wives were dead, Katherine (née Watkis m 1781 d 1724) and Ann (née Huelett m 1736).

A Clock & Case .	01 10 00
Chest .	00 07 00
2 Beds & bedsteads	02 10 00
a dresser & shelves	00 08 00
6 pewter dishes .	00 06 00
a table & 2 chairs	00 03 06
a grate 4s & a pott 2/6 .	00 06 06
a kettle 1/4 a barrell 1/6.	00 02 10
A Warming pan 6s 4 pewter plates	00 07 06
a water pail 1s frying pan 1s	00 02 00
. . . .	06 03 10

109. Ambrose Buckley

Trowman of Broseley, buried 23/IV/1758 (40y). Inventory (not dated) by William Spruce and Thomas Lloyd exhibited 6/VII/1758 by Mary Buckley relict and administratrix (née Adams m 1741). There were no children.

Kitchen

1 Clock .	01 10 00
1 Dress & shelves and Pewter upon it	01 10 00
1 Shelf with Delph upon it	00 01 06
2 Tables and 6 Chairs	00 04 04
Racks and furniture	00 03 04
1 Grate, 1 Fender, fire Shovel, Tongs and frying Pan	00 07 03
1 Warming Pan & 6 Pewter Porringers	00 06 00
1 Salt Box and a small Looking Glass	00 00 08

Chamber over do

1 Bed and Hangings	01 15 00
1 Chest and 2 Small Tables	00 11 06
3 Chairs and Small Looking Glass	00 04 06
2 old Boxes	00 01 06

Buttery

4 Barrells	00 12 00
6 Trenchers, 3 Wooden Trays & Tun Pail	00 01 02
1 Search, 1 Sieve, and an old Lanthorne .	00 01 08

Little Room over Do

| 1 Bed & 1 Chair. | 01 04 00 |

Brew House

3 Tubs, 1 Barrell.	00 03 04
1 Iron Pott, Kettle and Sauce Pan	00 02 10
1 Barge upon the River Severn	30 00 00
Debts due to the deceased	11 00 00
	50 00 07

110. William Hall

Weaver of Broseley, but apparently not buried there. Inventory 5/VIII/1758 by Marmaduke Roden* and Jno. Hartshorne exhibited 7/VIII/1758 for Mary Hall relict and administratrix.

In the Kitchen

A Dresser of Drawers & pewter frame & pewter thereon.	01 05 00
A Table & three Chairs & Twelve Trenchers	00 08 00
A fire Grate & Cheeks & Swail fire shovel & Tongs	00 15 00
A Join form & a Warming pan an Iron Mortar & Pestle.	00 06 06
An Iron Dripping pan & Lumber	00 02 06

In the Parlour

| A Long spining wheel & pair of Swifts an old Coffer | 00 05 00 |

In the Brewhouse

| Two small Iron Boylers two little Tubs & Water pail & Lumber. | 00 10 00 |

In the Cellar

| Two little Barrells a Horse a slob Dresser | 00 04 00 |

In the Workshop

| Three Weavers Looms & Gears thereunto belonging | 06 10 00 |
| Two old Looms at the Work House | 00 10 00 |

Above Stairs

Two old Beds & Bedding thereon	01 10 00
Two pairs of Bedsteads.	00 10 00
A small Coffer & four Chairs a little Spining Wheel	00 06 06
four pair of Course sheets overworn	00 12 00
A large Oak Chest one Box	00 08 06
Invenry Total	13 04 00

111. Richard Hartshorne

Carpenter of Broseley, buried 28/X/1760. Inventory 17/XI/1760 by Jno. Hartshorne exhibited 17/VII/1761 for Ann wife of George Hartshorne of Broseley daughter and administratrix. John Hartshorne of Benthall and Richard Simpson potter of Benthall signed the bond.

In the Kitchen

a clock and clock case	01	10	00
a Dresser of Drawers and Pewter Frame and the Pewter thereon	01	01	00
An Oval Table, Two small square Tables, six old chairs	00	17	06
A small fire grate ffire shovel & Tongs	00	06	06
An Iron Dripping Pan three Iron Candlesticks a Clever a flesh fork and old smoothing Iron	00	03	09
Two small Iron Potts & Potthooks a Brass Kettle and sauce pan	00	05	00
A Warming Pan a ffrying Pan a Pewter Candlestick and Porringer	00	02	06

Above Stairs

A Feather [sic] and Bolster, Bedstead, two old curtains	01	12	06
Three pair of hurden sheets one pair of Flaxen Do	00	12	00
Two Chests one Box and a stand	00	11	06
A little firkin, spiggott stean 5 glass bottles in the Pantry	00	01	06
A parcel of Carpenter's old Tools in and about the House	00	12	06
Total	07	11	03

112. Mary Beddow

Widow (probably of William Beddow d 1761) of Broseley, buried 7/VI/1762. Inventory (not dated) by Jno. Hartshorne exhibited by John Rushton *alias* Taylor son in law and executor 'in consideration of him taking care to support me ... while I live'. Will 5/VI/1762 left her grandson Francis Evans the winscott press or cupboard and her daughter Eleanor Bednall (?) the bed etc. 'she now maketh life on'.

In the Kitchen

One Fire Grate and Cheeks Fire Shovel and Tongs one Iron Pott and Pott Hooks two spits three Tin Pans	00	12	06
One Warming Pan on Brass Kettle one Tin Cover	00	05	00
A Dresser with Drawers and Shevles eight Pewter Dishes five Pewter Plate two Chairs one Table sixteen trenchers	01	10	00
A Childs Cradle a choping Knight a Little Barrell	00	04	06

In the Parlour

One Oval Table one kneading Tub one long Table a round Tub one Spinning Wheel two old Chairs a pair of scales and a Beam a Garden Rake and three Glass Bottles 01 05 00

In the Room Upstairs

One Bedstead with the Bed and Bed Cloathes one Press or Cupboard an old Drawer and Lumber 01 10 00

    05 07 00

113. Moses Watkiss

Collier of Broseley, buried 3/IV/1762 (65y). Inventory (not dated) by Jno. Hartshorne and John Instone exhibited 22/VI/1762 by Francis Hadden (wife's nephew) one of the executors. Mary Watkiss relict being the other (née Haddon m 1745). Will 8/III/1762 left everything to his wife Mary for life then to Thomas Watkiss brother and Francis Haddon.

In the Parlour and Cellar

one oval Table eight old Chairs	00 08 00
Two mashing Tubs two Coolers five Barrels and a joint stool .	01 06 00

In the Chamber above Stairs

three pair of Bedsteads one set of Curtains . . .	00 17 06
Three Feather Beds four feather Bolsters one Rug three Blankets three pair of Hurden Sheets over worn	01 04 00
Two Chests two small Tables two Chairs one Close Stool . .	01 00 06
Linnen of several sorts in one of the Chests . .	00 15 00
The deceased wearing Apparell of all sorts .	05 00 00

In the Kitchen

nine Pewter Dishes 12 Pewter Plates 6 Pewter Porringers a Pewter Tankard & Candlestick 3 Pewter Quarts 1 Mustard Pott . .	01 10 06
Fire Grate and Cheeks, Fire shovel & Tongs two Fire Plates .	00 16 00
One Warm a Brass Kettle a Tin Cullinder Tin Pan and Boiler .	00 07 08
One Iron Furnace in the Wall, a small Iron Pott a Marment four Iron Candlesticks	00 13 02
Two Pails one Bowl eighteen Trenchers	00 03 06
One Table two Dressers & Lumber one Frying Pan one spit .	00 04 06
Four old lumber Chairs	00 00 08

. . . . 14 01 00

114. Jonathan Oakes

Waterman of Broseley but apparently not buried there. Inventory (not dated and no appraisers named) witnessed by Edward Nash and Somerville Barrett exhibited 26/IV/1764 by Martha Oakes relict and administratrix.

Old Ropes 205 lbs at ½ .	00	08	06
Two Shrowds & Dead Eyes 50lbs at 2d .	00	08	04
One Main Stay 75 lb at 1d ½	00	08	11
Two Runners, Topsail sheet & pendale Strap 75 lb at 1d ½	00	08	11
One steam Block & Stay Block 98 lb at 2d ½	01	00	05
Two Topsail Sheet Blocks four Tackle Blocks 70 lb at 2d .	00	11	08
Four old Shrowds 80 lb at 1d	00	06	08
One Halling Line & a Quile of Ropes 65 lb at 1d.	00	05	05
One werp & a piece of a Horser 100lb at ½	00	04	02
One Windlass two Handlessis & a Cedger	00	15	00
One Sail & Sail Barrell	04	00	00
Two Planks	00	08	00
One Main Mast Top Mast Cap & Cross Trees & Mainyard	02	02	00

Household Goods

Two feather Beds one set of old Hangings &c	03	03	00
One Chest of Drawers & one Chest	01	00	00
One Hanging Press and one old Box	00	05	00
One Clock £1. 11s. 6d one Doz & half of Plates 5s	01	16	06
Five pewter Dishes 5s a Tin Cover &c 2s. 6d.	00	07	06
One Grate 10s. Two Tar Pawlings 5s	00	15	00
One Barrell one half Hogshead & one brewing Tub	00	07	00
Two Tables and five Chairs	00	06	06
One Iron plate two flesh forks one pair of Cobberts one Iron Spit and one Basting Spoon .	00	03	00
One Screen	00	01	06
Debts due to the Deceased about	10	00	00
	29	13	02

THE INVENTORIES OF LITTLE WENLOCK

115. Frances Baxter

Relict of George Baxter clerk, late minister of Little Wenlock but not apparently buried there. Inventory 23/III/1663 by Francis Smith, George Nicklis and Edward Jeffries exhibited 26/IV/1664 by Mary Baxter kinswoman and a principal legatee in the nuncupative will 5/XI/1663.

Impri's In the Hall
one Table board & frame	00	06	08
Itm. One Cupboard presse	00	13	04

It'm In the parler
two Small buffet Stooles, 1 joyne cheere & 1 little Table . .	00	06	08

It'm In the chamber over the Hall
1 old Trunke & chest	00	06	08
It'm In the Same chamber 1 presse	00	10	00

It'm In the Little Chamber
2 Coffers & a truckle bedd stedd.	00	06	00

It'm In the best chamber
1 peece of Waynscott called by the name of a bowe case . .	00	04	00
It'm One Oate meale boxe	00	00	06

It'm In the kitchen
1 Iron pott	00	13	04
It'm One little Cubboard.	00	02	06
It'm Three Iron broaches & 1 paire of Iron Cobberts . .	00	05	00
It'm One Which 1 stund & 1 Mitt	00	14	00

The Goods at Haughton apprized the day aforesaid
It'm Three Cowes & 2 Calves	07	10	00
It'm Eight dishes of pewter and 1 brazen Candlestick . .	00	17	00
It'm Two Brasse Panns	01	10	00
It'm One Brasse Pott and 1 possnett & Skimmer . .	00	16	00
It'm One dreepeinge pann	00	05	00
It'm One Pewter still wth a Ledden bottom . .	00	06	00

It'm Three Barrells	00 04 00
It'm One bedd 1 bolster & Three blanketts . . .	01 10 00
It'm All the Nappery	02 00 00
It'm Three Silver Spoones	00 08 00
It'm Two cushion stooles and 1 twill sheete . . .	00 04 06
Sum . .	19 19 02

116. William Green

Yeoman of Little Wenlock buried 6/II/1667. Inventory 17/II/1667 by Robert Hamnet, Will. Whistons, Richard Mathews and Podmore Peploe exhibited 3/III/1667 for Mary Green relict and administratrix.

Inprimis six oxen wherof three Harriots	17 00 00
Ite' nine cows	24 00 00
Ite' Six yong Cattell	06 00 00
Ite' one Mare, one colt	02 10 00
Ite' four yearling calves	03 00 00
Ite' eighteen ould sheepe and eight lambes . . .	05 00 00
Its. Corne and lent tilling in ye barne . . .	03 00 00
Ite' Corne mault and grain of all sorts in ye house . .	06 03 04
Ite' Hay	03 00 00
Ite' ffor butter and cheese	01 00 00
Ite' Beafe and Bacon	02 00 00
Ite' three feather beds and three feather boulsters with their furniture and two flock boulsters	02 00 00
Ite' two joyn'd bedsteads with four other bedsteads . .	04 00 00
Ite' Linnens & Napers ware of all sorts . . .	02 00 00
Ite' one chest six coffers and boxes	01 00 00
Ite' three table boards with formes and stooles . .	01 10 00

Ite' in ye parlour

one hanging presse & two joyn'd chayres	01 00 00
Ite' Brasse of all sorts	04 13 04
Ite' Pewter of all sorts	01 00 00
Ite' one iron plate behinde ye fire, one grate, two dreeping pans, three broaches and other iron ware	02 13 04

Ite' in ye house

one cupboard five chaires one table board & one cradle two wheeles	00 18 00
Ite' one weeting fat, five barrells stunds and all other trinen ware .	02 10 00
Ite' one mault mill & two garners	01 00 00

THE INVENTORIES OF LITTLE WENLOCK

Ite' four store swine	01	05	00
Ite' poultry of all sorts	00	03	04
Ite' one wain two tumbrell bodyes plowes, slead & harrowes	04	00	00
Ite' yokes chaines & all other implemts of husbandry	02	00	00
Ite' corne on ye ground	07	10	00
Ite' goods at ye three pigeons in Salop	04	00	00
Ite' Waring Apparell with money in his pocket	05	00	00
Ite' thing omitted	00	05	00
Ite' debtes spearate due upon specialty	53	00	00
Ite' debtes due wthout specialty	12	18	00
Suma totalis	193	14	04

117. Francis Woseley

Mason of Little Wenlock buried 17/I/1672. Inventory 7/IV/1673 by John Smitheman, George Hayward and John Fletcher exhibited 8/IV/1673 for relict and administratrix. Two of the appraisers were creditors. Widow Owseley assessed for 1 hearth.

Impr's In the house

one Table boarde & fframe	00	05	00
one Kettle one spitt one Iron pott	00	15	00
three pewter dishes	00	02	06
one chaire & stooles	00	01	06
one bed & Bedsteedes	01	00	00
ffower payre of hempen sheetes	01	00	00
one Barrell & a stund	00	03	00
Implem'ts of husbandry	01	00	00
one Cow & one yearling	03	10	00
two naggs	04	00	00
Corne growing upon the p'mises	01	00	00
Thinges fforgotten & not heere exprest	00	05	00
	12	17	00

debts That the decedent did owe as ffolloweth:

one debt due to the Noppll ffrancis fforester Esqr	03	00	00
one debt due to Will' Hayward gent	03	01	03
one debt due to John Chillton of Wyke	09	10	00
one debt due to Will Carter	03	00	00
one debt due to Richard Amies	05	00	00
one debt due to John Smitheman	03	00	00
one debt due to John ffletcher	01	01	00
	27	12	03

118. Richard Parton

Of Little Wenlock died and buried 28/II/1670. Inventory (not dated and no appraisers named) exhibited 14/III/1670 for Mary Parton relict and administratrix.

Imprimis One hayfer and one small Coole	03	00	00
Item Three mares with three pack Sadells.	03	10	00
Item one Swine .	00	05	00
Item four small dishes of pewter .	00	08	00
Item [deletion] .	00	04	00
Item one Cettell one chafeing dish and one skimer and four saucers of peuter	00	02	00
Item one candellstick and one flagone	00	03	00
Item trining ware vesells bouckes and mites	00	05	00
Item one Gine bed and a fither bed and boulst'r with one couering and one blanket .	02	00	00
Item three truckell bedes two twill shetes and one blanket and two chafe bedes	00	13	04
Item two tabell bordes and two formes .	00	10	00
Item two cuberts	00	05	00
Item two chayres	00	01	00
Item thre spining wheles .	00	04	00
Item the strackes of a ould payre of wheles	00	03	04
Item one plowe and carr one slede	00	03	00
Item six payre of hurden shetes and two payre of hempen shetes .	01	13	04
Item three flacksen pillow beares and seven flacksen napkins sixtene hurden napkins and foure tabell clothes .	00	13	04
Item Corne in the barne and hay and bucke	02	00	00
Item two gine chests and one box and five coffers	00	12	06
Item twelve slipings of yarne and six pound of hemp	00	13	04
Item one small spit and Cobarts and one grate	00	01	06
Item things of small value unvalued	00	02	06
Item the aparell of the desesed .	00	05	00
Toto of ye goodes	17	18	02

119. Mr. John Smitheman, senior

Yeoman of Little Wenlock, buried 5/X/1689. Inventory 9/X/1689 by Wm. Hayward, John Simmons and Richard Haberley exhibited 29/X/1689 by Margaret Smitheman relict, William Heyward junior gent and John Smitheman son joint executors. Will 18/IX/1689 left his wife Margaret the best bed and furniture and 10s. to buy a ring; his brother Francis Smitheman £10, the cottage in possession of Robert Powell, land called

THE INVENTORIES OF LITTLE WENLOCK

Powells Yard, formerly Forsley, a garden, hemp butt, the 3rd suit of clothes and the old scimitar and hanger; his son William lands called Stockings and Caplebrick, the 2nd suit of clothes, the sword and belt and £40; his daughter Mary lands called Claypit or Limekill Leasow, Coalpit Leasow, formerly Coalpit Close, the Quarrel and the Combe and £40; his daughter Lucy land called Hilly Meadow and £40; and his son John the best suit of clothes, the scimitar with the gold handle and belt and 10s. for a ring. William, Mary and Lucy to share the rest when of age.

Impr's Three Heifers one bullock & one bull	08	10 00
Barley in Crissetthayes barne	08	10 00
5000 of brick	02	10 00
6 Cowes one heifer & one year old bull	16	00 00
ffive Bullockes	11	10 00
Three Colts	04	10 00
four Calves	02	00 00
29 Sheep	03	10 00
2 little mares & 2 colts	03	00 00
6 year old beasts	06	00 00
three big swine & 6 shotes	04	10 00
Hard Corne in the barne	20	00 00
One bay of Oates	05	00 00
peas	01	05 00
30 strike of barly	02	15 00
Hay in the barne	15	00 00
waynes wheeles and all other the utensills & Implemts of Husbandry	10	00 00

In the parlour

Twelve Leatherne Chaires	02	08 00
Two Ovell Tables & Table Clothes	01	00 00

In the best Chamber

One Table 6 Chaires one bed and all the furnitre and the Hanging presse and one Coffer	05	00 00
One old Horse and one mare	07	00 00

In the midle Chamber

One bed bedsteeds and all ye furniture thereunto belonging Together one one Truckle bed and all the furniture of the Roomes	04	00 00

In the Garratts

The Cheeses Corne bottells and all other materialls belonging to them	05	00 00

In the Little Roome

One bed & bedsteads	01	10	00

In the Brew house

All the Barrells stunds wooden bottles mitts all other the Coopery ware with a long Coffer	03	00	00

In the Buttery

One Table one safe one Glasse Case 6 Chaires 10 barrells. .	03	00	00

In the milke house

One Salting Tubb pailes milk panns boles one Churne Shelves 1 Table	01	10	00
Linnens	03	00	00

In the Dwelling house

One Table 6 Chaires 2 formes 2 pair of Tonges Two fire Shovells all the brasses and pewter & one presse with five Iron spitts .	06	00	00
One malt mill	01	00	00
The deceased wareing apparell	10	00	00
One wach	01	10	00
One new sadle one bridle one pair of holsters one pair of pistolls .	02	00	00
One Little Gun	00	10	00
Things omitted and not menconed in this Inventory . .	02	00	00
. . . .	178	18	00

120. George Buttery

Of Huntingdon in Little Wenlock, buried 28/VI/1691. Inventory 19/X/1691 by Tho. Delves, Roger Walker and John Symons exhibited 22/X/1691 by Mary Buttery relict and administratrix. 1 hearth.

Impri's In ye Chamber over ye house

one feather bed & furniture	01	00	00
Item 2 stone of hemp in ye same room	00	06	00
Item 2 little wheels & one longe wheel	00	05	00
Item one Coffer	00	02	00

Item In the chamber over ye buttery

One truccle bed & 3 chests one small trunk . . .	01	00	04
3 table cloaths & 5 pair flaxen sheets	02	18	00
& 7 pair hempen & noggen	01	05	00
for other odd linen	00	17	00

THE INVENTORIES OF LITTLE WENLOCK

Item In ye buttery

one Joyned bed & furnitr	02	00	00
3 barrells 2 turnell & 3 stunds one Cupboard . .	01	05	00

Item In ye house

one press one table & one joyned form . . .	01	10	00
one joyned Chair & Seg chairs & 3 stools . .	01	03	00
Eleven Small pewter dishes 3 pewter chamber potts & 2 guns & 1 flaggon 3 pollingers one tandard one dozen of spoons & 2 salts .	01	12	00
Three brass potts 4 brass kettles one warming pann one skimer & ladle & one posnet	02	03	04
Two Iron dripping pans one Iron pott one posnet one Iron morter & pestell Two fryin pans 3 small broaches one Iron plate . .	00	12	00
One fire grate one fire pan & a pair of tongs one pair pot geels & 2 cobberts	00	03	00
One Small birding piece	00	02	00
One pail & one gallon measure & other trining ware .	00	02	06
One swine & 2 shotes	01	00	00
for hay	00	02	00
for wearing apparell boots bridle & sadle . . .	02	00	00
ffor things omitted	00	01	00
one bond desperate	—	—	—
. . . .	18	09	08

121. Edward Burgwyn

Yeoman of Little Wenlock, buried 7/V/1690. Inventory 7/V/1691 (*sic*) by Jo. Smitheman and George Glaesbrooke exhibited 8/V/1691 by Elizabeth Rushton *alias* Burgwyn wife of Francis Rushton and relict of Edward Burgwyn and administratrix.

In the House place

Impr's one Table & fframe	00	04	00
seaven pewter dishes & seven spoones . . .	00	14	00
five pewter porringers	00	03	00
one Iron pott lid two pewter salt sellers . . .	00	02	00
one pudding pan one pewter Candlesticke . .	00	01	04
one Iron dreeping pan	00	03	06
Two Iron potts	00	04	00
one Salt box	00	01	00
one pasty pann of tin	00	00	06
Two Smoothing Irons one Iron spitt & 2 Cobbards & two paire of pott Racks	00	04	00

In the parlour

One Table & ffoarme	00	01	06
one Joyne Stoole.	00	00	06
Two Turned Chaires	00	01	06
one Earthen bason	00	00	04
two stone Juggs .	00	00	08

In the Buttery

Three barrells	00	04	00
six mike bowles .	00	01	06
one Churne two stunds & other wooden ware	00	05	00
one Cheese tubbe two pailes & one piggin	00	02	00

In the Chamber over the house

one Joyne bed halfe Tester & one Truccle bed 6 blankets two feather beds two boulsters & three pillowes	02	00	00
two Cofferrs one Chest & two boxes & one little Truncke one Cradle .	00	16	00

In the Chamber over the buttery

One Chaffe bed & boulster one Red Rugg & one blankett	00	12	00
one saddle	00	04	00
Linnens of all sort	01	00	00
The deceaseds wearing apparrall .	01	00	00

In the Kitching

one needing tubbe one spinning wheele one Cheese presse two tutors	00	10	00
one old mare & old Cow	02	00	00
Implem'ts of husbandry .	00	10	00
Total	11	06	04

122. Richard Wheelwright

Yeoman of Little Wenlock, buried 12/I/1708. Inventory 2/III/1708 by John Smitheman and Maurice Hayward exhibited 21/VI/1709 for Priscilla Wheelwright relict and administratrix (née Owen m 1680, his second wife).

In ye dwelling house

One Table and fforme two Brasse kettles one Brasse chaffeing dish Two Brewing vessells two Mitts two Iron broaches one pair of Cobards two pailes one Churne three spining wheeles three potthucks and pott linkes one Iron Grate one pair of Tongs	03	13	00

In ye parlour

One Long Table and Two fformes	00	15	00
Twelve pewter dishes Eleaven plates 6 pewter Quarts one pinte & one pewter Chamber pott	12	10	00
One presse one Cupboard two Little Tables six chaires	01	03	00

In ye chamber

One ffeather bed and Boulster & ffurniture thereto belonging	03	10	00
One Ovall Table & one pillion	00	13	00

In ye Buttery

Seaven Barrells	01	03	00

In ye Outward Chamber

Two pair of Bedsteads & furniture	01	00	00
One square Table & one Joyne chair	00	04	00

In ye Inner Chamber

One pair of Bedsteads and furniture	01	00	00
one Chest and Table	00	10	00
Lynnens of all sorts	04	03	00
Beefe and Bacon	03	00	00
Two Stones of Hemp	00	06	00
Two Strikes of Muncorne	00	03	00
ffour strikes of pease	00	03	00
One Mare and one two year old Colt	03	10	00
Two Cowes two Heifers and two yearling Calves	10	10	00
Two Swine	01	00	00
One Hayrick	02	00	00
Barley in ye Barne	01	00	00
Things omitted and not meconed.	00	05	00
Sum total	42	16	00

123. Richard Jervis

Yeoman of Huntington in Little Wenlock, buried 2/IV/1715. Inventory 23/IV/1715 by Maurice Hayward and Richard Haberley, apparently not exhibited. Probate 20/IX/1715 to Martha Jennings sister in law and executrix. Will 24/II/1714 left his children Mary Jervis £20 and Richard Collier of Ketley Wood the cow at hire to Stephen Rodes. The rest was to be shared between Martha Jennings and Richard Jervis if she remained single.

Impr'is Two Mares and Two Horses	16	00	00
Two Yearlings	02	00	00

Two Two years old Bullocks	02	10 00
ffour Cows	16	00 00
One Barrenn Cow	02	10 00
Two store swine	01	00 00

In the Dwelling house

Brasse and pewter	01	15 00
One Iron pott & Marment	00	05 00
One Cupboard one Table one Joyne fforme 3 Chairs one Grate one ffire shovell one pair of Tongs	01	00 00

In the parlour

Two ffeather Beds with their Bedsteads & other furniture . .	05	00 00

In the Buttery

Two Barrells	01	00 00

In the Back Roome

One pair of Bedsteads & one old Chest	00	15 00
Implements of Husbandry	01	00 00
One pair of fflaxen and five pair of Hurden sheets with some other small Linnen	01	10 00
The Dec'ds Books & wareing Apparrell	02	00 00

In the Barne

Three thraves of Hardcorne and one of Oates . . .	01	00 00
Tot . .	55	05 00

124. William Whyston

Clerk Rector of Little Wenlock since 1690, buried 23/V/1713. Inventory 26/V/1713 by Maurice Hayward and Paul Peploe exhibited 23/VI/1713 for Samuel Whyston brother and administrator.

In ye Corne Barne

Hardcorne Unthreshed	02	00 00
Oates pease & barley	01	00 00

In ye Hay bay

Hay	01	05 00
one Hackney Saddle one pad one pack saddle one paire of Holmes one Collar one dragg	00	10 00

THE INVENTORIES OF LITTLE WENLOCK 251

Compost or Muck	01	05	00
Three Store Piggs	01	10	00
One Old Horse	01	05	00

In ye Schoole house

one mitt one old Barrell Two Tutors one Neading Trough & one Wash Tubb 00 07 00

In ye Kitching & back Kitching

Two Hogsheads 00 14 00
One brewing Tubb one Tunning dish one Turnell one Little Wheele one bench, 1 Spade 00 06 00
Two Pailes one Gaune one Butter Tubb one bench three bowles one pott one Marmt. one Skellett three Dozen of Trenchers four Noggins one Kipe on Coale box 00 14 00
One Table 00 08 00

In ye parlour

ffour Large pewter Dishes & four small dishes ffifteen plates Two Large Pewter Candlesticks three brasse Candlesticks three Iron Candlesticks four pewter porringrs one Mustard pott two Saltes one pye plate one pewter Chamber pott 00 10 00
Tinn Ware of all Sorts & one Lanthorne 00 04 00
ffive Small Dripping panns 00 12 00
Two Chaffeing dishes 00 01 08
One ffire shovell one paire of Tongs one Iron Grate one Cast back wo brasse Nobbs to ye Grate 00 15 00
ffour iron spitts ffour Flesh forkes one paire of Tongs one ffire shovell two basteing Spoones one sett of scewers one paire of Gobbards one Iron Grate 01 00 00
Earthen Ware of all Sorts & drinking Glasses . . . 00 05 00
one Mortar & pestell one barr fire shovell one fire plate on saw one Ax one Aze 00 07 06
one Clock & clock case & one salt box 01 00 00
one fiddle one old Cittern 00 05 00
Two Ovall Tables 8 Chairs one Side table one Skreen . . 00 14 00
one Warmeing pann 00 01 06
Six fflitches of bacon ffour fflitches of Beefe . . . 04 10 00

In ye Buttery

One halfe hoggshead & three small Barrells three boles & a Trea . 00 15 00
one Brasse pott & Masling Ketle 00 07 00

In ye Roome ovr ye Hall

Mault 01 05 00
one Litte Press 00 02 06
Hemp & fflax 00 09 00

one Halfe Strike & one peck	00	01	00
two Riddles & one Seeve	00	00	10
Pease & Wheate	00	06	06
Two Basketts	00	01	00
Two Hand Basketts	00	00	06
Two feather Bedds & furniture	05	00	00
Two Tables one Lookeing Glass	00	05	00
One paire of bedsteads & Hangings . . .	00	05	00

In ye parlour Chamber

one Feather bed & boulsters & other ffurniture thereto belonging	02	10	00
One Chest two Trunks one Little Desk one Close Stoole one Hanging press two Square Tables.	02	02	00
One Iron Grate	00	00	06
One Lookeing Glasse	01	00	00
One Little Trunk	00	00	06
Linnens of all sorts	03	00	00
Hemp Hurden & fflaxen Yarne	01	00	00
Eleaven Yards of Black Cloth	01	15	00
The Deceased's Wareing Apparell . . .	05	00	00
The Deceased's Libri of Books	02	10	00
Things omitted	00	05	00
tot . .	51	11	00

125. George Wheelwright

Yeoman of Little Wenlock, buried 20/II/1713. Inventory 15/III/1713 by Jo. Smitheman, Mau. Hayward* and Thomas Boycott exhibited 1/IX/1714 for Richard Wheelwright son and executor. Will 1/VII/1713 left his wife 'all I had with her which is now at interest on bond' and his daughter Sarah Roofe 1s. Residual legatees were his children Richard Wheelwright and Ann Jaundrell but it was all to remain in Richard's hands during the life of Ann's husband John Jaundrell who was never to get control of any of it even if Richard died first. Jaundrell became vicar of Madeley d 1753.

In ye Kitchen

One Table board one Joyne Skreen Two fformes Three Joyne Stoole three Chaires	01	05	00
Three Little Wheels & Long Spinning Wheel . . .	00	06	00

THE INVENTORIES OF LITTLE WENLOCK

One Child's Cradle	00	10	00
One Fire Shovell & paire of Tongs one Iron Grate	00	05	00
One ffrying pann Two pudding panns	00	04	00
Linkes & potthookes fflesh forkes one Basting Spoon one hacking Knife one Grid Iron	00	04	00
One Broach & Two Iron Cobbarts	00	02	00
Sixteen pewter Dishes & Seaven Pewter plates Six porringers two pewter Candlesticks one pewter Can One pewter Cupp	02	10	00
Tinnen Ware of all Sorts	00	03	06
One Iron Dripping pann	00	05	00
Two Iron potts	00	08	00
ffour Brass Kettles	01	00	00
One Brasse pan one brasse pott one Warmeing pan	01	00	00
ffive Stunds Three pailes one Churn One Gaun & Three Wooden Bottles	01	10	00
Two Wooden Coolers Three Small mitts for Milk	00	15	00
Beefe & Bacon	02	00	00

In ye Upper parlour

One feather bed & furniture	03	00	00
One other feather bed & furniture	03	00	00
Two Chests one Coffer one Box & one Desk one Cupboard & Some old Chaires	02	00	00

In ye Chamber over ye Upper parlour

One feather Bed & two Chaff beds & furnitur in ye Roome.	03	00	00

In ye Lower parlour

Two ffeather beds & two chaff beds one Chest one Trunk one box one Table & one old Coffer	03	00	00

In ye Buttery

Seaven Small Barrells & Drinke	01	10	00

In ye Chamber over ye Buttery

Six Chaires	00	06	00
Eight Strikes of Mault	01	04	00
Nine hurden Slippings of yarne ffive hempen slippings	00	10	00
Eight Cheese Vatts one Bowle for Milke one halfe Bushell	00	06	00
Cheeses	01	00	00
ffour Dozen of Trenchers	00	04	00
Linnens of All Sorts	05	00	00
The Deceased's Wareing Apparell & new Cloth to make him a Shute	03	10	00
Creditts due to ye Deceased	100	00	00
Eighteen Strikes Sewing on ye Ground	10	00	00

In ye Barne

The hardcorne	03	00 00
Oates	02	00 00
Hay	08	00 00
Implemts of Husbandry of all sorts	05	00 00
Six Cowes & Calves	20	00 00
Twenty five Sheep & thirteen Lambs	06	05 00
Six Oxen	24	00 00
One Mare & Two Colts	10	00 00
ffive Two yeare old heifers & Bullocks	10	00 00
ffour yeareling Calves	04	00 00
Two Store Swine	01	00 00
Things omitted & not menconed	00	10 00
Tot	243	12 06

126. John Fletcher

Yeoman/blacksmith of Little Wenlock, buried 10/I/1714. Inventory 17/III/1714 by Maurice Hayward and John Taylor exhibited 20/IX/1715. Will 7/I/1714 left his wife Jane all except the tools for life then to be shared among the children; his son William 'the tools & Implemts perteyning to ye trade of a blacksmith'.

In the Kitchen

One Table two fformes one Skreen four old chaires and one Cupboard	02	00 00
pewter of all sorts	02	10 00
Brass of all sorts	01	10 00
One Iron pott two Iron Kettles two Racks one other Iron pott one Grate Niggards three Broaches one ffryeing pann one dripping pann and Tongs	04	00 00
Woodden Ware in the Kitchen	00	15 00

In the parlour

One Ovall Table one long Table two Chests One fforme three Chaires one box One Bedd and ffurniture	03	00 00
The deceaseds Wareing Apparrell	02	00 00

In the Chamber over the house

Three old bedds & ffurniture	03	00 00
One Chest	00	06 08
20 Strikes of Barley	02	10 00
One other bedd and ffurniture	01	00 00

Six strikes of Wheat	01	00 00
Bacon and Beefe	03	00 00

In the Buttrey

Six Barrells and Two Churnes	01	00 00

In the Barne

Hard corne	03	10 00
Hay	02	10 00
Implemts of Husbandry	05	00 00

In the Stable

ffive horses & Mares and pack saddles and other Gears	20	00 00
ffour Oxen	17	00 00
ffour Cowes twoe Heifors and Twoe Twinter Bullocks	23	00 00
Twelve sheep	03	10 00
Twoe store piggs	01	00 00
Things omitted and not menconed	01	00 00
	105	11 08

127. William Wheelwright, senior

Yeoman of Little Wenlock, buried 19/IX/1714. Inventory 24/IX/1714 by Jo. Smitheman and the Tho. Boycott exhibited 20/IX?1715 for Margaret Wheelwright eldest daughter and Maurice Hayward. Will 4/IX/1714 left his daughters, Margaret £40, Ann £30, Bridget wife of Thomas Thirling and Sarah wife of William Ferreday 1s. each; his granddaughter Sarah Howle the cow called Nut; and his son William the freehold estate in Wellington and the rest of the estate unless he married Joan Fletcher. William Wheelwright blacksmith m Ann Smitheman 1667.

In the Dwelling house

One Table one presse one Cupboard Two fformes & one skreen	02	00 00
Seaven pewter dishes six pewter plates Two porringers one Chamber pott one pewter Candlestick one Tankard and one pewter Salt	01	05 00
Two Large Dripping pans	00	10 00
One pestell and Mortar	00	03 00
ffive Brasse Kettles Two Brasse potts one Chaffing dish two Brasse Candlesticks & Two Brasse Skelletts	04	00 00
Two Iron potts two Broaches one old Jack One fire shovell and Tongs one Grate Linkes and pott hucks one Marmitt one Iron Candlestick	01	10 00

In the Little Chamber

One ffeather Bed and furniture	02	10	00
One Chest	00	08	00
Two Brewing stunds	00	08	00
One steele Mill	00	10	00

In the parlour

One Bed and furniture	03	00	00
One Desk one Chest one Round Table three Chaires . .	01	00	00
The deceaseds Wareing Apparell	02	10	00
One Warming pann	00	03	06

In the Buttery

Six small Barrells & the Rest of the wooden ware. . .	01	10	00
One Cheese Tubb Milking pail one Long wheele . . .	00	04	00

In the Chamber Over the house

One ffeather Bed and furniture	02	00	00
Six pair of sheets	01	00	00
30 cheeses	01	10	00
Six Oxen four houses and Gears	40	00	00
Two Heifers	03	10	00
Three Calfes	01	10	00
Twenty sheep	04	00	00
Three Cows 9 li, four swine 1 li 10s 0d	10	10	00
One waine one Tumbrell & Implemts of Husbandry . .	06	00	00

Corne in ye Barn

Muncorne 10 li Barley 2 li 10s	12	10	00
Oates and Hay	10	10	00
15 Geese 10s things omitted 20s	01	10	00
Tot . .	116	01	06

128. William Wheelwright

Yeoman of Little Wenlock, buried 6/VII/1717. Inventory 23/VII/1717 by Maurice Hayward* and Thomas Boycott exhibited 30/VII/1717 for Margaret Wheelwright sister and administratrix.

In the Dwelling house

1 table 1 Cupboard 2 formes & 1 skreen	02	00	00
Seven pewter Dishes, 6 pewter plates 2 porringrs 1 Chamber pott, 1 pewter Candlestick 1 tankard 1 pewter Salt . . .	01	05	00

THE INVENTORIES OF LITTLE WENLOCK

Two large Dripping pans.	00 10 00
One Pestill & Mortar	00 03 00
ffive Brass kettels 2 brass potts 1 Chafing dish 2 brass Candlesticks & 2 brass Skelletts	04 00 00
Two Iron potts 3 broaches 1 old Jack one ffire shovell & tonges 1 grate Linkes & pothooks	01 10 00

In the Little Chamber

One ffeather bed & furniture	02 10 00
one Chest 8s 2 brewing stunds 8s	00 16 00
One Steell mill	00 10 00

In the Parlour

1 bed & furniture	03 00 00
One Desk 1 Chest 1 round table & 3 Chaires	01 00 00
The Deceds wearing apparell	02 00 00
One warming pan	00 01 00

In the Buttery

6 small barrells & the rest of the wooden ware	01 10 00
One Cheese Tub & milking pail	00 03 00

In the chamber over the house

one feather bed & furniture	02 00 00
ffive pair of sheets	01 00 00
30 cheeses	01 10 00
six oxen	24 00 00
ffive old horses & geeres	14 00 00
ffour yearling beasts	05 00 00
Three Calves	01 10 00
Six Sheep	01 10 00
ffour Cows	10 00 00
Two Swine	02 00 00
One waine one Tumbrell & Implements of husbandry	04 00 00

Corne on the ground

Hard corne	04 00 00
Barley	03 00 00
Pease	01 00 00
Oates	03 00 00
16 Geese	00 08 00
Things omitted & not mencioned	01 00 00
. . . .	97 16 00

129. Francis Parton

Yeoman of Little Wenlock, buried 18/IX/1728. Inventory 12/XI/1728 by Jo. Smitheman and Mau. Hayward exhibited 3/VI/1729 for Elizabeth Parton relict and administratrix.

In the Dwelling House			
One Long table and two forms	00	10	00
Six Old Chairs	00	02	00
One Small Joyned Skreen	00	03	00
One Iron Grate one plate one fire shovel and tons & Chains to hold pots on ye fire & other Iron ware & three Broaches	01	05	00
Nineteen Pewter Dishes 12 Pewter plates Spoons Porrengers & other pewter	02	00	00
Three Brasse Potts 2 Small Brasse Kettles 3 Brasse Candlesticks 2 Iron Candlesticks	01	00	00
One Old Cupboard & Some Delph ware & Glasses	00	05	00
One Old warming pann	00	01	00

The Chamber

One ffeather Bed & ffurniture	02	10	00
Two Chaffe Beds & ffurniture	00	10	00
One Table & Cupboard	00	03	00

In the Buttery & Milkhouse

Two Small Barrells and Milkpan & Bowls	00	10	00

In the Passage Room

One Tub two Pails & other Implments for ye Dairy	00	05	00

In the Kitchen

One Iron ffurnace	01	00	00
One Mill	01	00	00
Three Large Tubbs & other small vessells and two Coolers	01	10	00
One Old Cupboard	00	01	00

In the Other Buttery

Two Hogsheads & 5 Small Barrells	01	10	00

In ye Chamber over ye Dwelling House

One Straw Baskett	00	05	00

The New Room

One ffeather Bed Boulster & Hangings and other ffurniture to ye bed	03	00	00
One Oval Table and Six Chairs	00	10	00

THE INVENTORIES OF LITTLE WENLOCK 259

Two Chests & old Boxes	00	10 00
Linnen of all sorts	05	00 00

The fellows Room

One fflock Bed & ffurniture & other trumpery ware	00	10 00

In the Great Chamber

One ffeather Bed & Boulster two fflock Beds & ffurniture to ye Bed	03	00 00
The Deceased's wearing Apparrell	02	00 00
One Table one Chest three Old Coffers 1 fform	01	00 00

In the Corn Barn

One Mow of Hard Corn & Oates & Barley	25	00 00

In the Hay Barn & other Buildings

Hay and Clover	10	00 00
ffive Cows	17	10 00
ffour Oxen & five Bullocks	35	00 00
ffive Heifers	10	00 00
Eight Sheep	01	00 00
Implemts of Husbandry of all sorts	10	00 00
5 Calves	02	10 00
ffive Horses & Gearse	20	00 00
two Colts	05	00 00
Three Hoggs	03	00 00
Sum total	169	03 04

130. Edmund Gray

Yeoman of Huntington in Little Wenlock, buried 13/XII/1729. Inventory 22/I/1729 by Jo. Smitheman and William Shaen exhibited 16/VI/1730 for Bridget Gray relict and administratrix.

In the Dwelling House

One fire Shovel Tongs Iron Grate Niggard Links potthooks and A Cast plate Morter pestel a Chaffing dish three smoothing Irons & four spitts	01	00 00
Three Dripping panns	00	10 00
Eighteen pewter dishes & twelve plates	02	00 00
One Brasse pott & one Brass pann	00	10 00
One Clock & Old Jack	01	00 00
One Oval Table One Skreen & Six Chairs	01	00 00

One Dresser & Drawrs	00	10 00
Six Candlesticks	00	05 00

In the Wash House

One Cheese presse One Cheese Tubb two pails two Gawns three Iron potts one Iron Marment and one Brasse Kettle . .	01	10 00

The Little Room

One Table & Cupboard	00	02 06

In ye Buttery

ffour Barrells & one Hogshead	01	05 00
One Table four Mitts two Brewing Tubbs two Coolers one Churn & Six Cheese fatts	01	00 00

In the parlour

One ffeather Bed & furniture One Table one little Looking Glasse one Chest four Chairs three Boxes one Cupboard. . .	03	00 00

The Chamber over ye Parlour

Two Chests three Chairs & one Coffer	00	10 00
One ffeather Bed & furniture	02	00 00

In the Chamber Over the Kitchen

Two Old ffeather Beds four Chairs & one Chest . . .	03	00 00

In the Chamber Over ye Dwelling House

One Chaffe Bed two pair of Bedsteads one Malt Mill & one saddle pillion	02	00 00

In the House

Malt	00	15 00
Barley	01	00 00
Cheeses	01	00 00
One Long Table	00	05 00
The Deceased's Wearing Apparrell	02	00 00
Linnen of all Sorts	03	00 00
Hay in the Barnes	04	00 00
Hardcorn is the Barn	03	00 00
Oates	02	00 00
Pease	01	10 00
ffrench Wheat	00	06 00
six Cows	15	00 00
ffour two years old do	06	00 00
one three years Old Bullock	03	00 00

THE INVENTORIES OF LITTLE WENLOCK   261

One Bull	01	00	00
One Calfe	00	10	00
ffour Mares a Colt & one Lame Mare	20	00	00
One Stoned horse	10	00	00
Implemts. of Husbandry of all sorts	10	00	00
Two Swine	03	00	00
ffour piggs	01	00	00
Things Omitted & not mensoned.	01	00	00
Tot	110	08	00

131. George Fletcher, senior

Ropemaker of Little Wenlock, buried 22/V/1730. Inventory 22/V/1730 by Joseph and William Fletcher exhibited 16/VI/1730 for Mary Fletcher relict and administratrix.

One Old Bed with bedtick Boulster Rug and Blanketts	00	15	00
One Old Table & two fforms	00	07	06
One Old Wooden Cubboard	00	01	06
One Old Clock	00	10	00
Eight Segg Chairs	00	02	08
two Chaff Beds	00	10	00
One Oval Table	00	02	08
One old Chest & Coffer	00	05	00
One Old Brasse ffurnace.	00	10	00
Two Old Iron potts	00	03	00
One Brewing Tubb	00	02	00
two Old Barrells.	00	04	00
a small Long Table & fform	00	04	00
A Dresser w'th three draw'rs in	00	05	00
One Old Wooden skreen.	00	01	00
One Water Pail	00	00	06
Nine Small old pewter dishes	00	10	00
Nine Old pewter plates	00	03	00
One Old frying pan & pudding pann	00	01	06
One Old Brasse warming pann	00	01	06
One Dripping pann, old pudding plates & broach.	00	02	06
A Grate fire shovel & Tongs	00	02	06
A pewter Chamber pott & three porrengers & two tin pudding panns & a cover.	00	02	00
two Old Mares one 31 the other 21	05	00	00
Instruments etc belonging to Rope Making of all sorts	01	14	00
Tot	12	00	00

132. Francis Evans

Collier of Huntington Heath in Little Wenlock, buried 2/VII/1735. Inventory 15/VII/1736 by John Cowper and John Duddell exhibited 27/VII/1736 for Jules Evans son and administrator.

One old Clock and Case.	00	10	00
One old Table .	00	02	06
A Skreen, two old Chairs, and an old Ax.	00	04	05
Twenty Pounds of old Iron, two old Augers and an old Saw	00	02	02
One Cooler one Bench a pair of Potthooks and Links	00	03	05
One small furnace	00	10	00
One old Tub and 3 Boards	00	02	06
One pair of old Bedsteads	00	01	00
One old Box	00	00	03
A Pair of Bedsteads and one Hanging	00	04	06
A Bouch and an old Tub	00	01	00
Wearing Apparell	00	10	00
Two Grates	00	05	00
A Malt Mill	00	05	00
A Bucket Well Rope & Barrell	00	02	06
A Pair of old Bellows and a Hammer	00	01	00
An old Pitt Chain	00	00	08
six Young Geese.	00	05	00
Two old ones	00	03	00
	03	19	11

133. Roger Thresslecock

Yeoman of the Leasows in Little Wenlock, buried 1/IX/1742. Inventory 6/IX/1742 by Gab. Dixon and Math. Colly exhibited 7/IX/1742 for William Parton neighbour and John Howells son in law yeomen executors. Will 5/VI/1742 left his wife Margery everything for life then to his grandson Roger Thresslecock.

Three Carring Horses	12	00	00
Three other Carring Horses	04	10	00
Two Colts	03	10	00
Three Kine	10	00	00
Four Young beasts	08	00	00
Four Swine	03	10	00
Corn in the Barn	05	00	00
Oats	07	00	00
Yithords.	01	10	00

Hay	07	00	00
fflax	01	00	00
Implyments of Husbantry . . .	00	10	00
The Clock	01	10	00

In the Kitchen

Screen and Table form 2 pair of Cobbarts 2 Broches One Grate, One pair of Tongs, One fier Shovel	01	02	00
Two potts one Kettle	00	08	00
Six Chairs	00	03	00
One Cheese Tub a Pail, One Gaun, 2 Bottells 3 Dozen of Trenchers & four Cheesevatts	00	10	00

In the parlour

One Chest, One Table, one form.	00	12	00
five Dishes and Six plates	00	17	06
One Brass pott, One Kettle, One Warming pann . . .	00	11	00

In the Cellar

One Dreeping pan, One Chopping Knife Cleever . . .	00	08	00
four Barrells and one Tub	00	12	00
Three Weels	00	03	00

Milk house

One Cooler, one Churn, one Tundish, one mitt . . .	00	06	00

Roome Over the parlour

One Bed and Bedstead, One hangings for the bed . .	03	00	00
One Chest and Linnens	03	04	00

Roome Over the Kitchen

Three Beds & Bedsteads	03	00	00
One Boyler	00	05	00
All Lumber Computed	00	05	00
Wearing Apparell	01	10	00
. . . .	81	16	06

134. William Baugh

Of Little Wenlock, buried 17/V/1755. Inventory 21/V/1755, no appraisers named, but administrator signed*. His mother having renounced her right, it was exhibited the next day for William Baugh nephew. All goods were sold at auction by the overseers.

Two flock beds & bedsteads	01	10	00
Sheets & blanketts	00	06	00
two old Potts & a kettle	00	03	06
2 old Coffers	00	04	00
the dec'eds wearing Apparel	00	12	00
One barrel	00	01	06
One axe a reaping hook & a Scyth	00	03	00
a table & a dresser	00	10	00
	03	10	00

135. William Boycott

Butcher of Little Wenlock, buried 20/V/1709. Inventory 13/VI/1709 by Geo. Wheelwright and Maurice Hayward was exhibited 21/VI/1709 for Jane Boycott relict and administratrix (née Owen m 1681).

In the Dwelling house

One Skreen	00	04	00
Eight pewter dishes & other pewter	01	00	00
Bacon and Beefe	01	05	00
12 Cheeses	00	10	00
Two Brasse kettles 2 Iron potts	02	00	00
Two Broaches	00	02	00
Two smoothing Irons one dripping pan fire shovell tongs pott Linkes & pott Hucks and one Iron grate	01	00	00

In ye parlour

Three Joyne fformes one Chest Two Little Boxes three Little Tables	00	15	00
One Bed and ffurniture	01	05	00
Two Chaires one Warming pan	00	05	00
One other Bed being Chaffe & furniture	00	10	00

In ye Chamber Over ye house place

Two beds and furniture	01	00	00
Three Coffers three Basketts & one Little Box	00	10	00
Three wooden Bottles two dozen of Trenchers	00	03	00
Hard Corne and Mault	05	00	00

In ye Roome over ye parlour

Two Beds and all the furniture two Chests one Table	06	00	00
Two chaires	00	01	00
Linnens of all sorts	02	10	00
The deceased wareing Apparrell	02	10	00

In the Cellar

ffour Barrells two Mitts one Churne One Cheese Tubb and one Cheese press	01	05	00
All sorts of Implemts for Husbandry . . .	01	10	00
ffour Cowes two yearling heifers two two year's old Heifers one other Cow and Two Calfes	13	10	00
One Nag two Mares and 2 Colts	12	00	00
Seaven sheep two Lambs and two swine	02	00	00
things omitted and not menconed	00	10	00
Sum Tot . .	57	05	00

136. Thomas Cartledge

Potter of Little Wenlock, buried 1/V/1760. Inventory (not dated) by Edward Clarke and William Jones exhibited 8/VII/1760 for Abigail Cartledge relict and administratrix.

In the Kitchen some Old ffurniture	01	19	00
In the Parlour one old Chest of Draws old Table & Chairs .	00	19	00
Upstairs: Bedding	02	15	00
The Cellar two old Barrells	00	05	00
The Brewhouse some old Brewing Vessels	00	05	00
The new Workhouse Lath and Ware	01	14	06
The old Workhouse one Wheel and Ware	00	07	06
The Cattle	09	10	00
Two Piggs	00	18	06
Some Old Clothes and Linnen	01	00	00
. . . .	18	17	06

137. George Parton

Of Little Wenlock, buried 1/IV/1760. Inventory (not dated and no appraisers named) exhibited 4/V/1761 for Francis Parton son and administratrix.

One Grate one Pair of Tongs, 2 Flesh Forks, 1 scewer, one Pair of Pott Links	00	05	00

One Iron Boiler.	00	04	00
One Potts, one Iron Kettle and Sauce Pan	00	03	00
One old Tin Cullender & Cover Pepper Drudger.	00	00	08
One Iron Candlestick	00	00	03
One Long table, one Bench, one little Table, one hacking Block one turn up Table.	00	05	00
Three Ash Chairs & 2 old segg Bottom ones	00	02	06
One old Warming Pan.	00	02	06
Five old Pewter Dishes & fourteen Plates.	00	11	00
Eleven Trenchers	00	01	06
One Pail, one Gawn, one old Tub	00	02	06
One old frying Pan	00	00	08
One old Cooler.	00	02	06
One Chest, one old feather Bed and Bedsteads	00	14	00
One little Barrell and Bench	00	03	00
One old Bruing Tub, an old Churn	00	03	00
One Pair of Iron Racks.	00	01	06
One Pair of Bedsteads.	00	03	00
	03	05	07

THE INVENTORIES OF MADELEY

138. Francis Rushon

Husbandman of Madeley buried 16/III/1664. Inventory 27/IV/1665 by Edward Farrall and Richard Lynall, apparently not exhibited. On 14/XI/1664 Michael Richards and John Wolrich clerks were commissioned to take the oath of Mary Rushton relict and administratrix. Mary Blest *alias* Rushdon relict of Francis Rushton presented her account 22/X/1667. The Rushtons may have been non-conformists. In 1654 the birth of a child was recorded but not the baptism as was usual in the Madeley registers at that time.

Impr'is in ye Dwelling house

one Table Board & a forme	00	10 00
Item Too little Chaires a little Table & other odde things	00	03 04
Item one ioyned Cubbart.	00	05 00

In ye chamber over ye house

Too beds & beding thereunto belonging	01	00 00
Item two ioyned Chests	00	10 00
Item Linnen and Naperie of all sorts	02	00 00
Item Iron Implements app'taining to ye fire	00	10 00
Item 2 Spining wheeles	00	04 00
Item fore kine	10	00 00
Item three Heifors	04	00 00
Item two swine	00	10 00
Item one Mare	02	10 00
Item Timber for Coopers use	13	13 04
Item Corne in ye barne	01	05 00

in the chamber below

one bed and beding	00	10 00
Item three barrells one brewing stund a kneading tub and other Cowpery ware	00	16 00
Debts sperate & desperate	05	00 00
Item all other odde things omitted	00	03 00
Tot	43	09 08

139. Roger Evans

Of Madeley buried 4/IX/1665. Inventory 9/IX/1665 by Richard Astley and John Evans exhibited 2/XI/1665 for Margaret Evans relict and administratrix *(149)*.

Imprimis in the Parler
one Bedstead with curtaines & vallens one feather bed & boulster one chaffe bed and boulster one coverlett one blanckett one paire of sheets one warming pan one looking glase one table board one foarme one chaire & foure cushions, at 04 10 00

It' over the Dwelling house
two chaffe Beds two feather Boulsters thre pillows one Rugg Two Coverletts two Blanketts two Paire of Sheets one cheste 5 coffers one hanging candlesticke one chambr pott at . . 02 13 04
It' Linens. one paire of flaxen sheets two paire of Hempen, four or five paire of Hurden, two hempen table cloathes one dozen of napkins three pillowes bears one flaxen towell at . . . 02 13 04

It' Ov'r the Parlor
two great coffer one ould hodghead or pipe 5 or 6 ould tubbs, two straw whisketts three boards, two quartr of mault 4 or 5 Hundred of cheese a Parsell of linnen yarne & linnen cloath at . . 06 06 08

It' In the cockloft
one coffer and a few beanes at 00 02 00

It' In the buttery
one brasse pan one brasse pott foure brasse kettles 5 or 6 dishes of pewtr two or three barrels and some other treane ware . . 02 13 04

It' In the dwelinge howse
one cubbord one table board one forme two chaires 3 cushions three dishes of Pewtr, two Pewtr candlesticks one brass candlesticke one pewter salt one little brasse morter one iron mortr one iron dreeping pan two Spitts one paire of iron cobberts one iron pott & pot gailes one paire of tongs one fireshovel one iron backe one iron plate one grate wth andirons one fryinge pann . . . 02 10 00

It' In the kitchen or Bakehouse
one cheese presse one kneading trough one hatchell two spinninge wheeles 00 06 08

It' Coales 00 10 00

It' a wash tubb & stone trough	00	01 06
It' Corne & hay	02	10 00
It' foure cowes & one yearlinge heyfer . . .	11	10 00
It' three swine	01	05 00
It' Hempe wattered & unwatered. . . .	00	10 00
It' mony owing by specialty by severall men . .	31	00 00
It' wthout specialty of sevrall men . . .	08	00 00
It' desperatre depts of sevrall persons forty shillings or there abouts	02	00 00
It' His wearinge aparell & money in his purse . .	02	00 00
It' all other utensells and things fforgotten . .	00	06 08
. . . .	96	18 06

140. Humphrey Bowdler

Gent of Madeley 8/XI/1666. Inventory 18/IX/1666 by Michael Stephens, Andrew Langley gent, Michael Richards clerk and William Yopp gent exhibited 8/X/1666 by Audley Bowdler eldest brother and executor. Will 2/II/1659 referred to his father Henry d 1666, sisters Mary Jordan and Ann Richards (whose husband is one of the appraisers), and children Mary (b 1647), Audley (b 1651 *(169)*), Henry (b 1653) and Elizabeth (b 1657).

In the p'lor & Chambers

Tables Boards Stooles Chayres Bedsteads Coaffers Cubbards .	06	16 00
Bedds Beddinge & Bedd furniture	07	00 00

In the Chamber by the Buttery & Buttery

Two Safes & ffive Barrells	01	00 00

In the Store Chamber

Two old Coffers two Twiggen Basketts	00	10 00
hempe & fflax	03	05 00
A p'cell of hopps	03	00 00
howsehould pvison	04	00 00
Lynnens and all Napery ware	13	06 08

In the hall

A Table Board two fformes two Chayres	00	08 00
One Jack	00	10 00
Brasse and Pewter	04	00 00
A grate & Iron Back	01	00 00
A Silver Boale & Sixe Spoones	03	15 00

In the Deyry Howse & over the same

A Cheese presse 3 Placks 4 Shelves a dresser and Trynnen ware .	01	05	04

In the S'vants Chamber

One Bed & Bedcloathes	00	10	00

In the old Chamber

All Iron & Leaden ware	01	00	00
An old which & other old lomber	00	06	08
A weetinge vessell & other Wooden Vessells old . . .	01	05	00
A Sadle & Pillion	00	05	00
Waynes Plowes harrowes & other Implemts of husbandry wth Wayne & Plowe timber	10	00	00
Corne Grayne & ffodder and hay	40	00	00
Swyne & Powltery	06	00	00
Eight Oxen & tenn Cows & a Bull	53	00	00
An old mare & Colt	04	10	00
Six yonge Beasts	08	00	00
One Birdinge Gonne	00	05	00
The decedents wearinge Apparell	06	13	04
A lease of a Tenemt in Wike in the pish of Much Wenlock .	400	00	00
Old lumber in and about the howses	01	00	00
Som tot. .	582	11	00

141. William Ashwood

Nailer of Madeley Wood buried 18/VII/1667. Inventory 7/IX/1667 by Edward Davis and Edward Boden exhibited 10/IX/1667 for William Ashwood son. Administration had been granted 26/VIII/1667.

Imprimis In the Shop

Hombers, Stydyes, Bowes, and other Small tooles . . .	01	10	06
2 tabell Bordes, formes, stundes, mittes & other trumpery thinges .	01	07	00
Iron potts Brasse cettels a morter and a Grate . . .	00	15	00
Pewter	01	03	09
4 peire of Bedsteads 2 old Cubbords	01	00	00
Beds and beding and all other Small thinges omitted . .	00	10	00
All Debtes hopefull and Desperatt	02	10	00
. . . .	08	16	03

THE INVENTORIES OF MADELEY

142. Richard Brook

Trowman of Madeley died 24/V/1669 and buried two days later. Inventory 13/IV/1670 by George Eastop, John Forcebrooke and Thomas Corbett exhibited 25/IV/1670 for Joyce Brooke relict and administratrix.

Imprimis 2 table bords & fformes 2 Cubbords 3 bedsteeds & other brewing vessells & wooden ware .	03	10	00
Item beds of all sorts & ffurniture belong to them	07	10	00
Brass & pewter of all sorts	05	00	00
Iron ware of all sorts	01	10	00
Linnens of all sorts	03	00	00
Item a malt mill .	00	10	00
Item 7 kine & 3 young beasts	17	00	00
Item 7 swine	01	10	00
Item one vessell upon seavern called the Jonathan & all the ffurnyture belonging to it .	40	00	00
Item one old vessell by the name of ye Thomas and his furniture .	02	10	00
Item timber of all sorts .	05	00	00
Item Lymestone .	04	00	00
Item other things as yett omitted .	05	00	00
Item the apparell of ye deceased .	03	10	00
. . . .	99	10	00

143. John Yates

Of Madeley Wood buried 26/III/1670 at Gloucester (Madeley Parish register). Inventory 25/IV/1670 by George Eastop and Edward Lewis exhibited the same day for Ann Yates relict and administratrix. Edward Transum 'Navigator' also signed the bond. Also on the same day Michael Richards and William James clerks were commissioned to receive her oath as she was unable to travel to Ludlow.

Impr'is one Joyned bed with a feather bed two boulsters & curtains one Rugg	01	16	08
It' one standing bed without any tester over with a flock bed and ye boulsters and the bedding thereunto belonging	00	12	00
It' one low truckle bed with the things thereunto .	00	12	00
It' one halfheaded bedstead and ye furniture	00	16	00
Item two joyned Chests one Coffer one Joyned Chaire and a falling chaire table	01	03	00
It' one Joyned Cubboard & two Table boards w'th fframes	00	19	00

It' one other Table board one little board & two formes . .	00	17	00
It' linnen & napery of all sorts	02	16	00
It' brass and peauter of all sorts	04	06	08
It' fishing nets and the fishing boate	01	00	00
It' one malt mill and one planke of timber . .	00	18	06
It' all Implements of Iron in and about the House . .	00	13	04
It' all Cowpery ware and other woodden utensils . . .	01	15	00
It' Householud provision.	01	07	06
It' the decedents wearing Apparell of all sorts . . .	03	10	00
It' all other old lumber and odd things omitted . . .	00	02	06
Sume totall . .	25	05	02

144. John Hagar

Trowman/bargeman of Strutt Hill in Madeley, but buried 'according to his owne desire in his lifetime' at Buildwas 18/XII/1672. Inventory 3/I/1672 by James Colley and William Wheelright exhibited 18/III/1672 for Richard Hagar son and executor. Will 15/XI/1672, referred to his wife Katherine, sons Thomas, Richard and John, and daughters, Mary, Alice, Ann and Elizabeth. 2 hearths in Madeley Wood and town.

In the Hall

Imprimis Chaires & Stooles	00	10	00
Item Brasse & Pewter	10	00	00
Item Three Pottes, Two dreeping panns and three ffrying panns & all other Iron ware belonging to house keeping . . .	04	00	00

In the Parlower

It' One Bedstead & bedding belonging to the same . .	05	00	00
It' One Table board & Stooles	01	00	00

In all other Roomes belonging to the house

It' Six joyne bedsteeds & bedding belonging to the same . .	15	00	00
It' Three hoggesheads & all other Wooden ware . . .	02	10	00
It' ffower Oxen	12	00	00
It' ffive kine	10	00	00
It' ffive two year old beasts & two year old Calves . .	09	00	00
It' Three mares & one Nagg & their geares . .	16	00	00
It' ffore score & two sheep	12	00	00
It' six swine	02	13	04
It' Rye Muncorne & wheate in the house & barne . .	11	00	00
It' Barley and Oates	06	00	00
It' Six ffletches of Bacon.	03	00	00
It' Two Cowes killed in the house	03	00	00
It' Butter & cheese	04	00	00

It' All sortes of Linen & Nappie ware belonging to the house	08	00	00
It' Yarne & Towe	07	00	00
It' Wooll in the house	01	10	00
It' ffower Table Boards & two formes	02	00	00
It' Two Cubboards & Skreene	02	10	00
It' one Trunke three chests and three Coffers	02	00	00
It' All Implemts of husbandry belonging to the house	01	00	00
Item Corne growing upon the ground	08	00	00
It' Hay in the Barne	06	00	00
It' one Barge & all her Rigging	35	00	00
It' one house in Bentall pish belonging to the deed wherein Thomas Hagar & William Haynes doe now Inhabit	20	00	00
Ite' Bookes belonging to the dec'd	00	10	00
It' Powltry	00	06	08
It' one debt due to the decd from Mr. John Wooding Merchant in Bewdley.	05	00	00
It' thing forgotten & not herein apprised .	01	00	00
It' three suites of wearing app'ell of the dec'd	04	00	00
Sume totall	230	10	00

145. Joan Spencer

Widow of Madeley Wood buried 18/III/1673. Inventory 6/III/1673 (presumably before she died) by Ben Taylor, Willi. Ashwood and Timothy Turner exhibited 31/III/1674 for John Spencer forgemason, administration having been granted 23/III/1674. Assessed for 1 hearth.

In her dwelling house

A ioyned seat standing by the ffire place .	00	15	00
One iron ffurnace	01	00	00
Iron grates fire shovels and bellowes	00	05	00
Chaires stooles cushions Tables & frames & formes	00	10	00
Certaine Brewing vessells three hogesheads three barrells with all sorts of wooden ware	01	05	00
Beef Bacon with other household provission	01	00	00

In the Chambers over the house

Three Bedsteds and Bedding of all sortes with other furniture	03	00	00
Coffers and Boxes	00	10	00
Her wearing app'ell	02	00	00
Swine & poultry .	01	10	00
Things omitted & forgotten	00	05	00
Sume	11	10	00

146. John Lloyd

Of Madeley Wood buried 8/II/1675. Inventory 17/III/1675 by James Colly* and Ri. Sheppard exhibited 18/IV/1676 for Edward Lloyd gent of Madeley (trowman deleted) brother and principal creditor. The account listed debts of £79 including £22 8s. to Edward Dawley of Madeley but none to Edward Lloyd.

Impr' Lyinnings & Napery of all sorts vall'	06	00	00
It' Brass of all sortes whatsoev'r va'	03	10	00
It' Pewter of all sorts valued at	02	15	06
It' Iron ware of all sorts	01	16	00
It' six Beds w'th Bolsters & Pillows belonging thereunto valued at	11	05	00
It' all furniture of wollen belonging to the Bedding val'	05	10	04
It' six Bedsteads of all sortes whatsoever va' at	04	00	00
It' two Chests two Cubbarts one Truncke two Coffers & on Box valued	03	04	06
It' fower table Boardes one screene formes chaires & stoles of all sorts whatsoever valued at	02	13	04
It' on Carpett & chushions of all sorts whatsoever val'	01	03	00
It' Hogsheds & Barrells & all other sorts of wodden or trinning ware whatsoever valued at	02	15	00
It' Syder in the house at the tyme of his decease val' & other wynes	12	00	00
It' thirty dozen of Bottles or there aboutes val'	04	10	00
It' the decedents wearing apparrell val'	05	00	00
It' two little silver Cupps val'	01	00	06
Bricks quarries & tyles of all sorts whatsoever val'	02	10	00
It' debts oweing to the value of	03	00	00
It' all things or goodes whatsoever as yet unknowne & undiscovered valued at	04	00	00
Sum totall	76	13	02

147. John Sherratt

Chandler of Madeley Wood buried 6/VI/1676. Inventory 21/VI/1676 by Ben Taylor, Edward Boden and Robert Holland exhibited 6/VII/1676 by Elizabeth Sherratt relict and administratrix (née Lewis *alias* Davies m 1674). Listed in neither the Madeley Easter Book of 1662 nor the Hearth Tax Returns.

Impr's His wearing Apparrell Woollen & Linnen	06	00	00
It'm Money in his pockett at the time of his decease	00	13	04
It'm Desp'ate debts due & owing to the dec'ed at the time of his decease	66	00	00

THE INVENTORIES OF MADELEY 275

It'm Debts due & owing to the dec'd upon Specialty	200	00	00
It'm One riding Nagg w'th a Saddle and bridle	03	06	08
It'm Six sheep	01	00	00

In his workhouse

Impr's Candles ready made & Tallow pr'pared to make more Candle with wick yarne	10	00	00
It'm One ffurnace with all other necessaries belonging to his p'ssession	02	10	00
It'm things omitted & forgotten	00	10	00
Tot	290	00	00

148. Henry James

Bowyer of Madeley but apparently not buried there. Inventory (not dated) by Thomas Smetheman and Timothy Turner exhibited 4/V/1676 by Margaret James relict and executrix. Will 30/XI/1667 referred to 4 children all under age. The eldest John was left the house and tenement.

Item Two bedstids	00	12	06
Item table boards one Cobort two Joynd foremes	01	00	00
Item three bras pots one bras cettle one coldron one bras Candlestick	01	02	02
Item all manar of wollin and linin within the hoase	01	05	09
Item three ould coufors	00	06	08
Item nine small pewter dises one pewter Candlestick one Salte on Tankard	01	02	05
Item all maner of Iron ware about the house as Two broches one pare of Cobots one grate one pestle one small dreeping pan as potgales & all the rest in generall	00	08	11
Item Two bareles one neding tub & all maner of trining ware	00	10	02
The testators weareing apperell	01	00	00
to all	07	08	07

149. Margaret Evans

Widow of Roger Evans *(139)* of Madeley where she wished to be buried. Inventory 27/I/1676 by Thomas Smitheman senior and John Warren exhibited 27/III/1677 for Roberrt Darrall kinsman and executor. Will 9/X/1672 referred to, among others, a brother William Darrall, a son in law Thomas Evans and his children, Roger, Mary, Sarah and Ellinor, to whom she made specific bequests, including the bed in the parlour, a brass pot and a brass pan.

Impr: her wearing Apparrell both Linen and Wollen	00	10	00
It' readie money in the house	08	00	00
It' three coffers & one ioyne Cheat in the Roome over the house	00	13	04
It' two Chaffs beddes, one Blanket one Rugg one Coverlett and three small Pillowes	00	10	00
It' Seven paire of hurden sheets, one paire of fflaxen sheets, three pillowes beeres, halfe a dozen of hempen napkins, halfe a dozen of hurden Napkins, one hempen Table Cloth, three hurden table Clothes two hempen towells	01	10	00
It' two old coffers in the Roome at the Staire head	00	03	04
It' one chaffe bed one coulet & Bolster with a plaine Bedsteed	00	03	04
It' one large old coffer, one coulet, two Blanketts two feather Bolsters in the Roome over the Butteries and Parlor	00	10	00
It' a looking glasse in the same Roome	00	00	04
It' Brasse and Pewter	02	00	00
It' one fferkin and three old Barrells in the Butterie	00	03	04
It' one ioyned Press in the dwelling house	00	12	00
It' chaires and Stooles	00	02	06
It' one ffire shovell one paire of Tonges one iron dripping pann, one Iron morter and Pestell one Iron fire grate, two small iron plates behind and under the fire, two Iron broches, one paire of Potthookes, & Pott Linkes, one Clever and hacking knife one small Iron brandard	01	00	00
It' one paire of Bellowes	00	00	06
It' one table board & frame wth an old forme in ye house	00	03	04
It' Wooden Ware	00	05	00
It' one Bedsteed, one feather Bed, one Chaffe Bed, one old Blankett, one Bolster wth a sett of Curtaines made of Kidderminster Stuffe in the Parlor	01	00	00
It' one table board & frame wth a forme in the said Roome	00	03	04
It' Six cushions	00	01	06
It' Shelves with other trumperie ware lying up and downe in all Roomes of the said house	00	05	00
It' things omitted or forgotten	00	05	00
It' Debts due & oweing upon Specialie to the p'tie deceased	13	00	00
It' Desperate Debts due & oweing to the said p'tie at the time of her decease	04	00	00
Sums t'lis	27	09	10

150. John Cowper

Weaver of Madeley Wood. Inventory 29/VI/1680 by John Warren, William Smithiman and George Hutchingsonne* exhibited 19/V/11681 by Sarah and Mary Cowper daughters and administratrices, and not the executors,

William Ashwood and Timothy Turner, friends appointed to act in the will 5/V/1680. This referred to £40 in the hands of John Thomas, shoemaker of Claverley, the interest of which was settled on Mary Millward of Smallheath. 1 hearth at Madeley Wood.

Impr's The dec'ds wearing App'ell	01	00	00
It'm two Tables one forme Chaires & Stools in the dwelling house	00	13	04

It'm In the Parlor

one Table board one forme two Joyne bedsteds two feather beds foure blanks two couletts two bolsters two coffers one faire large chest wherein are six paire of sheets one warmeing pan one dozen of napkins & two table cloathes	05	00	00

In the little chamber

one bested & Matt	00	06	08
It'm Brasse & Pewter	02	10	00
It'm Wooden & Treine ware	01	00	00

It'm in the chamber over the dwelling house

Three bedsteds one feather bed two chaffe beds one chest & three coffers	02	00	00

It'm In the Shop

Two Weavers Loomes with geares thereto belonging . .	02	10	00
It'm Two cowes, two yearelings, three weaning calves . .	06	00	00
It'm Seven Ewes & five Lambes	01	10	00
It'm Ironware of all sorts	00	10	00
It'm Things omitted or otherwaies forgotten . . .	00	10	00
. . . .	23	10	00

151. Richard Twyford

Yeoman of Madeley Wood. Inventory 30/XI/1681 by Willi. Ashwood, George Glasbrooke and Robt. Holland exhibited 22/V/1682 by Luke Twyford son and executor. Will 29/IX/1681 left his daughter Mary £100, but only £50 if she married John Eckley. In fact she married William Roe *(168)* in 1684. Assessed for 2 hearths in Madeley Wood.

Impr'is In ye hall
one short Table & Carpett Seven Cheires And three Cushen . 00 16 08

Item In ye Chamber over the hall
one Joy'd bed wth furniture to it, one Chest, one Joynd Press,
1 Little Cubbard & A small table And five Cheires . . 05 00 00

Item In the Chamber over the buttery
one bed with furniture one Cheir And A table . . . 01 05 00

Item In ye Chichen
One table board And form one Joyn'd Stoole: three old Cheires
And two small hanging Cubbards. 00 13 04
Item Brass And pewter of all sortes And tinn Ware . . 03 13 06
Item All sorte of Iron ware 04 10 00

Item A little roome at ye Staire head over the Chichen
one bed And A small brass Clocke 02 00 00

Item In ye Chambr over ye Chichen
one bed with furniture, two Chests A Small Trunke, one Coffer
two boxes And one stoole 02 10 00

Item In ye Garrett over ye Chichen
one serv'ts bed And other Trumprey 00 13 04

Item The Chamb'r ove' ye brewhouse
One Servants bed 00 06 08
Item All sortes of Coopery And Tryning Ware As Barrells,
Tubs &c 01 10 00
Item All sortes of Linning And Apry ware . . . 04 00 00
Item All House provisions of all sortes 05 00 00
Item All sortes of Grain in the house & Barn thrasht And unthrasht
And hay in ye barn 16 00 00
Item Two old marres And two suckling Colts Seven Cowes and
Eight young Cattle 30 00 00
Item Husbandry Geares of all sortes (as) two small Cartes A small
paire of harrows And other Implemts of Husbandry . . 06 00 00
Item Swin And poltry 02 00 00
Item His wareing Cloathes And monys In his purse . . 04 00 00
Item Things omitted or otherwayes fforgotten . . . 00 10 00
Item owing upon bill 85 00 00
Item other desperate debts not Certainely knowne to me as yett:
About 30 00 00

In toto . . 204 18 06

152. William Ashwood

Blacksmith and trowman of Madeley Wood. Inventory 30/XI/1681 by William Ashwood exhibited 17/V/1682 by Mary Ashwood relict and administratrix. In 1688 she married Thomas Cullis widower of Benthall and father of Hugh Cullis *(16)*. 3 hearths.

Impr's In the dewelling house

one Cubbord, one fforme and three stooles	00	05	00

It'm In the Chamber over the house

Two Bedstids wth Beds & Coverings; one Table board; one Joyne forme; one ould Chaire & one Coffer	01	06	08

It'm In ye chamber over ye kichen

one ould Bedstid & bed	00	06	08

It'm In ye middle Parlour

one Joyne Bed & wth all furniture thereunto belonging one Table board, one forme & one Chest	01	13	04

It'm In the farther Parlour

one joyne bed & wth furntiure one Short Table; two small Cobboards, one Coffer; one Box & one Chaire	01	01	00

It'm In ye Chambr over ye Parlours

one Bedstid & A Chaire	00	06	08

It'm In ye kichen & Seller

all sorts of Coopery & Trinen ware	00	12	00
It'm All sorts of Brass & Pewter	01	08	00
It'm Two Iron potts & all other Iron ware	01	06	00
It'm Linens of all sorts wth linen yorne undressed	01	13	04

It'm In ye Shop

two pair of Bellows; two Anvels a beame & scales; & all tooles belonging to his trade	03	01	00
It'm ffoure small Cows	06	15	00
It'm Three Swine	01	02	00
It'm One ould Barge wth all materialls belonging thereunto vallued by ye iudgm't of a skillfull carpender	15	00	00
It'm Houshould provision of all sorts	01	00	00
It'm His Bookes & wearing Apparrell	01	10	00
It'm Things omitted or otherwais forgotten	00	03	04
toto	38	10	00

153. George Easthope, senior

Shipwright of Madeley Wood. Inventory 2/III/1681 by Willi. Ashwood, John Beddoe and John Wood exhibited 8/VIII/1682 for George Easthope, yeoman of Madeley son and administrator. 4 hearths in Madeley Wood.

Imp' In ye Kichin
one Short table Board	00	01	06

Item In ye old mans lodginge Roome
A Chest two old Chaires	00	06	08

Item In ye Chamber over ye parler
one Joyne bed w'th an old feather bed	00	09	00
Item two Chests And three Joyne Stooles a table board a Chaire .	01	00	09

Item In ye two Cocklofts
two halfe headed bedsteads	00	06	08
Item Ironware of all sorts	01	00	00
Item one paire of sheets two towels	00	03	04
Item his Chest & tooles	00	10	00
Item his wearing Apparrill	00	10	00
Lastly Things omitted and forgotten	00	02	06
totall is . .	04	09	08

154. Robert Yates

Trowman of Madeley but apparently not buried there. Inventory 12-19/XII/1677 by Edward Trensam and Thomas Aston exhibited 24/IV/1683 for Mary Yates relict and administratix *(175)*. Aston was her nephew. There is no entry in the Hearth Tax although he was listed in the Madeley Easter Book for 1662.

Imprimis foure bedds and bedding and ye furniture thereunto belonging	06	00	00
item Linnen & napery	03	00	00
item Chestes & cubboards table boards forms and chaires . .	02	01	00
item Brass & pewter and pewter of severall sorts & iron ware .	05	00	00
item ye decesants weareing reparell	03	10	00
item foure piggs & a mare	02	05	00
item ye Househould provision	00	18	08
item one ould Mault Mill	00	19	00
item Coopery ware of all sorts	00	15	04
item some smalle utincells	00	03	00
item money in bancke	00	07	00

item desperate debts out .	14	00	00
item for goods unpraised and forgotten .	00	02	06
Sum . .	38	11	06

155. Richard Beech

Labourer/collier of Madeley, buried 7/XII/1686. Inventory 20/XII/1686 by Edward Boden and Robert Holland exhibited 21/IV/1687 for Ann Beech relict and executrix. Will 29/XI/1686 left his daughters Mary and Joan and their husbands Thomas Bloomer and James Pool £12 each and his grandchildren Thomas Pool and Ann Bloomer 10s. each; i.e. £50 to be found out of an estate valued at only £12, so presumably there were assets not listed in his inventory.

Impr' In ye Chamb'r over ye house

one feather bed wth a flock bed and bedsteads & bed cloathes thereunto belonginge .	01	06	08
A Chest in ye same wth six seggen Chaires .	00	09	09

Item In ye Shire belonging to ye house

One feather bed & bedsteads wth bed cloathes thereunto belonginge .	01	00	02

Item In ye house

one table Board a bench two Cubberts wth a Table board at John Strattons. .	00	06	08
It' Two old Iron potts a warming pan a grate fire shovel and Tongs a broach a Dreepinge pan a frying pan a paire of Cobberts and pot geales a flesh forke and a bastinge Ladle .	00	15	00
It' Two small cettles wth a brass pott .	00	08	06
It' seven small pewter Dishes 6 spones 3 porringer Dishes a Salt Seller .	00	07	00
It' two small mitts 2 pailes a small brewing stoond 3 barrills .	00	13	08
It' two small swine .	00	15	00
Linings of all sorts Six paire of sheets one dozen of napkins a Table cloath and other things of small value .	00	18	06
It' Wearinge Apparrill .	00	17	06
It' p'vidyons in ye house .	00	12	00
It' A debt owinge to ye Testator at ye time of his death, by bond beinge desperate in in doubte to be recovered .	03	05	00
Lastly All things forgotten & unappraised an not herein before Appraised valued & Inventoried .	00	02	00
. . . .	12	07	05

156. Anne Richards

Widow of Michael Richards, vicar of Madeley (d 1671), buried 23/II/1688. Inventory 4/III/1688 by Thomas Lillie and Thomas Belcham exhibited 15/VII/1689. Nuncupative will 21/II/1688 left everything to her sister's children, Audley *(169)*, Henry and Mary Bowdler who were granted administration.

Impr's In the Chamber over the house

one bed with all things thereunto belonging	03	10	00
It'm one Chest two trunckes & two Desks	00	16	08
It'm one Chayre Table with a drawer under it	00	07	00
It'm one ould coffer & five small boxes at	00	03	06
It'm all pewter at	00	12	04
It' Brasse of all sorts	01	15	06
It' Chayres Stooles & Cuscions	00	10	00
It' all twiggen ware	00	01	06
It'm All manner of Bookes & papers	01	00	00
It'm a small spining wheele wth all things belonging	00	02	00
It'm an ould sword two paddle staves & some lead waites.	00	04	06
It' a small quantity of hopps	00	00	06
It' five yard & a halfe of black Cloath	00	13	00
It'm one ould bedtick & a boulster four Curtaynes wth a Vallian & 2 ould Carpetts	00	12	00
It' all linnen	02	00	00
It' a pair of ould Tables & waites	00	02	00
It'm hemp fflax & yarne .	01	00	00

It'm In ye dwelling house house

one Chayre Table wth a leafe of a table & other small things	00	08	00
It' all Iron ware	00	13	00
It' all trinnin ware	00	12	08
It' ould Bottles	00	01	00
It'm a screen & a table board	01	00	00
It' a halfe tester bed & a table	00	19	00
It' an ould Muskett	00	03	00
It' Coales in ye house	00	03	00
It' a lookeing glass	00	01	00
It' a silver spoone wth a small ringe	00	08	06
It' money in her pockett & owing to her	00	15	00
It' her Weareing Apparrell	04	00	00
It' three pewter dishes & a fflagon unpraysed above	00	05	06
It' ould lumber & thongs omitted or otherwise forgott	00	05	00
In toto .	23	05	02

157. Roger Tranter

Labourer of Madeley, buried 25/XI/1689. Inventory 10/XII/1689 by Thomas Eastopp, William Turner and John Beddoe exhibited 18/II/1689 for Ann Tranter relict and administratrix (presumably also of Richard Beech *(155)* as the two inventories appear to describe the same house).

Imp' In ye Chamb'r over ye house

2 halfe Bedsteads w'th Bedcloathes thereunto belonginge, ye one being a flock bed ye other a Chaff Bed	00	15	00
Ite' In ye same Roome two Chests	00	08	00

Item In a Small Shire belonginge to ye house

one ffeather Bed & Bedsteads w'th Bedcloathes thereunto belonginge	00	06	02

Item In ye house

one Table Board a forme two Cubbarts two old Iron potts a warming pann, a grate fireshovell & toungs a broach a Dreepinge pan a frying pan a paire of Cubbarts and pot gales a fleshorke and basting Ladles	01	11	04
It' tow small kettles w'th a brass pott	00	05	00
Ite' seven small pewter Dishes six spoones one salt seller	00	03	06
It' 2 small mitts 2 pailes one small brewing stoond 3 barrills	00	08	00
Ite' one swine or pig	00	10	00
It' Linings 6 paire of sheets a Table Cloath & one dozen of napkins and other things of small value	00	12	00
Ite' Wearing Apparrill	00	17	02
Item A debt owing to ye testator at ye time of his death, desperate & in doubt to be recouered	04	05	00
Lastly all things fforgotten & unprised and not herein before appraised valued or Inventored By us who were prizers ye day & year above written	00	01	00
	10	07	02

158. John Holland, senior

Yeoman of Madeley Wood, buried 16/IV/1690. Inventory 20/V/1690 by Sampson Crompton and William Ashwood exhibited 22/V/1690 by John Holland son, executor and sole legatee by the will 14/IV/1690. 6 hearths.

Imp' his Purse and Apparrell	21	10	00
Item one Joyn bedstead with a Truckle Bed w'th Two Beds and the ffurniture there unto belonging	02	10	00
Item Three Chests one Trunk one Deske.	01	16	08
Item In the Cocklofts twelfe old Bedsteeds fower old flock Beds with Eight bedings	02	15	00
Item one joyne press two side bords	01	02	06
Item five table bords two formes nine joynd stools three old Chaires.	02	00	00
Item three old cupbords.	00	07	00
Item a small p'sell of Brass Pewter and Iron ware.	01	05	00
Item old Coopery Ware.	00	03	00
Item one old Clocke	00	17	06
Item one small p'sell of Books	01	05	00
Item Wood Rails Tooles and several other material belonging to the Cole works	22	00	00
Item one Barge with all Tackle and materials thereunto belonging.	10	00	00
Item Due from Book Debts	19	11	00
Item Things forgotten or not mentioned.	00	05	00
Sum is.	97	07	08
Item In desperate Debts due upon Bills Bonds and otherwise	277	15	06
Total	374	18	02

159. Edward Boden

Collier of the Lloyds in Madeley, buried 7/VII/1691. Inventory 25/VII/1691 by Edward Lloyd, Robert Whitmore and Edward Cox exhibited 15/IX/1691 by Thomas and John Boden sons and joint executors. Will (not dated) left the following leasehold property:- to his wife Sarah and after to the eldest son Thomas 'The Lloyds'; to his second son John 'the house called the Green in Madeley Wood that I have repaired'; to his third son Edward 'the house for which I paid £30 which John Spencer built'. Thomas and John to have the three horses employed in the coalworks.

Impr' The decedents Weareing Apparrill.	04	10	00
It' 6 Beds bedsteeds and furniture	10	06	08
It' Linens of all sorts	03	16	08
It' Brass and pewter of all sorts.	03	10	00
It' one Clock	01	05	06
It' Iron Ware of all sorts.	01	05	10
It' 4 Tables, 3 Chests, 3 formes, 3 presses, one screen, one carpett, one trunk and chaires	04	19	08

It' three horses & one cow	. . . . .	07	05	00
It' Flax		01	02	00
It' Two Swine		00	18	06
It' Brewing vessells and all other things belonging Thereunto	.	02	13	04
It' Stock of drink in the house		02	04	06
It' for other small Things aboute ye house . . .		00	04	06
	In toto . .	44	02	02

Wife Elizabeth = with consent of landlord & paying rent due, the house in ye Lloyds in which I now live, for life, then to:
Eldest son Thomas = on same terms
Second son John = with consent of landlord, & paying rent due, the house I have repaired and the new building added unto in the place called the ground in Madeley Wood.
Third son Edward = £30 paid already to John Spencer for the tenance and right he had to a house in Madeley Wood then builded by his mother & himself, if landlord agrees, to go to third son Edward
If tenancy goes to another, hopes landlord will persuade tenant to repay £30 to Edward
Daughter Elizabeth, wife of William Smith of Bewdley = 50s
Sons Thomas and John = three horses now employed at ye coal works in Madeley now in my occupation to be divided betwixt them or the price for which they shall be sold in money
Wife Elizabeth = All goods of house for use. After her death to be divided between 3 sons, Thomas, John & Edward; she has power, if 3 sons agree to give one or more their share at any time during her life

160. William Ashwood

Trowman of Madeley Wood, possibly buried 16/VIII/1696. Inventory 4/V/1696 by John Hagar and Richard Bartholine exhibited 4/V/1696 *(sic)* for Sarah relict and executrix (née Hagar of Benthall m 1687). Will 11/I/1695 referred to three daughters, Jane, Mary and Sarah. Probably son of *(152)* and grandson *(141)*.

Impr's Item In ye little parler
One table bord one Cubbard one paire of Bedsteds wth a ffeather
bed & hangings and all things thereunto belonging wth two Seggon
Chaires 02 00 03

Item In ye next Roome
One press with cubborts one chest & other things of small
value 00 16 03

Item In ye Chambr upstaires
A Small ffeather bed wth an other Bed and other things of small value 00 15 06

Item In ye Roome called ye house
Brass and pewter of all sorts 01 03 04
Item Iron ware 00 10 00
Item Wooden ware of all sorts 00 14 04
Item Linings of all sorts 02 09 00

Item one Cow wth two Calves 05 00 00

Item one old Barge wth materialls thereunto belonging . . 13 00 06

Item In ye shop
Bellies and tools thereunto belonginge 03 00 02
Item one Store wth four small pigs 01 00 00
Item Hay 04 00 00
Item Debts desperate and hard to be recovered . . . 00 10 00
Item Things omitted or otherwise forgotten . . . 00 02 04

                                                   Totall is. . 35 01 06

161. William Maybury, senior

Of Madeley, buried 15/X/1703. Inventory 20/X/1703 by Law. Wellington and William Wheeles exhibited 22/VIII/1704 by Jane Holland *alias* Maybury daughter and administratrix. 2 hearths in Madeley Wood and town.

Im'ris One Sow Pigg 01 10 00
It' One Bed and Bolster one Blanket one Rugg . . . 01 07 00
It' one fflock Bedd two Bolsters ffive Blanketts and one Rugg . 00 05 00
It' one Bedstead in the Chamber 00 05 00
One Clock 01 10 00
One Table and Bench 00 05 00
One Chaire with Seggs & one other Chair . . . 00 01 06
One Coffer & one Desk 00 05 00

In the house
One Table & fforme 00 07 00
Two Barrells two brewing Tubbs one Paile and one neading Tubb on Tundish 01 00 00
One frying Pann and one pudding Pann one Cleever one bryling Plate 00 06 00
Two Pewter Plate one Salter 00 01 06
One Pott & one Posnett 00 04 00

THE INVENTORIES OF MADELEY   287

One Mortar and Pestill	00	03 04
One ffire Shovel one pair of Tongs & one Creeper before the fire	00	03 00
One pair Potlinks	00	00 06
One Sword & Belt	00	10 00
One pair of Bellows	00	00 09
One Plate to draw bread	00	01 00
One fflesh fork and basting spoon	00	00 06
One Box over the Table in the house	00	02 00
One Crach in the house with hucks	00	02 06
One pair of Cobirons	00	06 00
One Chest one Coffer to putt Sailte in	00	06 00
Two Pickfields Three Spades one Bill one iron Bake one Ax	00	08 00
One boyling ffurnace & Doore	00	13 00
Two pair of noggen sheets	00	08 00
One pair of Shears for the Garden	00	01 00
One hatt and Wigg	00	01 00
One new Coate Breeches and wastcoate	02	00 00
One old pair of Breeches & one old Coate	00	08 00
One Cast Grate	00	01 00
One fflaxen shirt & one hampen shir	00	03 00
One brass Possnett 8d 2 Ladders 2s	00	02 08
The Drall and Pott	00	01 00
	14	12 11

162. Benjamin Taylor

Vicar of Madeley, in his will be asked to be buried alongside his parents in the churchyard of Badger, Salop. Inventory 9/XI/1704 by Humphrey Greenowes of Sutton Maddocks and Thomas Parsons of Arleton in Worfield gents exhibited 9/II/1704 for Margaret Taylor relict and Jeremy Taylor son joint executors. Will 14/X/1704 left the farm at Astley Abbots to his wife and 1s. each to a daughter Margaret and a brother William of the Heath in Badger.

Imp's In his study

The study of Books	100	00 00
The Shelves in ye Study	00	05 00

Item In his Bed Chamber

One ffeather Bed wth ye furniture belonging to it.	04	00 00
Three Desks	01	00 00
One Box Grate	00	04 00
One Table	00	04 00
Three Stools & Two Chairs	00	05 00

Item In ye Green Chamber

Two ffeather Beds wth ye furniture	04	10	00
Three Chests, One Coffer ffower Trunks, Three Boxes	02	00	00
Napprey ware of all sorts	15	00	00

Item In ye Little Chamber

One ffeather Bed wth ye ffurniture	02	10	00

Item In ye Closett

Plate wth a Watch	09	00	00

Item In ye Lower Chamber

Two ffeather Beds wth ye ffurniture	07	00	00
One Table Two Chaires, One Trunk	01	00	00
Three Looking Glasses	00	05	00

Item In ye Parlour

One Oval Table, Six Russia Chairs, One ffoulding Bed Three picyures One Cupboard	05	00	00

Item The Closett in ye parlour

One Box One Cupboard Two ffowling pieces, Three pistolls	01	00	00

Item In ye Cheese Chamber

Two fflitchings of Bacon Cheese & Beer wth other pvision	08	00	00
Shelves, Two Witches, One Salt Box	01	00	00
Eight Barrells Six Halfe Hogsheads	01	10	00
Brass	04	00	00

Item In ye Kitchen Chamber

One Window Sheet, One Cheese press, Sacks & Baggs	01	00	00

Item In ye Kitchen

Trine Ware of all sorts	01	10	00

Item In ye Milk House

Shelves & One Table	00	10	00

Item In the Dwelling House

Iron Ware of all Sorts	05	00	00
Two Oval Tables six Chaires Two stools, One dresser	01	10	00
Pewter of all sorts	05	00	00
Hemp & fflax dressed & undressed	05	00	00
One Horse ffower Cowes Three Heyfors	15	00	00
Three swine	02	10	00
ffurniture for a Horse	00	10	00
Coles	01	10	00

Corne in ye Barn of all sorts	10	00	00
Hay	05	00	00
One Cart	01	10	00
Muck	00	15	00
One Malt Mill	00	10	00
Desperate Debts.	05	00	00
Wearing Apparrell & Money in his pockett	10	00	00
Things unseen & forgotten	01	10	00
Totall is.	240	18	00

163. George Glassbrooke, senior

Carpenter of the Furnace Bank in Madeley, buried 1/V/1709. Inventory 15/VI/1709 by Jo. Smitheman and Paul Peploe was exhibited 26/VII/1709 for George Deuxell yeoman of Madeley, son in law and administrator *(170)*.

In the dwelling house place
One brass Kettle one brass pann two brass pots one Cast Iron Morter two dripping pans seven pewter dishes one pewter candlestick one pewter Cann one brass Candlestick one frying pann two Iron spitts	04	05	00
One paire of Iron Racks.	00	10	00
Two Chaires and a Cupboard	00	05	00

In the little Chamber
One ffeather bedd and furniture.	03	00	00
One hanging press	00	10	00
One Clock and a Clock case	01	00	00
Bookes.	00	05	00
One ovall Table.	00	06	08
The dec'eds workeing Tooles	01	10	00

In the parlor
One Table and forme	00	05	00
one old Cupboard	00	05	00
one hand Iron one little Grate	00	05	00

In the Chamber over the parlor
One bedd and furniture.	02	10	00
one desk one old Coffer.	00	05	00
one Trunck one kneading mitt one other trunck and one Chest	00	10	00
Linnens of all sorts	01	00	00

In the Buttery
Two Barrells	00	10	00
	16	16	08

164. Edward Lloyd, senior

Trowman of Madeley, buried 30/VIII/1709. Inventory 29/X/1709 by Thomas Williams and Richard Bartlam exhibited 8/XI/1709 by Mary Lloyd widow and administratrix. The Madeley Easter book for 1704 recorded that he had paid tithes for four stalls of bees killed, four sheep, a fleece, three lambs and a barren cow. An Edward Lloyd, a poor labourer, possibly his grandfather, was drowned in the Severn in 1651 and buried at Madeley. Probably nephew of John Lloyd *(146)*.

Impr's

One Ould Trow wth all her appurtenances belonging to her to	10	00	00
One Ould Trow called the Eastop & all her appurtenances to	15	00	00
One Ould Barge called the Nicholls with all materialls belonging to her	13	00	00

In ye house

Two Tables a Screene & six Joyne stooles, a Joyne Chair w'th other lumber a grate an ould Gun, fier shovell & Tongues a Cleever . 01 12 00

In ye little Parlour

A paire of Bedsteads, wth a Bed & Bedding, Two Looking glasses, an ould Trunk a Table, a Press, a Bench, & Two Joyne stooles, a Coffer & a parcell of Bookes 02 10 00

In a litle Lower Roome

An ould Jack Iron Barrs & other Iron ware, an ould Table & Bench & other lumber 00 15 06

In a small Roome next ye Kitchin

An ould Bedstead wth Bed & furniture an ould Press wth other small lumber 00 06 08

An ould Brass furnace in ye Brewhouse wth other vessells of wood, one ould brass Pott, wth severall Pewter dishes, & ould Pewter Tinnware & an ould warming Pan . . . 02 10 00

In ye Store house or out Building

Severall ould halfe hogsheads, glass bottles wth other lumber, wheeles & other wooden ware of all sorts	01	01	08
A small parcell of Hay & two store piggs.	01	08	04

In ye Roome over ye house & two small roomes adjoyning to it

One Joyne Bed one half headed Bed & Bedsteads, wth Beding & furniture, two Tables & fifteene Chairs, & a Trunk, wth other Lumber & a Chest 03 11 04

In ye Cockloft

A Joyne Bed & furniture, six Chairs, a Chest a Carpett & six Cushions	01 14 08
A Chest & linen of all sorts as sheetes Napkins & other linen	02 12 06
In a debt certaine	05 00 00
In other doubtfull debts	10 00 00
In money in he house & wareing Aparell	03 10 00
other ould lumber & things forgotten	00 06 08
. . . .	74 19 04

165. James Smitheman

Gunsmith of Madeley, buried 17/X/1709. Inventory 16/XI/1709 by Audley Bowdler and John Heatherly was exhibited 1/VI/1710 for Thomas and Richard Smitheman brothers and executors. Will 1/XI/1709 left his brother Thomas a messuage in the possession of Richard Belcham and other property, to go to his brothers William and Richard if he died without issue and then to John Unett Smitheman gent of Little Wenlock son of John Smitheman.

Impr's in the Dwelling house

one Small ovell Table att.	00 05 00
Item 4 Seggen Chaires and a pair of bellows . . .	00 02 06
Item a little brass kettle, 1 Iron pott and 2 Iron pans att . .	00 07 06
Item one grate a fire shovell and tonges pot gales and a Coale hatchett	00 06 08

In the Chamber over the house

1 tester bed and stead with all things thereunto belonging . .	02 10 00
Item 2 Chests a desk and a little square table . . .	00 13 04

Item In the Cellar

4 barrells	00 10 00

Item in the barn

a borne bench and 9 bitt.	00 04 00
Item Coales	00 06 08

Item in the shop

1 Anvell, 1 vise and all other his working tooles . . .	07 00 00

Item Timber	00	10 00
Item his wearing apparell and moneys in his pockett . .	05	00 00
Item things omitted or otherwise forgotten . . .	00	01 00
In tot . .	18	06 04

166. Luke Twyford

Gent of The Lodge in Madeley, buried 23/XI/1711. Inventory 28/XI/1711 by Henry Bowdler and Mich. Stephens gents exhibited 22/I/1711 for John Atherly gent of Madeley friend and Richard Jones of Burrington in Hereford nephew in law executors. Will 19/XI/1711 left his niece Mary wife of Richard Jones the furniture in the chamber over the dwelling house 'where I usually live' and in the closet adjoining; his niece Mary wife of Richard Roe all other household goods; and godson Richard Pool the axe, spade, bill, broomhook, mattock and second suit of clothes. Roger Roe *(171)* and William Roe *(168)* are apparently his brothers in law; Richard Twyford *(151)* is his father.

Impr's In the kitchen

One Table board and fforme	00	05 04
One Joyn'd Skreen	00	06 08
One fowling peece	00	05 00
Two Cubberts & One Joyn'd stool & chair . . .	00	06 08
One Jack	00	05 00
One Iron Grate and stone dreeping pann	00	13 04
Two Iron broaches	00	03 00
Two pair of tongues and a fire shovell	00	02 00
One Iron cast plate	00	01 00
Two brasse Candlesticks	00	01 00
One Glasse Crate & one Cubbert	00	02 00
One pewter still	00	03 04
ffour Iron potlidds	00	02 00
One fleshforke	00	00 06

Item In the Parlour

One Round Table	00	06 08
One side table	00	02 00
Six chaires	00	01 06

Item In the pewter house

Seaven pewter dishes one warming pann Two small kettles three candlesticks Two Salts and one Cubbert	00	14 00

THE INVENTORIES OF MADELEY

Item In the Chamber over the Parlour

One little Table & chest	00	11	00
a fire shovell and tongues	00	01	06
One peece of linnen cloth	01	10	00
One bedsted Curtaines valence & Countpane	00	13	04
One Cubbert & looking glasse	00	03	06

In the Chamber over the Buttery

One Bed Bedstead Curtaines Valence two blancketts & Coverlitt & a little table	01	00	00

It' in the Brewhouse

One ffurnace and a boyler	01	00	00
One pair of Cast And-Irons	00	02	00
One Table	00	02	00
One Iron Mortar & pestell	00	05	00

Item In the little Chamber

One pair of bedstedds Curtaines & Valence	00	05	00

In the Chamber over the Kitchen

One Clock	01	00	00
One little box of drawers	00	02	00
Two Joyned Chests	00	13	04
Two Joyn'd stooles	00	01	00
One Close stool	00	01	00
One little Table	00	01	00
One bed & the furniture	01	10	00
Woolens and linnen in a Chest	01	15	00

In the Clossett

One desk	00	02	00
One looking glasse	00	03	00
Old bookes	01	00	00
Two little Cubberts	00	05	00
One Silver spoon & a pair of buckles	00	06	08

It' In the Barne

Barly	06	00	00
hay	03	00	00
Oates	01	10	00
ffetches	02	00	00
ffive Cowes	15	00	00
One Mare & One Colt	03	00	00
the Testatrs wearing apparrell	03	00	00
Ready money in the house	13	05	00
Thirty loads of Dung	01	10	00

It' In the Room over Mr Twyfords Chamber

One bed and Bedstead	00	10 00
One pair of Scales	00	05 00
In money oweing to the Testator by spcalty & otherwise . .	72	00 00
Tot . .	137	03 10

167. John Bayley, senior

Ground collier of Madeley Wood, buried 13/I/1711. Inventory 8/II/1711 by William Yeats and Samuell Bowdler exhibited 8/IV/1712 by Elizabeth relict and executrix. Will 13/III/1710 referred to children Edward, Joseph, Jonathan Bailey and Mary Jones.

Imprimis One old feather Bed & Boulster . . .	00	06 08
One small old flock Bed with a boulster & pillow. . .	00	04 00
One old Rug & 3 old Blankets	00	02 06
Three pair of old Hurden sheets	00	06 00
4 Chairs 1s 3 boxes 9d	00	02 00
1 Chest	00	02 06
One Table & frame with two formes	00	06 00
4 small pewter dishes	00	05 00
One Mitt one search one tunning dish	00	02 00
One Grate with tonges & fire shovel and Cheeks & Chains pothooks & 2 fleshforks	00	05 00
One small marmett	00	01 04
One old small table	00	01 00
One small firkin	00	01 00
. . . .	02	05 00

Is possest of a certain cottage or tenement in which I live, lately purchased of the assignees of Cumberford Brooke esq. Which is now divided into three several dwellings with garden places or plots of ground thereunto...

Wife Elizabeth Bayly = all that part of the cottage wherein I and she now live, being the cheife dwelling of the said house and lying at the east end thereof with all rooms, privileges &c. together with the brewhouse and garden adjoining

Youngest son Jonathan = the little Room and the cockloft over it with the grounds before the door & adjoining on the north side of the dwelling

Son Joseph = From the death of my wife, all before bequeathed to her for her life

Eldest son Edward = the middle part where he now lives being two rooms with a buttery place and garden to the same

Daughter Mary Jones = the Brewhouse and the Chamber over it and the little shop before the door; my son Joseph is to have the privilege of the Brewhouse att all times when he shall have occasion

168. William Roe

Yeoman of Madeley, buried 22/VII/1714. Inventory 26/VII/1714 by John Ashwood gent of Madeley and Roger Roe yeoman of Madeley exhibited 1/IX/1714 for Jeremy Taylor clerk (and vicar of Madeley) and William Phillips of Brockton executors. Will 12/VII/1714 left all to the executors to hold on behalf of the wife (Mary née Twyford presumably daughter of Richard Twyford *(151)* m 1684) provided that she brought up their daughter Elizabeth and stayed unmarried. Elizabeth to have £20, if she died before 21 then to his brother Benjamin Roe.

Imprim's in the kitchin
Two pewter dishes	00	05	00
one pott one brasse kettle	00	16	00
Bacon & Beefe	01	00	00

In the Dayry
Earthenware	00	02	06

In the Pantry
one cheese Tub & one churn	00	05	00

In the Celler
Three Barrells	00	07	00

In the Garretts
Cheese	05	00	00

In the Hall Chamber
one chest	00	04	00
one Bed & furniture	02	10	00
one Chair	00	01	00
one Box	00	01	00
Linnen of all sorts	03	05	00

In the parlor chamber
one Bed & furniture	03	00	00
one Chaire, one Table, one Stand	00	02	00
his wearing Apparrell mony in his pockett	02	10	00

In the Malthouse
one Malt Hill	01	00	00
one Saddle, one padd, one bridle	00	06	08
Raken & pikevills	00	02	00

Cheese presse & spade	00	03	00
three pailes four Gawns	00	05	00
Two Tubs one wheeting fatt	00	10	00
Mixed Corn	01	04	08
Barly	01	00	00
Malt	02	12	06
Oats	00	15	00
Charcoale	00	03	00

In the fields & about the house

nine Cows	25	00	00
Two Oxen	09	00	00
seaven calves	04	07	06
Six Two year olds	13	10	00
Six one year olds	07	10	00
Two horses, four mares and one colt	21	00	00
four small store piggs	00	12	00
four Larg store piggs	02	10	00
old oats in the Barn	01	10	00
one Waine & Wheels	02	10	00
Two Tumbrill boys & wheels	03	04	06
four plows, three sleads, one Tutot &c	00	12	06
Two pair of Harrows	00	12	06
flax & Hemp	00	13	04
four Geese	00	03	04
five yoakes & Geering	00	10	00
one coplate, suck & coultar	00	02	00
Two Chains	00	03	00
Two Torteries & a Cart rope	00	07	00
Horse geers	01	01	06
Cart Saddle & furniture	00	04	00
one grindle stone	00	04	00
Chaine & Buckett	00	03	00
Hay	38	00	00
Growing Barly	05	08	00
Growing oats	05	00	00
Growing pease	00	12	00
ffetches	00	03	00
Wheate & Rye	07	12	06
Three Sheep	01	00	00
Things omitted & forgotten	00	05	00
Tot	181	00	10

169. Audley Bowdler, senior

Yeoman of Madeley, buried 26/V/1715 (64y). Inventory 1/VI/1715 by Henry Bowdler senior and Richd. Phillips exhibited 12/VII/1715 for Isabel Bowdler relict and executor. Will 4/V/1714 left his eldest son Audley (b 1684) half the land and stock; his wife Isabel the other half for life and £700 from Audley, and she was residual legatee. If Audley died without heir then to the other sons and their heirs, Humphrey (b 1686), Richard (b 1692), Henry (b 1694) and Samuel (b 1696). Each of them was also to have £100 as was his daughter Ann Bowdler (b 1703).

Impr's 7 Cows at 8 li 10s p Cow.	24	10	00
3 Heifers in Calf.	08	13	04
3 Two years olf heifers & a bull stag	09	15	00
5 yearlings att	06	05	00
A mare & Colt .	07	00	00
3 Calfs .	01	10	00
A two year old Colt	03	00	00
3 Store Swine & 5 pigs .	03	10	00
6 Oxen & 2 Bullocks .	34	00	00

In the Parlour

1 Chest, 2 Tables, 6 Chaires seg bottoms 2 formes	02	15	00
6 Cushions	00	06	00

In the Chamber over the Parlour

3 Chests 2 Coffers a Desk & two boxes & 3 Trunks	03	00	00
2 Bedsteads & 3 feather beds wth Blanketts & Ruggs & hangings .	05	00	00

In the Chamber over the house

5 beds & bedcloathes a press a Table a Desk a Joyned Chair & 3 old Coffers a Cradle a nursing Chaire	06	05	00

In the Chamber next the house

2 Cupboards 1 Bed a Desk a Coffer & a small trunk, 4 Chairs	03	00	00

In the house

1 Table 1 Jack, 5 Joyned Stooles 1 Cupboard a Gunn 2 ffireshovels & 3 pair of Tonges	02	13	04

In the Dayry

Vessells of Wood Milk pans & other Utensills	01	15	00

In the Cheese Chamber

1 Cheat, 1 Trunk Beef & Bacon Cheese & Butter.	06	12	00

100 strike of Malt	17	00	00
70 strike of Corne	09	00	00
Oates & Pease, 18 strike	01	12	00
Implemt's of Husbandry, 2 waines, 2 Tumbrella a pair of small Harrows, an Ox Harrow, 2 Ploughs & Plough timber Spoakes & vellyes &c. a Role	16	10	00
Vessells of Brass Iron & Pewter & a malt mill	07	15	00

In the Buttery

2 hogsheads 4 half hogsheads & other barrels	01	10	00
Brewing Vessells, 1 old furnace in the Kitchen	02	02	06
Corn Growing on the ground Oates pease & Barley	15	00	00
Wearing Linnen of all sorts Hemp & fflax &c.	10	15	00
Moneys upon Bond	50	00	00
Wearing apparell & money in Pockett & books & other small things	15	00	00
	306	04	02

170. George Deuksell

Yeoman of the Furnace Bank in Madeley, buried 21/V/1717. Inventory 28/V/1717 by Maurice Hayward*, Tho. Stanley and Roger Thresslecock* exhibited 30/VII/1717 for George Deuksell son and Richard Langford executors. Will 17/V/1717 left his son George the tenement, copy and stock and his daughter Ann all the household goods except the clock. George was to pay her £100 when she married with the consent of the executors, but only £20 if not. Dewksell m Mary daughter of George Glassbrooke *(163)* before 1709. He was not listed in the Madeley Easter book for 1703 so presumably arrived in the parish after then.

Impr's in the Dwelling house place

Brass & pewter * Iron Ware	08	00	00
a Clock & Clock case	05	00	00
and the Dresser of Drawers & other furniture belinging to the house	03	00	00
One fowling piece	00	10	00

In the little Chamber

1 bed & furniture to it	03	00	00
One hanging press	02	00	00
Books tables & other furniture	02	00	00
And the wearing apparell of the Deced	08	00	00

In the Room over the little Chamber

one large Chest & a bed & other furniture	02	10	00
And the Cheese old & new	02	00	00

In the Parlour

1 large Chest & a Cupboard & a table board & other furniture	05	00	00
Item in Linnens fine & Course of all sorts	15	00	00

In the Buttery

Barrells & half hogsheads & other things	02	10	00

In the Chamber over the Parlour

two beds & other furniture	06	00	00

In the Chamber over the house

three beds & 2 Chests & other furniture	09	00	00

In the worke house

the tools belonging to the trade of a Carpenter	06	00	00
A Grinding stone & other things out of doors	00	10	00
and two stall of Bees	00	13	04
and a parcell of yarne	04	10	00
Eight sheep	02	00	00
One Mare	05	00	00
Two piggs	01	05	00
ffive Cows, 3 yeare olds & 2 Calves	23	00	00
The Implemts of husbandry	02	00	00
and the growing Corne & lent tilling	04	00	00
	122	08	04

171. Roger Roe

Yeoman of Madeley, buried 17/I/1718. Inventory 19/I/1718 and 7/II/1718 by William Sansom sen*, Thomas Stanley, Thomas Farmer and William North exhibited 10/II/1718 for Mary Jones his daughter wife of Richard Jones 'fabr' ferrar' administratrix.

Impr's Six Cowes each three pound ten	21	00	00
Item three Bullocks	10	00	00
6 two Yeare olds	10	00	00
5 Calves	05	00	00
Item three Colts & a ould Mare	03	10	00

three Working Mares	07	10	00
Item In the Out Barne 45 Strike of Barley	04	10	00
Item in the Stable one horse	06	00	00
Item In the Barne at the house 11 loads of hay	11	00	00
Item a Cart & Tumbrill 3 plows & Slead	04	10	00
thirty Thrave of Corn 45 Strike	07	10	00
55 Strike of Barley	05	10	00
6 Strike of pease	00	15	00
fforty Strike of Oates	03	00	00
a fatt pigg	01	15	00
4 Store Piggs	01	08	00
2 Tumbrill draughts & a Wayne body	00	06	00
2 Harrows	01	05	00
All odd Implemts of husbandry vist. Yoakes, Old Iron, Geares for 5 horses, 2 Ox Chaines, 2 Sythes & a Wayne Rope	02	00	00
A Saddle and a padd	00	15	00

Item In the Parlour

on Table	00	08	00

In the Chamber over the parlour

one ffeather bed, one blankett, one Matt, and 2 bolsters not apprized before	01	00	00
2 Chaires	00	02	00
Wearing Apparrell	01	10	00

It'm In the Chamber over the Buttery

57 Cheeses	03	05	00

It'm In the house

One Clock & Case	02	00	00

It'm In the Brewhouse

Ten Strike of Barley and four baggs	01	00	00
5 Tubbs, 2 Barrells & other Ware	01	00	00

In the Wash house

Pewter and all in that Roome	00	10	00
	122	19	00

Things forgott wch were nott Apprized in the Inventory taken & apprized ffebruary the 7th 1718 by us.

Money due from the p'ishioners of Madeley	10	00	00
2 Yeares hemp	01	00	00

THE INVENTORIES OF MADELEY 301

In the Corne Chamb'r

2 Whiches	00	05 00
Two Strike and half of Corne	00	07 00
2 pitchforkes & a Rather.	00	01 00

In the Malt Roome

4 Cheese Shelves	00	04 00

In the Brewhouse

Old Iron, 2 Grid Irons, one peele, One Ringe and a Barr.	00	02 06
A Sack and feathers	00	02 00

In the Milkhouse

3 Bowles, 6 Cheese ffatts	00	07 00

In the Kitchen

2 ffrying panns .	00	03 00
A round Table and a Warming Pann	00	07 00
2 Paire of Bellowes and a ffire plate	00	03 00
4-6 old Iron	00	02 06
A Lanthorne	00	01 00
A Small Wheell & Erwings	00	01 06
2 brass Candlestickes	00	02 00
A pillion and Cloath	00	06 00

In the Closett at the Staire head

five pair of Sheetts, & a dozn of Napkints 3 Table Cloaths & other Linnen .	01	00 00
A Hand saw 12d, a pair of shoes 3s	00	04 00
24 slipins of hemp Yarne	00	15 00
A Coffer and 2 Boxes, wth all other things in the sd Roome	00	02 06

In a Clossett in the Garrett

one Bowle, one dozn Trenchers .	00	01 06
½ strike of beanes	00	02 06
Tinn Ware 2s, A Box Iron 18d .	00	03 06
A Mattock, one Ax & a Bill	00	03 00
6 Ducks.	00	02 06
2 Geese and a Gander .	00	03 00
15 Cockes and hens	00	07 00
. . . .	16	19 00

In the Chanber over the Kitchen

2 Beds and one pair of Steads & hangings, One Chest, One hanging press, wth all in the sd Roome .	04	00 00

It'm in the Chamber over the Kitchen Chamber

2 Bed steds and a servants Bed	00	10	00
Beefe and Bacon	02	00	00
ffor the Cropp of Corne on the Land	13	06	08
. . . .	19	16	08
. . . .	16	09	00
. . . .	122	19	00
Tot . .	159	14	08

172. Roger Downes

Brassfounder of Madeley Wood but not apparently buried at Madeley. Inventory 28/X/1719 by Samuel Bowdler and Willm. Hodgkis exhibited 1/V/1720 for Jeremy Taylor clerk of Madeley and John Smitheman gent of Little Wenlock executors. Will 5/X/1719 referred to his children Arthur, Roger, Ann and Jane Downes, his wife Sarah and his sister Ann Heath. Also to £30 due from the estate of Abraham Darby.

Impr's In the work House

Flasks & Implem'ts & Tules Old Brasse & Molds. . .	01	10	00

It' In the chamber over the work House

Three Vices and Two Lathes	01	00	00
Six Dozen of New Cocks at 14s p Dozen . . .	04	04	00
Twelve Dozen of Cocks in the Rough	01	16	00

It' In the dwelling House

One Brasse Pot	00	10	00

It' In the Cup Board in the Parlour

Three Dozen & a Halfe of Cocks	01	15	00
It' Thirteen Thrave of Corne	01	19	00
It' A Parcell of Flax watered	04	00	00
It' Weareing Apparell	01	10	00
Tot . .	18	04	00

Son Arthur Downes = £10 when the money that is due to me from Mr Thomas Baylies administrator of Abraham Darby shall be paid

Son Roger Downes = £10 likewise
Daughter Ann = £5 to be paid at the same time
Daughter Jane Downes = likewise at the same time
Sister Ann Heath, widow = £2
Loving wife Sarah Downes = residual legatee
Jeremy Taylor of Madeley, clerk, & John Smitheman of Little = executors

173. Adam Crompton

Coalminer/collier of Broseley, but buried at Madeley 26/III/1723. Inventory 5/IV/1723 by Samuel Bowdler and Johannes Clemson* exhibited 18/IV/1723 by Elizabeth Crompton relict and executrix, though his will appointed his brother Thomas Crompton as executor. Will 13/III/1722 referred to 4 children Thomas, Jeremiah, who was killed in a coalpit in 1740, Adam and Mary. None was baptised at Broseley, all were under age.

Impr's in the little lower Room at the East End of the House

ten pewter dishes six pewter Porringers; five plates and other odd things on the pewter Bench	00	12	00
Three Iron dripping Pans and other iron Ware . . .	00	06	08
one old Chest and nine Chaires	00	05	00

Item in the Maine Kitchen

one joined Chest, three Tables on ffoarm two stooles five Iron Potts, and other odd things	01	00	00

Item in the Parlor

two round Tables seven chaires	00	13	00

Item in the Brewhouse

one press one chest, three stands one cooler two pailes one Vatt .	00	15	00

Item in the Chamber over the main Kitchen

one ffeather bed & steads and ffurniture, two old Coffers one old trunk	00	13	04
Eight pair of course sheets, one pair fine do, six napkins & other Linnens	01	00	00

Item in the Chamber oer the East End

Two flock bedds and steads and other ffurniture . . .	00	10	00

Item in the Cellar

five barrells & one Hogshead	00	12	00

His Wearing Apparell &c.	.	.	.	.	.		00	15	00
Money in his Pockett	.	.	.	.	.		00	05	06
overlookt several odd things	.	.	.	.	.	.	00	05	00
.	.	.	.	.	.	.	07	12	06

Eldest son Thomas - 1s & eastward end of the house in which I now reside after my wife's decease, with brewhouse belonging, & parlour beyond,. + largest iron dripping pan, one joined chest

Second son Jeremiah - 1s & westward end of the house: 2 rooms below and 2 rooms abovestairs + one joined chest

Youngest son Adam - 1s & piece of ground called Barnyard with barn standing thereon at age of 21y + one joined chest

Jeremiah to have to his part of the house part of the garden which is one the over side the house nominately that part from the Cockpit to the Codling trees & box tree from the hedge downward.

Daughter Mary - to receive £20 from Thomas & Jeremiah and a pair of joined bedsteds

174. William Cludd

Weaver of Madeley, buried 8/VI/1726. Inventory 16/VI/1726 by William Blest and Sampson Stretton exhibited 4/VII/1727 for Ann Cludd relict and Richard Tennant son in law executors. Will 18/VIII/1722 left his wife Ann (m 1698 Ann Tennant widow) the freeland in Madeley for life and after to Richard Tennant.

Impr's

In the Chamber over the house

One Chest	.	.	.	.	.	.	00	06	00
an old Table	.	.	.	.	.	.	00	02	06
a pair of Bedsteads bed bloster blanketts and Coverlett	.		02	05	00
an old Trunk and four pair of Sheets a coarse tablecloth and six Napkins .	.	.	.	.	.	.	00	17	00

In the Cockloft

a pair of Bedsteads a coarse Chaff Bed a Blankett and Coverlett	.	.	.	.	.	.	00	06	00
a long spinning Wheel	.	.	.	.	.	.	00	02	00
a stone of hemp .	.	.	.	.	.	.	00	03	00
an old Covver	.	.	.	.	.	.	00	00	06

In the Room over the old parlor

an old pair of Bedsteads Chaff Bed Blanketts and Coverlid	.	00 05 00

THE INVENTORIES OF MADELEY

In the new parlor

a pair of Bedsteads a Bed Bloster pair of Sheets Blankett Coverlid & Hangings	02	05	00
ffour Chairs	00	01	06

In the House place

Six pewter dishes six pewter porringers a pewter cann & Chamberpott & Candlestick	00	14	06
a Dish frame	00	01	06
three Tin pans	00	01	06
Iron Dripping pan	00	01	06
Two Iron pudding pans brass Skymmer Basting Spoon a Tin Broiler Cullender Cover Dredger & Eg Slice	00	03	06
Iron Broach Grate Niggards ffire Shovel and two pair of Tongs	00	04	00
a Table ffoarm	00	00	04
a dozen a half of Trenchers	00	01	06
a Hanging Cupboard	00	01	06

In the Brewhouse

two Iron marmotts an Ironpott & pott lid	00	03	00
a ffrying pann	00	01	00
two pails on Gawn 2 wooden bottls six wooden piggins an old Cheese press a sieve & searce	00	04	09

In the Cellar

two brewing Tubs a Cooler a Churn three Barrells a Tundish	00	11	00

In the Shop

Three Looms thirty Linnen & Woollen Gears Warping Bar & Trough & Quill Wheel	05	10	00
	14	12	07

175. Mary Yates

Widow of Robert Yates 154 of Madeley, 'murthered by one George Jenkes and others', buried 6/VII/1687. 'A true and perfect note or Inventory of what goods. Mary Yates. was possest of within the house now found' (not dated and no appraisers names) exhibited 13/III/1687 for Thomas Aston son of her brother William Aston deceased principal legatee, granted administration with the two executors, John Cock brother in law and Thomas Newton friend of Buildwas. Will 27/VIII/1681 left Elizabeth Hill kinswoman, 'a shirt and smock of hemp, a couple of dressings and a Quoife and a cinamon coloured petticoat and a little brass pot'; and Elizabeth Miles cousin two pair of hurden sheets, one pewter dish and six pewter spoons. Residual legatees were Thomas Aston and her two sisters Elizabeth wife of John Cock and Ann wife of Thomas Littleford.

Impr's One feather bed And bedsead And All thearetoo belonging to the value of	02	00	00
It' Three table boards two chests And Two coufers computed And Impraised	01	00	04
It' one Mare to the value of	01	06	08
It' One gilt And Two pigs at	00	10	06
It' one smale iron furnes And one Little iron pot at the value of	01	10	00
in the Lord of the Maners hands			
It' two feather bedds and two flock bedds with the App'ten' thereunto belonging	07	00	00
It' Linnens of all sorts	01	04	00
It' brasse pewter and Ironware of all sorts	02	00	00
It' Desp'ate Debts	02	00	00
Sum	18	11	06

176. Edward Owen, senior

Wareman of Madeley Wood, buried 11/XII/1727. Inventory 1/VI/1728 by Sam Bowdler and James Owen* exhibited 16/VII/1728 by Ann Owen relict and Edward Owen son joint executors. Will 23/X/1727 left his wife Ann the dwelling house in Madeley Wood containing the house part, kitchen and buttery with rooms over them, with the garden before the door which reaches to the wall separating it from the orchard, with free passage to the little house standing in the orchard (then to son Edward); his son Edward the other part of the house with the stable at the west end and the orchard. If he died without issue to daughters Mary and Elizabeth Owen and if they were without issue to Thomas son of daughter Sarah (m 1715 Thomas Withington of Shifnall) and Edward Boden son of daughter Jane. Edward Owen was to work the trow not sold with the barge called 'the Edward' and the two boats and Ann Owen to have an equal share of the profits.

Impr's

In the Chief Kitchin

Pewter, Brass and Iron wares, with other ffurniture valu'd.	02	10	00

Item *In the Buttery*, ffour Barrels, a Long Wheel and Six glass Bottles 00 10 00

Item *In the Parlour*, One Skreen, One Oval Table, Six Chairs & other ffurniture 00 15 00

Item *In the Brewhouse*, ffive Brewing vessels . . . 00 11 00

Item *In the Chamber* over the Brewhouse, two ffeather beds with steads & other furnit'e One hanging press one chest, two Cupboards, two Trunks two little Boxes two Chairs 05 00 00

Item *In the Middle Chamber*, One Clock and Case, One fflock bed & ffurniture, One Chest & One Trunk 03 14 00

Item *In the Parlour Chamber*, one ffeather bed & its ffurnit'e . 04 00 00
In do One Chest, One Chest of Drawers, ffive Chairs and other ffurniture 01 16 00
Ten pair of Sheets vizt ffour fflaxen & six Hemp . . . 02 00 00
Table Linen with other useful Linen 00 16 00
Item The deceased's Wearing Apparel and Cash in Pocket. . 03 10 00
Item One horse, and one pigg (or swine) 02 05 00
Item Two Trows and one Barge with all materials thereunto belonging 60 00 00
Item Two small Boats 05 00 00
Item Things overlook'd & unseen by us the Appraisers . . 01 00 00

. . . . 93 07 00

177. William Eardley

Engineer of Madeley Wood, buried 20/III/1728. Inventory 27/III/1729 by Thomas Hughes and Francis Boden exhibited 2/VI/1729 for Hanna Eardley relict, executrix and residual legatee. Will 16/III/1728 left his son in law John Moss £10.

Impr's

In ye parlour 1 Small Table 00 05 00
6 Chaires 00 02 06

It' In ye Kitchen

6 Small pewter dishes, & 2 old plates 00 10 00
One Dripping pann, One Tinn pann & One Iron Mortar & pestle. 00 05 06
One Warming pann, One Small Table 00 03 00
One Iron Grate & other Materills thereunto belonging . . 00 06 00

It' In ye Celler

3 Small Barrells & 2 pailes	00	05 00
3 Tubbs & one Stand, 2 Small Iron potts, 2 Small Kettles, & 2 Spinning Wheells	00	12 00
2 pailes, 18 Trenchers	00	02 00

It' In ye Back Chamber

One ffeather Bed, One fflock Bed, 1 pair of Bedsteads,	02	10 00
2 Blanketts & 1 Rugg and 1 sett of Curtaines thereunto belonging	00	05 00
One Chest	00	05 00

It' In ye Chamber over ye Kitchen

One Clock	00	10 00
One Chest & 6 Chairs, 1 Small Table	00	10 00

It' In ye parlour Chamber

a ffeather Bed wth other ffurniture	02	00 00
One old Trunk and 6 pair of Sheets	00	12 00

It' Wearing Apparrell	01	10 00
Money	00	05 00
	11	12 00

178. John Doughty

Carpenter of Madeley Wood, buried 18/IV/1728. Inventory 24/IV/1728 by John Pufford and Sam Bowdler exhibited 14/V/1728 for Martha Doughty relict and administratrix.

Impr's

In the Parlour

a Clock and Case	02	10 00
An Ovall table 8s a Case of Drawers not finished 7s 6d Chairs 3s	00	18 06
2 Small tables	00	07 00

Item In the Out Kitchen

i Skreen	00	07 00
i Small table & 6 Chairs	00	04 00
7 pewter dishes i doz: & half of plates	01	06 00

Item In the East Chamber

i bed & sheds with rug & blanketts	01	10	00
A Chest & box & a pair of Bedsteads	00	15	00

Item In the Middle Chamber

i Bed & furniture	02	00	00
3 Chests 8s a Close Stool 2s/6d	00	10	06
5 boxes	00	05	00

Item In the Back Chamber

2 flok Beds with other furniture	00	13	04
A Small Wheel	00	01	06

Item In the Buttry

a Skreen 2 barrells & other Wood Ware	00	08	06

Item In the back kitchen

i table	00	03	00
A Mitt & 2 tubs a pail a Cupboard	00	06	00
Iron & tin ware & earth ware	00	08	00
A Warming pan & copper can	00	03	00
2 pair of Sheets	01	02	06
Table Linnen with other ordinary house Linnen	00	10	00

Item In the Shop

all the working tools	01	10	00
Boards Rails Spars & plank	03	00	00

A Pig	00	06	00
Wearing Apparell	01	10	00
Money	00	05	00
Things Overlookd	00	04	00
Book debts	15	06	07
Totall	36	10	11

179. Richard Cox

Collier of Madeley Wood, but apparently not buried at Madeley. Inventory 24/XI/1731 by Robert Fox of Foxholes* and Thomas Edwards exhibited 12/IX/1732 for Elizabeth Cox relict and administratrix.

Impr's In the house place

An old Dresser & shelves	00 01 00
Eleven pewter dishes	00 18 00
Ten old plates & some other old pewter	00 03 06
A Wooded Skreen	00 03 00
A fflower search	00 00 06
Six Old seggen Chairs & a Little Old Table	00 01 09
Three Marments & a little old Brass kettle	00 04 06
An Old Warming pann	00 01 00
An old Candle Box Broiler Tuning dish & Baster	00 00 06
Earthen dishes & Muggs &c.	00 00 09
A ffrying pann	00 00 06
Three Old Candlesticks	00 00 03
A Grate, ffire Shovell, Tongs, Niggotts, Spitts & plate to stand before the ffire, & Maid	00 04 06
An Old Wooden Mortar & a Little pestle	00 00 04
ffour old Tin Tobacco dishes	00 00 02
An Old paile	00 00 06

In the parlor

An Old Ovall Table & Joyned fform	00 03 00
ffive Seggen Chairs	00 01 00
A Round handle Baskett	00 00 04

In the Celler

One Hogshead & three half Hogsheads	00 15 00

In the Chamber over the house

One ffeather bed, steads, Hangings, Blankets Bolsters & pillows	01 05 00
An Old Wooden Chest, Coffer & Box	00 02 06
An Old pewter Chamber pott	00 00 06
Six pair of Old Hurden Sheets & a Table Cloth	00 12 00

In the Chamber Over the Parlour

An Old Sap Bedsteed &c	00 02 00
An Old Hanging press & Coffer	00 03 06
Seven Old Chairs	00 02 00
A Little Old Spinning Wheell	00 00 06

In the Brewhouse

Two Brewing Tubbs	00 06 00
Two other Small Tubbs	00 03 00
An old Kneading Tubb	00 01 06
An old Barrell & a Cleansing Seive	00 00 06
An Old Iron ffurnace	00 04 00

Two plankes	00	00	03

Wearing apparrell

One Coat Wastcoate & Britches	00	07	06
Two Shirts	00	03	00
Shoes & Stockings	00	02	00
Tot	06	16	10

180. Edward Cludd

Collier of Madeley, buried 8/II/1732. Inventory 10/IV/1732 by William Wood and Thos Edwards exhibited 11/VII/1732 for Benjamin Cludd brother and executor. Will 1/I/1731 left daughters Mary, Margeret (m Robert Rodes), Margery (m Richard Clifton) and Alice Cludd spinster 1s. each and all goods and chattels to be shared; eldest daughter Ann (m 1722 Robert Reynolds *alias* Phillips) the cottage; if she has no children then to daughter Joyce (m Joseph Taylor) and then to the other daughters. Impr's

In the house place

One Oval Table	00	02	06
An Old Iron pott & 3 small Marments	00	02	00
A small Maslen Kettle two Iron Candlesticks A Basting Spoon Bellows Iron and Heeters	00	04	06

In the parlore

One Old fashioned wooden Cupboard	00	01	00
An Old Bedstead a Small desk two Barrells	00	03	06
A Little Round Mitt a wooden Mortar a Little Tub and water pail	00	02	06

In the Chamber

One bed Boulster three Blaketts & steads A small Square Table A Long Wheel Little Wheel kneading trough Two Coffer & a Chest	01	00	00
ffour stones of Hemp	00	08	00
An Iron Grate Niggards a pair of pott Hookes fire shovel & Tongs	00	04	06
Eight pewter dishes two porringers One Tankard Nine Spoons and a Candlestick	00	12	00
A Tin dredger Sawsepan & ten wooden Trenchers	00	00	08
One pair of Hempen Sheets three pair of Hurden Sheets One Old Hurden Sheet One Hurden Table Cloth a pillows ped & four Napkins	00	15	00

A side of pork a Cheese and a piece of Beefe	.	.	.	00 03 00
Wareing Apparrell	.	.	.	.	.	00 10 00
	Tot	.	.	04 09 02

181. Mark Henworth

Miller of Madeley, buried 6/IX/1729. Inventory 29/IX/1729 by Edward Littleton and John Shiston exhibited 19/VII/1732 by Ann Henworth relict and executrix. Will 3/IX/1729 left his son John and two unnamed daughters 1s. each and his wife Ann all else including book debts and money. In 1707 Henworth was recorded as paying for Bowdlers mill in the Madeley Easter book.

Impr'is

In the Kitchen or House place

Six Pewter dishes five plates, three porringers, a posset cup Candlestick & a doz of wooden Trenchers	00 13 00
A Table & form, a ffire Grate, Shovel & Tongs, a spit, frying pan warming pan a Little Kettle, a Little pot, a Marment and two Chaires	00 16 00

In the Buttery

Two Barrells, two Tubs a Churn a Milking Gawn a pail and an old ffurnace	00 04 06

In the Little Chamber

One bed, bedsteads, Clothes an old Trunk & Chaire	00 16 06

In the other Chamber

A bed with bedsteads, Clothes, a Chest, a Box, a Close Stoole and an old Chair	00 18 06

In the Parlour

A Bed with bedsteds, Clothes, Chest and two Chairs	01 01 00
An old Spining Wheel and Linnen	01 10 00

In the Meadow

An old Mare almost dead of a ffistula	00 05 00
Hay and a Pigg	00 19 00
ffor old lumber & things not seen	00 05 00
Wearing Apparell ready money & debts good and bad	01 10 06
Tot	08 19 00

182. Edward Owen

Trowman of Madeley Wood, buried 31/V/1732. Inventory 21/VI/1732 by Edward Ward exhibited 25/IX/1734 by Elizabeth Owen relict (née Hallen 1728) and Cornelius Holland and father in law, two of the executors. The third was Thomas Stanley. Will 26/V/1732 left his wife all goods for the maintenance of their son Edward until he was of age; his brother James £5; and his two sisters Sarah Withington 1 guinea and Mary Fletcher half a guinea. Son of Edward Owen *(176)*.

In the Kitchen

One Fire Grate and Ears, 1 Fire Shovel and Tongs one perkettery and Fender with one plate .	01	05	00
One Gridiron & Chafind Dish One Brass Scumer & Spoone One Fryind pann and 1 Doz of Iron scures . . .	00	04	08
5 Brass Candle Sticks and Snuffers, One Brass Druger Box and Brass Peper Box.	00	07	00
2 Iron Spitts one Driping pann and puding pann One Box Iron and One Brass Sauce pann	00	09	02
One Tin Cullendore 1 Driping pann one Druger One Puding pann one Candlebox and Tundish	00	04	00
2 Lanthornes and one Doz Potty pans	00	02	06
13 pewter Dishes Weight 67 li	02	04	00
2 Dozen and 2 pewter plates and one Solver . .	01	01	00
One Brass Warming pann 5 shills 7 pewter Porengers 2 shills .	00	07	00
One punch Bole and Other Bristoll Earthen Wares . .	00	02	00
A Dresser of Drawers and Six Ash Chairs . . .	01	00	00
One Ovall Table 1 Square Table and two Cupboards . .	00	15	00
3 pair of fire Bellows and 2 fire Brushes . . .	00	03	06
One Bacon Crach 2 Shills. and Hat Brush 3 pence . .	00	02	03

In the Brue House

One Iron furnace and Boyler	00	15	00
17 Trenchers one Dog Wheele and Chaine . . .	00	05	00
One Iron Pott and pottlids and potthucks . . .	00	03	00
3 Benches and one Cleansing Sive	00	01	00
1 Copper Sauce pan 1 Water paile and Gawn . . .	00	02	00
1 Copper Can 1 Cooler & Mashing Tub	00	06	00

In the Parlour

A Clock & Case 40 Shills 1 folding screene 5 shills . .	02	05	00
4 Black Chairs 2s 6d one Child Chair 1 shilling . .	00	03	06
A Small Spining Wheele 2s 6d. One Iron Grate & Ears One pair of hand Irons Brass 7s 6d. One Wheather Glass One pewter Wine Quart & pint 8s 6d one Side Table and Drawers 2s . .	00	03	06
One Slate Table 5 shills 10 Pictures and a Map 2 Shills . .	00	07	00

In the Parlour Chamber

One flock Bed Curtains and bed Cloaths .	01	10 00
One Deale hanging Press	00	15 00
Two Turky Chairs 2 Leather Chairs & 2 Cushing Stols .	00	08 00

In the Kitchen Chamber

One feather Bed Hangings and Bed Cloaths . .	02	00 00
5 Chairs 7 Shills One Chest 7s 6d 2 Maps & 2 Pictures 6d .	00	16 00

In the Best Roome

One feather Bed & bed Cloaths with Hangings . .	02	10 00
6 Chairs 6 Shills. one Map & 7 pictures 1 shilling . .	00	07 00
One Chest of Drawers and one Dressing Table . .	00	15 00
Two Brass hand irons and one Brass fender . .	00	02 00
A Looking Glass.	00	06 00

Linnings of All Sorts Vist.

One Diaper Table Cloath and one Doz Napkins . .	00	16 00
7 pair Hempen Sheetts £1 15s. one horden pair 3 shillings .	01	18 00
5 Horden Table Cloaths & one Doz Napkins . .	00	08 00

In the Garrett

one feather Bed & Bed Cloaths	00	15 00

In the Celler

One half Hogshd	00	05 00
One 3 Quatr Vessell with Eight Iron hoops . .	00	10 00
One Small firkin and one Quarter Vessell. . .	00	02 06
One Store Pigg	00	15 00
The Great trow at Gloucester	70	00 00
The Midle Trow	60	00 00
The Little Trow	30	00 00
One Long Stock Boat	02	10 00
A Silver Watch pockett Money and Wearing Apparell . .	02	10 00
Things out of sight & forgott	00	05 00
. . . .	213	12 07

183. John Goodman

Of Madeley, buried 29/XII/1733. Inventory 9/I/1733 by Matt Astley and Richard Henshaw exhibited 15/I/1733 by Constance relict and administratrix.

THE INVENTORIES OF MADELEY

Impr's In the House

A Grate Fire Shovell, Tongs & Niggards	00	05	00
A Maid, Pot Links, Fry Pan and Hand pan . . .	00	03	06
A Jack Spit and dripping Pan	00	10	06
A Chest 3 Chairs a Bench A Salt Box A Buffet stool & A pair Bellows	00	07	06
A Cock and Case	00	15	00

Item In the Parlour

Two Tables and Six Chairs	00	12	00
Eight pewter Dishes Nine plates two salves & a Mustard pot .	00	17	06
One Dozen of Hemp part of it spun	00	06	00
Two Baskitts	00	00	08
A Warming pan, A Brass Candlestick & Snuffers, 2 skimmers A Brass Spoon A Mortar & pestill	00	08	00
Twelve pair of sheets fine and coarse	03	00	00
Two Huggaback Table Cloths and twelve Napkins . .	00	11	00
Ten coarse Table Cloths & hand Towells	00	03	00
A parcell of old Books	00	05	00

Item in a little pantry

three spinning Wheels	00	07	00

Item in 2 little Sellers

A Hogshead 4½ Hogsheads 3 small Barrells A Horse they stand on	01	15	00

Item in the Brewhouse

Two Coolers	00	12	00
Two Brewing Tubs and one Cheese Tub	00	10	00
A Churn Milk pales & some small Wood Vessells . .	00	10	00
A Cheese press and A little Table	00	10	00

Item in the Malt Chamber

A Skreen a parcell of Barley & Hair Cloth . . .	02	00	00

Item in the Store Chambers

A parcell of Wheat & Some Peas	04	00	00
A Malt Mill some Malt and A parcell of Oats . .	02	05	00
A parcell of Cheese	01	10	00
Beef and Bacon	01	10	00

Item In the Parlour Chamber

A Bed Bolster Beadsteads & Hangings 2 Blanketts A Quilt 6 Chairs a Table Window Curtains a Glass Trunk and fender . .	03	10	00

Item in Kitching Chamber

A Bed Bolster 2 Blanketts a Quilt Bedsteads & Hangings . .	02	10	00

It'm in the Garret over

A Bed Bolster Bedstead 2 Blanketts A Rug & A Coffer . .	01	01	00

It'm in ye other Garrets

2 Beds 2 Bolsters A Bedstead & 3 Blanketts . . .	00	15	00
A parcell of Glass Bottles	00	05	00
A Box Iron 2 Smoothing Irons a Chopping Knife some Iron Chandlesticks A Lanthorn & some Tin Ware . . .	00	05	00
A Mesuring Hoop A parcell of Sives & Riddles and some Bags	00	10	00
Item One Brass Kettle 2 Iron potts 2 Iron Kettles . .	01	00	00
Half A Dozen Knives & Forks	00	02	06
Item Two Waggons	11	10	00
Two Tumbrills and Two Carts	10	10	00
Two Ploughs two pair of Harrows & a Hopper . . .	02	15	00
Eleven pair of Horse Gears	03	00	00
Wheat in the Barn Unthrash'd	06	00	00
A parcell of Barly & Oats unthrash'd	01	10	00
Hay & Straw	07	00	00
Nine Sheep	02	05	00
Six Cows and one Calf	22	18	00
Two Twinter Heffer & 4 Year olds	07	00	00
Six Drawing Horses	23	00	00
A Mare A Filly & a Foal.	06	00	00
Three Waggon Mares	06	00	00
A Guilt and A Store Pig	01	05	00
Old Iron & Lumber Unseen	01	00	00
The deceased's Sadle Bridle & wearing Apparell . . .	02	00	00
Totall . .	146	17	02

184. William Easthope

Labourer/ground collier of Madeley Wood, buried 1/III/1742. Inventory 28/XII/1743 by William Hinton shopkeeper of Madeley Wood and John Meeson gent of Little Dawley exhibited 3/VII/1744 for Ann Easthope relict and executrix. Will 26/II/1742 left his wife Ann all lands, tenements and annuities for life then to his nephew Richard son of John Bayley. Son of John Easthope *(186)*.

THE INVENTORIES OF MADELEY

8 pewter dishes & 12 old plates	01	05	00
one old Brass & one Iron pot	00	06	06
one Tin Dripping pan	00	00	09
one Iron Grate fender Shovells and Tongs	00	07	06
one Spitt one Iron Dripping pan	00	02	00
4 Brass Candlesticks	00	04	00
one old Warming pan	00	02	00
1 old Clock and Case	00	15	00
1 Deal Chest	00	04	00
1 Dresser & Shelves	00	10	00
1 parcell of Old Drawers	00	01	06
Earthen Ware and Glasses	00	02	00
1 Oval Table	00	04	00
Six Chairs with wooden bottoms	00	03	00
1 Brass Dish Stand	00	02	00
3 Little Barrells	00	03	00
1 Chopping knife	00	00	06
1 Feather bed bolster pillows 3 blanquets 1 Old Coverlid and Steads	02	00	00
one Glass	00	04	00
A Little Square Table	00	02	00
Three Old Tables & 1 Dozen of Trenchers	00	03	09
1 Spade & Wire Riddle	00	02	00
Six pair of old hempin Sheets	00	12	00
one Cow	03	00	00
one Two year old heifer or young Cow	02	00	00
1 Yearling Calfe	01	00	00
Wearing Apparrell and Cash	05	00	00
	19	06	06

Daughter in law Ann Easthope, widow: parlour & rooms over it, with liberty of keeping a cow with hay & grasse in lands belonging to me for life.

Grandson Richard Bailey: Barn & that part of the yard it stands in, next the Rails from the place where the Old Hedge formerly Divided it, with Liberty of Erecting Scaffolds or Ladders at any time for repairing in the other part of the yard.

Rest of lands & tenments (& that devised to Ann Easthope after her decease) with goods & chattles to grandson John Bailey

Except the next falling of the Coppy Wood of the Dingle which I give to my Grandaughter Mary Bailey, she leaving the standard trees that were left last fall.

185. John Boden, the younger

Coalminer of the Green in Madeley Wood, buried 1/XI/1746. Inventory 15/XI/1746 by Wm. Botteley, John Boden and Edward Boden exhibited 9/IX/1747 for Ann Boden relict and executrix. Will 24/X/1746 left his wife Ann the house and his son Michael another house in the possession of widow Glazebrook, the room he normally slept in and two sheep in return for looking after Ann's sheep.

Impr's The Deceaseds Wearing Aparell	00	10	00
It' two Tables	00	02	00
It' A Small Screen	00	01	00
It' Chairs	00	01	00
It' pewter	00	06	06
It' A Warming pan an Old one	00	00	06
It' An Iron Driping pan	00	01	00
It' Tin Weare	00	00	08
It' Two Old Candlesticks	00	00	02
It' an Old Hanging press	00	03	00
It' two Old fflock Beds	00	14	00
It' two Old Chests	00	05	00
It' Old Blanchting	00	05	00
It' Lining of all Sorts	00	10	00
It' Old Bedsteads	00	05	06
It' 2 Old Barrells	00	03	06
It' fier Shovel & Tongs Grate & pot Links	00	03	06
It' 6 Small Weltch Sheep	00	15	00
	04	07	04

186. John Easthope

Yeoman of Madeley Wood, buried 23/VII/1746. Inventory 30/VII/1746 by John Mason and Jno. Hartshorne exhibited 5/VIII/1746 for John Bayley executor. Ann Easthope widow daughter in law was also executrix. Will 2/XI/1743 left the said Ann the parlour and the room over and the liberty to keep a cow in hay and grass on his land; his grandson Richard Bayley the barn and the part of the yard 'that stands next the rails from the place where the old hedge formerly divide it'; and his granddaughter Mary Bayley the next falling of copy wood in the Dingle leaving the standard trees. Father of William Easthope *(184)*.

In the Kitchen

A Dresser & Shelves	00	02	06

THE INVENTORIES OF MADELEY

Six Pewter Dishes seven Pewter Plates three Pewter Porringers one Pewter Salver one Pewter Candlestick and Salt	00	16 00
One Brass Pan ffive Brass Kettles a Brass Pott & Skillet all old Brass	00	16 00
A Table & fform	00	03 00
An Iron Mortar & Pestle.	00	02 06
An old Jack & two spitts and Iron dripping Pan	00	06 00
A ffire Shovel & Tongs w'th other odd Lumber	00	01 06

In the Room over the Kitchen

Two Bedsteads & old Curtains	00	10 00
One ffeather Bed & Bolster and Bedding thereunto belonging	01	10 00
One Bed of flocks & feathers & Bedding thereon.	00	10 00
An old Wainscoat Chest & 3 pair of sheets therein	01	00 00
An old Chair Lumber	00	01 06
One other ffeather Bed & Bedstead being in two other Rooms	00	12 00
The dec'eds Wearing Apparel and all other Linnen unmentioned	01	01 06
	07	12 06

187. John Harper

Yeoman of Madeley, buried 25/III/1749. Inventory 7/IV/1749 by John Mason and Joseph Hussey exhibited 19/IX/1749 by John Harper executor. Richard Harper of the Hem was also executor. Probate 19/IX/1749. Will 25/VII/1748 made John Harper son of George Harper of the Wike near Shifnal sole legatee on condition that he looked after his aged parents.

Goods in the House Imprimis

1 small Grate & Cheeks, Fire Shovel Tongs & Fender	00	07 06
13 pewter dishes.	01	06 00
8 pewter plates	00	04 00
4 pewter porringers	00	02 00
1 old pewter Tankard	00	01 00
5 pewter spoons, 2 tin pudding pans & 1 Tin Cover	00	01 06
1 pewter salt, 1 Tin Tun Dish & 1 Warming pan	00	02 06
1 Small Pewter Frame	00	02 00
2 Brass Ladles & 1 Scimmer	00	02 00
1 Large Brass Kettle & 1 small Do	00	07 06
1 Small Maslin Kettle & 1 Small brass Candlestick	00	01 00
1 Marment 1 old Pot	00	01 06
2 Iron Spits 1 Tin Dripping Pan & 1 Iron Drippin Pan	00	06 00
1 Old Mortar & Pestil	00	01 06

1 old Chafing Dish & Bellows	00 01 00
2 Doz of Wood Trenchers	00 02 00
1 Little Cupboard	00 01 00
1 old Long Table, 1 Form, 2 joint Stools & 1 Side Bench . .	00 07 06

Goods in the Parlour Item

1 Chaff Bed, 1 old pr of Bedsteds, 1 Bolster, 1 Blanket & Coverlid	00 10 00
1 old Chest 4 old Chairs	00 10 00
1 Table Frame & Form	00 05 00
7 old Horden Sheets	00 10 06
3 Horden Table Cloths 1 Hemp Do . . .	00 04 06
8 Old Hand Towels, 1 Yard of Coarse new Cloth . .	00 05 00
1 Old Cloth Basket, 1 Hand Basket	00 01 06

Goods in the Entry Item

1 Small Churn & Churn Staff	00 04 00
1 small Cheese Tub & Milk Bowl	00 03 06
1 Mattock 1 Spade 1 Ax 1 Bill	00 04 00

Goods in the Milk House Item

3 Small old Barrels 1 old Butter Scale	00 06 00

Goods in the Brewhouse Item

3 old Tubs 1 old Strike	00 08 00
1 Kneeding Tub & Cheese press	00 04 00
1 Old Copper Furnace	01 00 00
3 Pails, 2 Spining Wheels.	00 05 00

Goods in the Brewhouse Chamber Item

Old iron &c	00 01 06

Goods in the Room over the House Item

1 Old Feather Bed 1 old Chaff Bed 1 pr of Bedsteds & Hangings 1 Bolster, 2 Blankets 1 Covrlid	01 10 00
2 Chests 3 Old Coffers 1 Box	01 10 00
2 p'r of Flaxen sheets, 2 p'r of Hemp Do 13 horden Napkins 1 Pillow bere	02 00 00
1 p'r of old Boots	00 04 00
1 Flitch & half of Bacon	01 10 00

Goods in the Room over the Parlour Item

1 old Feather Bed, 2 Bolsters one Pillow 2 old Blankets & Coverlid 1 pr old Bedsteds	01 10 00
2 p'r Coarse Horden Sheets	00 10 00

1 old Chest 1 old Box 1 Old Table	00	05 00
5 Stone of Hemp	00	12 06
1 Strike & Half of Corn	00	03 09
2 Straw Wiskets 1 Old Sack	00	04 00

Outward Stock Item

2 Cows	07	00 00
2 Tuns of Hay	03	00 00
Things unseen	00	05 00
Wearing Apparel	02	10 00
. . . .	31	14 03

188. Thomas Boden

Ground collier of Madeley Wood, buried 1/XI/1750. Inventory 20/XI/1750 by Robert Palmer and John Jones exhibited 30/VII/1751 for Elizabeth Boden relict executrix and sole legatee. Will 30/X/1750.

In the Dwelling House &c

One Press or Cubboard two Salt boxes One Screen . .	00	18 06
One Turn up Table one Joint Stool	00	04 00
One Dresser and Shelves.	00	07 00
Two Benches Six Chairs One Coffer . . .	00	13 06
One Oval Table a Small Desk	00	12 06
Three pair of Bedsteads one Chest . . .	01	14 00
One Table the leaf 8 Square	00	02 00
One feather Bed Two Sheets 3 blankets One Rug and a Set of Curtains in the back Room	02	05 00
One Flock bed 2 blankets One Rug and Red Curtains . .	01	05 00
A Long Spinning Weel	00	02 00
One pair of Flaxen Sheets & pillow Beer . . .	00	15 00
One pair of hempen Sheets 2 pair of Hurden Sheets . .	00	16 00
One Table Cloth Six Ells of Hempen Cloath . .	00	09 06
One Search two Small Tubs and a Barrell . .	00	04 11
One Pot one Marment one Kettle and Cover one frying pan .	00	05 00
One Iron Dripping pan one Tin Dripping pan 2 Spitts .	00	06 00
One Smoothing Iron 1 Iron holder 1 Cullendor 1 Tundish .	00	02 01
One firegrate and Cheeks a fireshovel & Tongs a fire plate Links and a Pestell	00	10 00
One Roasting fork 2 brilers 2 Tin pans one Cover . .	00	01 09
12 Tin patty Eight pewter dishes 11 pewter plates. .	01	02 00
Six Trenchers 9 Glass bottles	00	02 04

3 Washing pans 2 Tickney dishes.	00	01	00
One pail One bowl one Small Looking Glass 1 Chopping knife	00	02	06
Ten Small Earthen Cups and a Mustard pott	00	00	10
Eight old books and two Brushes	00	01	09
One Old Cupboard a Mantle peice and a Dresser.	00	04	00
One old furnace.	00	02	00
Sum Total	13	10	02

189. Mary Clemson

Widow of Madeley, buried 25/IV/1753. Inventory 30/IV/1753 by Thomas Guest junior and Robert Hawkins exhibited 7/V/1753 for Elizabeth (wife of William Hodgkiss) and Elianor wife of William Fennell daughters and executrices. Will 19/IV/1753 left her daughter Elizabeth Hodgkiss all the tools belonging to ropemaking and the spinning house, rope yard and piece of land adjoining provided she followed that employment, otherwise to eldest son William Clempson, and she was to pay 20s. p.a. to be divided among all the children, herself included and the rent to the Lord of the Manor; her youngest daughter 'what is in her possession'; and all the children to share the rest.

An old Press Cubboard two old Tables	01	02	00
Old Pewter of All sorts	00	08	00
An Oval Table and six Chairs with seg Bottoms	00	11	00
A feather Bed Bedsteads Hangings and Bed Cloaths	02	10	00
An old Desk an old trunk and a Close Stool	00	02	06
ffive p'r of sheets a Table Cloth & six Napkins	01	07	00
Three small Barrells for Drink	00	10	06
An old Furnace .	00	04	06
A Grate fender & purgator and other Iron Ware .	00	10	06
One other Bed & Bedsteads	01	08	06
The Reversion of a Chattle Lease.	01	01	00

Materials belonging to Ropiers Business

One Engine a Jack Hook & Engine Barr w'th other Ironwork	01	09	03
Six Iron Bolts an Iron Crow & a Brake	00	12	06
A Half Hundred Weight & a Copper Pan.	00	19	10
Two old Scale Beams & Boards .	00	02	00
an old ax a wheel & winces Brass Boards & a Old Hammer	00	06	03
A Slead four Carts & other wood work belonging to the Works	00	05	00
Book Debts good & bad to the value of .	42	00	00
An old Skreen * a p'r of Racks	00	01	06
Tot	55	11	10

190. John Jones

Forgeman of Coalbrookdale in Madeley. Probably buried 15/III/1747 a week after making his will. Inventory 21/VI/1754 by Jno. Summerland and Richd. Prichard exhibited 24/VI/1754 for Mary Jones relict and executrix who died in 1755. Will 7/III/1747 made her sole legatee.

One feather Bed Bed Cloaths & Curtains.	01	10	00
Two pair of old Bedsteads six Chairs	00	09	04
Two Tables a Chest & two Boxes	00	14	03
Linnen of all sorts	01	01	06
A Dresser & Shelves with the Pewter	01	10	06
A Warming Pan a frying pan and tin ware	00	04	02
four Candlesticks three old Pictures	00	01	00
A fire grate and purgatory	00	18	06
A Spitt and Coberts	00	02	06
four Barrells a Mash Tub & Kneading Mitt	00	18	09
Some other old furniture and Lumber	00	03	06
Book debts ab't.	00	18	00
Divers other Goods sold since the Deceased's for ab't	08	00	00
Tot	16	12	00

191. Edward Thomas

Coalminer of Madeley Wood, buried 21/VI/1754. Inventory, not dated, by Robert York and Will. Dicken exhibited 3/VII/1755 for Elizabeth Thomas relict and executrix. Will 5/VI/1754 left his wife Elizabeth the dwelling house he lived in with the cook house, half the garden and the household goods, also the brew house late dwelling house of Edward Holland and the other half garden until his son Edward of age and a piece of land to the east of the cook house and the garden called the Further Orchard until his daughters Joan and Sarah of age.

In the Kitchen

A Fire Shovel Tongs Grate & Cheeks	00	10	06
Pothooks Fry pann & chafin dish	00	04	00
Fire shovel Tongs brass basting spon & fire plate.	00	06	00
A warming pann pudding pann & Candlesticks	00	07	04
A Brass Box & pepper Box	00	00	10
Dresser with drawers & shelves.	00	15	00
Twenty Pound weight of pewter.	00	10	00
Eighteen Trenchers	00	02	00
Tables Chairs and a stool	00	03	08

A Tin dripping & Salt Box	00 01 08
Other pewter and Earthen Ware	00 01 09

In the parlour

an ovel Table & looking Glass	00 06 00
Four old chairs	00 01 00

In the Brewhouse

An old Iron Furnace	00 05 00
Table pails a Gaun & two Iron Potts	00 10 00
Six Barrells & Stillings	00 18 00
A Bed Bolster & Hangings	01 10 00
A Chest old Trunk and a chair	00 06 08
Another Fether Bed Bolster & Bedsted	01 00 00
A Flock Bed Bolster & Steeds	00 06 06
A little Box and an old Wheel	00 02 06
Sheets and Table Linnen	00 12 00
Wearing Apparrell & Moneyt in Pockett	01 07 06
Lumber & things overseen & forgott	00 02 03
	10 09 03

192. Thomas Rowley

Blacksmith of Madeley but apparently not buried there. Inventory (not dated) by Thos. Dovey and Jno. Dickens exhibited 23/IX/1755 for William Hallen creditor.

First The deceaseds Wearing Apparrell	00 10 00
New Barr Iron in the Shop	01 08 11
Hammers punches & Studdys	00 11 08
New Shoes Links New Rod & old Iron	01 10 02 ½
old shoes scraps & old iron & eleven ordinary clouts	00 19 07
Files Flews a Bromhook and other old things in the Window	00 02 06
A Scrue Plate and a Nail Studdy	00 04 01
A Cast Mould and a Grinding Stone with a Iron spindle	00 08 09
Two Anvill Blocks an old Cofferr and a Shoeking Box	00 04 00
A parcell of Coal in the shop	00 14 00
A Large Anvill	03 00 00
A smiths pair of Bellows	02 02 00
A Vice	00 12 00
New Iron in the house	01 10 00
	13 07 00 ½

193. John Palmer

Master collier of Madeley Wood, buried 20 May 1759. Inventory dated 4 June 1759 by Josh. Hatton and Humphrey Jandrell. Will dated 12 April 1756, probate 28 June 1759.

In the Kitchen

A Grate racks fire shovel and Tongs	02	02	00
A round Table 2 Square Tables	00	14	00
5 Wood Chairs 1 Elbow do	00	07	00
A Dresser wth Drawers & Shelves	01	10	00
One Dozn of Pewter Dishes	01	10	00
1 Dozn and half of plates	00	10	00
4 pewter Quarts and 1 pint	00	06	00
A Knife Box Salt Box and frying Pan	00	03	06
2 Iron Spitts 2 Iron Plates & Warming pan	00	09	00
A Jack and Appurtenances	00	18	00
An Iron ffender 3 Brass Candlesticks & 3 Iron do	00	09	00
An Iron Crane and pot hooks 2 smoothing Irons	00	10	00
A Sauce pan Kettle & small looking Glass	00	05	00
2 Iron Potts	00	05	00

Big Parlour

A Writting Desk and Book Case	01	01	00
A Square Cupboard 6 Wood Chairs 1 round Table	00	08	00
A Lookg Glass and Map	00	05	00

Little Parlour

6 Wood Chairs 1 Elbow do and round Table	00	10	06

In the Shop

A Dresser wth 2 Drawers	00	04	00
A Counter wth 4 Drewers	00	06	00
A Cupboard wth Drawers	00	04	03

In the Passage

One Clock and Case	01	15	00

Best Chamber

1 ffeather Bed Bedstead & hanging & Quilt & Blankets	00	10	00
4 Chairs 1 stools a Chest Table and looking Glass	01	05	06

Little Chamber

1 ffeather Bed Bestead & hanging Coverlid & Blanketts	04	05	00
A small lookg Glass &c.	00	01	06

Over the Kitchen

| One Bed Bedsteads hangings Quilt & Blanketts | . | . | . | 03 | 15 | 00 |
| A Chest Close Stools & 2 Wood Chairs | . | . | . | . | 01 | 02 | 06 |

In the Cellar

3 Barrells and 2 Tubbs	.	.	.	.	.	00	18	00
Books Debts	.	.	.	.	.	.	65	00	00
.	.	.	.	.	.	.	.	96	09	09

Son John Palmer - £30
Brother Robert Palmer & Henry Onions of Dawley Green, Master Collier - rest of estate in trust for:
Daughter Abigail - for life my tenement in Madeley Wood at Lake Head which belonged to my father Robert Palmer & now in the possession of Edward Yates
Daughter Eleanor - life interest in land called the Tuckies held by lease from John Wase of Broseley
Daughter Mary - to enjoy income &c from Aston Leasow in parish of Madeley which I hold from Francis Phillips of Brockton, Salop, and have erected a house & other dwellings on it
Thomas Danks of Madeley Wood, father of my wife Mary left her life interest in house he dwelt in called the Old House; if it goes to Abigail, Elenor to have house at Lake Head

194. Richard Pritchard

Yeoman/shopkeeper of Coalbrookdale in Madeley, buried 10/III/1759. Inventory 24/III/1759 by Saml. Hallen and Jos. Hatton (both also witnessed the will) exhibited 27/VI/1759 for Hannah Prichard mother and executrix. Will 24/IX/1757 left her 'all shop goods and book debts and cash'.

Swanskins Linseys & flannens	.	.	.	.	.	02	12	00
Tamies fustians & checks	.	.	.	.	.	01	00	00
Hanckerchiefs buttons & thred	.	.	.	.	.	00	15	00
Cottens linnens & gartering	.	.	.	.	.	02	03	06
Counter & drawers	.	.	.	.	.	00	03	00
packthred & brushes	.	.	.	.	.	00	02	06
Stockings & caps	.	.	.	.	.	01	00	00
Coffee & tea	.	.	.	.	.	.	00	16	00
Childrens stays	.	.	.	.	.	.	00	05	00
Horse & sadle	.	.	.	.	.	.	03	00	00
Wearing apparel & Money	.	.	.	.	.	04	00	00
.	.	.	.	.	.	.	.	15	13	00

195. George Thomas

Of Coalbrookdale in Madeley, but apparently not buried there. Inventory (not dated) by Walter Parker (who also witnessed the will) and Will Dicken exhibited 8/VII/1760 by Mary Thomas relict and executrix. Will 5/I/1760 left his wife Mary the house garden and orchard in Coalbrookdale for life or until remarriage. After it was to be divided. His son George was to have the house orchard and garden to the south end of the house from the footpath at the upper end thereof to the brook at the bottom and his daughter Hannah Thomas the brewhouse or out kitchen adjoining the south end of the house and the garden to the hedge at the side of Walter Parkes garden from the footpath to the brook; the two to be divided from top to bottom in a straight line by quicksets but George was to have access to the pump in front of the brewhouse. The will of his father John Thomas who died in 1760 referred to the footpath from George's house through the ground of his other son John to the common way, stating that it was to be used as a footpath only.

Grate ffire shovel and Tongs	00	05	06
Pewter fframe and Pewter	01	00	00
a Table and Chairs	00	04	00
Candlesticks & small Iron Ware	00	02	00
In the Parlor 6 Chairs and a Table	00	07	06
In the Brewhouse one Iron Furnace and 3 Tubs	00	10	00
In the Cellar a Wood Horse and 4 Little Barrels	00	08	00
In the Room over the Kitchen a Bed and Hangings	01	10	00
2 Chairs and a Table	00	04	06
In the Room over the Parlor a Bed and Hangings	02	06	00
4 Chairs a Table and Looking Glass	00	10	00
A Chest and some Linnen	00	15	06
Wearing Apparel and Cash in Pocket	01	18	00
Old Lumber and Things unseen	00	05	06
	10	06	06

196. William Botteley

Collier/publican of Madeley Wood, buried 24/V/1762. Inventory (not dated) by Abraham Ford exhibited 23/VI/1762 by John Botteley brother in law and John Nicklass son in law executors. Will 4/IV/1762 referred to his children Thomas, James, Sarah Bottely, Joan and Margaret.

In the Kitchen
A Grate Dresser and other Furniture 03 10 00

In the Parlour
A table, Cupboard, Chairs, &c. 01 10 00

In the New Room
old Benches Shelves and other Lumber 01 00 00

In the Celler
six Barrells and two Stillings 01 05 00

In the Room over the Kitchen
Bed Coverlid Blankets Chest Chairs &c. 04 00 00

In the Room over the Parlour
Bed Coverlid Box &c. 02 10 00

In the Room over the New Room
Chest, Box, &c. 01 10 00

In the Brewhouse
Brewing Tubs and Benches 02 10 00

In the deceased Pockett 00 10 00

. . . . 18 05 00

Son Thomas b. 1736 - Kitchen, cellar & parlour, together with part of the garden belonging to the same, the kitchen, cellar and parlour being part of the dw ho wherein I now live, and garden to go or be parted from an outside door known by name of the little room door to a fill Board Tree at the bottom of the garden bounding to the brook opposite to Amram Styches's dwelling

Son James b. 1739 - Other part of the dwelling house, known as the little room, with the room over it and the brewhouse, with the other part of the garden bound on one side by Thomas Botheley's share and on other side to the Waste on the North.

Son Thomas - A little bed fixed under the window at the stairs head over the parlour

Son James - The other bed in the farther room known as the servant's bed, joining up to the hanging press

Daughter Sarah Botteley b. 1730 - 6 pewter dishes and 6 pewter plates, with a piece of new cloth for napkins not made, with a bed and all furniture thereto belonging in the chamber over the little room and the chest in the same

Daughters Joan b. 1728, Sarah and Margaret b. 1734 - All remaining household goods chattels & stock of drink equally

GLOSSARY

This glossary is designed simply to define words used in this this volume, although it draws on evidence from the large numbers of other Shropshire probate inventories that have been transcribed and analysed. The nature of the language used in inventories, and definitions of words used in specialised contexts are discussed elsewhere, notably in Trinder, B., 'The Wooden Horse in the Cellar', in Arkell, T., Evans, N. and Goose, N., 2000, *Till Death do us Part*, Oxford, Leopard's Head Press. Specialist terms relating to mercers and dyers are defined in Cox, J. and Trinder, B., 1980, *Yeomen and Colliers in Telford*, Chichester: Phillimore. The glossary includes definitions for all words likely to be unfamiliar, and we have tried to cover every phonetic variation in spelling which is capable of causing confusion.

Andiron.—In the plural, a set of moveable iron plates used to contract the area of a grate and support logs. In the West Midlands, a pair of fire dogs fixed together with horizontal bars to form a grate.

Apry ware.—Napery ware, i.e. linens.

Archill.—A dyestuff, the lichen *rocella tinctoria*, or orchilla-weed, producing a violet dye.

Argill.—Any clay-like substance, but in the context of a clothier's inventory probably alum, used as a mordant in dyeing, or possibly argol, the crude cream of tartar deposited during the fermentation of wine, used as an addition to mordanting baths with alum to brighten colours.

Barm tub.—A tub used for the fermenting stage of the brewing process.

Beer/Pillow Beer.—A pillow case, or possibly a cloth in which to wrap a pillow.

Bellis.—Bellows.

Bing.—A receptacle for storing grain or a manger.

Bodies.—Boddice, a pair of stays or corsets.

Bond lase.—Boned lace (i.e. lace made with a bobbin).

Bouch.—Bucket.

Bow case.—A cupboard set in wainscotting.

Brandard.—A three-legged stand in a fireplace on which utensils without legs were placed.

Broach.—A narrow tapering iron rod or pin, especially the rod on a spit.

Cadis (Caddis).—A worsted yarn, or ribbons made from such yarn, used for garters and girdles.
Calico.—A light cotton cloth, on which designs were often printed, originally imported from India but made in England by the 17th century.
Chopp.—Shop.
Close stool.—A commode.
Cobbards/Cobbarts/Cobirons.—Irons which supported a spit, usually two iron bars with knobs at one end, which rested on the back of the grate. Sometimes used to mean andirons, and sometimes a kind of cradle for firewood.
Cock.—Tap.
Cooler.—A staved tub, particularly one used to cool the wort in brewing, or in the dairy to receive warm milk.
Coopery ware.—Items made by a cooper.
Counterfeit.—An item made of a base metal, usually pewter, chased with a pattern or wrought.
Cowpery ware.—Coopery ware.
Cratch.—A hurdle-like construction, which might be a manger mounted on a wall, a frame hung from a kitchen ceiling from which joints of bacon were suspended, or a frame to which teasles were attached in finishing woollen cloth.
Creeper.—A small iron dog, of which a pair would be placed between the andirons in a grate. Alternatively a small iron frying pan with three legs.

Dale.—Deal.
Dead-eye.—A block with three holes driled in it used for extending the shrouds (qv) on a sailing ship.
Delphware.—Earthenware, usually of good quality, of the style customarily made in the Dutch city of Delft, but in practice usually made in England.
Dimity.—A stout cotton cloth, woven with raised stripes and fancy figures.
Drall.—Probably a variation of *thrall*, a term which usually signifies a stand designed to tilt a barrel, which could also have applied to one which tilted a pot.
Dredge.—Mixed grain—usually oats and barley, sometimes malted for brewing.

Elfatt(e).—Ale vat.
Erwing.—Yarn Wind (qv).

(F)fat(t).—Vat.
Fellies. Segments of the exterior rim of a wheel.
Fenering.—Veneering.
Ferret.—A stout tape of cotton or silk, used for garters amongst other purposes.
Furnace.—A large metal pot, particularly one used for brewing, dyeing or boiling, and usually set in masonry.
Fustic(k).—A dyeing material. Old fustic is *Morus tinctorus* or *Chlorphora Tinctoria*, imported from the Americas, used on wool and mordanted with copper and iron

to give fast olive yellow, combined with logwood, mader and indigo to produce olive brown and, ultimately, black. Young fustic, *Ctonus Coggyria,* actually a much older material, produced orangy yellow when mordanted with alum or tin but these were not fast to light and its use was discontinued as old fustic became available.

Gaun/Gawn.—A ladle, particularly used in dairies, originally one that held a gallon.
Gears.—Heddles, the wires through which warp is passed on a loom; or a horse's harness, either for ploughing or haulage.
Gine.—Join, Joined or Joint (qv).
Goanr.—Probably a gallon.
Gunn.—Gaun.

Hackle.—Hatchell (qv).
Handiron.—Andiron.
Handle cratch.—A frame in which teasles were set for raising the nap on woollen cloth before it was sheared.
Hatchell.—A comb-like instrument used to separate the long and short fibres of flax.
Hawser.—A tow line for a ship.
Hetchell.—See Hatchell
Hempot.—Hamper.
Hogshead.—A cask with capacity for 48 gallons of ale or 54 gallons of beer (i.e. 1½ barrels), but a hogshead of wine contained 63 gallons.
Hogshit.—Hogshead.
Holland.—Linen cloth, usually of high quality, of a type that originally came from the Netherlands.
Homber.—Hammer.
Hoop.—A tub or half-barrel, particularly one used for measuring quantities, in Shropshire usually a peck.
Hopper.—A basket in which a sower carries seed.
Howlster.—Holster.
Hurden.—A coarse linen or hempen cloth made from the hurds, the pieces of flax or hemp separated by combing with a heckell.

Inkle.—A kind of linen tape, or the thread from which it was made.

Jersey.—Synonym for worsted.
Join/Joined/Joint.—Furniture made by a joiner.

Kedger.—A small anchor.
Kilderkin/Kinderkin.—A cask holding 16 gallons of ale or 18 gallons of beer.
Kinching.—A loop or bundle of yarn.

Latten ware.—A form of brass.
Lodging bed.—A bed for guests at an inn or similar establishment.
Logwood.—A dyestuff, the heartwood of *haematoxylon campechianum,* imported from the Caribbean, ground in logwood mills, and used to dye cloth black.
Long wheel.—A spinning wheel used for wool.

Maid.—An object on which other objects are placed—the term can refer *inter alia* to a clothes horse, or to trivets.
Malt mill.—A device, usually operated by hand, used for crushing malt before brewing.
Mandrell.—A pick, sharp-pointed at each end, used in getting coal.
Marment/ Marmet.—An iron cooking utensil, smaller than the ordinary cooking 'pot'.
Maslin.—A kind of brass, or mixed grain, muncorn or dredge.
Maundrell.—Mandrell (qv).
Mitt.—A half-barrel or tub, often used in a dairy.
Muncorn.—Mixed grain, a winter crop, usually a mixture of wheat and rye intended to produce flour for bread-making.

Niggard.—A false bottom for a grate, intended to reduce fuel consumption.
Noggs, Noggen, Noggin.—The coarse fibres of flax or hemp.

Paddle stave.—A spade-shaped implement used in the mashing stage of the brewing process.
Perkettery.— Purgatory (qv).
Pickell/Pickfield/Pike evil.—A pitchfork.
Piggin.—A small wooden vessel or pail with one stave longer than the rest to serve as a ladle.
Pillion.—A saddle, especially a light one for a woman, or a special cushion attached to the rear of an ordinary saddle to enable a second person to ride a horse.
Pipe.—A large cask containing 126 gallons of wine, 128 gallons of ale or 144 gallons of beer.
Pish.—Parish.
Placks.—Planks.
Porringer.—A basin, especially one used for porridge.
Portmanteau.—A trunk for clothing.
Posnet.—A small metal cooking pot with a handle and three feet.
Potash.—A crude form of potassium carbonate used for several purposes in finishing woollen cloth.
Pottinger.—Porringer (qv).
Powdering tubb.—A tub for salting or pickling meat.
Press.—A cupboard usually a large one with shelves. The term is sometimes synonymous with cupboard. A hanging press is a wardrobe.

GLOSSARY

Purgatory.—A receptacle for ashes beneath or in front of a fire.

Quill Wheel.—A wheel for winding weft for a loom.

Rather.—A cart rail or rathe.
Riddle.—A sieve.
Rindle ware.—Possibly items made from bark.

Sagen.—Seggen (qv).
Say.—A fabric resembling serge, often partly of silk.
Schlice.—Slice (qv).
Scotch cloth.—A cheap fabric resembling lawn, by repute originally made of nettle fibres.
Scribbling.—The first stage in the treatment of fleece wool, during which the fibres are straightened before the process of carding can begin.
Segg/Seggen.—Made from rushes.
Shroud.—In this collection, a set of ropes attached to the head of the mast of a sailing ship which relieved the lateral strain on the mast, but more commonly a sheet in which a corpse was wrapped.
Shute.—Suit.
Skellet/Skillet.—In the north of England a metal cooking vessel, usually with three feet and a long handle, but in Shropshire usually a utensil made of beaten brass or copper, without legs, and more akin to a saucepan or frying pan.
Skimmer.—An iron implement for taking ash from a hearth, or, more commonly, a metal spoon for taking fat from a boiling pot or for use in the dairy.
Skormer.—Skimmer (qv).
Slice.—A fire shovel.
Slipping.—A skein of yarn.
Slob bench.—A working surface on which processes involving liquids could be carried out.
Specialty.—In relation to debts—recoverable at law.
Sperate/Sperial.—Debts of which there is hope of recovery. Sometimes confused with specialty (qv).
Spig(g)ot.—A wooden pin used to stop the venthole of a barrel or cask.
Standing bed.—A substantial bed, usually, by implication, a four-poster, and usually with space beneath for a truckle bed.
Steel Mill.—A malt mill (qv) but could also mean a device for producing a spark by rotating a steel disc against a flint.
Stilling.—A rack for barrels.
Stuff.—A cloth with no nap or pile, usually light in weight, and often dyed, patterned or printed, made in Kidderminster, amongst many other places in the period covered by these inventories.
Stun/Stund.—A half-barrel or tub used in brewing or in the dairy.

Sway.—A crane over a fire.

Swift.—A lightweight reel, usually of adjustable diameter upon which skeins of yarn can be placed in order to be wound off.

Taffity (i.e. Taffeta).—A name that means different kinds of fabric at different times. In the 17th century it usually referred to silks used for ribbons. Taffeta of whatever kind usually had warp and weft of different colours.

Teasle.—The burr-like head of *dipsacus fullonum* used in finishing woollen cloth.

Thrave.—A measure of straw or of unthreshed grain, usually either 12 or 24 bundles.

Tickneyware.—Coarse earthenware in the style of that made at Ticknall, Derbyshire.

Torterie/Tortree.—An item of horse harness.

Treen.—Wooden ware, usually turned—i.e. dishes, plates &c.

Truckle bed/Trundle bed.—A low bed, usually on casters, often stored when out of use under a standing bed (qv).

Tuger ware.—Probably items made by tugging—i.e. wickerware or basketware.

Tundish/Tuning dish/Tunning dish.—A funnel, usually of wood, used in brewing or in a dairy.

Turnell.—A half barrel or tub, sometimes oval-shaped.

Vallyes.—Fellies (qv).

Warping bar.—A roller on which warp yarn is measured when ready for weaving.

Weanling.—An animal, usually a calf, in the process of weaning.

Weeting Vat.—A wetting vat used in malting.

Which/Witch.—A wooden bin for grain.

Windlace/Windlace/Winlass.—A hand-operated winding drum, which in the context of this book might be used for raising minerals from a pit, or for lowering and raising the mast of a sailing ship.

Worsted.—Yarn or cloth made from long staple wool which is combed rather than carded.

Yarn blades/Yarn winds/Yarwingles.—Pairs of blades for winding yarn.

Yealing Vat.—Ale Vat.

Yithords.—A crop, perhaps vetches, or possibly *yether*, a variant of *yedder*, an osier, or a pliant rod used for binding a hedge.

BIBLIOGRAPHY

1. Works on probate records and other archives, and published collections of inventories

Ambler, R.W. and Watkinson, B. and L., *Farmers and Fishermen: the Probate Inventories of the ancient parish of Clee, South Humberside, 1536-1744* (1985), Hull: Centre for Regional and Local History, University of Hull.

Bewdley Historical Research Group, *Bewdley in its Golden Age: Life in Bewdley 1660-1760* (1991), Bewdley: Bewdley Historical Research Group.

Brown, A. and Cox, N., *Husbandry and Huswifery: Life and Work in Cressage c1535-c1750* (1993), Nottingham: Nottingham Trent University in association with the University of Wolverhampton.

Brinkworth, E.R.C. and Gibson, J.S.W., *Banbury Wills and Inventories Part I: 1621-1650* (1985), Banbury: Banbury Historical Society.

Brinkworth, E.R.C. and Gibson, J.S.W., *Banbury Wills and Inventories Part II: 1621-1650* (1976), Banbury: Banbury Historical Society.

Collet-White, J., *Inventories of Bedfordshire Country Houses 1714-1830* (1995), Bedford: Bedfordshire Record Society.

Cox, N., 'The Distribution of Retailing Tradesmen in North Shropshire 160-1750', *Journal of Regional and Local Studies,* vol. 13 (1993), pp.4-22.

Cox, N. and J., 'Probate Inventories: the Legal Background, Part I', *The Local Historian,* vol. 16 (1984), pp. 133-45.

Cox, N. and J., 'Probate Inventories: the Legal Background, Part II', *The Local Historian,* vol. 16 (1984), pp. 217-28.

Cox, N. and J., 'Valuations in Probate Inventories: Part I', *The Local Historian,* vol. 16 (1985), pp. 467-78.

Cox, N. and J., 'Valuations in Probate Inventories: Part II', *The Local Historian,* vol. 17 (1986), pp. 85-100.

Cox, N. and J., 'Probate 1500-1800: a system in transition' in Arkell, T., Evans, N. and Goose, N., *Till Death do us Part* (forthcoming - 2000), Oxford: Leopard's Head Press.

Hall, E., *Michael Warton of North Bar House, Beverley: an Inventory of his possessions with some other inventories for the area of Beverley and Hull* (1986), Hull: University of Hull.

Holman, J. and Herridge, M., *Index of Surrey Probate Inventories 16th - 19th Centuries* (1986), Epsom: Domestic Buildings Research Group (Surrey).

Johnson, J.A., *Probate Inventories of Lincoln Citizens 1661-1714* (1991), Lincoln: Lincolnshire Record Society.

Lansberry, H.C.F., *Sevenoaks Wills and Inventories in the Reign of Charles II* (1988), Maidstone; Kent Archaeological Society.

Machin, R., *Probate Inventories and Manorial Excepts of Chetnole, Leight and Yetminster* (1976), Bristol: University of Bristol Department of Extra-mural Studies.

Matthews, G.F., *Shropshire probates in the Prerogative Court of Canterbury 1700-49* (1928).

Moore, J.S., *The Goods and Chattels of our Forefathers: Frampton Cotterell and District Probate Inventories 1539-1804* (1976), Chichester: Phillimore.

Perkins, E.R., *Village Life from Wills and Inventories: Clayworth Parish 1670-1710* (1979), Nottingham: Centre for Local History, University of Nottingham.

Priestley, U. and Fenner, A., *Shops and Shopkeepers in Norwich 1660-1730* (1985), Norwich: Centre for East Anglian Studies.

Reed, M., *Buckinghamshire Probate Inventories 1661-1714* (1988), Aylesbury: Buckinghamshire Record Society.

Spavold, J., *In the Name of God, Amen: Everyday Life in South Derbyshire 1535-1700* (1992), Ashby de la Zouch: South Derbyshire Local History Research Group.

Steer, F.W., *Farm and Cottage Inventories of Mid-Essex 1635-1749* (1969), Chichester: Phillimore.

Swinburn, H., *A Brief Treatise on Testaments and Last Wills* (1640), London: Company of Stationers.

Tate, W.E., *The Parish Chest*, 3rd edition (1969), Cambridge: Cambridge University Press.

Trinder, B., 'La vie d'une région en cours d'industrialisation: le Bassin houiller du Shropshire 1660-1760', in CILAC, *L'étude et la mise en valeur du Patrimoine Industrial* (1985), Paris: Éditions du Centre national de la Recherche Scientifique.

Trinder, B., 'The Wooden Horse in the Cellar', in Arkell, T., Evans, N., and Goose, N., *Till Death do us Part* (forthcoming - 2000), Oxford: Leopard's Head Press.

Trinder, B. and Cox, J., *Yeomen and Colliers in Telford: the Probate Inventories of Dawley, Lilleshall, Wellington and Wrockwardine* (1980), Chichester: Phillimore.

Vaisey, D.G., *The probate inventories of Lichfield and District 1568-1680* (1969), Stafford: Staffordshire Record Society.

Vickers, N., *A Yorkshire Town in the Eighteenth Century: the Probate Inventories of Whitby 1700-1800* (1986), Studley: Brewin.

Weatherill, L., 'Probate Inventories and Consumer Behaviour in England 1660-1740' in Martin, G.H. and Spufford, P., *The Records of the Nation* (1990), London: British Records Society.

2. Works on material culture and industrial communities

Braudel, F., *Civilisation and Capitalism 15th-18th Century, I, The Structures of Everyday Life: the Limits of the Possible* (1981), London: Fontana.

Braudel, F., *Civilisation and Capitalism 15th-18th Century, II, The Wheels of Commerce* (1982), London: Fontana.

Braudel, F., *Civilisation and Capitalism 15th-18th Century, III, The Perspective of the World* (1984), London: Fontana.

Brears, P., *The Kitchen Catalogue* (1979), York: Castle Museum.

Brears, P. and Harrison, S., *The Dairy Catalogue* (1979), York: Castle Museum.

Brewer, J. and Porter, R., eds., *Consumption and the World of Goods* (1994), London: Routledge.

Eden, G., ed., *The Recipe Book 1659-1672 of Archdale Palmer ... of Wanlip ... Leicestershire* (1985), Wymondham (Leics.): Sycamore.

Elliott, D.J., *Shropshire Clock and Watchmakers* (1979), Chichester: Phillimore.

Evans, C., *Labyrinth of Flames: Work and Social Conflict in early industrial Merthyr Tydfil* (1993), Cardiff: University of Wales Press.

Flinn, M.W., *The History of the British Coal Industry II, 1700-1830* (1984), Oxford: Clarendon Press.

Garner, F.H. and Archer, M., *English Delftware*, 2nd edition (1972), London: Faber.

Gloag, J., *English Furniture*, 6th edition (1972), London: Black.

Gough, R., *The History of Myddle*, ed. D. Hey (1981), Harmondsworth: Penguin.

Hatcher, J., *The History of the British Coal Industry I, Before 1700* (1993), Oxford: Clarendon Press.

Hatcher, J. and Barker, T.C., *A History of British Pewter* (1974), London: Longman.

Hey, D., *The Fiery Blades of Hallamshire: Sheffield and its Neighbours 1660-1740* (1991), Leicester: Leicester University Press.

Holme, R., *The Academy of Armoury* (1688), Chester: privately published.

Homer, R.F. and Hall, D.W., *Provincial pewterers: a study of the craft in the West Midlands and Wales* (1985), Chichester: Phillimore.

Hudson, P. and King, S., 'Rural Industrialising Township and Urban Links in Eighteenth Century Yorkshire', in, Clark, P. and Corfield, P., *Industry and Urbanisation in Eighteenth Century England* (1994), Leicester: Centre for Urban History, University of Leicester, pp.41-79.

Hussey, D.P., Milne, G.J., Wakelin, A.P. and Wanklyn, M.D.G., *The Gloucester Coastal Port Books 1575-1765: A Summary* (1995), Wolverhampton: University of Wolverhampton School of Humanities and Social Sciences.

Ladurie, E. Le Roy, *Montaillou: Cathars and Catholics in a French village 1294-1324* (1980), Harmondsworth: Penguin.

Malmgreen, G., *Silk Town: Industry and Culture in Macclesfield 1750-1835* (1985), Hull: Hull University Press.

Owen, H., *Two Centuries of Ceramic Art in Bristol* (1873), London: Bell: Daldry.

Pountney, W.J., *The Old Bristol Potters* (1920), Bristol: Arrowsmith.

Prior, M., *Fisher Row: Fishermen, Bargemen and Canal Boatmen in Oxford 1500-1900* (1982), Oxford: Clarendon Press.

Roberts, H.D., *Downhearth to Bar Grate; an illustrated account of the evolution in cooking due to the use of coal instead of wood* (1987), Avebury: Wiltshire Record Society.

Rowlands, M., *Masters and Men in the Small Metalware Trades of the West Midlands* (1975), Manchester: Manchester University Press.

Sambrook, P., *Country House Brewing in England 1500-1900* (1996), London: Hambledon.

Spufford, M., *Small Books and Pleasant Histories: Popular Fiction and its Readership in seventeenth century England* (1981), Cambridge: Cambridge University Press.

Spufford, M., *The Great Reclothing of Rural England: Petty Chapmen and their wares in the seventeenth century,* London: Hambledon.

Stratton, M. and Trinder, B., *Industrial England* (1997), London: Batsford.

Thomas, K., *Man and the Natural World: Changing Attitudes in England 1500-1800* (1984), Harmondsworth: Penguin.

Thompson, E.P., *The Making of the English Working Class* (1963), London: Gollancz.

Thompson, E.P., *Customs in Common* (1993), London: Penguin.

Trinder, B., *The Blackwell Encyclopedia of Industrial Archaeology* (1992), Oxford: Blackwell.

Trinder, B., 'The Archaeology of the British Food Industry 1660-1960: A Preliminary Survey', *Industrial Archaeology Review,* vol.15 (1993), pp. 119-39.

Trinder, B., 'Revolutions in the Food Industry', in Canadian Society for Industrial Heritage, *From Industry to Industrial Heritage: Proceedings of the Ninth International Conference on the Conservation of the Industrial Heritage,*

1994 (1998), Ottawa: National Museum of Science and Technology, pp.111-18.

Turner, T., *The Diary of Thomas Turner 1754-1765* ed. D.Vaisey (1984), Oxford: Oxford University Press.

3. Books and articles relating to the Coalbrookdale Coalfield

Alfrey, J. and Clark, K., *The Landscape of Industry: patterns of change in the Ironbridge Gorge* (1993), London: Routledge.

Bagshaw, S., *History, Gazetteer and Directory of Shropshire* (1851), Sheffield: Bagshaw.

Cossons, N. and Trinder, B., *The Iron Bridge: Symbol of the Industrial Revolution* (1979), Bradford-on-Avon: Moonraker.

Cox, N., 'Imagination and innovation of an Industrial Pioneer: the First Abraham Darby', *Industrial Archaeology Review*, vol. 12 (1990), pp. 127-44.

Fiennes, C., *The Journeys of Celia Fiennes* ed. C.Morris (1947), London: Cresset.

Forest, H.E., *The Old Houses of Wenlock* (1914), Shrewsbury: Wilding.

Green, C., *Severn Traders: The West Country Trows and Trowmen* (1999), Lydney: Black Dwarf.

Hayman, R., 'Lloyds Engine House, Ironbridge', *Transactions of the Shropshire Archaeological Society*, 4th series, vol. 72 (1997), pp. 38-51.

Higgins, D., Morriss, R. and Trueman, M., *The Broseley Pipeworks: an archaeological and historical evaluation* (1988), Telford: Ironbridge Gorge Museum Trust.

Jones, A., *Finds Tuypologies; Pottery I: The Coarse Earthenwares* (1988), Telford: Ironbridge Gorge Museum Trust.

Jones, A., Higgins, D. and Truman, M., *11 Benthall Lane* (1987), Telford: Ironbridge Gorge Museum Trust.

Jones, K., Hunt, M.W., Malam, J. and Trinder, B., 'Holywell Lane; A Squatter Community in the Shropshire Coalfield', *Industrial Archaeology Review*, vol. 6 1982), pp.163-85.

Muter, G., *The Buildings of an Industrial Community: Ironbridge and Coalbrookdale* (1979), Chichester: Phillimore.

National Trust, *Benthall Hall, Shropshire* (1965), London: Country Life.

O'Riordan, C., 'Sequestration and Social Upheaval: Madeley, Shropshire and the English Revolution', *West Midland Studies*, vol. 18 (1985), pp. 21-31.

Powell, J. and Vanns, M., *Archive Photograph Series: South Telford* (1995), Stroud: Chalford.

Randall, J., *Handbook to the Severn Valley Railway* (1863), Madeley: privately published.

Randall, J., *Broseley and its Surroundings* (1879), Madeley: Randall.

Randall, J., *A History of Madeley* (1880), Madeley: Wrekin Echo.
Smith, S.B., *A View from the Iron Bridge* (1979), London: Thames and Hudson.
Stamper, P., *The Farmer feeds us all* (1989), Shrewsbury: Shropshire Books.
Stamper, P., *Historic parks of Shropshire* (1995), Shrewsbury: Shropshire Books.
Trinder, B., ed., *A Description of Coalbrookdale in 1801 A.D.* (1970), Telford: Ironbridge Gorge Museum Trust,
Trinder, B., *The Industrial Revolution in Shropshire*, 2nd edition (1981), Chichester: Phillimore.
Trinder, B., *The Darbys of Coalbookdale*, 2nd edition (1992), Chichester: Phillimore.
Trinder, B., *The Most Extraordinary District in the World*, 2nd edition (1988), Chichester: Phillimore.
Trinder, B., *The Industrial Archaeology of Shropshire* (1996), Chichester: Phillimore.
Trinder, B., 'The First Iron Bridges', *Industrial Archaeology Review*, vol. 3 (1979), pp. 112-121.
Trinder, B., 'Coalport Bridge: a Study in Historical Interpretation', *Industrial Archaeology Review*, vol. 3 (1979), pp. 153-57.
Trinder, B., 'The Shropshire Coalfield', in, Clark, P. and Corfield, P., *Industry and Urbanisation in Eighteenth Century England* (1994), Leicester: Centre for Urban History, University of Leicester, pp.33-40.
Victoria History of Shropshire, Vol. IV, Agriculture (1989), Oxford: Oxford University Press.
Victoria History of Shropshire, Vol.X, Wenlock, Upper Corvedale and the Stretton Hills (1999), Oxford: Oxford University Press.
Victoria History of Shropshire, Vol. XI, Telford (1985), Oxford: Oxford University Press.
Wanklyn, M.D.G., 'Industrial Development in the Ironbridge Gorge before Abraham Darby', *West Midland Studies*, vol. 15 (1982), pp. 3-7.
Wanklyn, M.D.G., 'John Weld of Willey: Estate Management 1631-1660', *West Midlands Studies*, vol.4 (1970-71), pp.63-71.
Wanklyn, M.D.G., 'Urban Revival in Early Modern England: Bridgnorth and the River Trade 1660-1800', *Midland History*, vol. 18 (1993), pp.37-64.

INDEX OF SUBJECTS AND PLACES

Figures in italics (e.g. *92*) refer to inventories. Other figures refer to pages in the Introduction.

Ackleton, Worfield, Shropshire, *162*
Acreages of crops, 49, *68*
Alabaster, 26, 28
Ale, *26, 36, 68, 69, 102, 128, 135*
Ale vats, *58, 94, 103*
Aliases, 12
Anchors, *26, 83*
Andirons, *103, 139, 163, 166*; brass, 7, *182*
Annuities, 54
Anvils, *6, 36, 52, 73, 152, 165, 192*
Appraisers, 11-13
Apry ware, *5, 29, 35, 151*
Argill, *59*
Ash: boards, *13*; chairs, *19, 98, 137*
Ashballs, *104*
Augers, *81, 132*
Axes, *19, 20, 33, 56, 124, 132, 134, 161, 171, 187, 189*

Backhouses, *47, 106*
Back rooms, *123*
Bacon, *23, 43, 68, 102, 116, 122, 124, 125, 128, 144, 145, 162, 183, 187*
Bacon cratches, *94, 182*
Bags, *162, 171, 183*
  of malt, *42*
Baking, 59
Bakehouses, *139*
Bank, money in, 16, *154*
Bars, *124*
Barges (and vessels—*see also* boats, trows), *26, 29, 30, 37, 45, 75, 83, 85, 96, 100, 109, 144, 152, 158, 160, 176*; small, 7; worn-out, *83*; *Edward, 176*; *Elizabeth, 34*; *Jonathan, 142*; *Joyce, 48*; Nicholls, *164*; *Primrose, 34*; *Thomas, 142*; *Walton, 48*
Barge chests, *26, 27, 96*
Barge owners, *see* Trowmen
Bark, *86*
Barley, *9, 10, 13,* 50-51, *53, 80, 119, 122, 124, 125, 126, 127, 129, 130, 144, 166, 168, 169, 171, 183*
Barm tub, *13, 94*
Barns, *7, 9, 13, 53, 68, 79, 80, 86, 119, 122, 123, 125, 126, 127, 130, 133, 151, 162, 165, 166, 183*; corn barns, *124, 129*; hay barn, *129*
Barrels, *5, 6, 7, 8, 12, 13, 16, 17, 18, 21, 26, 36, 36, 39, 46, 47, 48, 56, 58, 60, 64, 66, 67, 69, 75, 76, 82, 84, 102, 103, 110, 113, 114, 115, 116, 119, 120, 121, 122, 124, 125, 126, 128, 131, 133, 135, 136, 137, 138, 140, 145, 148, 155, 157, 161, 162, 165, 169, 170, 171, 173, 174, 177, 181, 187, 189, 190, 191, 193, 195, 196*; with drink, *16, 69*; damnified, *14*; for winding pit, *81*; for winding well, *131*; for windlass, *85*
Barrows, *70*
Basins, wooden, *82* (*see also* Brass, Pewter)
Baskets; *70*; domestic, *33, 57, 124, 183*; at mines, *20, 58, 92*; butchers' baskets, *135*; clothes baskets, *187*; hand baskets, *124, 187*; round handle baskets, *179*; straw baskets, *129*; twiggen baskets, *10, 140*; *see also* Flasket, Which
Basketmakers, 36
Basters, *179*
Basting ladles and spoons, *19, 36, 114, 125, 155, 157, 174, 180*; brass, *85, 100*; iron, *46*
Beam (with scales), *10, 112, 152, 189*
Beanfet, *107*
Beans, *139*
Beds, 64-66; board, *49*; chaff, *10, 23, 28, 30, 31, 79, 91, 118, 121, 125, 129, 130, 135, 139, 149, 150, 157, 174, 187*; feather, *2, 3, 5, 7, 8, 9, 10, 13, 19, 22, 23, 25, 28, 30, 31, 33, 36, 42, 46, 48, 57, 59, 60, 65, 69, 71, 72, 73, 75, 76, 80, 83, 84, 85, 87, 91, 92, 94, 95, 96, 97, 98, 100, 102, 103, 106, 107, 111, 113, 114, 116, 118, 121, 122,*

341

123, 124, 125, 127, 128, 129, 130, 139, 143, 149, 150, 153, 155, 160, 162, 163, 167, 169, 171, 173, 175, 176, 177, 179, 182, 184, 186, 187, 188, 189, 190, 191, 193; feathers, with weight given, 79; flock, 7, 8, 9, 14, 19, 22, 30, 33, 34, 36, 37, 40, 46, 48, 58, 59, 60, 76, 79, 91, 92, 100, 107, 129, 134, 143, 157, 161, 167, 173, 175, 176, 177, 178, 183, 185, 186, 188, 191; folding, 162; high, 51; lodging, 6, 12, 65; low, 51; low truckel, 143; servants', 47, 151, 171; standing, 3; standing without any tester, 143; truckel, 3, 25, 34, 47, 51, 53, 76, 79, 86, 115, 118, 119, 120, 121, 158
Bed chambers, 162
Bedsteads: half-headed, 34, 44, 76, 142, 153, 157, 164; half-headed joined, 57, 121; half-tester, 156; joined, 57, 76, 116, 120, 142, 144, 151, 152, 153, 158, 164; lumber, 98; mean, 65; plain, 5, 149; sap, 179
Bed ticks, 49, 131
Beef, 68, 116, 122, 124, 125, 128, 145, 183
Beer, 60, 162
Bees, 40, 49, 170
Bellows: domestic, 13, 19, 30, 47, 59, 145, 149, 161, 165, 171, 180, 182, 183, 187; smiths', 6, 52, 73, 152, 160, 192
Belt (for sword), 161
Bend ware, 82
Benthall (Shropshire), 5, 1-21, 79, 144; church, 3
Best chamber, 182
Bewdley (Worcestershire), 34, 144
Bibles, 19, 50, 94
Bills (i.e. tools, *see also* Forest bills, Hedging bills), 33, 80, 161, 171, 187
Bings, 13
Blacksmiths, 6, 34-5, 52, 125, 152, 160, 192
Blankets, 3, 7, 9, 10, 13, 19, 22, 30, 34, 40, 42, 46, 53, 55, 57, 58, 59, 60, 71, 73, 75, 79, 80, 84, 85, 94, 95, 97, 98, 100, 103, 107, 113, 115, 118, 121, 131, 134, 139, 149, 150, 161, 166, 167, 169, 171, 173, 174, 177, 178, 179, 180, 183, 184, 185, 187, 188, 193, 196
Blanketing, 185
Blocks (in rigging), 114
Blue room, 87
Boards, 13, 35, 37, 58, 94, 98, 139, 178, 189; for use by glazier, 89; for use by pipemaker, 84; *see also* Dubbing boards, Sheer boards, Planks
Boats, 12, 18, 25, 26, 101, 176; fishing boat, 143; stock boat, 182
Boddices, 23

Boilers, 12, 16, 19, 36, 54, 59, 66, 78, 80, 82, 88, 91, 116, 133, 135, 166; iron, 106, 110, 137, 182
Bolsters, 2, 10, 13, 19, 42, 46, 48, 44, 49, 65, 71, 76, 91, 96, 97, 98, 100, 101, 102, 106, 107, 115, 121, 122, 129, 131, 139, 143, 146, 149, 150, 156, 161, 167, 171, 174, 179, 180, 183, 184, 186, 187, 191; Chaff, 139; feather, 5, 7, 34, 57, 79, 94, 95, 102, 103, 111, 113, 116, 118, 124, 139, 149; flock, 34, 79, 116
Bolts (for ropemaking), 189
Bonds, 3, 7, 25, 32, 35, 38, 39, 41, 46, 73, 79, 120, 175
Book cases, 193
Books (*see also* Bibles), 6, 19, 22, 47, 51, 56, 62, 63, 67, 70, 74, 79, 91, 123, 124, 144, 152, 156, 158, 163, 164, 166, 169, 176, 183, 188; studies of, 41, 162
Boots, 120, 187
Boring benches, bits, rods, 98, 141, 165
Bottles, 119, 146; glass, 13, 41, 55, 89, 91, 103, 106, 111, 146, 156, 164, 176, 183, 188; wooden, 79, 80, 119, 125, 174
Bouches, boucks, 118, 132
Bow case, 115
Bow haulers, 27-28
Bowls, 99, 113, 119, 124, 171; milk bowls, 98, 119, 121, 125, 129, 187
Bowyer, 43, 148
Box, with linen, 67
Box of drawers, 166
Box grate, 162
Box irons, 94, 100, 103, 171, 180, 182, 183
Box over the table, 161
Brake, 189
Brandards, 13, 149
Brasil, 59
Brass (kettles, pans, pots, *passim*) 67; andirons, 7, 182; basting spoons, 36, 59, 80, 85, 100, 102, 174, 182, 183, 191; brewing kettles, 42; box, 191; candlesticks, 19, 21, 30, 40, 56, 67, 75, 85, 89, 94, 103, 115, 124, 126, 127, 129, 139, 148, 163, 166, 171, 183, 184, 187, 193; cauldron, 148; chafing dishes, 59, 122, 126, 127; clock, 151; dish-stand, 184; dredger, 182; fender, 182; furnace, 16, 98, 103, 131, 164; jack, 101, 103; knobs on grate, 124; ladles, 7, 60, 120, 187; mortars and pestles, 19, 30, 139, 183; old, 172, 186; pepper boxes, 182, 191; posnets, 120, 161; saucepans, 111, 182; scales, 64; skilletts, 126, 127, 186; skimmers, 7, 91, 102, 115, 120, 174, 182, 183, 187; snuffers, 59, 182, 183; warming pans, 46, 56, 59, 60, 73, 85, 90, 100, 102, 103, 120, 128, 131, 133, 182

INDEX OF SUBJECTS AND PLACES 343

Brassfounder, 22, *172*
Bread, 50, 78, *95*; plate to draw bread, *162*
Breeches, *161, 179*
Brewhouses, *10, 12, 13, 21, 53, 58, 65, 67, 69,* 75-79, *76, 77, 80, 85, 86, 87, 91, 94, 95, 98, 101, 102, 103, 110, 119, 136, 151, 164, 166, 171, 173, 174, 176, 179, 182, 183, 187, 191, 195, 196*
Brewing, 76-78
Brewing stunds, *42, 138, 155, 157*
Brewing furnaces, *see* Furnaces
Brewing tubs, *10, 33, 53, 67, 83, 100, 114, 125, 130, 131, 137, 161, 174, 183, 196*
Brewing vessels, *13, 17, 25, 28, 47, 57, 60, 66, 69, 86, 87, 107, 122, 136, 145, 159, 169, 175, 176*
Bricks, *13*, 23, *81, 119, 146*
Bridles, *13, 36, 51, 86, 94, 120, 147, 168*
Bridgnorth, Shropshire, 28, 30, 33, 42, 71
Bristol, *26,* 28-29, 67
Bristol ware, *182*
Broaches, *7, 8, 16, 28, 29, 30, 31, 36, 37, 48, 53, 58, 59, 60, 64, 116, 120, 125, 126, 127, 128, 129, 133, 155, 157*; iron, *56, 57, 59, 115, 122, 148, 149, 166, 174*
Broilers, *179, 188*
Broom hooks, *19, 80, 192*
Broseley, 2-5, 7, *15, 22-114,* 23-24, 39; Broseley Wood, 37
Brushes, *188, 194*; fire brush, *182*; hat brush, *182*
Buckets, *132*
Buckles, *166*
Buffet stools, *38, 87, 115, 183*
Buildwas, Shropshire, 79
Bullocks, *3*
Bureau, *13*
Butchers, 39, *135*
Butter, *43,* 47, *53,* 78, *116, 144, 169*
Butter scale, *187*
Butter tubs, *91, 124, 168*
Butteries, *10, 12, 13, 17, 19, 25, 33, 36, 53, 59, 66, 75, 82, 87, 91, 96, 97, 99, 106, 109, 119, 120, 121, 122, 123, 124, 126, 127, 128, 129, 130, 139, 140, 149, 163, 166, 169, 170, 171, 176, 178, 182*
Buttons, *194*

Cadice, *23*
Calico, *23*
Candle boxes, *10, 71, 80, 84, 91, 96, 179, 182*
Candles, *13,* 34, 67, *147*
Candlesticks, *191*; hanging, *139*; *see also,* Brass, Iron, Pewter, Sconce
Caps, *194*

Carpenters, *1, 35,* 35-36, *98, 99, 111, 152, 163, 170, 178*
Carpets, *22, 29, 41,* 67, *146, 151, 159, 164*
Carts, *3, 22,* 52, *118, 151, 162, 171, 183, 189*; cart rope, *168*; dung cart, *47*
Case of drawers, *178*
Case for glasses, *55*
Casks, *16, 37*
Cassocks, *41*
Cattle, *29,* 45-7, *136*; barren cow, *123*; breend cow, *88*; bulls, *10, 13, 47, 53, 119, 130*; bull stag, *47, 169*; bullocks, *3, 47, 119, 123, 128, 129, 171*; calves, *10, 13, 53, 68, 115, 118, 119, 126, 127, 128, 129, 130, 160, 168, 170, 171, 183*; cows, *1, 3, 6, 9, 13, 28, 32, 34, 44, 53, 68, 76, 79, 80, 85, 115, 116, 117, 119, 122, 123, 125, 126, 127, 128, 129, 130, 139, 150, 151, 159, 160, 162, 166, 168, 169, 170, 171, 183, 184, 187*; cows, killed in house, *144*; heifers, *68, 118, 119, 122, 127, 129, 138, 162*; heifers in calf, *169*; kine, *25,* 30, *42, 47, 133, 138, 142, 144*; milking cow, *19,* 99; old cow, *98, 105, 121*; oxen, *9, 10, 22, 44, 47,* 52-3, *53, 116, 125, 126, 127, 128, 129, 168*; rearing calves, *3*; red cow, *88*; small cows, *152*; three-year-old bullocks, *130*; twinter bullocks, *125*; two-year-olds, *130, 144, 168, 171*; weaning beasts/calves, *4, 47, 150*; welch kine, *4,* 47; yearlings, *44, 47, 68, 117, 123, 126, 150, 168, 169, 170, 183*; yearling calves, *30, 36, 116, 122, 128, 144, 184*; young beasts, *4, 25, 133, 140*; young cattle, *13, 116, 142, 151*
Cauldron, *148*
Cellars, *6, 16, 18, 21, 36, 47, 54, 57, 58, 66, 67, 69, 72, 75, 76, 77, 79, 80, 85, 86, 87, 92, 94, 95, 98, 101, 102, 103, 110, 113, 133, 136, 152, 165, 168, 173, 174, 177, 179, 182, 183, 193, 195, 196*; ale cellar, *13*; small beer cellar, *13*
Chafing dishes, *67, 118, 124, 130, 182, 187, 191*
Chaff, *see* Beds, Bolsters, Pillows
Chains, *13, 22, 116, 168*; and bucket, *168*; and dog wheel, *182*; in fireplace, *167*; to hold pots on fire, *129*; ox chains, *171*; pit chain, *132*
Chairs; 61-2; arm, *21*; ash/ash-bottomed, *19, 98, 137, 182*; black, *182*; boarded bottoms, *94, 95*; cane, *13*; child's, *182*; common, *12*; easy, *13*; elbow, *91, 193*; green, *39*; joined, *1, 9, 10, 14, 19, 34, 45, 51, 80, 82, 115, 116, 120, 122, 142, 143, 164, 169*; joined elbow, *80*; leather, *119, 182*; nursing, *15, 169*; plain wood, *21*; Russia, *162*; seg/seggen, *7, 19, 21, 56, 57, 59, 76, 82,*

94, 95, 98, 120, 131, 137, 155, 160, 161, 165, 169, 179, 189; Turkey work, 57, 182; turned, 121; twiggen, 26; wainscot, 99; wood, 9, 193; wooden-bottomed, 184
Chaise, 45
Chalk, 86
Chambers, 54-55
Charcoal, 57, 76, 168
Chattel Leases, *see* Leases
Check (fabric), 194
Cheeks (of grate), 36, 64, 80, 82, 89, 92, 116, 119, 126, 127, 128, 130, 139, 144, 162, 168, 169, 170, 171, 180, 183
Cheese, 78
Cheese boards, 10
Cheese chambers, 10, 13, 47, 162, 169
Cheese plates, 9
Cheese presses, 10, 13, 79, 99, 121, 130, 139, 140, 162, 168, 174, 183, 187
Cheese shelves, 171
Cheese toaster, 108
Cheese tubs, 9, 47, 99, 121, 126, 127, 130, 133, 168, 183, 187
Cheese vats (Cheese fats/ Cheswitts), 9, 10, 47, 79, 80, 128, 130, 133, 171
Chests; 62-3; deal, 184; joined, 1, 14, 42, 71, 75, 76, 80, 81, 138, 143, 149, 166, 173; oak, 110; old wooden, 179; wainscot, 186; with hemp, 47; with linen, 83, 85, 86, 87, 95, 101, 102, 113, 164, 186; with linen and warming pan, 150; with woollens and linen, 166
Chests of drawers, 55, 59, 66, 68, 72, 74, 77, 79, 85, 87, 91, 94, 97, 98, 101, 103, 105, 106, 114, 176, 182
Chest upon a chest, 98, 136
Children's rug, linens, 33
Chimney piece, 101, 103
China (i.e. porcelain), 47, 64
Chopper, 135
Chopping knife, 91, 100, 112, 133, 183, 184, 188
Churn staff, 187
Churns, 9, 10, 19, 36, 79, 88, 98, 119, 121, 122, 125, 128, 130, 133, 137, 168, 174, 181, 183, 187
Cider, 146
Cittern, 124
Clay (for tobacco pipes), 13, 71
Cleavers, 19, 30, 46, 76, 79, 91, 111, 133, 149, 161, 164; iron, 135
Clergy, 37-8, 41, 45, 124, 162
Clocks, 6, 12, 13, 16, 22, 25, 29, 36, 41, 47, 50, 58, 66, 68, 69, 71-2, 107, 109, 114, 130, 131, 133, 158, 159, 161, 166, 175, 177; brass, 151; case, 82; repeating, 13; with

cases, 8, 20, 63, 72, 73, 74, 77, 80, 84, 85, 89, 91, 94, 95, 98, 101, 102, 104, 108, 111, 124, 132, 163, 170, 171, 175, 176, 178, 182, 183, 184, 193; with weights and line, 56
Close stools, 13, 19, 47, 58, 64, 76, 80, 85, 98, 101, 113, 166, 178, 181, 189, 193
Closets, 13, 47, 72, 80, 86, 162, 166, 171; writing closet, 87
Clothes basket, 187
Clothiers, 42
Clothing, 72-5
Clouts, 192
Clover, 129
Coal, coal mining, 13, 16-21, 22, 23, 26, 27, 29, 45, 56-7, 61, 79, 130, 156, 158, 162, 165, 192
Coal box, 124
Coal hatchet, 164
Coal wagon, 13, 22, 29
Coalbrookdale, Shropshire, 6, 21-4, 28, 31, 39, 75, 194, 195
Coats, 161, 179
Cob-irons, 28, 36, 37, 42, 46, 48, 58, 85, 88, 94, 95, 98, 114, 120, 121, 122, 124, 133, 155, 157, 190; iron, 57, 73, 115, 125, 139, 148
Cock-lofts, 6, 9, 10, 57, 58, 66, 80, 139, 153, 158, 164, 174
Cocks (i.e. taps), 172
Cocks (i.e. poultry), 171
Coffee, 60, 194
Coffee pot, 107
Coffers, 62-3; to put salt in, 161; with yarn, 63
Collars (for horses), 13, 124
Colliers (*see also* Master Colliers), 5, 18-21, 25, 29, 36, 46, 56, 92, 104, 108, 155, 158, 159, 167, 173, 179, 180, 185, 188, 191, 196
Colter, 168
Colts, 17
Combs, 13, 59
Compost, 22, 41, 52, 124
Convenient house, 10
Cooking, 57-58
Coolers, 8, 12, 13, 18, 19, 42, 75, 76, 85, 91, 94, 95, 98, 102, 103, 113, 129, 130, 132, 133, 135, 137, 173, 174, 182, 183; wooden, 125
Cooling vat, 53
Cooper, 36, 138
Coopery ware, 5, 22, 38, 42, 45, 47, 60, 62, 70, 119, 138, 143, 151, 152, 154, 158; timber for, 138
Copper, 66, 68, 80, 101; cans, 59, 178, 182; candlesticks, 59; furnaces, 66, 80, 187; pan, 189; saucepan, 103, 182
Cords (for beds), 96, 103

INDEX OF SUBJECTS AND PLACES

Corn (*see also* Mixed Corn, Hard Corn), *3, 9, 13, 22, 30, 42, 47,* 50, *53, 68, 79, 116, 117, 118, 128, 133, 138, 139, 140, 144, 151, 162, 169, 170, 171, 172, 187;* for bread, *95*
Corn chamber, *171*
Cottons, *194*
Counter (in shop), *87, 193, 194*
Counterfeit dishes, *31*
Counterpanes, *55, 166*
Coverlets, *2, 3, 10, 13, 19, 22, 40, 42, 58, 59, 71, 73, 76, 80, 107, 139, 149, 150, 166, 174, 184, 187, 193, 196*
Cradles, *7, 33, 51, 59, 66, 91, 98, 112, 116, 121, 128, 169*
Cranes (over fires), *98, 193*
Cratches, 17, *57, 60;* bacon cratches, *94, 182;* handle cratch, *59;* joyne cratch, *49;* with hooks, *161*
Cravatts, *59*
Creepers, *71;* before the fire, *161*
Cressethayes, Shropshire, *119*
Crests (i.e. ridge tiles), *81*
Crossbow, *22*
Crow, iron, *189*
Cupboards, 62-3, *71, 81, 95, 125, 127, 128, 140, 152, 154, 166, 182, 187, 188;* hanging, *10, 151, 174;* joined, *42, 44, 46, 57, 80, 138, 143;* old-fashioned, *180;* press, *115;* square, *193;* standing, *47;* with drawers, *7, 94, 193;* wooden, *131*
Curtains (for beds), *19, 22, 46, 49, 55, 59, 67, 75, 80, 84, 87, 89, 94, 95, 106, 111, 113, 139, 143, 156, 177, 182, 186, 188, 190;* green, *103;* Kidderminster stuff, *149;* red, *188;* yellow, *59; see also* Window Curtains
Curtain rods, *49*
Cushion stool, *115*
Cushions, *10, 22, 25, 36, 41, 47, 51, 64, 80, 146, 149, 164, 169*
Cutlery, 61; *see also* Knives, Spoons

Dairies, *3, 13,* 47, *47, 59,* 78, *129, 140, 168, 169*
Dale (deal): boards, *13;* boxes, *13, 55;* chest, *184;* hanging press, *182*
Dead eyes, *114*
Deal, *see* Dale
Debts, *22, 23, 26, 28, 30, 34, 36, 44,* 53-4, *66, 77, 79, 88, 95, 98, 104, 109, 114, 117, 128, 144, 146, 181;* book debts, *51, 178, 189, 190, 193;* desperate, *12, 13, 35, 40, 46, 57, 73, 76, 138, 139, 141, 147, 149, 151, 154, 155, 162;* hopeful, *141;* by specialty, *33,* 47, *116, 147* 149, *166;* sperate, *12, 13, 116, 138; see also* Bills, Bonds
Decanter, *91*

Delph ware, 69, *96, 102, 109, 124;* basins, *95, 103;* dishes, *97, 103;* jugs, *91;* plates, *91, 103, 104*
Desks, *9,* 61, *73, 87, 124, 126, 127, 128, 156, 158, 161, 162, 163, 165, 166, 169, 180, 188, 189;* spice desk, *55;* writing desk, *98, 193*
Diaper, *see* Napkins, Table cloths
Diddlebury, Shropshire, 4
Dimity, *23*
Dining room, *13*
Dish frame, *174*
Dish stand, *184*
Doctors, 38
Dog wheel, 57-8, *182*
Drag, *124*
Drawers, *184;* in counter, *193, 194; see also* Cupboards, Dressers, Tables
Dressers (mining equipment), *20*
Dressers (furniture), *12, 17, 21,* 63-4, *68, 73, 75, 76, 78, 79, 83, 84, 86, 87, 89, 92, 94, 95, 96, 97, 98, 99, 100, 101, 102, 103, 104, 106, 108, 109, 110, 111, 112, 113, 130, 131, 134, 162, 170, 179, 182, 184, 186, 188, 190, 191, 193, 196*
Dressing tables, *10, 86, 182*
Dripping pans, *13, 19, 21, 29, 36, 42, 48, 53, 56, 58, 63, 74, 85, 90, 92, 115, 116, 121, 124, 126, 127, 128, 130, 135, 155, 157, 173, 182, 183, 184;* iron, *9, 59, 73, 80, 83, 100, 102, 110, 111, 120, 125, 139, 148, 149, 174, 185, 186, 187, 188;* stone, *186;* tin, *91, 94, 188*
Dubbing board, *59*
Ducks, 49, *171*
Dung, *166*
Dwelling house (i.e. room), *6, 10, 16, 17, 18, 37, 39, 45, 51, 58, 73, 97, 119, 122, 123, 127, 128, 129, 130, 138, 139, 145, 152, 156, 162, 163, 165, 170, 172, 188*
Dyeing, 42

Ears of grate, *182*
Earthenware, *3, 13, 60, 62, 63,* 69, *79, 80, 94, 101, 124, 168, 178, 184, 191;* basin, *121;* cups, *188;* dishes, 26, *179;* mugs, *179;* mustard pot, *188;* plates, *79;* punch bowl, *182; see also* Bristol ware, China, Tickney war, Whiteware
Egg slice, *174*
Elfate, *see* Ale Vat
Engine (for ropemaking), *189*
Engineer, *177*
Entry (part of house), *51, 187*
Erwings, *see* Yarn Blades and Winds
Esquires, 36

Feathers, *13*, 49, *49*, 77, *95*, *171*; see also Beds, Bolsters, Pillows
Fellies, *10*, *169*
Fellows' room, *129*
Fenders, *13*, *80*, *91*, *98*, *101*, *102*, *107*, *109*, *182*, *183*, *184*, *187*, *189*; brass, *182*; iron, *103*, *193*
Fenring (veneering) stuff, *98*
Ferrets (i.e. ribbons), *13*
Ferries, 27
Files, *73*, *192*
Fire backs: cast, *124*; iron, *34*, *47*, *139*, *140*
Fire brushes, *13*, *182*
Fire pan, *120*
Fireplaces, 56-8
Fire plate, *13*, *21*, *82*, *85*, *88*, *94*, *95*, *99*, *100*, *107*, *113*, *129*, *171*, *179*, *182*, *191*, *193*; cast iron, *18*, *19*, *130*, *166*; iron, *26*, *58*, *114*, *116*, *120*, *149*
Fire shovels, *2*, *8*, *13*, *18*, *19*, *30*, *34*, *46*, *47*, *48*, *53*, *55*, *56*, *58*, *59*, *60*, *64*, *65*, *78*, *80*, *82*, *84*, *85*, *88*, *89*, *91*, *94*, *96*, *97*, *98*, *100*, *103*, *106*, *107*, *110*, *111*, *112*, *113*, *119*, *123*, *124*, *125*, *127*, *128*, *129*, *130*, *131*, *133*, *135*, *139*, *145*, *149*, *155*, *157*, *161*, *164*, *165*, *166*, *167*, *169*, *174*, *179*, *180*, *181*, *182*, *184*, *185*, *186*, *187*, *188*, *191*, *193*
Fire slices, *6*, *29*, *36*, *37*, *42*, *44*
Firkins, *106*, *111*
Fishing boat, 33, *143*
Fishing nets, *24*, 33, *143*
Fistula, *181*
Flails, 53
Flannel, *79*
Flasks (used by brassfounder), *172*
Flax, *10*, *11*, *13*, *30*, *41*, 51-2, 73-5, *102*, *124*, *133*, *140*, *156*, *159*, *168*, *169*, *172*; dozen of, *10*; dressed, *13*, *162*; flaxen yarn, *37*; hatchelled, *10*; pounds of, *30*; watered, *172*
Flesh forks, *19*, *36*, *44*, *46*, *48*, *53*, *82*, *88*, *91*, *94*, *100*, *111*, *114*, *124*, *125*, *128*, *137*, *155*, *157*, *166*, *167*
Flocks (i.e. stuffing for bed), *49*, *95*; see also Beds, Bolster
Flutes, 55
Fodder, *29*, *68*, *140*
Folds, *85*, *86*, *94*
Footrids, *58*
Forest bills, *82*
Forgemen, *190*
Forks (for hay), *76*
Frigates, *75*
Frying pans, *2*, *19*, *21*, *21*, *30*, *33*, *42*, *46*, *48*, *56*, *59*, *64*, *78*, *85*, *88*, *91*, *94*, *96*, *103*, *108*, *109*, *120*, *125*, *126*, *139*, *144*, *155*, *157*, *163*, *174*, *179*, *181*, *182*, *183*, *190*, *191*

Furnaces, *9*, *12*, *36*, *51*, *80*, *91*, *107*, *132*, *166*, *169*, *188*, *189*; boiling, *161*; brass, *193*, *131*, *164*; brass in wall, *16*, *98*; brass and lead, *57*; brewing, *54*, *66*, *94*; candlemaking, *147*; copper, *66*, *80*, *187*; dyer's, *59*; iron, *51*, *67*, *86*, *87*, *101*, *102*, *103*, *129*, *175*, *179*, *182*, *191*, *195*; iron in wall, *76*, *113*
Furnace Bank, *163*, *170*
Fustian, *194*
Fustic, *59*

Gails, see Pot Gails
Gallon Measure, *120*
Gardens, *13*, *112*, *161*,
Garden chamber, *25*
Garners, *116*
Garretts, *13*, *18*, *53*, *67*, *79*, *94*, *101*, *102*, *119*, *151*, *168*, *171*, *182*, *183*; men's, *13*
Gartering, *194*
Gauns, *10*, *21*, 47, *79*, *80*, *91*, *98*, *100*, *124*, *125*, *130*, *133*, *137*, *164*, *168*, *169*, *174*, *182*; bend, *31*; gallon measure, *120*; lading, *76*; milking, *19*, *98*, *181*; pewter, *33*, *34*, *36*, *40*, *42*, *120*
Gears (for looms), *83*, *110*, *150*, *174*
Geese, 49, *126*, *127*, *132*, *168*, *171*
Gentlemen, *22*, *47*, *53*, *55*, *67*, *140*, *166*
Gins (horse), *25*
Girth (for horse), *94*
Gitchfield, Broseley, 19
Glass, *89*; see also Looking glasses
Glass case, *119*
Glass crate, *57*, *66*, *166*
Glass frame, *79*
Glass ware (and drinking glasses), *13*, *41*, *47*, *62*, *63*, 69-70, *74*, *79*, *91*, *94*, *102*, *103*, *124*, *129*, *184*
Glazier, 43, *89*
Globe, *91*
Gloucester, *182*
Glover, 41, *86*
Gloves, *23*, *86*
Goanr (of butter), *43*
Gobbards, see Cob-Irons
Gold, 68, *73*; money, *13*; piece, *55*; plate, *22*; rings, *13*, *51*, *62*, *102*
Golden Ball, 6
Grates, *7*, *8*, *16*, *18*, *19*, *20*, *21*, *28*, *29*, *30*, *31*, *34*, *36*, *37*, *42*, *43*, *44*, *46*, *47*, *48*, *53*, *55*, *57*, *58*, *60*, *64*, *65*, *67*, *71*, *73*, *75*, *78*, *80*, *83*, *84*, *85*, *88*, *89*, *91*, *92*, *94*, *95*, *97*, *98*, *99*, *100*, *101*, *102*, *103*, *104*, *106*, *107*, *108*, *109*, *110*, *111*, *112*, *113*, *114*, *116*, *120*, *123*, *125*, *128*, *127*, *129*, *130*, *131*, *132*, *133*, *137*, *139*, *140*, *141*, *145*, *155*, *157*, *163*, *164*, *165*, *167*, *174*, *179*, *180*,

INDEX OF SUBJECTS AND PLACES

181, 182, 184, 185, 187, 188 189, 191, 193, 196; box, *162*; cast, *161*; iron, *2, 13, 6, 57, 59, 79, 82, 122, 124, 129, 148, 149, 166, 177, 82*; pipemaking, *71, 84*
Green chamber, *162*
Gridiron, *80, 125, 171, 182*
Grindstone, *168, 170, 192*
Grocery, *51*
Guinea box, *78*
Gun case, *13*
Guns, *13, 22, 73, 91, 164*; birding guns/pieces, *47, 120, 140, 162*; fowling guns/pieces, *166, 170*; *see also* Gauns, Muskets, Pistols
Gunsmiths, 35, *164*
Gutters, *81*

Hack, *19*
Hacking block, *137*
Hacking knives, *36, 125, 149*
Hackney saddles, *91, 94, 124*
Hackney stable, *13*
Hair cloth, *183*
Half barrels, *135*
Half bushels, *128*
Half hogsheads, *18, 21, 73, 80, 85, 95, 101, 103, 107, 114, 162, 169, 170, 182*
Half pecks, *76*
Half strikes, *80, 124*
Halls, *10, 13, 25, 33, 36, 38, 47, 52, 53, 75, 86, 115, 124, 140, 144 , 151, 168*; little hall, *59*
Hammers, *73, 141, 192*
Hampots, *94*
Handle cratch, *59*
Handirons, *see* Andirons
Handkerchiefs, *194*
Hand pan, *183*
Hanger (for sword), *55*
Hanging cupboard, *10, 151, 174*
Hanging press, *16, 21, 36, 57, 75, 82, 85, 90, 99, 101, 114, 116, 119, 124, 163, 170, 171, 176, 179, 185*; deal, *182*
Hangings, *6, 10, 13, 16, 76, 79, 85, 91, 95, 98, 101, 102, 107, 109, 114, 129, 133, 160, 169, 174, 179, 182, 183, 187, 189, 193, 195*; blue, *99, 103, 107*; coarse cloth for, *107*; overworn, *60*
Hard corn, *119, 123, 124, 125, 126, 128, 129, 130*
Harness, *41, 52*
Harrows, *22, 52, 79, 80, 116, 140, 151, 168, 169, 183*; ox harrow, *169*
Hatchells, *139*
Hats, *161*; brush, *182*
Haughton, Shifnal, Shropshire, 8, *115*
Hauling lines, *58, 114*

Hawsers, *114*
Hay, *9, 10, 13, 41, 47,* 51, *80, 86, 90, 105, 116, 118, 120, 124, 125, 127, 128, 133, 135, 139, 140, 160, 162, 164, 166, 168, 181, 183, 187*; in barns, *22, 47, 53, 119, 129, 130, 144, 151, 171*; loads of, *18, 171*; in mow, *129*; in ricks, *3, 19, 63, 74, 122*; in stable, *72*
Heaters (for box irons), *100, 103, 180*
Hedge shears, *19*
Hemp, *13, 28, 30, 32, 41, 42, 47, 48,* 51-2, 73-5, *79, 102, 118, 120, 122, 124, 128, 139, 140, 156, 168, 169, 171, 174, 180, 183, 187*; dozens of, *183*; dressed, *13, 42, 47, 162*; kinchings of, *30*; pounds of, *118*; seed, *42*; stones of, *120, 122, 174, 180, 187*; two years', *171*; yarn, *28, 37, 48, 128, 171*
Hens, *171*
Hereford, diocese, 7
Heriotts, *116*
Hillings, *6, 22,* 51, *77*
Hoes, *13*
Hogsheads, *5, 6, 8, 9, 13, 18, 21, 25, 26, 36, 39, 47, 48, 58, 76, 79, 98, 101, 103, 124, 129, 139, 144, 145, 146, 169, 173*; of drink, *26, 36*
Holland (fabric), 23
Holly Groves, Broseley, Shropshire, *57*
Holsters, *119*
Homes, *124*
Hoops, *13*; bark, *13*; iron, *182*; measuring, *183*
Hoppers, *183*
Hops, *42, 67,* 77, *81, 94, 102, 140, 156*; sacks of, *67, 94*
Horse litter, *41,* 45
Horses, 20-1, *22, 28,* 43-5, *65, 80, 86, 123, 125, 126, 129, 162, 168, 176, 194*; almost dead, *181*; blind, *105*; carring, 44-5, *133*; colts, *10, 22, 25, 58, 65, 116, 119, 122, 128, 130, 140, 166, 16, 169, 171*; drawing, *183*; filly and foal, *183*; for gins, *25*; lame, *103, 130*; mares, *3, 4, 6, 10, 13, 25, 53, 54, 55, 58, 65, 79, 80, 105, 116, 118, 121, 122, 123, 125, 128, 130, 131, 135, 138, 140, 144, 151, 154, 166, 168, 169, 170, 171, 181, 183*; nags, *15, 117, 144*; old, *9, 13, 79, 90, 91, 124, 126, 135, 140, 151, 171, 181*; packhorses, 44, *118, 125*; riding nags, *147*; stallions, *10*; stoned, *130*; sucking colts, *151*; waggon horses, *79, 183*; wain horses, *79*; working horses, *3,* 45, *65, 171*; yearling colts, *4*
Horses (for barrels), *76, 91, 94, 110, 195*
Horseshoes, *192*
Houses/house places, *9,* 54-6, *116, 117, 120, 121, 130, 144, 149, 155, 157, 160, 151, 164, 169, 171, 174, 179, 180, 181, 183, 187*
Huckaback (fabric), *183*

Hunting horn, *55*
Huntington, Little Wenlock, Shropshire, *120, 123, 130*
Hurden cloth, *70*; yarn, *13, 28, 30, 124, 128*; *see also* Napkins, Sheets, Towels
Husbandmen, 13-14, *138*
Hutches, straw, *30*

Ill vat, *see* Ale Vat
Inkles, *23*
Innkeepers, *6*, 40, *72*
Inventories, values, 10-11
Iron, 68; bar iron, *52, 54, 192*; bars, *164*; boilers, *106, 110, 137, 182*; brandreth, *149*; cast iron, *8, 106, 130, 161, 163, 166*; candlesticks, *36, 46, 59, 80, 91, 94, 97, 100, 103, 111, 113, 124, 127, 129, 137 180, 183, 193, 195*; fenders, *103, 193*; furnaces, *51, 67, 86, 87, 101, 102, 103, 129, 175, 179, 182, 191, 195*; grid irons, *171, 182*; holder for smoothing irons, *188*; jacks, *9, 59, 91*; kettles, *43, 44, 90, 109, 126, 137*; language, 16-17; marments, *34, 76, 80, 103, 130, 174*; mortars and pestles, *73, 102, 103, 110, 120, 139, 148, 149, 163, 166, 177, 186*; old iron, *132, 171, 183, 187, 192*; pans, *73, 75, 76*; plate, *120*; posnet, *120*; pots, *2, 5, 13, 18, 21, 29, 33, 34, 36, 42, 43, 44, 51, 56, 57, 58, 65, 67, 73, 75, 78, 80, 81, 84, 90, 94, 95, 97, 98, 99, 100, 102, 104, 109, 111, 112, 113, 115, 117, 120, 121, 123, 125, 126, 127, 128, 130, 131, 135, 139, 141, 144, 152, 155, 157, 165, 173, 174, 175, 180, 182, 183, 184, 193*; pot lids, *121, 166, 174, 182*; pudding pans, *174, 182*; saucepans, *109, 135, 137*; skewers, *182*; ware, *3, 5, 8, 10, 12, 13, 22, 23, 24, 25, 29, 31, 35, 36, 38, 39, 41, 42, 43, 44, 45, 51, 52, 60, 62, 63, 65,66, 67, 68, 72, 74, 76, 77, 86, 95, 102, 106, 116, 129, 138, 142, 143, 144, 146, 148, 150, 151, 152, 153, 154, 156, 158, 159, 160, 162, 164, 170, 173, 176, 178, 189*; weights, *64*; *see also* pressing Irons, Smoothing Irons
Iron manufacture, 21-2
Ironstone, *13, 20*, 21, *58*

Jacks, *6, 7, 8, 10, 13, 16, 22, 36, 41, 47, 51, 53, 58, 59, 63, 67, 69, 74, 79, 80, 85, 94, 98, 107, 127, 128, 130, 140, 163, 164, 166, 169, 183, 186, 193*; brass, *101, 103*; iron, *9, 59, 91*; leather, *40*
Jack hook (for ropemaking), *189*
Jersey (fabric), *59*
Jews, 38
Joined furniture: bedstead, *1, 5, 34, 36, 37, 42, 46, 48, 57, 116, 118, 121, 143, 150, 151, 152, 153*; bench, *57, 80*; chairs, *1, 9, 10, 14, 19, 34, 45, 51, 80, 82, 115, 116, 120, 122, 142, 143, 164*; chests, *1, 14, 42, 71, 75, 76, 80, 81, 138, 143, 149, 166, 173*; cradles, *7, 66*; cratch, *49*; cupboards, *42, 44, 46, 57, 80, 138, 143*; forms, *1, 9, 10, 42, 44, 47, 53, 81, 110, 148, 152, 179*; presses, *33, 44, 149, 151*; screens, *57, 75, 76, 80, 128, 129, 166*; seat; *145*; stools, *18, 19, 22, 36, 57, 71, 76, 80, 91, 95, 113, 121, 151, 153, 166, 187, 188*; tables, *1, 57, 71*; trunk, *22*; ware, *1, 22, 24, 29*

Kettles, *see* Brass, Iron
Kidderminster stuff, *149*
Kilderkins, *76, 80*
Kinchings (of yarn), *30*
Kipe, *124*
Kitchens, *3, 9, 12, 13, 19, 21, 34, 36, 40, 47, 51, 53, 57, 59, 66, 67, 69, 72, 75, 76, 77, 79, 80, 82, 83, 84, 85, 86, 87, 88, 89, 90, 91, 92, 94, 95, 96, 98, 101, 102, 103, 106, 109, 110, 111, 113, 115, 121, 124, 125, 126, 129, 133, 136, 139, 151, 152, 153, 162, 164, 166, 168, 171, 177, 181, 182, 186, 191, 193, 196*; back kitchens, *57, 91, 124, 178*; chief kitchen, *176*; main kitchen, *173*; old kitchen, *94*; out kitchen, *173*
Kneading mitts, *37, 80, 163, 190*; troughs, *44, 47, 124, 139*; tubs, *13, 21, 58, 82, 84, 95, 100, 106, 121, 138, 148, 161, 187*
Knife box, *193*
Knives, *13, 135*
Knives and forks, *13, 183*

Labourers, 13-14, *134, 155, 157, 184*
Lace, *23*
Ladders, *13, 82, 94, 161*
Lanthorns, *91, 109, 124, 171, 182, 183*
Larder, *13*
Lathe (for brass founder), *172*; (for potter), *136*
Latten ware, 16, *62, 63, 74*
Laundry work, 79
Lawyers, 38
Lead, *57, 115*; weights, *156*
Leaden ware, *140*
Leases, *17, 41, 49, 54-5, 60, 62, 77, 79, 85, 91, 103, 140, 189*
Leather, *86*
Lent tilling, *68, 116, 170*
Lichfield, diocese, 7-8
Limestone, *13, 23, 142*
Linen: apparel, *11, 147, 149, 169*; bed, *6*; child's, *33*; cloth, *13, 25, 74, 104, 139, 166, 194*; coarse, *1, 170*; fine, *170*; gears (for

INDEX OF SUBJECTS AND PLACES

loom), *174*; house, *178*; table, *12, 64, 66, 191*; yarn, *15, 32, 36, 102, 152*; *see also* Hempen, Hurden, Sheets, Napery Ware, Napkins, Towels
Lines (for barges), *26, 58, 70, 114*
Links, *see* Pot Links
Linsey, *194*
Literacy, 12
Litter (for horse), *41*
Little Wenlock, Shropshire, 6-7, *115-37*
Livery cupboard, 17
Locksmith, 73
Lodging rooms, *91, 153*
Loft, *35*
Logwood, *59*
Looking glasses, *6, 12, 13, 19, 47, 51, 58, 62, 66, 67,* 71, *72, 74, 77, 79, 85, 86, 94, 101, 102, 107, 109, 124, 130, 135, 139, 149, 156, 162, 164, 166, 182, 183, 188, 191, 193, 195*
Looms (for weavers), *59, 82, 110, 150, 174*
Ludlow, Shropshire, 38, 45, 67

Madeley, Shropshire, 6, *34*, 39, *138-96*
Madeley Wood, *141, 143, 152, 153, 158, 160, 167, 172, 176, 177, 178, 179, 184, 186, 191, 193, 196*
Maids (utensils), 16-17, *91, 98, 179, 183*
Malt, *13, 42,* 51, *68, 73,* 76-7, *80, 116, 124, 128, 130, 139, 168, 169, 183*; bags of, *42*; quarters of, *139*; stones of, *73*; strikes of, *6, 80, 128, 169*
Malt chambers/rooms, *171, 183*
Malt houses, *10, 80, 168*
Malt mills, *13, 28, 57, 58, 67, 69, 73, 80, 94, 116, 119, 130, 132, 142, 143, 154, 162, 168, 169, 183*
Mandrells, *5, 20, 92*
Mantelpiece, *188*
Manure, 52
Maps, *98, 182*
Mariners, *see* Trowmen
Marments, *8, 19, 37, 53, 73, 88, 104, 113, 123, 124, 127, 167, 179, 180, 181, 187, 188*; iron, *34, 76, 80, 103, 130, 176*; in wall, 73, 76
Marmulets, *71*
Mash(ing) tubs, *21, 94, 95, 102, 103, 113, 135, 182, 190*
Mashing staff, *94*
Maslin, *10,* 50
Maslin kettles, *124, 180, 187*
Masons, 43, *91, 117*
Master colliers, *58, 79, 81, 94, 132, 193*
Masts, *75, 83, 85*
Mats, *95, 103, 150, 171*; seggen, *49*
Mattocks, *19, 80, 171, 187*

Meadow, *181*
Meal tub, *106*
Meat, 59-60
Mercers, *23,* 39, *39, 51, 64*; See also Shopkeepers
Mercery, *51*
Middle rooms, *40, 85*
Milk: bowls, *98, 119, 121, 125, 129, 187*; cans, *19*; houses, *10, 25, 80, 88, 119, 129, 133, 162, 171, 187*; gauns, *19, 98, 181*; pails, *3, 79, 119, 126, 127, 128, 129, 181, 183*; pans, *59, 119, 129, 169*; vessels, *3, 10, 28, 44, 47*
Mill, *129*; *see also* Malt Mills
Miller, 40, *181*
Mitts, *5, 6, 16, 46, 53, 56, 57, 79, 118, 119, 122, 124, 130, 133, 155, 157, 167, 178*; kneading, *9, 37, 58, 60, 64, 78, 80, 147, 163, 190*; little round, *180*; for milk, *125*; wooden, *80*
Mixed Corn, *168*; *see also* Maslin, Muncorn
Money, 53-4
Mortars, *141*; brass, *139*; iron, *57, 166*
Mortars and pestles, *36, 53,* 58-9, *124, 139, 161, 187*; brass, *19*; iron, *19m 46, 59, 103, 120, 149, 186*; *see also* Pestles
Mortgages, 54, *94*
Moulds: brassfounder's, *172*; smith's, *192*; tobacco pipe maker's, *71, 84*
Mow (i.e. rick), *129*
Much Wenlock, Shropshire, 5, 9, *140*
Muck, *13, 22, 41,* 52, *118, 124, 162*; loads of, *79, 80*
Muncorn, *13,* 50, *79, 122, 127, 144*
Murder, *175*
Music, 38, 70-1
Muskets, *156*

Nailers, *54, 141*
Nails, *54*
Napery ware, *1, 3, 22, 24, 45, 115, 116, 138, 143, 144, 146, 154, 162*
Napkins, *6, 21, 23, 30, 39, 42, 45, 47, 54, 56, 57, 5, 75, 79, 80, 85, 91, 103, 104, 107, 135, 139, 150, 155, 157, 164, 171, 173, 174, 180, 182, 183, 189*; diaper, *59*; flaxen, *59, 76, 118*; hempen, *37, 149*; hurden, *7, 37, 59, 11, 149, 187*; overworn, *12, 14*
Neck cloth, *50*
New houses, *15, 40*
Newport, Shropshire, 67
New rooms, *40, 129, 196*
Niggards, *126, 130, 174, 179, 180*
Noggen, noggs, *28, 34, 37, 79*; pounds of, *28, 37*; yarn, *34*
Noggins, *124*

Oak: bark, *86*; chest, *110*; oval table, *91*, *94*
Oars, 26, *75*
Oatmeal box, *115*
Oats, 9, *10*, *13*, 50-51, *53*, *68*, *80*, *90*, *144*, *166*, *168*, *169*, *171*, *183*
Okum, *45*
Outhouses, *89*, *164*
Oxen, *see* Cattle

Pack saddles, *94*, *118*, *124*, *125*
Pack thread, *194*
Paddle Staves, *156*
Pads, *36*, *51*, *94*, *124*, *168*, *171*
Pails, *7*, *10*, *30*, *31*, *36*, *37*, *42*, *43*, *44*, *56*, *57*, *76*, *80*, *85*, *91*, *98*, *107*, *113*, *119*, *120*, *121*, *122*, *124*, *125*, *128*, *130*, *133*, *137*, *155*, *157*, *161*, *168*, *173*, *174*, *177*, *179*, *181*, *191*; bend, *82*; dairy, *129*; milking, *3*, *79*, *119*, *126*, *127*, *128*, *129*, *181*, *183*; tun, *109*; water, *13*, *21*, *96*, *99*, *108*, *110*, *131*, *180*, *182*
Pantries, *59*, *66*, *79*, *86*, *87*, *98*, *106*, *111*, *168*, *183*
Paper, *156*
Paper prints, *67*
Parlours, *6*, *9*, *10*, *13*, *25*, *33*, *34*, *36*, *40*, *47*, *54*, *57*, *67*, *72*, *76*, *77*, *80*, *83*, *85*, *86*, *87*, *90*, *91*, *94*, *95*, *98*, *101*, *102*, *103*, *110*, *112*, *113*, *115*, *116*, *119*, *121*, *122*, *123*, *124*, *126*, *127*, *28*, *130*, *133*, *136*, *139*, *140*, *144*, *149*, *150*, *153*, *160*, *162*, *163*, *166*, *168*, *169*, *170*, *171*, *172*, *173*, *176*, *177*, *178*, *179*, *180*, *181*, *182*, *18*, *187*, *191*, *195*, *196*; big and little, *193*; middle and further, *152*; new, *174*; old, *79*, *174*; upper and lower, *125*
Passage boat, *93*
Passage room, *129*, *193*
Pastry room, *13*
Patty pans, *107*, *182*
Peas, *13*, 51, *119*, *122*, *124*, *126*, *130*, *168*, *171*, *183*
Pecks, *76*, *80*, *124*
Peels, *36*, *171*
Pepper boxes, *182*, *191*
Pestles, *148*, *166*; iron, *139*; *see also* Mortars and Pestles
Pewter, 67-8; basins, dishes, plates, *passim*; bench, *173*; cans, *7*, *8*, *11*, *65*, *128*, *163*, *174*; candlesticks, *7*, *19*, *30*, *33*, *36*, *37*, *40*, *56*, *57*, *59*, *79*, *91*, *94*, *103*, *111*, *113*, *121*, *124*, *126*, *127*, *128*, *139*, *148*, *163*, *166*, *174*, *180*, *181*, *186*; chamber pots, *7*, *19*, *21*, *30*, *34*, *36*, *40*, *56*, *58*, *83*, *120*, *122*, *124*, *126*, *12*, *131*, *174*, *179*; cups, *21*, *128*; flaggons, *33*, *34*, *36*, *37*, *40*, *42*, *56*, *57*, *120*, *156*; frames, *59*, *79*, *80*, *84*, *86*, *87*, *89*, *90*, *91*, *94*, *95*, *96*, *100*, *101*, *102*, *103*, *104*, *106*, *110*, *111*, *187*, *195*; gauns, *33*, *34*, *36*, *40*, *42*, *120*; half pints, *58*; house, *166*; mustard pots, *19*, *79*, *94*, *103*, *113*, *124*, *183*; old, *189*; pie plate, *124*; pints, *8*, *58*, *84*, *103*, *122*, *182*, *193*; porringers, *7*, *21*, *30*, *33*, *34*, *36*, *37*, *46*, *58*, *59*, *79*, *83*, *84*, *85*, *88*, *97*, *98*, *103*, *111*, *113*, *120*, *124*, *126*, *127*, *128*, *129*, *131*, *155*, *173*, *174*, *180*, *181*, *182*, *186*, *187*; posset cup, *181*; pots, *33*, *34*; prices per pound, *79*, *94*, *182*, *191*; quarts, *21*, *34*, *58*, *84*, *95*, *103*, *113*, *122*, *193*; salts, *19*, *33*, *34*, *36*, *40*, *56*, *57*, *58*, *70*, *99*, *103*, *120*, *121*, *124*, *126*, *127*, *139*, *148*, *155*, *157*, *161*, *186*, *187*; salvers, *59*, *94*, *95*, *103*, *182*, *183*, *186*; skimmer, *118*; spoons, *33*, *56*, *78*, *88*, *98*, *120*, *129*, *180*, *187*; stills, *115*, *166*; tankards, *14*, *19*, *21*, *30*, *57* *58*, *82*, *88*, *103*, *113*, *120*, *126*, *127*, *148*, *180*, *187*; wine quart, *182*
Pictures, *62*, *63*, *66*, *69*, 71, *74*, *79*, *87*, *89*, *91*, *94*, *98*, *100*, *101*, *102*, *162*, *182*, *190*
Piggins, *78*, *121*, *174*
Pigs (and swine), *1*, *3*, *4*, *5*, *6*, *7*, *8*, *9*, *10*, *13*, *25*, *26*, *28*, *30*, *39*, *41*, *47*, 49, *53*, *54*, *56*, *56*, *60*, *63*, *66*, *69*, *72*, *74*, *86*, *118*, *120*, *122*, *126*, *127*, *130*, *133*, *136*, *138*, *139*, *140*, *142*, *144*, *145*, *151*, *152*, *154*, *157*, *159*, *160*, *162*, *170*, *176*, *178*, *181*; bacon swine, *42*; big swine, *119*; fat, *171*; gilts, *183*; hogs, *10*, *68*, *129*; middling swine, *63*; shuts, *11*, *120*; small swine, *155*; sow, 4, *86*, *88*, *161*; store, *23*, *42*, *8*, *73*, *80*, *85*, *86*, *93*, *94*, *102*, *116*, *123*, *124*, *125*, *128*, *160*, *164*, *168*, *171*, *182*, *183*
Pike evils, *19*, *91*, *161*, *168*, *171*
Pillions, *13*, *86*, *122*, *130*, *140*, *171*
Pillow bears, *6*, *7*, *30*, *43*, *47*, *85*, *91*, *139*, *149*, *180*, *187*; feather, *102*
Pillow cases, *103*
Pillows, *7*, *10*, *13*, *19*, *55*, 65-6, *76*, *85*, *94*, *102*, *103*, *121*, *139*, *146*, *149*, *167*, *179*, *184*, *187*; feather, *102*
Pins, 23
Pipe clay, *13*
Pipe makers, *19*, *71*, *84*, *106*
Pipes (i.e. casks), *36*, *139*
Pistols, *13*, *91*, *98*, *119*, *162*
Pitch, *45*
Planks, *75*, *94*, *114*, *140*, *143*, *178*, *179*; walnut, *98*
Plate (i.e. gold or silver), *41*, *53*, *67*, *68*, *162*
Plates, *see* Pewter, Earthenware, Fire Plates, &c.; bryling, *161*; to draw bread, *161*

INDEX OF SUBJECTS AND PLACES 351

Platters, *43*
Ploughs, *22*, *47*, 52, *79*, *116*, *118*, *140*, *168*, *169*, *171*, *183*; plough timber, *47*, *140*, *169*
Poker, *13*
Pool Quay, Monts., 32
Porch, *47*
Pork, *98*, *180*
Port books, 2, 25, 29
Portmanteau, *13*
Posenhall, Shropshire, *4*, *5*, *10*
Posnets, *8*, *115*, *161*; *see also* Brass, Iron
Posset cup, 60, *181*
Potash, *59*
Pot gails, *29*, *37*, *44*, *89*, *120*, *139*, *148*, *155*, *157*, *165*
Pot hangers, *28*, *30*
Pot hooks, *30*, *57*, *73*, *111*, *112*, *122*, *125*, *127*, *128*, *130*, *132*, *137*, *149*, *167*, *180*, *182*, *191*, *193*
Pot links, *36*, *57*, *80*, *91*, *94*, *122*, *125*, *127*, *128*, *130*, *132*, *137*, *149*, *161*, *183*, *185*, *188*
Pottery, 23
Poultry, *13*, *49*, *80*, *86*, *116*, *140*, *144*, *145*, *151*; *see also* Cocks, Ducks, Hens, Geese
Powdering tubs, *13*
Preen Farm, Broseley, *80*
Press (dyer's), *59*
Press cupboard, *189*
Press irons, *50*; *see also* Smoothing Irons
Presses (i.e. cupboards), *34*, *104*, *107*, *112*, *115*, *119*, *122*, *124*, *127*, *159*, *160*, *164*, *169*, *188*; joined, *33*, *44*, *149*, *151*; See also Hanging Presses
Prints, *101*, *107*
Property, 53-4
Pudding pans, *125*, *182*, *191*
Punch (tool), *182*
Purgatories, *85*, *99*, *101*, *103*, *107*, *182*, *189*, *190*

Quarries (i.e. floor tiles), *146*
Quarryman, *20*
Quarter barrels, *80*, *98*, *103*, *107*
Quill wheel, *174*
Quilts, *13*, *94*, *95*, *98*, *107*, *183*, *193*

Racks, *13*, *29*, *47*, *53*, *91*, *109*, *121*, *126*, *137*, *163*, *189*, *193*
Rails, *178*
Railways, 20, *58*, *92*, *158*
Rakes, *13*, *19*, *80*, *91*, *161*, *168*; dressing rakes, *19*, *112*
Rapier, *55*
Reaping hook, *134*
Red chamber, *66*
Red room, *87*

Rent, 15
Retailing, 39-40
Ribbons, *23*
Ricks, *see* Corn, Hay, Mows
Riddles (wire), *13*, *94*, *124*, *183*, *184*
Rind ware, *29*
Ring and bar, *171*
Rings, *41*, *55*, *156*; gold, *13*, *51*, *62*, *102*; signet, *22*
Roasting fork, *188*
Roller (agricultural), 52, *80*; stone, *13*
Ropemakers, 33-4, *131*, *189*
Rugs, *7*, *13*, *19*, *34*, *42*, *46*, *53*, *57*, *58*, *75*, *80*, *84*, *85*, *91*, *94*, *96*, *97*, *100*, *103*, *107*, *113*, *139*, *143*, *149*, *161*, *167*, *169*, *177*, *178*, *188*; child's, *33*; indifferent, *71*; overworn, *60*; red, *80*, *121*; spotted, *76*, *103*
Rye, 50, *144*, *168*

Sacks, *67*, *94*, *162*, *171*, *187*
Saddles, *13*, *36*, *51*, *55*, *79*, *86*, *119*, *120*, *121*, *140*, *147*, *168*, *171*; hackney saddles, *91*, *94*, *124*
Sad irons, *102*
Safes, *119*, *140*
Sails, *14*, *26*, *34*, *75*, *85*, *114*
Salt, 59-60
Salt boxes, *13*, *80*, *91*, *98*, *109*, *121*, *162*, *183*, *191*, *193*; coffer, *161*
Salting bench, *106*
Salting tub, *119*
Saws, *124*, *132*, *171*
Say (fabric), *23*
Scales, *10*, *59*, *64*, *73*, *91*, *98*, *112*, *152*, *166*, *189*; butter, *187*
School house, *124*
Sconce, *59*
Scotch cloth, *23*
Screens, *1*, *51*, *5*, *62*, *83*, *88*, *114*, *126*, *146*, *164*, *176*, *178*, *183*; folding, *59*, *75*, *96*; joined, *76*; wainscot, *85*; wooden, *131*
Screws (for pipemaking), *71*, *84*
Scribbling horse and cards, *59*
Sculleries, *19*, *59*, *86*
Scythes, *13*, *19*, *134*, *171*
Searches, *91*, *84*, *167*, *174*; flour, *179*
Seat by fireplace, *145*
Sellars, *see* Cellars
Servants, *11*, 37
Servants' chambers, *66*, *86*, *87*, *98*, *140*
Severn, River, *2*, 8, 11, *12*, 13, 16, *18*, 20, 25-33, *27*, 75, *83*, *85*, *95*, *96*, *100*, *101*, *142*
Shafts, *70*, *75*
Shear board, *59*
Shears: Clothier's, *10*; garden, 13, *161*; hedge, *19*; tailor's, *59*

Sheep, *4, 10, 11, 13, 28, 30,* 47-49, *47, 68, 119, 125, 126, 127, 128, 129, 144, 147, 168, 170, 183;* ewes, *150;* lambs, *116, 128, 150;* old, *116;* Welsh, *185*

Sheets, *passim,* 65-6; coarse, *39, 104, 110, 173, 183;* coarse hurden, *84;* fine, *85, 173, 183;* fine hemp, *84;* flaxen, *7, 14, 39, 71, 75, 76, 94, 111, 120, 123, 139, 149, 176, 187, 188;* hempen, *7, 37, 39, 42, 46, 59, 71, 73, 75, 76, 80, 91, 94, 100, 103, 117, 118, 120, 139, 176, 180, 182, 184, 187, 188;* hurden, *7, 10, 21, 37, 42, 59, 71, 73, 75, 76, 77, 79, 80, 81, 91, 94, 96, 103, 111, 118, 123, 136, 139, 149, 167, 179, 180, 182, 187, 188;* noggen, *120, 161;* overworn hurden, *85, 113;* twill, *115, 118; see also* Winnowing Sheets

Shifnal, Shropshire, *34*
Shipwrights, 27, *153*
Shires (i.e. outhouses), *155, 157*
Shirts, *50, 161*
Shoemakers, 40
Shoes, *171, 179*
Shopkeepers, 39-40, *69, 87, 194; see also* Mercers
Shops, *6, 10, 51, 52, 54, 66, 69, 71, 73, 82, 84, 86, 87, 89, 97, 106, 150, 152, 160, 165, 174, 178, 193*Shovells, *5, 20, 33, 92*
Shrewsbury, Shropshire, *34, 67, 71, 116*
Shrouds (for barges), 27, *114*
Sieves, *174, 183;* cleansing, *94, 179, 182*
Sign post, *28*
Signet ring, *22*
Silver, 68, 73; bowls, *25, 47;* buckles, *166;* cups, *19, 25, 47, 146;* money, *13;* pins, *51;* plate, *15, 29, 62;* spoons, *13, 19, 25, 47, 77, 115, 156, 166;* tankards, *47, 77;* tobacco box, *47;* watches, *13, 20, 79, 182*
Skewers, *94, 137;* iron, *182;* plate of, *95;* set of, *124*
Skillets, *80, 107, 24, 126, 127, 186*
Skimmers, *7, 30, 37, 75, 80, 91, 95, 102, 107, 115, 120, 174, 182, 183, 187*
Skins, *85*
Slates, *94, 182*
Sleds, 52, *116, 118, 168, 171, 189*
Slippings (of yarn), *30, 34, 37, 102, 118, 128*
Slobs, slob benches, *71, 84, 91, 94, 97, 98;* slob dressers, *99, 102, 110*
Smoking rooms, *13, 72*
Smoothing irons, *10, 36, 44, 46, 59, 80, 91, 111, 121, 130, 183, 188, 193;* cast metal, *103; see also* Box irons, Pressing irons, Sad irons
Snap reel, *59*
Snuffers, *59, 182, 183*

Soap, *64*
Soaping tub, *13*
Spades, *5, 13, 19, 33, 76, 80, 98, 124, 161, 184, 187;* used in cheese making, *168*
Spars, *178*
Spice desk, *55*
Spiggot, *11*
Spindle (for grindstone), *193*
Spinning wheels, *19, 31, 33, 6, 58, 60, 80, 91, 99, 102, 103, 112, 116, 118, 121, 122, 133, 138, 164, 177, 181, 183, 187, 191;* little, *76, 79, 82, 98, 120, 124, 128, 179, 180;* long, *98, 110, 127, 128, 174, 176, 180, 188;* small, *34, 156, 171, 178*
Spits, *13, 18, 19, 21, 42, 46, 79, 83, 85, 88, 91, 94, 95, 97, 98, 9, 103, 107, 112, 117, 130, 139, 179, 181, 183, 184, 186, 188, 190, 193;* iron, *71, 73, 75, 76, 80, 89, 102, 114, 119, 121, 124, 163, 182, 187*
Spokes (for wheels), *169*
Spoons, *37, 56, 120, 157; see also* Basting spoons, Pewter, Silver
Spring crops, 50-1
Stables, *79, 80, 86, 90, 91, 94, 102, 126*
Stairs, Staircases, Stairheads, *9, 12, 13, 23, 47, 73, 75, 76, 81, 86, 89, 90, 91, 94, 96, 101, 110, 111, 112, 113, 149, 151, 171*
Stallions, *10*
Stalls (of bees), 40, *170*
Standing cupboard, *47*
Standing presses, *36, 51*
Starching room, *13*
Status, 13-15
Stay (for barge), *114*
Stays (garments), *194*
Steam engines, 18
Stean, *111*
Steel irons, *106*
Steel mills, *54, 57, 66, 126, 127;* or malt mill, *57;* to grind malt with, *54*
Steelyards, *see* Stilliards
Stilliards, *79, 135*
Stillings, *135, 191, 196*
Stills, *13, 47, 115, 166*
Stockings, *179, 184*
Stocks, *10*
Stone ware, *121*
Store chambers, *140, 183*
Store house, *164*
Strakes (of wheels), *118*
Straw, *79, 90, 183;* baskets, *129;* whiskets, *139, 187*
Strethill, Madeley, Shropshire, *144*
Strike measure, *103, 187*
Studdy (i.e. tool), *141, 192*
Study (i.e. room), *162; see also* books

INDEX OF SUBJECTS AND PLACES

Stund, *7, 42, 46, 48, 115, 116, 119, 121, 122, 125, 128*; brewing, *42, 127, 128, 138, 155, 157*
Suck (part of plough), *168*
Suits (clothing), *128*
Sutton Maddock, Shropshire, *162*
Swail, Sway, *91, 107, 110*
Swanskin (fabric), *194*
Swifts (used in weaving), *110*
Swine, *see* Pigs
Swords, *13, 55, 156, 162*

Table cloths, *12, 14, 21, 23, 30, 39, 43, 46, 47, 54, 56, 57, 79, 80, 91, 103, 118, 120, 135, 150, 155, 157, 171, 179, 188, 189*; coarse, *107, 174, 183*; damask, *94*; diaper, *59, 182*; flaxen, *59, 76, 94*; hempen, *37, 71, 139, 149, 187*; huckaback, *183*; hurden, *94, 149, 180, 182, 187*; linen, *7*; long, *85*
Tables, *passim*, 60-1; chair tables, *143, 156*; folding, *84*; joined, *1, 57, 71*; long, *9, 13, 14, 58, 112, 121, 125, 129, 130, 131, 137*; oval, *10, 13, 47, 51, 55, 66, 69, 72, 73, 75, 79, 85, 86, 91, 94, 95, 97, 98, 99, 101, 102, 104, 11, 112, 113, 119, 122, 124, 125, 129, 131, 162, 163, 165, 176, 178, 179, 180, 182, 184, 188, 189, 191*; oval oak, *91, 94*; pairs of, *13, 47, 51, 156*; round, *6, 25, 57, 59, 127, 166, 171, 173, 193*; short, *151, 152, 153*; side, *13, 14, 19, 36, 47, 75, 124, 166, 182*; slate, *182*; square, *12, 55, 73, 76, 85, 89, 95, 98, 100, 101, 103, 111, 122, 124, 165, 180, 182, 184, 193*; turn-up, *137, 188*; with leaf, *188*; with slate in leaf, *94*; writing, with stone in leaf, *85*
Tafity (fabric), *23*
Tailors, 41, *44, 50, 136*
Tallow, *66, 105, 147*
Tallow chandlers, 34, *38, 63, 66, 74, 105, 147*
Tansey, *194*
Tapes, *13*
Tar, *45*
Tarpaulins, *83, 114*
Tea, *45*, 60
Teachers, 38-9
Tea kettles, *67*
Teasells, *59*
Thread, *23, 194*
Three Pigeons, 116
Tick, *49, 131, 156*
Tickneyware, *69, 188*
Tiles, *81, 146*
Timber, *33, 142, 165*; cooper's, *138*; plough, *47, 140, 169*; wain, *140*; *see also* Boards, Planks

Tinware, *13, 19, 41, 51, 54, 60,* 68-9, *79, 85, 87, 91, 99, 101, 102, 103, 124, 128, 151, 171, 178, 183, 185, 190*; boiler, *113*; broiler, *174*; can, *78*; candlebox, *84, 91, 96, 180*; colendar, *80, 84, 94, 103, 113, 137, 174, 182*; cover, *58, 80, 100, 114, 137, 187*; dredger, *174, 180*; dripping pan, *57, 91, 94, 100, 184, 187, 188, 191*; pan, *36, 64, 95, 97, 103, 113, 174, 177, 188*; pasty pan, *121*; patty pan, *57, 79, 98, 188*; pudding pan, *131, 187*; tundish, *187*
Tobacco, *64*; dish, *179*
Tobacco pipe-making, *13, 19,* 23-4, *71, 84, 106*
Tongs, *passim*: smith's, *6*
Tools: agricultural, 53; brassfounder's, *172*; carpenter's, *98, 99, 111, 163, 170*; collier's, *5, 25, 29, 56, 81, 92, 158*; edge tools, *22*; glover's, *86*; gunsmith's, *165*; locksmith's, *73*; mason's, *91*; nailer's , *54, 141*; pipemaker's, *19, 71, 84, 106*; ropemaker's, *131, 189*; shipwright's, *153*; smith's, *6, 36, 52, 152, 160, 192*
Tortree, *168*
Tow, *102, 144*
Towels, *6, 7, 30, 37, 91, 96, 100, 153*; flaxen, *139*; hand, *88, 183, 187*; hempen, *149*; hurden, *94*
Tray, Trea, Try, *79, 80, 124*; wooden, 109
Treen, Trinen ware, *3, 41, 118, 120, 139, 140, 148, 150, 151, 152, 156, 162*
Trenchers, *13, 57, 59, 64, 78, 87, 91, 95, 96, 109, 110, 113, 124, 125, 133, 135, 171, 174, 177, 180, 182, 184, 188, 191*; wooden, *21, 181, 187*
Trowmen, *7, 8, 12, 14, 16, 17,* 25-33, *26, 30, 34, 37, 45, 48, 49, 70, 75, 83, 85, 95, 96, 100, 101, 107, 109, 114, 142, 144, 164, 176, 182*
Trows, *7, 8, 17, 25, 75, 83, 85, 100, 101, 107, 164, 176, 182*; Eastop, 164; Frances, 101; John, 101, 107
Tubs, *6, 9, 16, 48, 56, 58, 64, 75, 76, 77, 85, 98, 110, 129, 132, 133, 137, 168, 171, 177, 181, 193, 195*
Tuger ware, 16, *62, 63, 74*
Tumbrels, *3,* 52, *80, 126, 127, 171, 183*; body, *116*
Tun (i.e. turning) barrel, *81*
Tun pail, *109*
Tundishes, *13, 19, 21, 53, 58, 80, 88, 98, 99, 103, 107, 124, 133, 161, 167, 174, 179, 188*; tin, *187*; wooden, *57*
Turnell, *120, 124*
Turners' ware, *22, 60, 62, 63, 74*
Tutors (i.e. tools for flax & hemp dressing), *121, 124, 168*

Twiggen baskets, *10*, *140*; ware, *156*
Twill, *49*, *115*

Valances, *46*, *55*, *59*, *80*, *139*, *156*, *166*
Vats, *173*; *see also* Ale Vats, Cheese Vats, Weeting Vats
Vessels: on river, *see* Barges, Boats, Frigates, Trows; household, *see* Brass, Pewter, Tinware &c
Vetches, *10*, *13*, *166*, *168*
Vices, *19*, *89*, *165*, *172*, *192*

Wafer irons, *59*
Wages, *11*
Wagon wheels, *9*, *119*, *168*
Wagons: agricultural, *52*, *79*, *183*; railway, *13*, *20*, *22*, *29*, *92*
Wains, *22*, *47*, *52*, *116*, *119*, *125*, *17*, *148*, *168*, *169*; body, *171*; rope, *171*; timber, *140*
Wainscot: bow case, *115*; chair, *99*; chest, *186*; press, *100*; screen, *85*
Waistcoats, *161*, *179*
Waiter, *91*
Walnut plank, *91*
Warming pans, *7*, *9*, *19*, *21*, *30*, *37*, *40*, *53*, *57*, *59*, *60*, *66*, *83*, *88*, *92*, *94*, *97*, *99*, *100*, *102*, *112*, *113*, *120*, *124*, *127*, *128*, *133*, *135*, *137*, *139*, *150*, *155*, *157*, *181*, *183*, *185*, *187*, *190*, *191*, *193*; brass, *46*, *85*, *90*, *182*; in chest, *150*
Warping bar and trough, *174*
Wash houses, *130*, *171*
Wash tubs, *13*, *18*, *58*, *124*, *139*
Washing pan, *188*
Watches, *55*, *61*, *71-2*, *119*, *162*; silver, *13*, *20*, *79*, *182*
Watermen, *see* Trowmen
Water pails, *13*, *21*, *79*, *108*, *110*, *131*, *180*, *182*
Water tub, *21*
Watering pan, *13*
Weapons, *73*
Weather glass, *182*
Weavers, 41-2, *74*, *82*, *110*, *150*, *174*
Wedges, *5*
Weeting vats, *47*, *116*, *168*
Weeting vessel, *140*
Weights, *59*, *73*, *156*; half hundredweight, *189*; iron, *64*; for jack, *103*; lead, *156*
Wellington, Shropshire, 13, 42

well rope, *132*
Wenlock, borough, 2, 13
Wet larder, *13*
Wheat, *10*, *13*, 50, *79*, *80*, *124*, *125*, *144*, *168*, *183*
Wheelbarrows, 52
Wheels: potter's, *136*: *see also* Carts, Waggons, Spinning Wheels
Whiches, *115*, *162*, *171*; corn, *47*
Whisketts, *139*, *187*
White ware, *41*
Wick yarn, *66*, *146*
Wig, *161*
Winches, *189*
Windlasses, 27, *85*, *114*
Window curtains, *13*, *41*, *59*, *66*, *76*, *102*, *183*
Wine, *146*, *182*
Wings (of grate), 2, *46*, *73*, *78*, *94*, *98*, *100*, *102*, *103*
Winnowing sheet, *162*
Woad, *59*
Women, 15-16, 73-9, 80
Wooden ware, *1*, *2*, *4*, *6*, *7*, *8*, *9*, *10*, *13*, *23*, *24*, *28*, *30*, *32*, *33*, *36*, *42*, *43*, *45*, *51*, *54*, *65*, *66*, *68*, 70, *73*, *76*, *121*, *126*, *127*, *128*, *142*, *144*, *145*, *149*, *150*, *160*, *164*, *169*, *178*
Woodhouse, Broseley, Shropshire, *47*
Wool, *11*, *13*, *30*, 75, *86*, *144*
Woollens, *37*, *146*, *148*, *149*, *166*; bedding, *24*, *37*, *146*; cloth, *14*, *49*, *104*; clothing, *147*, *149*; gears for loom, *174*
Workhouses, *86*, *136*, *147*, *170*, *172*
Workshop, *110*
Writing closet, *87*
Wyke, Shropshire, *10*, *79*, *117*, *140*

Yard, *98*
Yarn, *41*, *63*, *74*, *77*, *118*, *144*, *152*, *156*, *170*; in coffer, *63*; flaxen, *37*, *124*; hempen, *28*, *37*, *48*, *124*, *128*, *171*; hurden, *13*, *28*, *30*, *124*, *128*; linen, *25*, *32*, *36*, *74*, *86*, *102*, *152*; noggen, *34*; woollen, *30*, *59*
Yarn blades, winds (Erwingles, Herringles, Yarwingles, &c), *13*, *80*, *82*, *172*
Yealing vat, *see* Ale vat
Yeomen, 14, *86*, *69*, *7*, *116*, *119*, *121*, *122*, *123*, *126*, *127*, *128*, *130*, *139*, *168*, *170*, *171*, *186*, *187*
Yokes, *116*, *168*, *171*

INDEX OF NAMES OF APPRAISERS AND OTHERS MENTIONED IN INVENTORIES AND THE INTRODUCTION

Names of those included in the List on pp. 88-115 are not included in this index.

Figures in italics (e.g. *92*) refer to inventories. Other figures refer to pages in the Introduction.

Acton: John, *82*
Adams: William, *24*
Addenbrooke: Thomas, 38
Amies: Richard, *117*
Andrews: John, 5
Angle: Margaret, *28*; Richard, 28
Armstrong: family, 29
Arunshire: John, *31*
Asbury: Richard, *72*
Ashwood: John, *168*, William, *145*, *151*, *152*, *153*, *158*, Mr., 79
Astley: Matthew, *183*; Richard, *139*
Aston: Thomas, 35, *57*, *58*, *154*

Ball: William, *97*; family, 30
Barker: Ralph, *31*
Barnett: Somervill, *114*
Barnfield: John, 2
Barrett: Francis, *62*, *67*, *72*; Henry, 30; Samuel, 38
Bartholm: Richard, *160*, *164*
Bate: Thomas, 87
Batley: John, 5
Baugh: William, *34*
Bayliss: Thomas, 22
Beard: Eustace, 7, 8, *70*; John, *16*, 85, *95*; Richard, 34, *95*, *101*; family, 31-2
Beddow: John, *153*, *157*; Thomas, *46*, 77
Belcham: Thomas, *156*
Bell: John, *96*
Benbow: John, *12*; Nowell, *28*; Richard, *42*; family, 29
Benthall: Lawrence, 36; Philip, *11*, *13*, 36-7; Richard, *13*, 36-7
Bird: Richard, *23*

Bithell: William, *66*
Blackshaw: Daniel, *69*
Blest: Thomas, *174*
Boden: Edward, *141*, *147*, *155*, *185*; Francis, *177*; John, 15
Bowdler: Audley, 22, *140*, *165*; Henry, 51, *166*, *169*; Samuel, *167*, *172*, *173*, *176*, *178*
Bowen: John, *28*
Boycott: Thomas, *125*, *127*, *128*
Bradley: Edward, *57*; Ralph, 2; William, 37, 45
Bromley: William, 79
Brooke: Sir Basil, 6
Brookes: Humphrey, *31*
Brown: John, *71*
Browne: Ralph, 5
Bryan: Thomas, *108*
Buckley: Mary, *109*; William, *36*, *40*, *54*; family, 29-30
Bullock: Charles, *99*
Burrows: Mary, *98*; Samuel, *91*, *94*

Carrington: William, *86*
Carter: William, *117*
Chilton: John, 10, *117*
Clarke: Edward, *136*
Clemson: Jonathan, *173*
Cleobury: John, *108*
Cocke: William, *39*
Colley: Joseph, *144*, *146*; Matthew, *133*; Richard, 4
Cope: Thomas, 8
Corbett: Richard, *98*; Thomas, 33, 38, 41, *142*; William, *62*, *67*
Cowper: John, *131*; Richard, 29
Cox: Edward, *50*, *55*, *159*

Crompton: *Elizabeth*, 79; John, *178*; Richard, *64*; Sampson, *46*, *158*; family, 30
Cullis: family, 30

Darby: Abraham I, 6, 21-2, 31, 77
Darrall: Edward, *138*
Davi(e)s: Edward, *23*, *141*; James, *34*; John, 38
Dawes: John, *30*
Day: Mary, *17*, *18*
Delves: Thomas, *120*
Dicken: William, *191*, *195*
Dickens: John, *192*
Dixon: Gabriel, *133*
Dodson, family, 32
Dovey: Thomas, *192*
Duddell: John, *132*

Easthope: George, *142*, *143*; Thomas, *167*
Eaves: John, *34*
Edge: Henry, *28*
Edwards; Elizabeth, *79*; Francis, *79*; Joyce, *79*; Nevill, *53*; Thomas, *8*, *46*
Eele: Eleanor, 15; Martin, 22
Evans: Elizabeth, *61*; John, *139*; Paul, *78*; Samuel, *60*; Thomas, *8*, *46*
Everall: Thomas, *34*

Farmer: Thomas, *13*, *171*
Fiennes: Celia, 1
Fletcher: John, *117*; Joseph, *131*; William, *131*
Ford: Abraham, *186*
Forester: Francis, *117*; family, 6-7
Fosbrook: John, *142*
Fox: Richard, *179*

Gears: John, *1*; Margaret, *15*; Richard, *15*
German (*see also* Jarman): William, *40*, *41*
Gittins: William, *21*
Glasebrooke: George, 121; 151
Gough: Eleanor, *28*
Gower: Dorothy, *75*
Green(e): Thomas, *9*; —, *13*
Grenowes: Humphrey, *162*
Griffiths: Thomas, *63*
Guest: Robert, *45*, *54*; Thomas, *189*
Gwilliam: Thomas, *149*

Haberley: Richard, *119*, *123*
Hagar: John, *160*
Hains: John, *44*
Hall: William, *105*
Hallen: Samuel, *194*
Hamnet: Richard, *116*
Hare: John, *84*, *101*
Harper: Ralph, *11*; Richard, *71*
Harrison: James, *30*; Nicholas, *36*, *69*; Ralph, *46*; Thomas, *67*, *72*; William, *52*
Hartshorne: Charles, *16*, *85*; George, *3*, *6*; James, *49*; John, *14*, *15*, *18*, *20*, *37*, *71*, *75*, *84*, *85*, *89*, *94*, *95*, *96*, *97*, *98*, *99*, *100*, *102*, *103*, *104*, *106*, *110*, *111*, *112*, *113*, *186*; Morris, *15*, *26*; Ralph, *6*; Samuel, *64*, *73*; Thomas, *3*, *11*, *12*, *60*, *65*, *73*
Hatton: Joseph, *193*, *194*
Hawkins: Robert, *189*
Hayward: George, *117*; Maurice, *122*, *124*, *125*, *126*, *128*, *129*, *170*; Nathaniel, *123*; William, *117*, *119*
Head: Elizabeth, *97*
Heatherley: John, *165*
Henshaw: Richard, *79*, *80*, *183*
Hewlett: John, *79*; Thomas, *13*
Hill: Edmund, *46*
Hinksman: John, *68*
Hinley: John, *135*
Hinton: William, *184*
Hitchingsonne: George, *150*
Hodgkiss: William, *172*
Holland: Robert, *147*, *151*, *155*
Horton: Robert, *22*
Hughes: Thomas, *7*, *14*, *177*
Humphreys: Megan, *44*
Hussey: Joseph, *187*
Huxley: Francis, *23*

Instone: John, *19*, *73*, *79*, *91*, *113*; Samuel, *58*, *79*

James: John, *46*
Jarman (*see also* German): William, *27*, *28*, *30*
Jaundrell: Humphrey, *192*
Jefferies: Edward, *115*
Jones: John, *89*, *188*; Richard, *34*, *47*; Thomas, *43*; William, *78*, *136*
Justice: Margaret, 16

Kitchen: Jacob, 39

Langley: Andrew, *140*; John, *68*; family, 4
Lewes (Lewis): Edward, *29*, *163*; William, *90*, *92*
Lillie: Thomas, *156*
Littleford: John, *65*
Littlehales: Richard: *9*; Samuel, *13*
Littleton: Edward, *181*
Lloyd: Edward, *52*, *159*; Thomas, *109*; William, *76*
Lynall: Richard, *138*

Mackarell: Thomas, *86*
Maire: *see* Mayer
Mann: Francis, *46*
Manning: Richard, *55*

INDEX OF NAMES OF APPRAISERS

Mason: John, *180, 187*
Matthews: John, *3*; Richard, *116*; Robert, *40*; Thomas, *72*
Mayer: John, *27*
Meeson: John, *184*
Millichop: John, *28*; Nowell, *28*
Morrall: Christopher, *51*; Kester, *46*
Morris: John, *88*; William, *90*

Nash: Edward, *114*; Francis, *30, 56*
Niclis: George, *115*
North: Francis, *44*; William, *171*

Oakes: Sarah, *96*; family, 30
Oliver: Thomas, *46, 50*
Oswald, family, 32
Owen: James, *176*; family, 31

Palmer: Robert, *188*
Parker: Michael, *22*; Walter, *195*
Parsons: Thomas, *162*
Parton: Charles, *42*; Francis, *137*
Patten: John, *82*
Pearce (Pearse): William, *77, 79, 92, 105*
Peploe: Paul, *124, 163*; Podmore, *116*
Pew: *see* Pugh
Phillips: George, *31*; Richard, *49, 169*; William, *4, 35, 54*; family, 32-3
Pitt: Richard, *13*; Thomas, *19*
Pool(e): Sarah, *83*; William, *75*
Potts: Thomas, *83*
Preene: John, *46*
Price: Timothy, *21*
Pritchard: Richard, *190*
Pufford: John, *178*
Pugh: John, *48*
Pursell: Edward, *79*

Reynolds: Richard, *66*
Rhodes: Catherine, *93*; Edward, *93*; Robert, *46*
Richards: Michael, *140*
Roden: Marmaduke, *110*; Richard, *71*; Samuel, *71*
Roe: Roger, *168*
Rose: Thomas, *22*
Rowley: Edward, *93*; George, 18
Rutter: Samuel, *5*; William, *33, 37*

Sansom: William, *171*
Savage: Richard, *81*
Shaen: William, *130*
Shaw: Thomas, *103*
Shepherd: Richard, *1, 22, 146*
Sherborne: Amos, *74*

Shiston: John, *181*
Simons, Simmons: Edward, *39*; William, *100*; *see also* Symons
Slicer: John
Smith: Edward, *46*; Francis, *115*; George, *20*; Richard, *60*
Smitheman: John, *117, 121, 122, 125, 127, 129, 130, 163*; Thomas, *148*; William, *150*
Southorn: *see* Suthorne
Spruce: William, *109*
Squire: John, *74*
Stanley: Thomas, *170*
Stephens: Michael, *59, 82, 106, 166*
Stretton: Samson, *174*
Summerland: John, *190*
Suthorne: Thomas, *46*
Symons: John, *120*

Taylor: Benjamin, *147*; Henry, *24*; John, *126*; Sarah, *30*
Teece: Thomas, *40*
Thresstlecock: Roger, *170*
Tiler: Humphrey, *34*
Tomkis: Samuel, *135*
Transom: Edward, *45, 154*
Turner: Jonathan, *70*; Timothy, *145, 148*; William, *157*

Vahan (Vaughan): Moses, *46*

Waller: Roger, *120*
Walton: John, *26, 43*
Ward: Edward, *182*; William, *53*
Warren: John, *149, 150*
Weaver: Elizabeth, *79*; John, *81*; Richard, *13, 76, 79, 80, 88*
Weld: George, 30
Wellings: Thomas, *10, 46*
Wellington: Lawrence, *161*
Wheeler: Thomas, *79*; William, *161*
Wheelwright: William, *144*
Whitefoot: Elizabeth, *91*
Whiston: William, *116*
Whitmore: Robert, *159*
Williams: Thomas, *32, 34, 48, 56, 83, 164*
Willis: Edward, *59*
Wood: John, *153*; William, 180
Woof(e): Richard, *9*
Wyke: Isaac, *63*; Jacob, *102*

Yates (Yeats): Jane, *107*; William, *167*; family, 33
Yopp: William, *140*
York: Robert, *191*